FREEDOM
NOT FAR
DISTANT

Published with Funds from
Friends of the Society,
the Estate of Edward J. Grassmann,
and an
Anonymous Gift
Dedicated to the Memory of
Delia Brinkerhoff Koster

FREEDOM NOT FAR DISTANT

A Documentary History of Afro-Americans in New Jersey

Compiled and edited

by

CLEMENT ALEXANDER PRICE

A joint project of the
New Jersey Historical Society
and New Jersey Historical Commission

NEWARK 1980
New Jersey Historical Society

© 1980 by The New Jersey Historical Society
Library of Congress catalog card number 80-14781
ISBN 0-911020-01-2

Printed in the U.S.A. by the Harvard Printing Company
Orange, New Jersey

Library of Congress Cataloging in Publication Data

Freedom not far distant.
  (The Collections of the New Jersey Historical
Society ; 16)
  Bibliography: p. 334
  Includes index.
  1. Afro-Americans—New Jersey—History—Sources.
2. New Jersey—Race relations—Sources. I. Price,
Clement Alexander, 1945- II. New Jersey Historical
Society. III. New Jersey Historical Commission.
IV. Series: New Jersey Historical Society. Collec-
tions ; 16.
E185.93.N54F73   974.9'00496073   80-14781
ISBN 0-911020-01-2

To My Parents
JAMES LEO PRICE, SR.
and
ANNA CHRISTINE PRICE,
Who Were My First History Teachers

THE COLLECTIONS OF
THE NEW JERSEY HISTORICAL SOCIETY
Volume XVI

*In print.

Table of Contents

Note on Illustrations

Dr. James Still (Philadelphia, 1877), frontispiece.

15 Medford Township office and home of Dr. James Still. Engraving in *Combination Atlas Map of Burlington County* (Philadelphia, 1876), p. 62.

16 Peter Lee. Photograph, n.d. NJHS.

17 Benjamin Jackson. Drawing by John Collins (1814–1902). Courtesy of the Burlington County Historical Society.

18 John Wood. Photograph, ca. 1900. NJHS.

19 Mrs. Sophronia Wood. Photograph, ca. 1900. NJHS.

20 Alpha Company No. 1, Knights of Pythias, Atlantic City. Photograph in Joseph H. Morgan, *History of the Knights of Pythias . . . State of New Jersey* (n.d., n.p.), p. 65.

21 Colored Branch of the YMCA in Orange. Photograph, 1901. NJHS.

22 Signal Training, U.S. Colored Troops. *"Over Here," Camp Dix, New Jersey* (Baltimore, Md., n.d.), p. 63.

23 Non-commissioned officers, Second Support Company, New Jersey Militia. Photograph, ca. 1918. Courtesy of Clement A. Price.

24 Gouldtown school children. Photograph, 1924. NPL.

25 Lawnside Volunteer Fire Department. Photograph, 1968. NPL.

26 Newark street scene. Photograph, 1930s. NPL.

27 Newark, WPA Federal Theatre Project. Photograph, 1936. NJHS.

28 Trenton, road workers. Photograph, 1930s. NJHS.

29 Newark, WPA Household Training Project. Photograph, ca. 1938–39. NJHS.

30 James D. Carr. Photograph, 1892. Courtesy of Rutgers University Archives.

31 Paul Robeson, Photograph, ca. 1919. NPL.

32 Marion Thompson Wright. Photograph, n.d. Courtesy of Moorland-Spingarn Research Center, Howard University.

33 Harold A. Lett. Photograph, 1965. NPL.

34 Anna Monroe in the Bethany Baptist Church, Newark. Photograph, 1947. NJHS.

35 Pickets at the State House in support of the Trenton Six. Photograph, 1951. Courtesy of the Schomburg Center for Research in Black Culture, New York Public Library, Astor, Lenox and Tilden Foundations.

36 "The Morning After," Springfield Avenue, Newark. Photograph, 15 July 1967. Associated Press Photo.

Foreword

T HE degree of ignorance on the part of most Americans about Afro-American history is astonishing and, undoubtedly, one of the reasons efforts to improve race relations have traditionally had such little success. Many northerners, for example, still believe that racial problems which exist in the North are insignificant in comparison to those in the South. The South, they say, has a peculiarly dismal racial history; racial problems in the North are new. I am often saddened, in fact, to hear supposedly well-educated citizens—black and white—say that slavery existed only in the South, certainly not in New Jersey. Ask a high school student in your neighborhood which states had slavery. Alas, most are likely to start with North Carolina and move southward.

But Professor Price is concerned with much more than slavery. The vast collection he has assembled of the words of scores of people who have shaped the lives of Afro-Americans in New Jersey is replete with insights about New Jersey's history and politics. Take Newark, for instance, New Jersey's largest city. It has become the metaphor for America's urban decay. Sixty percent of its land is tax exempt. The unemployment rate is more than twice the national average, only 10 percent of the housing is owner occupied, and many of the schools are totally dysfunctional. It is more devastated now than when the rioting occurred there in 1967.

When Newark exploded, several other cities like Englewood, Plainfield, Paterson, and Asbury Park did as well. It was evident, as found by the special commission appointed by then Governor Richard Hughes to investigate the disturbances, that there was a particularly deep and extreme frustration among black New Jerseyans. In the aftermath of the widespread rioting, Governor

Hughes tried to have the legislature provide aid to help restore the cities—a special package of more than $25 million. The plan was turned down by lawmakers. A smaller measure of around $5 million was approved. But what was it used for? To increase the salaries of police officers. The police may indeed have needed more money—but the way the whole affair unfolded told powerful messages about the hardship of blacks in the state, the unwillingness of government to respond, and the weakness of black leadership. One learns so much from this work about the unerlying hopes and disappointment—the sometimes earnest efforts as well as indifference of officials throughout a long history and the list of failed policies—it is impossible not to apply some of that wisdom to more immediate concerns.

Consider, for instance, the way geographical divisions in the state have affected the fate of Afro-Americans in New Jersey. During slavery the northern part of the state, influenced by adjacent New York, supported the slave system. The southern part, influenced by Quakers in Philadelphia, fought for the abolition of slavery. Despite the ironic shift of ideological orientation, the north and south division in New Jersey has weighed heavily in the development of social policy and helps to explain historically and contemporaneously why New Jersey leaders have been so deeply divided on the issue of race.

In many ways the documents alone sufficiently illuminate many dark areas of Afro-American history. Whether it is John S. Rock appealing for the humanitarian treatment of blacks; Paul Robeson chronicling black life in Princeton; Harold A. Lett recounting his many years in the struggle for equality; or Amiri Baraka arguing for a fundamental change in the nation's social and economic system—the voices are powerful.

Professor Price's interpretation adds more. He examines the claims of voices contained in the documents and evaluates official responses. The result is a history not only of blacks in New Jersey, but a history of a state and a nation. Back in the 1970s, civil rights groups in New Jersey lobbied to have a bill passed to require that black history be taught in public schools. It was not an easy fight, but it was eventually won in 1973. As I read Professor Price's work, I thought of how very much more persuasive the arguments could have been.

Robert Curvin

Preface

THIS book attempts to relate three centuries of Afro-American history in New Jersey through selected documents and connecting narrative. A work of this sort, of course, is somewhat limited by its format in that individual documents provide a circumscribed view of the complex nature of history. Documents may be easily misinterpreted, moreover, without an understanding of the larger context of human events. Despite these shortcomings, an examination of historical records is indispensable to an understanding of human thought and action. For this reason, I have made every effort to select documents which acquaint historians, students, and general readers with the course of Afro-American history in New Jersey, and also provide an understanding of black concerns beyond this state's borders.

Although New Jersey has had a relatively large black population since the eighteenth century, there is a distressing lack of knowledge about the role of Afro-Americans in the state's development. To some extent, this pervasive ignorance results from an inherent bias in the source material. But, more important, it is the result of the way blacks have been viewed by the rest of American society. At no time have many New Jerseyans realized that the blacks in their midst contributed to the economic and political institutions, the ideals and culture which are central to the state's way of life. New Jersey blacks have had a peculiar and unenviable status which has improved slowly and only with a veritable crusade for racial justice lasting centuries. In a sense, this book serves as a contribution to our growing understanding of the problems posed to democracy by the historic mistreatment of Afro-Americans. This is also a needed chapter in the story of Afro-American protest and agitation, and the role blacks have played in making democratic ideals possible in a racially charged society.

In 1850, John S. Rock, a distinguished black lawyer in Boston and a native of Salem, New Jersey, called on the state's white residents to enfranchise his people. He attacked the popular notion that blacks were incapable of participating in a democratic society and wrote:

> If we, who have always been with you, do not understand something of the regulations of this country, how miserably ignorant are the thousands of voters who arrive in this country annually, who know nothing of this government, and but little of any government! There is no just plea, and apology for you to shut every avenue to elevation, and then complain of degradation; what else can be expected, while we are looked upon as *things*, and treated worse than unthinking animals?

As Rock's appeal and other documents in this volume show, Afro-Americans have never accepted the lowly position forced upon them in New Jersey. That they have sought equality so long has made this desire for racial justice indisputable. Their struggle for freedom has been inextricably linked to the elevation of blacks throughout the country. Documents repeatedly underscore the unswerving devotion of New Jersey blacks to equality and justice, which, though rooted in our democratic traditions, has enriched the lives of all New Jerseyans.

This volume includes documents shedding light on two central themes in New Jersey history—racial prejudice and exploitation on the one hand, and the resistance by blacks and whites of good will to racial injustice on the other. While not every potential area of interest could be explored, I have carefully selected sources basic to an understanding of black history in New Jersey, drawing on a wide range of documentary materials: legislative acts; pro- and anti-slavery petitions and writings; memoirs; organizational records; letters; newspapers; state publications; treatises; oral history interviews; court decisions; public testimony; and poetry.

Chapter introductions aim to place the documents in historical context, giving the reader an overview of the forces that shaped race relations and the way New Jersey blacks thought and acted. In addition, each document is introduced and annotated to highlight its importance, identify authorship, and, when appropriate, alert the reader to inherent fallacies and prejudices. Most documents are printed in full, but some lengthy documents have been abridged to save space, with deletions indicated by ellipses. While names of signatories have been deleted from petitions, I have retained the original spelling and capitalization. At the head of each document is a bibliographic citation.

This work has been a collaborative effort in many respects. Its completion has been made possible by the generous assistance of the staffs of The New Jersey Historical Society and the New Jersey Historical Commission. Bernard Bush, Director of the Commission, carefully read the entire manuscript and provided many helpful comments and criticisms of the various drafts. To him I am deeply grateful. I am also indebted to Paul A. Stellhorn, the Assistant Director of the New Jersey Committee for the Humanities; William C. Wright, Head of the Archives and History Bureau, New Jersey State Library; Joan C. Hull, Director, as well as Robert M. Lunny and Clifford L. Lord, former Directors of The New Jersey Historical Society; Donald Sinclair, Curator of Special Collections, Alexander Library, Rutgers University; Charles F. Cummings, Supervising Librarian, James Brown, Senior Librarian, as well as Robert L. Blackwell and James S. Osborne of the New Jersey Reference Division, Newark Public Library; Robert C. Morris, Head of Special Collections, Teachers College, Columbia University; Henry N. Drewry, Director of the Office of Teacher Preparation and Placement, Princeton University, and Chairman of the New Jersey Historical Commission; and Ronald J. Grele, Research Director, New Jersey Historical Commission.

From its outset, the project has been enthusiastically encouraged by the Afro-American Committee of The New Jersey Historical Society. Its members were involved in the editorial committee's early meetings, and they provided moral support as work neared completion. I extend special thanks to Vera Brantley McMillon, the committee's indefatigable chairwoman, renowned for her many accomplishments in Newark; Jack Brown; William M. Ashby; and Miriam V. Studley, who served beside her. My work has always received helpful encouragement from Bruce Cohen, Worcester State College; Lee Hagan, Jersey City State College; Larry A. Greene, Seton Hall University; and my Rutgers University colleagues, Seth M. Scheiner and Elliot A. Rosen.

I am especially grateful to the following individuals, libraries, and institutions for their permission to reprint manuscripts and published works: Mr. Amiri Baraka and the Sterling Lord Agency, for the selection from *The Practice of the New Nationalism,* 1972, and poems "Young Soul" and "Beautiful Black Woman,"

1969; the Association for the Study of Afro-American Life and History, Inc., Washington, D.C., for "An Address from the Coloured Convention . . ." in Marion Thompson Wright, "Negro Suffrage in New Jersey, 1776–1875," *Journal of Negro History,* 1948; the trustees of the Burlington County Historical Society, for documents pertaining to slave kidnapping intercepted at Little Egg Harbor, 1803; the Carnegie Institution of Washington, D.C., for selections from Elizabeth Donnan, *Documents Illustrative of the History of the Slave Trade to America,* 1932; the Newark Public Library, for the interview with Harold A. Lett, 1974; the New Jersey State Council on the Arts, for poems from the Creative Writing Program, *Prison Poetry,* 1973; the New Jersey State Library, Bureau of Archives and History, for manuscript petitions supporting slavery, 1774, and manumission, 1775; the Princeton University Press, for letters from Rev. C. N. Grandison and William H. Maxwell to Woodrow Wilson in Arthur Link, ed., *The Papers of Woodrow Wilson,* vols. 21 and 22, copyright 1976; Mr. Paul Robeson, Jr., for excerpts from Paul Robeson, *Here I Stand,* 1958; the Rutgers University Archives, for the letter from James D. Carr to William H.S. Demarest, 1919; the Special Collections, Alexander Library, Rutgers University, for the manuscript document pertaining to the removal of Harey, 1818; the trustees of the Somerset County Historical Society, for "The Revolutionary War Record of a Somerset County Slave," *Somerset County Historical Quarterly,* 1914; the National Urban League, Inc., for Beatrice A. Myers and Ira De A. Reid, "The Toll of Tuberculosis among Negroes in New Jersey," *Opportunity,* 1932, and Lester B. Granger, "Mayor Hague and the Negro," *Opportunity,* 1938. Picture credits are given in the Note on Illustrations after the Table of Contents.

I should also like to acknowledge the assistance of Roderick Harrison, formerly of Princeton University, who began the project as co-editor. Don C. Skemer, Editor of Publications at The New Jersey Historical Society, guided this book from manuscript into print, with assistance from Delight W. Dodyk and King Morrison. Finally, to Cozetta L. Williams of East Orange, I extend my sincerest appreciation for her enthusiastic support through the laborious process of compiling and editing this book.

Abbreviations

Leaming and Spicer

Aaron Leaming and Jacob Spicer, *The Grants and Concessions, and Original Constitutions of the Province of New Jersey* . . . (Philadelphia, 1752).

New Jersey Archives

William A. Whitehead, et al., eds., *Archives of the State of New Jersey*. ser. 1-2 (Newark, N.J. and other places, 1880–1949). "Prepared and edited by authority of the State of New Jersey, at the request of The New Jersey Historical Society."

New Jersey Laws

Acts of the . . . General Assembly of the State of New Jersey (Trenton, N.J., 1776–1884); continued as *Acts of the . . . Legislature of the State of New Jersey* (Trenton, N.J., 1845-   ).

I

Birth of a Slave Society

FROM the beginning of its history as an outpost of European civilization, New Jersey was a multi-racial society and one of the most culturally diverse colonies in British North America. In the seventeenth century the area, at first called New or Nova Cæsaria by the English, was settled by various Old World groups, including Dutch, English, Swedes-Finns, Germans, French, and Scotch-Irish immigrants. New Jersey offered to its first generation of European settlers a refuge from economic privation, interminable wars, and religious intolerance. New Jersey was for many a new beginning in human freedom. The setting was receptive to the bold venture of these first immigrants. New Jersey was well endowed with wonderfully strange creatures. Its rich soil, navigable rivers, and vast forests appeared both economically attractive and visually pleasing to most settlers.

The land of New Jersey, though abundant, was not immediately for the taking. European explorers and settlers found a rich, complex culture in the Lenni-Lenape natives who had settled along the Delaware River and its tributaries. The Lenni-Lenape, whose settlement in the region went back as much as five thousand years, became the first group to suffer the indignities of European colonization in New Jersey. As more colonists arrived, the natives lost their lands, faced exploitation under slavery, and succumbed to the diseases brought by Europeans. The beginning of New Jersey's history under the Dutch and later the English brought an end to the native population's independence. Many of them, perhaps realizing the futility of co-existence with the land-hungry white settlers, migrated west in search of uncontested lands. Those who remained behind adopted the ways of Anglo-American civilization and gradually lost their distinctiveness in New Jersey society.[1]

Africans, whose presence in the New World extends back to the early age of European exploration, were the next non-European group to become victims of colonization. While it is not certain exactly how long Afro-Americans have been in New Jersey, Dutch farmers had surely brought black slaves to the west banks of the Hudson before the first tide of English settlers arrived in the latter half of the seventeenth century. The earliest record of African slaves in the colony was made in 1680 in Shrewsbury, Monmouth County, where Colonel Lewis Morris owned between sixty and seventy blacks.[2] In 1665, New Jersey's first constitution, the Concessions and Agreement, prescribed the conditions under which colonists settled the region; and it strongly supported the introduction of slaves to the colony. [doc. 1] Although most New Jersey blacks in the seventeenth century were slaves, there were some free men and women of African ancestry. In 1687 two free blacks from New York—John DeVries II, the son of a black woman and a Dutch man, and Claes Emmanuel, the son of an African by the name of Manuel van Angola—were among the early settlers in the upper Hackensack River valley. Their descendants later sold their landholdings and migrated to the Ramapo Mountains. A small number of free blacks also came to the other parts of New Jersey after they were freed by their Dutch owners in New Netherland.[3]

New Jersey became a British colony in 1664 with the conquest of New Netherland, a vast region encompassing the Hudson and Delaware valleys. Before military victory was assured, King Charles II granted New Netherland, which included New Jersey, to his brother James, duke of York. In the same year, James conferred the colony on John Lord Berkeley and Sir George Carteret, under whose auspices the Concessions and Agreement was issued. In 1674 the colony was divided into East Jersey and West Jersey, two separate political and territorial entities. The division led to sharp conflicts and contrasts which shaped New Jersey's treatment of Africans and its larger sense of identity and purpose.[4]

In East Jersey, which originally comprised Bergen, Essex, Middlesex, and Monmouth counties, the most important institutions were closely intertwined with New York City's economic and social life. That city's liberal importation of African slaves during the colonial period encouraged East Jerseyans to do likewise. The fertile lands of the Passaic and Raritan river valleys could be readily exploited through slave labor. In East Jersey, as in other colonial areas where exploitation of Indian slaves and white indentured laborers proved woefully inadequate, landowners and merchants turned to African slaves to fill their needs. East Jersey's early economic vitality owed much to the labor of blacks. Governor Philip Carteret's encouragement of the slave trade, moreover, attracted slaveholding British planters from the Caribbean island of Barbados and Dutch farmers from New York. In Monmouth and Bergen counties, where they settled, slavery bolstered the economy, as it also did in Perth Amboy, Middlesex County, the center of the colony's slave trade. Toward the end of the seventeenth century most of the inhabitants of that port city depended upon black slave labor.

The religious outlook of East Jersey was also a powerful inducement to the development of slavery. In this region, Puritans and later Anglicans generally saw slavery as a necessary economic tool, and they wielded the most political and economic influence. By the early eighteenth century the Church of England implicitly supported the slave system. Anglican concessions to African laborers, including the rites of baptism and marriage, did little to improve their status. The white-over-black system of labor, the treatment of blacks accused of crimes, and the social relations between the two races were not fundamentally altered by the conversion of Africans to Christianity; and it did not enhance their chances of obtaining freedom. An East Jersey law enacted in 1703 stated that freedom for Christian slaves was "a groundless Opinion and prejudicial to the Inhabitants of this Province." The measure provided that Christian baptism should "not be any reason or cause for letting them, or any of them at Liberty." Under these conditions East Jersey became, according to Peter Chandler, a businessman from Connecticut, "the land of slavery" by the end of the American Revolution. In some areas, notably the settlements in Bergen County and Perth Amboy, contemporary accounts observed that it was rare for a white family to be without African slaves. On the eve of the Revolution, black slaves comprised ten to twelve percent of East Jersey's population.[5]

African slavery existed in the West Jersey counties of Burlington, Gloucester, Salem, and Cape May, but the institution never had as much support there as in East Jersey. The settlement of large numbers of Quakers, whose religious ideals made them increasingly opposed to slavery, militated against its development in the region.[6] The Society of Friends affirmed human equality before God and believed that an "inner light" within all men and women would, if heeded, direct them to a righteous way of life. These were radical notions in colonial America, guiding the Quakers to treat their African brethren with considerable kindness. Quakers also released their slaves from bondage in proportionally greater numbers than did other Christians, and were the first to protest against the inherent evil of the institution.[7] [doc. 2] Unlike East Jersey, moreover, where labor was critically short during the colonial period, West Jersey settled white laborers in sufficient numbers to obviate the introduction of slaves. The combination of a rural economy based upon free labor with an aggressive religious credo opposed to slavery fostered the development of free black communities acutely aware of their human dignity. At the beginning of the American Revolution only about four and a half percent of West Jersey's population was African.[8]

The contrasts between the East and West Jersey views of slavery continued long after the two colonies were reunited in 1702. East Jersey, economically the more developed province, imported an ever-increasing number of Africans during the first half of the eighteenth century. Slavery continued in the western region also, but not without increasingly effective protests from Quakers. The conflict over the immorality of human bondage took on a deeper meaning as the western hinterland came under the influence of Quaker-dominated Philadelphia, while the eastern section of the colony was drawn tightly into the orbit of slaveholding New York.

Despite its economic advantages in colonial New Jersey, slavery created a social and legal dilemma for the white population. The major problem confronting colonists was that slaves were chronically troublesome and, in some extraordinary cases, very dangerous. Contemporary sources reveal that although blacks were heavily outnumbered by the white population and were at the mercy of colonial peace powers, they were not passive. Even the most trusted of them attempted to run away, committing acts of vandalism or violence against their masters which threatened the well-being of whites, if not the foundation of slavery. Thievery by slaves was an especially prevalent problem. Slaveholders often complained of livestock and other valuable goods stolen and sold by enterprising Africans. Slaves were accused of plotting the more frightening crimes of murder and insurrection. The punishment which they were accorded by colonial courts suggests that whites regarded their illegal action as dangerously subversive.

New Jersey lawmakers desperately sought to prevent unlawful activity by Africans and to keep them under control. In order to prevent theft, a measure was enacted in 1682 which prohibited business transactions with slaves. In 1694 and 1695 the East Jersey legislature enacted slave codes for the regulation of crimes by slaves and misdeeds by the small free black population. The 1695 law established special courts to hear cases involving slaves. [doc. 3,4] As the eighteenth century opened, the treatment of blacks in the legal system became more severe, evidenced in part by an increase in the number of crimes carrying the death penalty for black offenders. A measure enacted in 1703 prescribed castration and death of "any Negro, Indian or Mallato [who would] attempt by force or persuasion to Ravish or have carnal knowledge of any White Woman, Maid or Child. . . ." Ten years later a comprehensive slave code was adopted which extended the separate slave court system throughout the colony.[9] [doc. 5]

The slave codes were not only a reflection of the extreme difficulty that whites had in controlling the black population. In practical terms they established a separate and unequal system of justice for blacks, strikingly similar to the harsh treatment of the race in the southern colonies. In 1694 a black man convicted of murder was sentenced in this manner by a Monmouth County judge: ". . . thy right hand shall be cut off and burned before thine eyes. Then thou shalt be hanged up by the neck till thou art dead, dead, dead; then thy body shall be cut down and burned to ashes in a fire, and so the Lord have mercy on thy soul, Cæsar."[10] This undeniably severe form of punishment, which other slaves were forced to witness, was also employed in Middlesex and Bergen counties. In 1730 a black was burned for the murder of an itinerant tailor in Perth Amboy. For the crime of attempted arson a slave in Bergen County was burned at the stake. Six years later two blacks were burned at Hackensack after being convicted of setting fire to several barns.

East Jersey's pro-slavery attitudes and harsh treatment of blacks continued in the eighteenth century, though anti-slavery feeling began to rise in some segments of the population. As in the past, Quakers spurred this nascent anti-slavery expression. It was a New Jersey Quaker, John Woolman (1720–72) of Mount Holly, Burlington County, who wrote one of the earliest attacks on slavery with a wide impact in British North America: *Some Considerations on the Keeping of Negroes* (1754). [doc. 6] Later generations of abolitionists in New Jersey and beyond would employ similar arguments. During the colonial period, however, few New Jersey slaveholders other than Quakers heeded Woolman.[11] Support for the institution was stronger in New Jersey than in any other northern colony. When the New Jersey Assembly passed a bill imposing a duty on slave importation, the Council rejected it for fear that any limitation on the slave trade would undermine economic stability. **[doc. 7]** It would take another century before the anti-slavery forces in the state struck down the last vestiges of slavery. During that time the people of New Jersey lived with an ever-increasing uneasiness over the peculiar institution in their midst. In a society born out of the hope for individual freedom, the bondage of so many of its inhabitants was New Jersey's greatest moral contradiction; and, for men and women of good will, its greatest challenge.

---

1 CONCESSIONS AND AGREEMENT, 1664/65

The Concessions and Agreement was of immense importance to the early European settlement of New Jersey and the introduction of African slaves into East Jersey. It offered to Christian dissenters, who constituted a majority of early European settlers in the colony, religious freedom and the right to be left alone, and it boldly sanctioned the notion that the New World held the promise of economic independence and individual freedom. Yet, this remarkable charter also laid the economic and social foundations upon which slave society developed. Under its provisions every freeman who accompanied Governor Philip Carteret on the "first voyage" to New Jersey in 1665 was promised a headright (land grant) of 150 acres, with decreasing acreages promised to those who came in succeeding years. Lesser grants were made to "weaker servants" (women and children) and to indentured servants upon the completion of their term of service. Additional grants were made to settlers who brought indentured male servants and slaves into East Jersey. In some cases ownership of slaves doubled the settler's land grant. This inducement was especially attractive to slaveholders from New England, New York, and Barbados, where black slavery had been firmly established. The growing number of slaveholders who settled in

East Jersey came to wield considerable economic and political power. Meanwhile, the paradox of slavery in an ostensibly free society became all the more clear and disturbing.

John Lord Berkeley and Sir George Carteret, "The Concessions and Agreement of the Lords Proprietors of New Cæsaria, or New Jersey, To and With All and Every the Adventures and All Such as Shall Settle or Plant There," Leaming and Spicer, pp. 20-23.

. . . And that the Planting of the said Province may be the more speedily promoted.

I. [ITEM.] We do hereby grant unto all persons who have already adventured to the said Province of *New-Cæsarea* or *New Jersey,* or shall transport themselves, or servants, before the *first* day of January, which shall be in the year of our Lord *One Thousand Six Hundred Sixty-five,* these following proportions, viz: To every freeman that shall go with the first Governor, from the port where he embarques, or shall meet him at the Rendezvous he appoints, for the Settlement of a Plantation there, arm'd with a good musket, bore twelve Bullets to the Pound, with ten Pounds of Powder, and twenty Pounds of Bullets, with Bandiliers and Match convenient, and with six Months Provision for his own Person arriving there, One Hundred and Fifty acres of Land English Measure; and for every able Servant that he shall carry with him, arm'd and provided as aforesaid, and arriving there, the like quantity of One Hundred and Fifty Acres English Measure: And whosoever shall send Servants at that Time, shall have for every able Man Servant he or she shall send, armed and provided as aforesaid, and arrive there, the like quantity of One Hundred and Fifty Acres: And for every weaker Servant, or Slave, Male or Female, exceeding the Age of fourteen Years, which any one shall send or carry, arriving there, Seventy five Acres of Land: And for every Christian servant, exceeding the Age aforesaid, after the expiration of their Time of Service, Seventy five Acres of land for their own use.

II. ITEM. To every Master or Mistress that shall go before the first day of *January,* which shall be in the year *One Thousand Six Hundred Sixty five;* One Hundred and Twenty Acres of Land. And for every able Man Servant, that he or she shall carry or send, arm'd and provided as aforesaid, and arriving within the time aforesaid, the like quantity of One Hundred and Twenty Acres of Land: And for every weaker Servant or Slave, Male or Female, exceeding the Age of fourteen Years, arriving there, Sixty Acres of Land: And to every Christian Servant to their own use and behoof Sixty Acres of Land.

III. ITEM. To every free Man and free Woman that shall arrive in the said Province, arm'd and provided as aforesaid, within the second year, from the first Day of *January* 1665 to the first Day of *January* One Thousand Six Hundred Sixty six, with an intention to plant, Ninety Acres of Land English Measure: And for every Man Servant that he or she shall carry or send, armed and provided as aforesaid, Ninety Acres of Land of like Measure.

IV. ITEM. For every weaker Servant or Slave, aged as aforesaid, that shall be so carried or sent thither within the second Year, as aforesaid, Forty five Acres of Land or like Measure: And to every Christian Servant that shall arrive the second Year, Forty five Acres of Land of like Measure, after the Expiration of his or their Time of Service, for their own use and behoof.

V. ITEM. To every free Man and free Woman, armed and provided as aforesaid, that shall go and arrive with an intention to plant, within the third Year from *January* 1666 to *January* 1667, armed and provided as aforesaid, Threescore Acres of Land of like Measure: And for every able Man Servant, that he or they shall carry or send within the said Time, armed and provided as aforesaid, the like quantity of Threescore Acres of Land. And for every weaker Servant or Slave, aged as aforesaid, that he or they shall carry or send within the third Year, thirty Acres of Land: And to every Christian Servant so carried or sent in the third Year, thirty Acres of Land of like Measure, after the expiration of their Time of Service. All which Land, and all other that shall be possessed in the said Province, are to be held on the same Terms and Conditions as is before mentioned, and as hereafter in the following Paragraphs is more at large express'd. PROVIDED ALWAYS, that the before mentioned Land and all other whatsoever, that shall be taken up and so settled in the said Province, shall afterward from Time to Time for the space of thirteen Years from the Date hereof, be held upon the conditions aforesaid, continuing one able Man Servant or two such weaker Servants as aforesaid, on every Hundred Acres a Master or Mistress shall possess, besides what was granted for his or her own Person: In failure of which upon other disposure to the present Occupant, or his Assigns, there shall be three Years given to such for their compleating the said number of Persons, or for their sale or dispositions of such part of their Lands as are not so People'd within such time of three Years. If any such persons holding any Land shall fail by himself his Agents, Executors or Assigns, or some other way to provide such number of Persons, unless the general Assembly shall without respect to poverty, Judge it was impossible for the party so failing, to keep or procure his or her number of Servants to be provided as aforesaid; in such case we the Lords to have Power of disposing of so much of such land as shall not be planted with its due number of Persons as aforesaid, to some others that will plant the same. PROVIDED ALWAYS, That no person arriving in the said Province, with Purpose to settle (they being Subjects or naturalized as aforesaid) be denied a grant of such Proportions of Land as at the time of their arrival that are due to themselves or Servants, by Concession from us as aforesaid; but have full Licence to take up and settle the same, in such order and manner as is granted or prescrib'd. All Lands (notwithstanding the Powers in the Assembly aforesaid) shall be taken up by Warrant from the Governor, and confirm'd by the Governor and Council, under a seal to be provided for that purpose, in such order and method as shall be set down in this Declaration, and more at large in the Instruction to the Governors, and Council . . . .

2 QUAKERS PROTEST SLAVERY, 1693

Few white colonists in seventeenth-century New Jersey opposed the importation of Africans who had been captured and enslaved on their native soil, since black labor was considered crucial to the fragile, undeveloped colonial economy. Not only did the proprietary and provincial leadership sanction and encourage the slave trade, but religious authorities also believed that slavery was a necessary, though distasteful, economic institution.

The Quakers could not so easily satisfy their conscience. In the 1693 document printed below, Philadelphia Quakers offered the first anti-slavery protest in North America. The Quakers, as victims of persecution in Restoration England, practiced a religion emphasizing human brotherhood. With remarkable compassion they acknowledged Africans as "a real part of Mankind" and capable of Christian salvation. Some white colonists undoubtedly agreed that blacks were members of the human family, but prevailing racial attitudes and economic considerations worked powerfully against a harmonious relationship between Europeans and Africans. Even when blacks embraced Christianity, their status was usually unchanged. Christian baptism, while perhaps providing some measure of spiritual comfort for the African, rarely led to freedom. Except for the Quakers, white Christians generally ignored the inconsistencies between their religious precepts and the injustices endured by blacks.

At a time when there were few restraints on slavery's development, the "Exhortation" represents a rare expression of religious idealism. One is struck by the foresight of late-seventeenth-century Quakers. The authors of this progressive document could not have known that their arguments against racial intolerance would be used repeatedly before the end of the eighteenth century. Although the "Exhortation" was printed in Philadelphia, West Jersey Quakers were deeply influenced by this and other humanitarian tracts. To be sure, Quakers continued to own slaves, but their belief in human equality fostered an empathy for the African that was unparalleled in the doctrine of other Christian denominations. By 1776 slaveholding Quakers in Pennsylvania and western New Jersey were not permitted to attend Friends meetings. This did not end the bondage of Africans in those areas, but it suggests that the Quakers, with the exception of blacks themselves, were the most vehemently anti-slavery group in the colony.

"The First Printed Protest against Slavery in America:
An Exhortation & Caution to Friends Concerning Buying
or Keeping of Negroes," Pennsylvania Magazine
of History and Biography **13 (1889): 265-70.**

Seing our Lord Jesus Christ hath tasted Death for every Man, and given himself a Ransom for all, to be testified in due time, and that his Gospel of Peace, Liberty and Redemption from Sin, Bondage and all Oppression, is freely to be preached unto all, without Exception, and that *Negroes*, *Blacks* and *Taunies* are a real part of Mankind, for whom Christ hath shed his precious Blood, and are capable of Salvation, as well as *White Men*; and Christ the Light of the World hath (in measure) enlightened them, and every Man that cometh into the World; and that all such who are sincere *Christians* and true Believers in Christ Jesus, and Followers of him, bear his Image, and are made conformable unto him in Love, Mercy, Goodness and Compassion, who came not to destroy men's Lives, but to save them, nor to bring any part of Mankind into outward Bondage, Slavery or Misery, nor yet to detain them, or hold them therein, but to ease and deliver the Oppressed and Distressed, and bring into Liberty both inward and outward.

. . . And to buy Souls and Bodies of men for Money, to enslave them and their Posterity to the end of the World, we judge is a great hinderance to the spreading of the Gospel, and is occasion of much War, Violence, Cruelty and Oppression, and Theft & Robery of the highest Nature; for commonly the Negroes that are sold to white Men, are either stollen away or robbed from their Kindred, and to buy such is the way to continue these evil Practices of Man-stealing, and transgresseth that Golden Rule and Law, *To do to others what we would have others do to us.*

Therefore, in true *Christian Love,* we earnestly recommend it to all our Friends and Brethren, Not to buy any Negroes, unless it were on purpose to set them free, and that such who have bought any, and have them at present, after some reasonable time of moderate Service they have had of them, or may have of them, that may reasonably answer to the Charge of what they have laid out, especially in keeping Negroes Children born in their House, or taken into their House, when under Age, that after a reasonable time of service to answer that Charge, they may set them at Liberty, and during the time they have them, to teach them to read, and give them a Christian Education.

Some Reasons and Causes of our being against keeping of Negroes for Term of Life.

First, Because it is contrary to the Principles and Practice of the *Christian Quakers* to buy Prize or stollen Goods, which we bore a faithful Testimony against in our Native Country; and therefore it is our Duty to come forth in a Testimony against stollen Slaves, it being accounted a far greater Crime under *Moses's* Law than the stealing of Goods: for such were only to restore four fold, *but he that stealeth a Man and selleth him, if he be found in his hand, he shall surely be put to Death, Exod.* 21.16. Therefore as we are not to buy stollen Goods, (but if at unawares it should happen through Ignorance, we are to restore them to the Owners, and seek our Remedy of the Thief) no more are we to buy stollen Slaves; neither should such as have them keep them and their Posterity in Perpetual Bondage and Slavery, as is usually done, to the great scandal of the *Christian Profession.*

Secondly, Because Christ commanded, saying, *All things whatsoever ye would that men should do unto you, do ye even so to them.* Therefore as we and our Children would not be kept in perpetual Bondage and Slavery against our Consent, neither should we keep them in perpetual Bondage and Slavery against their Consent, it being such intollerable Punishment to their Bodies and Minds, that none but notorious Criminal Offendors deserve the same. But these have done us no harm; therefore how inhumane is it in us so grievously to oppress them and their Children from one Generation to another.

Thirdly, Because the Lord hath commanded, saying, *Thou shalt not deliver unto his Master the Servant that is escaped from his Master unto thee, he shall dwell with thee, even amongst you in that place which he shall chuse in one of thy Gates, where it liketh him best; thou shalt [not] oppress him, Deut.* 23. 15,16. By which it appeareth, that those which are at Liberty and freed from their Bondage, should not by us be delivered into Bondage again, neither by us should they be oppressed, but being escaped from his Master, should have the liberty to dwell amongst us, where it liketh him best. Therefore, if God extend such Mercy under the legal Ministration and Dispensation to poor Servants, he doth and will extend much more of his Grace and Mercy to them under the clear Gospel Ministration; so that instead of punishing them and their Posterity with cruel Bondage and perpetual Slavery, he will cause the Everlasting Gospel to be preached effectually to all Nations, to them as well as others . . . .

Fourthly, Because the Lord hath commanded, saying, *Thou shalt not oppress an hired Servant that is poor and needy, whether he be of thy Brethren, or of the Strangers that are in thy Land within thy Gates, least he cry against thee unto the Lord, and it be sin unto thee; Thou shalt neither vex a stranger nor oppress him, for ye were strangers in the Land of Ægypt, Deut.* 24. 14, 15. *Exod.* 12. 21. But what greater. Oppression can there be inflicted upon our Fellow Creatures, than is inflicted on the poor Negroes! they being brought from their own Country against their Wills, some of them being stollen, others taken for payment of Debt owing by their Parents, and others taken Captive in War, and sold to Merchants, who bring them to the *American* Plantations, and sell them for Bond Slaves to them that will give most for them; the Husband from the Wife, and the Children from the Parents; and many that buy them do exceedingly afflict them and oppress them, not only by continual hard Labour, but by cruel Whippings and other cruel Punishments, and by short allowance of Food, some Planters in *Barbadoes* and *Jamaica,* 'tis said, keeping one hundred of them, and some more, and some less, and giving them hardly any thing more than they raise on a little piece of Ground appointed them, on which they work for themselves the seventh days of the Week in the after-noon, and on the first days, to raise their own Provisions, to wit, Corn and Potatoes, and other Roots, &c. the remainder of their time being spent in their Masters service; which doubtless is far worse usage than is practised by the *Turks* and *Moors* upon their Slaves. . . . Surely the Lord doth behold their Oppressions & Afflictions, and will further visit for the same by his righteous and just Judgments, except they break off their sins by Repentance, and their Iniquity by shewing Mercy to these poor afflicted, tormented miserable Slaves!

Fifthly, Because Slaves and Souls of Men are some of the *Merchandize of Babylon* by which the Merchants of the Earth are made Rich; but those Riches which they have heaped together, through the cruel Oppression of these miserable Creatures, will be a means to draw Gods Judgments upon them; therefore, *Brethren,* let us hearken to the Voice of the Lord, who saith, *Come out of* Babylon, *my People that ye be not partakers of her Sins, and that ye receive not her Plagues; for her Sins have reached unto Heaven, and God hath remembered her Iniquities; for he that leads into Captivity shall go into Captivity, Rev.* 18. 4, 5 & 13. 10.

Given forth by our Monthly Meeting in Philadelphia, *the* 13*th day of the* 8*th Moneth,* 1693. *and recommended to all our Friends and Brethren, who are one with us in our Testimony for the Lord Jesus Christ, and to all others professing* Christianity.

3   LAW CONTROLLING SLAVES, 1694

Though New Jersey colonial slavery was not as harsh as that of the southern colonies, an examination of laws regulating blacks shows that the institution was not benign and blacks were tightly held in bondage. The following law was passed by the East Jersey legislature in reaction to the growing problem of theft by slaves. It forbade slaves to carry guns unless accompanied by their masters or white men authorized by their masters, and it prohibited slaves from keeping swine not their masters' property. Violation of these provisions subjected slaveowners to a fine. In addition, the act prescribed fines for harboring slaves more than two hours, a provision which may have been directed against unauthorized use of the slave's labor and aid to runaways. This 1694 act made it legal for any person to apprehend a slave who was five miles from his master's domicile. White men, regardless of their social status, were thus granted discretionary power over slaves and made responsible for the perpetuation of slavery.

An Act Concerning Slaves,
Leaming and Spicer, pp. 340-42.

WHEREAS complaint is made by the Inhabitants of this Province, that they are greatly injured by Slaves having liberty to carry Guns and Dogs, into the Woods and Plantations, under pretence of Guning, do kill Swine. BE IT ENACTED by the Governor, Council and Deputies in General Assembly met and assembled, and by the Authority of the same, that no Slave or Slaves within this Province after Publication hereof, be permitted to carry any Gun or Pistol, or take any Dog with him or them into the Woods, or Plantations, upon any pretence whatsoever; unless his or their Owner or Owners, or a white Man, by the order of his or their Owner or Owners, be with the said Slave or Slaves, upon the penalty of *Twenty Shillings* for the first Offence, and for the second Offence, *Thirty Shillings,* and so for every Offence after so committed *Ten Shillings* more; the one half to the informer that Shall Prosecute the same to effect, the other half to the use of the Poor belonging to the Town where the fact was committed, to be recovered as as Action of Debt; *Forty Shillings* or under to be tryed at the Court of small Causes in the Town where the fact was committed, and above *Forty Shillings* to be try'd by the County Court where the fact was committed; the said Action to be commenced against the Owner or Owners, of the aforesaid Slave or Slaves so Offending; and after Judgment obtained against the said

Owner or Owners, Execution to be levied upon their Bodies or Estates, for the Satisfaction of the said Penalty so recovered as aforesaid with cost. AND BE IT FURTHER ENACTED by the Authority aforesaid, that no Person or Persons within this Province, shall suffer his or their Slave or Slaves, to keep any Swine, but what are of their Owners mark, upon the penalty of *Twenty Shillings* for every Swine otherwise marked; to be recovered of the Owner or Owners of the said Slave or Slaves as aforesaid. And Whereas it is found Injurious to many of this Province having Slaves, that their Slaves are withheld by the Countenance, Harbouring and Entertaining of them by many of the Inhabitants thereof, without their Owners consent. BE IT ENACTED by the Authority aforesaid, that any Person or Persons on whom it can be proved, that they do presume to suffer any Slave to be or remain in his House, not Licensed by his Owner as aforesaid, by the space of two Hours, shall forfeit the Sum of *five shillings,* and so proportionately for a longer Time, to the Owner wrong'd thereby; and that it shall be lawful for any Person to apprehend and take up as a Runaway, any Slave that shall be found five Miles from his Owners Habitation, or Town of his abode, without a Certificate for the same, and upon returning the said Slave or Slaves, to the said Owner or Owners, he or they so apprehending and returning as aforesaid, shall have paid them by the Owner or Owners of the said Slave or Slaves within Ten Miles distance, *five shillings*; if within Twenty Miles, and more than Fifteen Miles from the said Owners Habitation, *Ten Shillings* per head, and if further, than *six-pence per mile* more to be paid and recovered as aforesaid. AND BE IT FURTHER ENACTED by the Authority aforesaid, that if any Person or Persons shall lend, give or hire out to any Slave, or Slaves, Pistol, Gun or Guns, the said Person or Persons so lending, giving, or hiring, shall forfeit the said Pistol, Gun or Guns, or *Twenty Shillings* to the Owner of the said Slave or Slaves, to be recovered as an Action of Debt as aforesaid.

4   SLAVE COURTS ESTABLISHED, 1695

Before the passage of the following act in 1695, blacks and whites faced trial, if not similar treatment, in the same East Jersey courts. This law established special slave courts where "Negroes, or other Slaves" accused of a felony or murder, were tried before three justices of the peace of the county and a jury of twelve men. In keeping with an earlier slave law passed in 1694 **[doc. 3],** the act also prescribed fines against imprudent owners whose slaves were convicted of theft. Harsh justice was meted out in these special slave courts from 1695 until 1768, when the New Jersey legislature abolished them.

An Act Concerning Negroes,
Leaming and Spicer, pp. 356-57.

BE IT ENACTED by the Governor, Council and Representatives in General Assembly met and assembled and by the Authority of the same, that when any Negro, Negroes, or other Slaves, shall be taken into Custody for Felony or Murder, or Suspicion of Felony or Murder, that three Justices of the Peace, of that County where the fact is committed, one being of the Quorum, shall with all conveniency meet and try the said Slave or Slaves, and upon Conviction by a Jury of Twelve lawful Men of the Neighbourhood, pronounce the Sentence appointed for such Crimes, and Sign the Execution. BE IT FURTHER ENACTED by the Authority aforesaid, that if any Negro, Negroes, or other Slaves shall steal, or be found stealing, any Swine, or other Cattle, Turkeys, Geese, or any other kind of Poultry and Provisions whatsoever, or any kind of Grain, and shall be convicted thereof before two Justices of the Peace, one whereof being of the Quorum, the Master or Mistress of such Negroes, or other Slaves, shall within Ten Days after Conviction, pay the Value of what he or they have Stolen to the Party from whom the same is Stolen, and in default to be levied by distress and sale of Goods, of the said Master or Mistress, by a Warrant from the Justices before whom such Conviction is made directed to the Constable of the Town where the Master or Mistress resides: And the said Negro or Negroes or other Slaves, being so convicted, shall be publickly punished with corporal Punishment, not exceeding Forty Stripes, the Master or Mistress of such Negro, Negroes or other Slaves, to pay the Charge thereof.

5 TIGHTENING SLAVE REGULATIONS, 1713

New Jersey enacted the following legislation in the aftermath of a 1712 slave revolt in New York City in which nine persons were killed and several injured. The specter of slave revolt nearby unnerved whites and further contributed to the erosion of black rights in New Jersey. The 1713 act mandated harsh penalties for slave crimes and misdemeanors, while extending the use of

separate courts for slaves throughout the province. Under its provisions, slaves could be whipped by any person if they were found
five miles from their master's premises. A similar fate was
prescribed for escaped slaves who entered New Jersey from
another province. The section of the law dealing with murder,
rape, and arson was closely patterned after New York's severe
slave code. So that slave owners would not attempt to help blacks
elude punishment, the measure provided that they were to be compensated for slaves who were executed. Theft by slaves was
punishable by public whipping. Slaves, moreover, were prohibited
from holding property—New York was the only other northern
colony to take such action.

This act generally reflected the prevailing racial attitudes
toward Africans. As free men and women, the law claimed that
they were "an idle, slothful people," who were a burden to
the colony. To discourage their manumission, owners were
required to post a security of 200 pounds and to pay a yearly sum
of twenty pounds to each slave they manumitted. Under these
conditions, the voluntary manumission of slaves was made financially prohibitive.

An Act for Regulating Slaves,
Samuel Neville, comp., *The Acts of the*
General Assembly of the Province of New Jersey,
2 vols. (Philadelphia and Woodbridge, N.J.,
1752–61), I:18-24.

Sect. 1. *BE IT ENACTED by the Governor, Council and General
Assembly, and by the Authority of the Same,* That all and every Person
or Persons within this Province, who shall at any Time after Publication
hereof, Buy, Sell, Barter, Trade or Traffick with any *Negro, Indian* or
Mulatto Slave, for any Rum, Wine, Beer, Sider, or other strong Drink,
or any other Chattels, Goods, Wares or Commodities whatsoever, unless
it be by the Consent of his, her or their Master or Mistress, or the Person
under whose Care they are, shall pay for the first Offence Twenty Shillings, and for the Second, and every other Offence, Forty Shillings,
Money according to the Queen's Proclamation, the one Half to the Informer, the other Half to the Use of the Poor of that Place where the
Fact is committed, to be recovered by Action of Debt before any one of
Her Majesty's Justices of the Peace.

2. *AND BE IT FURTHER ENACTED by the Authority aforesaid,*
That all and every Person or Persons within this Province who shall find
or take up any Negro, or Mulatto Slave or Slaves, five Miles from his,

her or their Master or Mistresses Habitation, who hath not Leave in Writing from his, her or their Master or Mistress, or are not known to be on their Service, he, she or they, so taken up, shall be whipt by the Party that takes them up, or by his Order, on the bare Back, not exceeding Twenty Lashes; and the Taker up shall have for his Reward *Five Shillings,* Money aforesaid, for every One taken up as aforesaid, with reasonable Charges for carrying him, her or them home, paid him by the Master or Mistress of the Slave or Slaves so taken up; and if above the said five Miles, *Six Pence per Mile* for every Mile over and above, to be recovered before any one Justice of the Peace, if it exceeds not *Forty Shillings,* and if more, by Action of Debt in the Court of Common-Pleas of the County where the Fact shall arise.

3. *AND BE IT FURTHER ENACTED by the Authority aforesaid,* That if any Negro, Indian or Mulatto Slave, of or belonging to any other Province shall come into this Province without License under the Hand of his, her or their Master or Mistress, or that is not known to be upon his or her Business, every such Negro, Indian or Mulatto Slave shall be taken up by any Person within this Province, and be whipp'd by the nearest Constable of the Place where the said Slave shall be taken up, not exceeding Twenty Lashes on the bare Back, and to be committed by a Warrant from the next Justice of the Peace, to the Goal of that County, and the Person so taking them up, and carrying them to be whipp'd, shall have for his Reward *Ten Shillings,* Money aforesaid, for each Slave, and the Constable *Three Shillings* for whipping each Slave, to be paid by the Master or Mistress of such Slave or Slaves, and to remain in Prison till it be paid, with all reasonable Charges that may accrue thereby.

4. *BE IT FURTHER ENACTED by the Authority aforesaid,* That all and every Negro, Indian or other Slave, who after the Publication of this Act shall murder, or otherways kill (unless by Misadventure, or in Execution of Justice) or conspire or attempt the Death of any of Her Majesty's Leige People, not being Slaves, or shall commit any Rape on any of the said Subjects, or shall wilfully burn any Dwelling-House, Barn, Stable, Out-House, Stack or Stacks of Corn or Hay, or shall wilfully Mutilate, Maim or Dismember any of the said Subjects, not being Slaves, as aforesaid, or shall wilfully Murder any Negro, Indian or Mulatto Slave within this Province, and thereof be convicted before three or more of Her Majesty's Justices of the Peace, one whereof being of the *Quorum,* who are hereby required and impowered to hear and determine the same, in Conjunction with five of the Principal Freeholders of the County wherein such Fact shall be committed, without a Grand Jury, seven of whom agreeing, shall give Judgment, and Sign the Execution, according to this Act, and he, she or they so offending, shall suffer the Pains of Death in such Manner as the Aggravation or Enormity of their Crimes (in the Judgment of the Justices and Freeholders aforesaid) shall merit and require.

5. *BE IT FURTHER ENACTED by the Authority aforesaid,* That upon Complaint made to any one Justice of the Peace against any Indian, Negro or Mulatto Slave or Slaves, who have or are supposed to have committed any of the Murders, Rapes, Maims, &c. mentioned in this Act, the said Justice shall immediately issue out his Warrant to the next Constable, to apprehend the said Offender or Offenders, and for all or any Person or Persons to come before him, that can give Evidence; and if upon Examination it appears that the Person or Persons are Guilty, he shall commit him or them to Prison, and also shall Certify to the next two Justices, the said Cause, and to require them, by Virtue of this Act, to associate themselves to him, which the said Justices are hereby required to do, and they so associated, are to issue their Summons to five Freeholders, acquainting them with the Cause, and appointing them the Time and Place the same shall be heard and determined; at which Time and Place the Justices are hereby impowered to appoint some Person to prosecute the said Offender or Offenders, and the Person appointed shall prefer an Accusation in Writing, specifying the Time, Place and Nature of the Offence, as near as conveniently may be, to which Accusation the Offender or Offenders shall be obliged to plead, and upon Refusal to plead, the like Judgment shall be given against the Person or Persons so accused, as if convict by Verdict or Confession. And upon Pleading thereto the Justice shall proceed to Tryal, in Conjunction with the said Freeholders so summoned as aforesaid, to which Freeholders no Peremptory Challenge shall be allowed. And if upon hearing the Matter (the said Freeholders being first sworn by the said Justices, to judge according to Evidence) they shall adjudge the Negro, Indian or Mulatto Slave or Slaves Guilty of the Offence complained of, they shall give Sentence of Death upon him, her or them, as aforesaid, and by their Warrant cause immediate Execution to be done by the common or other Exccutioner, in such Manner as they shall think fit. *Provided,* That the Evidence of Indian, Negro or Mulatto Slaves shall be admitted and allowed on Trials of such Slaves on all Causes criminal.

6. And whereas such Negro, Indian or Mulatto Slave is the Property of some of Her Majesty's Subjects in this or the neighbouring Provinces, *BE IT THEREFORE ENACTED,* That any Master or Mistress of any Negro, Indian or Mulatto Slave, supposed to be guilty, as aforesaid, may, upon their desiring the same, have a Jury to try the said Slave returned by the Sheriff, and the said Master or Mistress may have Liberty to make such Challenges to the Jury as is admitted to be made in other Cases of the like Nature.

7. And whereas such *Negro, Indian* or *Mulatto* Slave, so put to Death, will be a great Loss to the Owner of the same, who was no Way assisting, countenancing or abetting his said Slave in the Mischief done and perpetrated by the said Slave, and may induce the Owner to transport the said Slave out of the Province, by which Means the said Slave will be secured from the Punishment to be inflicted on him for his said Crime,

and other *Negro, Indian* or *Mulatto* Slaves encouraged to do the like Mischief, in Hopes of the same Security: For preventing of which for the future, and that the Owner of any *Negro, Indian* or *Mulatto* Slave may not be under any Temptation or withdrawing and securing the said Slave from the Prosecution of Justice, BE IT ENACTED, by the Governor, Council, and General Assembly, and by the Authority of the same, That every Owner of any *Negro, Indian* or *Mulatto* Slave (such Owner residing within this Province) shall for each Man Slave executed for any of the Crimes aforesaid, receive the Sum of *Thirty Pounds,* Money according to the Queen's Proclamation; and for every Woman Slave, executed as aforesaid, the Sum of *Twenty Pounds,* Money aforesaid; to be levied, collected and paid, in Manner following, *to wit,* The Constables of every Town and District within this Province, shall deliver a List of all the *Negro, Indian* or *Mulatto* Slaves, within their and each of their several and respective Districts, both Men and Women, above the Age of Fourteen, and under Fifty Years, which are not disabled or uncapable of performing their Master of Mistress's Service, unto the Justices at their Courts of General Quarter Sessions of the Peace in every County, in the Months of *May* and *June,* yearly and every Year, who shall order the Clerk of the Peace to file the same; and when any *Negro, Indian* or *Mulatto* Slave shall happen to be executed, for any Crime, the Justices of the Peace of the County where the Fact is committed, or any Three of them, One being of the *Quorum,* at the Desire of the Master or Mistress of such *Negro, Indian* or *Mulatto* Slave, shall meet together, and call for the aforesaid List from the Clerk of the Peace, and, according to said List, they shall assess the Value of the said Slave or Slaves so executed, equally on the Heads contained in the said List, *To wit, Thirty Pounds,* Money aforesaid, for a Man, and *Twenty Pounds* for a Women, or less, as the Justices, in their Discretion, shall think fit, and shall appoint a Collector, to collect and receive the same, of which Assessment, made as aforesaid, and the Time of Payment thereof, the Constables shall give Notice to the Masters, or Mistresses, of such *Negro, Indian* or *Mulatto* Slaves, within their and each of their several and respective Districts within said County, and upon Refusal or Delay of Payment, the said Collector shall deliver a List of the said Deficients to any Justice of the Peace of the said County, who shall make out Warrants to the Constables of the several Towns and Districts to distrain for the same, and the said distress to sell at a Public Out-cry, and pay the said Assessment to the said Collector, and *Eighteen Pence* to himself for the Charges of such Distress, and return the Overplus (if any be) to the Owner; and the said Collector shall pay the said Money so collected, to the Master of Mistress of said *Negro, Indian* or *Mulatto* Slave so executed, as aforesaid, and take his or her Receipt for the same, which he shall deliver to the Justice, at their next Sessions of the Peace, to be filed by the Clerk of the said Court.

8. And the Justices of the Peace are hereby allowed *One Shilling* for

every Warrant of Distress, as aforesaid, the Collector, for his Trouble shall have *One Shilling* in the Pound, for all Money collected and paid by him by Virtue of this Act, and each Constable shall have *Three Shillings* for giving Notice as aforesaid.

9. *AND BE IT FURTHER ENACTED,* That if any *Negro, Indian* or *Mulatto* Slave shall attempt to ravish any white Woman or Maid, or that shall presume to assault or strike any free Man or Woman professing Christianity, any two Justices of the Peace, are hereby authorized to inflict such corporal Punishment (not extending to Life or Limb) upon such Slave or Slaves so offending, as to the said Justices shall seem meet.

10. *AND BE IT ENACTED by the Authority aforesaid,* That if any *Negro, Indian* or *Mulatto* Slave, shall steal to the Value of *Six Pence,* or above, and under *Five Shillings,* and be thereof convicted before two Justices of the Peace, one whereof being of the *Quorum,* such *Negro, Indian* or *Mulatto* Slave, shall be whipped on the bare Back, at the Publick Whipping-place with Thirty Lashes, by the Constable of such Township or Place where the Offence was committed, or by such Person as he shall appoint. And that if any *Negro, Indian* or *Mulatto* Slave, shall steal to the Value of *Five Shillings,* or above, such Slave be whipped, on the bare Back, Forty Stripes, as aforesaid, by the Constable as aforesaid, the which Constable shall receive, for whipping of each Slave, *Five Shillings,* to be paid by the Master of Mistress of the Slave, and in Default of Payment, to be levied by Warrant from any Justice of the Peace, out of the Goods of the said Master or Mistress . . . .

12. *BE IT FURTHER ENACTED,* by the Authority aforesaid, That no Person or persons whatsoever, shall hereafter employ, harbour, conceal, or entertain other People's Slaves at their Houses, Out-houses, or Plantation, without the Consent of their Master or Mistress, either signified to them verbally, or by Certificate in Writing, under the said Master or Mistress's Hand, excepting in Distress of Weather, or other extraordinary Occasions, upon the Forfeiture of *Forty Shillings,* for every Time they are so entertained and concealed, to be paid to the Master or Mistress of such Slave or Slaves (so that the Penalty for entertaining such Slave, exceeds not the Value of said Slave.) And if any Person or Persons whatsoever, shall be found guilty of harbouring, entertaining or concealing of any Slave, or assisting to the Conveying them away, if such Slave shall happen to be lost, dead, or otherways rendered unserviceable, such Person or Persons so harbouring, entertaining, concealing, assisting or conveying them away, shall be also liable to pay the Value of such Slave to the Master or Mistress, to be recovered by Action of Debt, in any Court of Record within this Province.

13. *BE IT FURTHER ENACTED,* by the Authority aforesaid, That no *Negro, Indian* or *Mulatto* that shall hereafter be made free, shall enjoy, hold or possess, any House or Houses, Lands, Tenements or Hereditaments, within this Province, in his or her own Right, in Fee Sim-

ple of Fee Tail, but the same shall escheat to her Majesty, her Heirs and Successors.

14. AND whereas it is found by Experience, That Free *Negroes* are an idle, slothful People, and prove very often a Charge to the Place where they are, *BE IT THEREFORE FURTHER ENACTED,* by the Authority aforesaid, That any Master or Mistress, manumitting and setting at Liberty any *Negro* or *Mulatto* Slave, shall enter into sufficient Security unto her Majesty, her Heirs and Successors, with two Sureties, in the Sum of *Two Hundred Pounds,* to pay yearly and every Year to such *Negro* or *Mulatto* Slave, during their Lives, the Sum of *Twenty Pounds.* And if such *Negro* or *Mulatto* Slave, shall be made free by the Will and Testament of any Person deceased, that then the Executors of such Person shall enter into Security, as above, immediately upon proving the said Will and Testament, which if refused to be given, the said Manumission to be void, and of none Effect.

6 JOHN WOOLMAN ON RACIAL JUSTICE, 1754

The anti-slavery campaign in colonial New Jersey needed an articulate and energetic advocate. Such a man was John Woolman (1720–72), a Mount Holly tailor and storekeeper and a Quaker who came to the anti-slavery cause early in life. At twenty-three, Woolman was troubled when his employer asked him to prepare a bill of sale for an African slave. Subsequent travels through the southern colonies convinced him of the immorality of slavery. During his travels in New Jersey and the southern colonies, he attacked the evils of the institution, chastised his fellow Christians for their treatment of the Indians, and urged pacifism. His was an early American chronicle of lost causes. Yet, Woolman's speeches and writings were not without impact during the colonial period. He was an apostle of racial justice at a time when most whites were indifferent to the idea. Like the authors of the 1693 "Exhortation" [see doc. 2], Woolman defended the humanity of Africans; most of his contemporaries believed that whites and blacks had no common origins. Woolman and his early anti-slavery mentors implored Quakers to free their slaves. In the following abridged essay, Woolman presents an anti-slavery argument that was surprisingly well developed for its time. He was perhaps the first American writer to probe the question of racial prejudice in colonial society. Woolman believed, as did most of his contemporaries, that whites were endowed with "distinguished Gifts" which were denied to blacks; but he urged his race to use their superiority for good ends. For Woolman, unlike other early abolitionists, white prejudice and the stigma of bondage produced African slothfulness, ignorance, and depravity. This correlation became one of the most common arguments adduced by nineteenth-century abolitionists.

John Woolman, *Some Considerations on the Keeping of Negroes* (Philadelphia: Printed by James Chattin, 1754).

Forasmuch as ye did it to the least of these my brethren, ye did it unto me.—Matt. xxv.40.

As Many Times there are different Motives to the same Actions; and one does that from a generous Heart, which another does for selfish Ends:—The like may be said in this Case.

There are various Circumstances amongst them that keep *Negroes*, and different Ways by which they fall under their Care; and, I doubt not, there are many well disposed Persons amongst them, who desire rather to manage wisely and justly in this difficult Matter, than to make Gain of it.

But the general Disadvantage which these poor *Africans* lie under in an enlight'ned Christian Country, having often fill'd me with real Sadness, and been like undigested Matter on my Mind, I now think it my Duty, through Divine Aid, to offer some thoughts thereon to the Consideration of others.

When we remember that all Nations are of one Blood, *Gen.* iii. 20. that in this World we are but Sojourners, that we are subject to the like Afflictions and Infirmities of Body, the like Disorders and Frailties in Mind, the like Temptations, the same Death, and the same Judgment, and that the Alwise Being is Judge and Lord over us all, it seems to raise an Idea of a general Brotherhood, and a Disposition easy to be touched with a Feeling of each others Afflictions: But when we forget these Things, and look chiefly at our outward Circumstances, in this and some Ages past, constantly retaining in our Minds the Distinction betwixt us and them, with respect to our Knowledge and Improvement in Things divine, natural and artificial, our Breasts being apt to be filled with fond Notions of Superiority, there is Danger of erring in our Conduct toward them.

We allow them to be of the same Species with ourselves, the Odds is, we are in a higher Station, and enjoy greater Favours than they: And when it is thus, that our heavenly Father endoweth some of his Children with distinguished Gifts, they are intended for good Ends;

but if those thus gifted are thereby liften up above their Brethren, not considering themselves as Debtors to the Weak, nor behaving themselves as faithful Stewards, none who judge impartially can suppose them free from Ingratitude.

When a People dwell under the liberal distribution of Favours from Heaven, it behoves them carefully to inspect their Ways, and consider the Purposes for which those Favours were bestowed, lest, through Forgetfulness of God, and Misusing his Gifts, they incur his heavy Displeasure, whose Judgments are just and equal, who exalteth and humbleth to the Dust as he seeth meet . . . .

To consider Mankind otherwise then Brethren, to think Favours are peculiar to one Nation, and exclude others, plainly supposes a Darkness in the Understanding: For, as God's Love is universal, so where the Mind is sufficiently influenced by it, it begets a Likeness of itself, and the Heart is enlarged towards all Men. Again, to conclude a People froward, perverse, and worse by Nature than others (who ungratefully receive Favours, and apply them to bad Ends) this will excite a Behaviour toward them unbecoming the Excellence of true Religion.

To prevent such Error, let us calmly consider their Circumstance; and, the better to do it, make their Case ours. Suppose then, that our Ancestors and we had been exposed to constant Servitude in the more servile and inferior Employments of Life; that we had been destitute of the Help of Reading and good Company; that amongst ourselves we had had few wise and pious Instructors; that the Religious amongst our Superiors seldom took Notice of us; that while others, in Ease, have plentifully heap'd up the Fruit of our Labour, we had receiv'd barely enough to relieve Nature, and being wholly at the Command of others, had generally been treated as a contemptible, ignorant Part of Mankind: Should we, in that Case, be less abject than they now are? Again, if Oppression be so hard to bear, that a wise Man is made mad by it, *Eccl.* vii.7. then a Series of those Things altering the Behaviour and Manners of a People, is what may reasonably be expected.

When our Property is taken contrary to our Mind, by Means appearing to us unjust, it is only through Divine Influence, and the Enlargement of Heart from thence proceeding, that we can love our reputed Oppressors: If the *Negroes* fall short in this, an uneasy, if not a disconsolate Disposition, will be awaken'd, and remain like Seeds in their Minds, producing Sloth and many other Habits appearing odious to us; with which being free Men, they, perhaps had not been chargeable. These, and other Circumstances, rightly considered, will lessen that too great Disparity, which some make between us and them.

Integrity of Heart hath appeared in some of them; so that, if we continue in the Word of Christ [previous to Discipleship, *John* viii.31.] and our Conduct toward them be seasoned with his Love, we may hope to see the good Effect of it: The which, in a good Degree, is the Case with some into whose Hands they have fallen: But that too many treat them otherwise, not seeming conscious of any Neglect, is, alas! too evident. . . . Had these People come voluntary and dwelt amongst us, to have called them Strangers would be proper; and their being brought by Force, with Regret, and a languishing Mind, may well raise Compassion in a heart rightly disposed: But there is Nothing in such Treatment, which upon a wise and judicious Consideration, will any Ways lessen their Right of being treated as Strangers. If the Treatment which many of them meet with, be rightly examined, and compared with these Precepts, *Thou shalt not vex him nor oppress him; he shall be as one born amongst you, and thou shalt love him as thyself,* Lev. xix.33. Deut. xxvii.19. there will appear an important Difference betwixt them.

It may be objected there is Cost of Purchase, and Risque of their Lives to them who possess'em, and therefore needful that they make the best Use of their Time: In a Practice just and reasonable, such Objections may have Weight; but if the Work be wrong from the beginning, there's little or no Force in them. If I purchase a Man who hath never forfeited his Liberty, the natural Right of Freedom is in him; and shall I keep him and his Posterity in Servitude and Ignorance? "How should I approve of this Conduct, were I in his Circumstances, and he in mine?" It may be thought, that to treat them as we would willingly be treated, our Gain by them would be inconsiderable: And it were, in divers Respects, better that there were none in our Country.

We may further consider that they are now amongst us, and those of our Nation the cause of their being here; that whatsoever Difficulty accrues thereon, we are justly chargeable with, and to bear all Inconveniencies attending it, with a serious and weighty Concern of Mind to do our Duty by them, is the best we can do. To seek a Remedy by continuing the Oppression, because we have Power to do it and see others do it, will, I apprehend, not be doing as we would be done by . . . .

It appears, by Experience, that where Children are educated in Fulness, Ease and Idleness, evil Habits are more prevalent than is common amongst such who are prudently employed in the necessary Affairs of Life: And if Children are not only educated in the Way of so great Temptation, but have also the Opportunity of lording it over their Fellow Creatures, and being Masters of Men in their Childhood, how can we hope otherwise than that their tender Minds will be possessed with Thoughts too high for them? Which, by Continuance, gaining Strength, will prove like a slow Current, gradually separating them from (or keeping from Acquaintance with) that Humility and Meekness in which alone lasting Happiness can be enjoyed.

Man is born to labour, and Experience abundantly showeth that it is for our Good: But where the Powerful lay the Burthen on the Inferior, without affording a Christian Education, and suitable Opportunity of improving the Mind, and a treatment which we, in their Case, should approve, that themselves may live at Ease, and fare sumptuously, and lay up Riches for their Posterity, this seems to contradict the Design of Providence, and, I doubt, is sometimes the Effect of a perverted Mind: For while the Life of one is made grievous by the Rigour of another, it entails Misery on both . . . .

If we call to Mind our Beginning, some of us may find a Time, wherein our Fathers were under Afflictions, Reproaches, and manifold Sufferings.

Respecting our Progress in this Land, the Time is short since our Beginning was small and our Number few, compared with the native Inhabitants. He that sleeps not by Day nor by Night, hath watched over us, and kept us as the Apple of his Eye. His Almighty Arm hath been round about us, and saved us from Dangers.

The Wilderness and solitary Deserts in which our Fathers passed the Days of their Pilgrimage, are now turned into pleasant Fields; the Natives are gone from before us, and we established peaceably in the Possession of the Land, enjoying our Civil and religious Liberties; and, while many Parts of the World have groaned under the heavy Calamities of War, our Habitation remains quiet, and our Land fruitful.

When we trace back the Steps we have trodden, and see how the Lord hath opened a Way in the Wilderness for us, to the Wise it will easily appear, that all this was not done to be buried in Oblivion; but to prepare a People for more fruitful Returns, and the Remembrance thereof, ought to humble us in Prosperity, and excite in us a Christian Benevolence towards our Inferiors . . . .

Whoever rightly advocates the Cause of some, thereby promotes the Good of all. The State of Mankind was harmonious in the Beginning, and tho' sin hath introduced Discord, yet, through the wonderful Love of God, in Christ Jesus our Lord, the Way is open for our Redemption, and Means are appointed to restore us to primitive Harmony. That if one suffer, by the Unfaithfulness of another, the Mind, the most noble Part of him that occasions the Discord, is thereby alienated from its true and real Happiness.

Our Duty and Interest are inseparably united, and when we neglect or misuse our Talents, we necessarily depart from the heavenly Fellowship, and are in the Way to the greatest of Evils.

Therefore, to examine and prove ourselves, to find what Harmony the Power presiding in us bears with the Divine Nature, is a Duty not more incumbent and necessary, than it would be beneficial . . . .

To conclude, 'Tis a Truth most certain, that a Life guided by the Wisdom from above, agreeable with Justice, Equity, and Mercy, is throughout consistent and amiable, and truly beneficial to Society; the Serenity and Calmness of Mind in it, affords an unparallel'd Comfort in this Life, and the End of it is blessed.

And, no less true, that they, who in the Midst of high Favours, remain ungrateful, and under all Advantages that a Christian can desire, are selfish, earthly, and sensual, do miss the true Fountain of Happiness, and wander in a Maze of dark Anxiety, where all their Treasures are insufficient to quiet their Minds: Hence, from an insatiable Craving, they neglect doing Good with what they have acquired, and too often add Oppression to Vanity, that they may compass more.

O that they were wise, that they understood this, that they would consider their latter End! Deut. xxxii. 29.

---

7 DUTY-FREE IMPORTATION OF SLAVES, 1744

A generation before the American Revolution popularized libertarian principles, there was an attempt in New Jersey to curb the continued importation of African slaves. Some colonial leaders feared that black slaves, most of whom had been seasoned in the West Indies, threatened the security of white society. This view gained wide currency in 1741 after the New York slave conspiracy. Growing occurrences of slave crimes and the ever-present threat of insurrection made colonists re-examine the institution's merits.

As early as 1714, in a statute designed to foster white immigration, the Assembly laid a duty of ten pounds on every slave brought into New Jersey. The act expired in 1721, after which the free importation of Africans was permitted for the next forty-eight years. During that period the western counties unsuccessfully attempted to pass a duty in the colonial legislature. In 1744 a bill ("for Laying a Duty on Indian, Negroe and Molatto Slaves, imported into this Colony") passed the Assembly but was rejected by the Council of New Jersey. It was common for these two bodies to differ on the complicated question of import duties; the Assembly was the more representative body and thus inclined to support popular concerns. Obviously, the Assembly sought to tax slavery out of existence through this bill. The Council, however, feared that the proposed ten-pound duty on slaves would intensify the colony's labor shortage. At the time, many whites had been recruited for a British military expedition against the Spaniards in the West Indies, and immigration had diminished due to war in Europe and development of the linen industry in Ireland. Not until 1769, when the colony was in danger of becoming a haven for slave trading, because New York and Pennsylvania had duties on slaves, did New Jersey place a fifteen-pound duty on imported blacks.

Representation of the Council of New Jersey to Governor [Lewis] Morris—containing reasons for rejecting Severals Acts, etc., *New Jersey Archives,* ser. 1, 6:222-23.

The next Bill rejected by the Council, was, *A Bill for laying a Duty on Indian, Negroe and Molatto Slaves, imported into this Colony.*

This Bill the Council considered abstractedly from any instructions your Excellency has in relation to the African Company,[1] which many of the Gentlemen of the Assembly we suppose are not unacquainted with, and only weighed the Advantages and Disadvantages that would arise to the People of this Colony upon that Bill's passing into a Law. By that Bill was plainly intended an intire Prohibition of all Slaves being imported from foreign Parts, no less than a Duty of Ten Pounds being imposed on all grown Slaves imported from the West-Indies, and Five Pounds on all those directly imported from Africa. Upon the most mature Consideration the Council were of Opinion, that if that Bill, or any other Bill, discouraging the Importation of Slaves, should at this time pass into a Law, the People of this Province in general (a few Labourers only excepted) and the Farmers in particular, would be great Sufferers by it, and that for the following Reasons.

1. It is well Known, that a great Number of Labourers went out of this Province on the late Expedition to the West Indies, and that very few of them have returned; That many, for some Time past, have been going, and still are going, on the Privateering Account; by which Means Labourers Wages are become very high, and the Farmers, Trading-Men and Tradesmen, are greatly straitened for want of Labourers to carry on their Business.

2. It is also well Known, that since the Manufacture of Linnens has arrived to any tolerable Perfection in *Ireland,* we have had very few Servants or Labourers from that Island, and have no Reason to expect many for the Time to come.

3. The present War throughout the German Dominions, and between almost all the Powers on the Continent of *Europe,* give us Reason to expect no Assistance from that Quarter. And as our Sovereign is deeply engaged in a war with many powerful Princes, we have as little Reason to expect any Number of Servants from the Island of *Great-Britain.* Wherefore we conceive, that it would be more for the Interest of the People of this Colony to encourage at this Time the Importation of Slaves, than by a Law to prohibit them altogether, and therefore we rejected that Bill.

---

1. Chartered in 1672, the Royal African Company was granted a monopoly over the English slave trade in Africa until 1682.

II

Africans in a Strange Land

OUR knowledge of slave society in colonial New Jersey is severely limited by the paucity and bias of contemporary sources. Slaves rarely, if ever, committed their thoughts to writing. Bondage and racial prejudice fostered illiteracy and silenced much of the African's inner turmoil. When whites sought to describe the culture and social habits of blacks, their outlook was heavily clouded by cultural arrogance. Africans were viewed as uncivilized and pagan in their native lands. "Selfishness, absolute and lawless selfishness, is the master passion of their hearts," claimed the Reverend Samuel B. How of New Brunswick in 1855, "—a selfishness which regards neither justice, nor humanity, nor decency, nor friendship;—a selfishness which is universal, and which produces falsehood, theft, fraud, drunkenness, gluttony, and debauchery." There was, he said "no confidence between man and man. Every man must be the sole guardian of his own rights, his own interest and property, and defend them against the evil designs of all around him."[1] How's unfavorable view of African society was not uncommon. Most whites believed that the African's enslavement, though admittedly distasteful, afforded Christian salvation but held neither hope of eventual freedom nor social equality. That view reveals more about prevailing white attitudes than black manners and mores.

Contemporary records shed some light on the lives of Africans in New Jersey prior to the Revolution. Although most blacks were inarticulate by contemporary standards and constituted a small minority in most communities, they were seldom viewed with indifference. Colonial newspapers, legal and legislative records, and personal papers often touch on the peculiar problems caused by blacks. These sources make it clear that blacks as laborers had a considerable impact on New Jersey's economy and white society. Slaves displayed heroic qualities and never lost their desire for freedom. They resisted attempts to make them a docile labor force, running away and committing acts of vandalism and more serious crimes. Although contemporary observers often viewed their disorderly conduct as an expression of innate lawlessness, the severity and frequency of slave crimes suggest a deeper meaning. Slaves, on the whole, never became convinced that bondage was their natural condition and provided a constant challenge to the continuation of slavery.

After more than twenty years of revisionist historiography on slavery, it is now generally acknowledged that the blacks who were brought to the New World came from dynamic cultures and civilizations in West Africa. In their societies, Africans were accustomed to hard work and a systematic division of labor. Their agricultural economies, observes historian Kenneth Stampp, "in some places approached the complex organization of a plantation system."[2] Africans were used effectively on American sugar and tobacco plantations largely because of skills acquired in their native land. The practice of slavery in African societies, used as a rationale for slavery in the Americas, was, like all forced labor systems, potentially brutal; but it was not as destructive and demeaning as chattel slavery in the New World. In Africa even slaves were considered members of society.

Tribal customs wove intricate and subtle relationships between family members and gave stability and reverence to kinship in African society. Their religious practices, as historian John Blassingame has noted, were "a complex synthesis of magic, nature worship and belief in a Supreme Being."[3] Many African religious traditions survived in the New World. They blended with Christianity and gave the slave's "new religion" a vital role in surviving generations of bondage. As more Africans were brought into the colonies, their cultural baggage was more effectively, but not completely, stripped from them. In short, Africans in the New World retained a link with their native land through values, ideas, relationships, and behavioral patterns.[4]

New Jersey played a significant role in Afro-American colonial history. Blacks were imported there in larger numbers than any other northern colony, and their treatment was generally harsher than in other colonies whose economies were based primarily on white labor.[5] This does not suggest that Jerseymen were more hostile to blacks than were whites in other colonies. Rather, slavery as a social and economic institution withstood legal and moral challenges in New Jersey because of the colony's peculiar political development and the value of the institution to continued economic growth. [doc. 1] Frances Pingeon has shown that Africans brought with them skills that were highly valued by white colonists. Blacks tended to be excellent hunters and farmers. Dutch and Barbadian planters in the colony frequently entrusted black slaves with livestock.[6]

Blacks were also skilled iron forgers, miners, loggers, and woodworkers—trades which were practiced in Africa long before the beginning of the Atlantic slave trade. To these skills were added others learned under slavery. In contrast to slavery in the southern colonies, where a developing plantation system concentrated blacks in routine agricultural work, New Jersey blacks acquired proficiency in many non-agrarian crafts. The ferry at Lambertville in Hunterdon County used eight slaves. At the Andover Iron Works in Sussex County, as historian Leonard Stavisky noted in his study of black craftsmanship in colonial America, slaves "produced superior iron wares which were eventually accepted for high quality on the basis of brand name alone."[7] The principal labor performed by black men in colonial New Jersey was agricultural, but during the winter months their owners often gave them other responsibilities or sold their labor to white employers. Black women were generally domestic workers, although they were sometimes called upon to perform agricultural work.

In the realm of folk arts, too, blacks in New Jersey were distinctive and talented. Although many of their creative abilities were kept hidden from their owners, their dance and music were well known in the colony. During the early 1700s, dance contests between New York and New Jersey blacks helped make New York's Catherine Market a social mecca. Considered to be better dancers than the "country slaves" of New Jersey and Long Island, the local New York slaves were partisan favorites at such affairs.[8] Slaves retained many African musical traditions, and observers in New Jersey underscored their proficiency. In his study of Afro-American music, Amiri Baraka has argued that the "Negro's way in this part of the Western World was adaptation and reinterpretation. The banjo (an African word) is an African instrument, and the xylophone, used now in all Western orchestras, was also brought over by the Africans . . . ; the only so-called popular music in the country of any real value is of African derivation."[9] The colonists sought to preserve the music of the Old World in New Jersey, but in time their new environment and African influences spawned a distinctly American brand of popular music.

Numerically, blacks were always a minority. In 1726, there were approximately 2,581 blacks in a total population of 32,422; in 1738, New Jersey's total population of 47,364 contained only 3,981, and by 1745, blacks numbered 4,606 in a population of 61,383. On the eve of the Revolution, blacks accounted for between ten and twelve percent of the population.[10]

Since New Jersey never developed a plantation system as in the southern tobacco colonies, slaves were in much closer contact with their owners, and the influence of white society was undoubtedly greater. In some communities, according to contemporary observers, race relations were not universally strained. In 1894 the Reverend John Bodine Thompson of the Reformed Church in Readington recalled that Dick and Rose and Sam and Kate "used to come back occasionally to the farm on which they lived as slaves to visit their 'Young Missey,' as they called her, and to exchange reminiscences of earlier days, which brought tears of alternate joy and sorrow both to her eyes and to theirs."[11] In Hunterdon County the private lives of slaves and their owners seemed quite close. Some benevolent owners considered slaves not merely property but members of their families. Blacks took on the surnames of their owners and participated in local festivities, especially at Christmas and when the militia drilled in June.[12] Probably the most striking manifestation of interracial contact in New Jersey was the extensive evidence of miscegenation. The records of the colonial period made many references to mulattoes in the black population, though it is clear that they were not accorded any more liberties or privileges than slaves of pure African ancestry.[13] [see chap. 1, doc. 5, 7]

Christianity contributed to the acculturation of Afro-Americans. During the eighteenth century and especially the religious revival known as the Great Awakening (1739–44), slaves were converted in ever-increasing numbers. Slaves took the sacrament in Lutheran, Dutch Reformed, Presbyterian, Methodist, and Baptist churches, and, in relatively large numbers, joined the Society of Friends. Cyrus Bustill (1732–1806) of Burlington, a distinguished free black, became a Quaker and was married in a Friends ceremony. Mingo Whano of Bethlehem Township, a man of African nobility before his enslavement, was also a Quaker convert, as was William Boen of Mount Holly.[14] **[doc. 2]** On rare occasions black Christians were allowed to preach before white congregations. There is also evidence that they were subjected to the moral rigors of the religion; in Hunterdon County a black woman was released from the Hopewell Baptist Church because she gave birth to "a bastard child."

Familial ties of blacks in New Jersey, as in other slave colonies, were subservient to the financial and personal needs of their owners. Although some slaves were married in Christian ceremonies, these unions were not protected from the abuses of the slave system. The family under these conditions, as Arthur Zilversmit observed in his study of slavery in the northern colonies, was a precarious institution.[15] The greatest threat to stable unions between blacks was the colonial slave trade. Families rarely remained together when slaves were sold. Children were usually, but not always, sold with their mother. There seems to have been a correlation between the slave family's stability and its master's moral convictions. Quaker religious principles worked against the destruction of family ties; some owners sought to keep parents and children united when they were sold. But in most areas of the colony little consideration was given to the welfare of black families. **[doc. 3]** Afro-Americans, nevertheless, sought to preserve their families even if it meant escaping from bondage to be reunited with loved ones.

Slavery in New Jersey, as elsewhere, denied to Afro-Americans most opportunities for social mobility. Rarely could slaves use their skills to acquire money and purchase their freedom. As a result of the limits placed upon slaves, many of them attempted to escape from their owners, using deceit and various forms of rebelliousness as alternatives to a life of perpetual bondage. The odds were great against successful escape from slavery. Under the threat of prosecution for aiding runaways, few whites and perhaps not many blacks would befriend an escaping slave. A successful flight to freedom required reliance on the slave's wits, favorable circumstances, and, least reliable of all, luck. Slaves fled despite cruel physical hazards and unknown circumstances awaiting them at the end of the journey. Fearing the loss of valuable property, colonial slaveholders advertised rewards for captured slaves. The rewards posted in local newspapers reveal that Africans were often ingenious in flight. Usually an escaping slave would make his or her dash for freedom alone, although on occasion small groups escaped. From the available sources, it seems that warm weather brought a flurry of escape attempts. Some enterprising blacks, much to the chagrin of their owners, absconded with clothes, livestock, and weapons. Newspaper notices also reveal that slaves were often competent in the use of English as well as other European languages, but the clever runaway knew that he should mask such skills in order to avoid suspicion. They also forged manumission certificates to facilitate their trek through the colony. Most were young men in their twenties and thirties, but older men also eluded their masters. Relatively few rewards were posted for women, perhaps as a result of the difficulty of escape with children, the lesser value of women to their owners, and the comparatively lighter work given to female slaves. [doc. 4]

Fugitive slaves were the most troublesome problem for slaveholders during the colonial period, but the threat of rebellion was always their greatest fear. There were few slave uprisings in New Jersey; but whites, encouraged by the popular notion that Africans were dangerous, lived in fear that blacks, if given the opportunity, would rise up against them. In 1734 the fears of a black insurrection were intensified when an alleged uprising was uncovered near Somerville. [doc. 5] During the so-called Negro Conspiracy in New York in 1741, whites in Hackensack, Bergen County, meted out a swift and harsh punishment to those suspected of complicity in the scheme. When two blacks accused of setting fire to barns in Bergen County were burned at the stake for their alleged participation in the unsuccessful plot, an observer noted: "The People thereabout are greatly alarmed, and Keep under Arms every Night, as well as at New-York."[16]

The persistent fear of slave uprisings and the unwelcome competition which slavery posed to white workers encouraged the colonial legislature to use import duties in an effort to restrict the number of blacks. [see chap. 1, doc. 7] While such efforts were unsuccessful in New Jersey until 1769, New York and Pennsylvania enacted legislation toward that end. As a result, New Jersey faced the threat of large numbers of blacks being unloaded in the colony, a dangerous prospect which Governor Josiah Hardy outlined in correspondence with the Board of Trade in 1762. Prior to the passage of the 1769 measure placing duties on slave importation, New Jersey became a leading area for slave trading in the mid-Atlantic colonies and the soil upon which scores of Africans began their lives in North America.

1 BLACK CARGOES, 1761–64

Without an import duty on slaves until 1769, New Jersey became a major slave trading area in the northern colonies. Ships carrying slaves directly from the coast of western Africa, or from Barbados and other sugar colonies in the Caribbean archipelago, docked in New Jersey ports, particularly Perth Amboy and Cooper's Ferry (now in Camden). Their human cargoes were advertised in local newspapers, as shown below, and then sold to New Jersey buyers and slave traders from neighboring Pennsylvania and New York. In May 1762 the schooner *Sally* was anchored at Cooper's Ferry, boasting "a parcel of likely Men and Women Slaves, with some Boys and Girls of different Ages" from the region of the River Gambia. More than two centuries later, Alex Haley would trace his family back to one of his enslaved ancestors, Kunta Kinte, who was taken from the village of Juffure in Gambia.

**Elizabeth Donnan, ed., *Documents Illustrative
of the History of the Slave Trade to America*
(Washington, D.C., 1932), 3: 454-56.**

May 28, 1761.

Just imported from Barbadoes, in the Ship *William and Mary,* George Nicholson, Master, and now lodged at Mr. Daniel Cooper's Ferry, on the Jersey Shore.

A Negroe Man, and two New Negroe Boys, who are to be sold by Willing, Morris and Company. The Purchaser to pay the Duty lately imposed by Act of Assembly, if brought into this Province.

Aug. 6, 1761.

To be Sold, On Board the Schooner *Hannah,* lying in the River Delaware, very near Mr. Daniel Cooper's Ferry, West New Jersey, opposite the City of Philadelphia, a Cargo of likely Negroes, just imported in said Schooner, directly from the Coast of Guinea. For terms of sale apply to Thomas Riche, David Franks, or Daniel Rundle.

Oct. 22, 1761.

Just imported in the Sloop *Company,* Captain Hodgson, from the Coast of Africa, A Parcel of Likely Negroe Slaves; Which may be seen on board said Sloop, lying off Cooper's Ferry. For Terms, apply to Samuel and Archibald M'Call, and James Wallace and Company.

May 27, 1762.

Just imported from the River Gambia in the Schooner *Sally,* Bernard Badger, Master, and to be sold at the Upper Ferry (called Benjamin Cooper's Ferry), opposite to this City, a parcel of likely Men and Women Slaves, with some Boys and Girls of different Ages. Attendence will be given from the hours of nine to twelve o'clock in the Morning, and from three to six in the Afternoon, by W. Coxe, S. Oldman, and Company. N.B. It is generally allowed that the Gambia Slaves are much more robust and tractable than any other slaves from the Coast of Guinea, and the more Capable of undergoing the Severity of the Winter Seasons in the North-American Colonies, which occasions their being Vastly more esteemed and coveted in this Province and those to the Northward, than any other Slaves whatsoever.

Sept. 20, 1764.

Just imported in the Brigantine *Africa*, Francis Moore, master, from the coast of Guinea, and to be sold by Thomas Riche, In New Jersey, opposite Philadelphia, A few likely Negro men, women, boys and girls, very reasonable for cash or short credit. N.B. The said Riche will attend the Sale from 10 to 1 o'clock, and from 2 till 5 in the afternoon.

2   ONE BLACK MAN'S LIFE, 1735–1824

The *Anecdotes and Memoirs of William Boen* is among the earliest accounts of a black New Jerseyan's life. Boen (1735–1824) was born in Rancocas near Mount Holly, Burlington County, where Quakers constituted a sizeable portion of the population and its most influential inhabitants. This work recalls his life under slavery, his conversion to Christianity, and his freedom. Boen became a Quaker at the age of eighty after a life of exemplary Christian virtue and plain living. He refused to use food or clothing produced by slave labor and dressed in the simple manner of John Woolman, with whom he was intimately acquainted. In the following selection, Boen's own words and testimony by members of the Mount Holly Friends Meeting in 1824 underscore his devotion to a Christian life in a society blighted by slavery.

Anecdotes and Memoirs of William Boen, A Coloured Man, Who Lived and Died Near Mount Holly, New Jersey . . . **(Philadelphia, 1834), pp. 3-8.**

William Boen was a coloured man, who resided near Mount Holly, New Jersey. Like many of his brethren of the African race, in those days, he was from his birth held as a slave. But though poor and ignorant, in his early days, he was cared for, as all others are, by the universal Parent of the human family. He became a pious, sober, temperate, honest, and industrious man; and by this means, he obtained the friendship, esteem, and respect of all classes of his fellow-men, and the approbation and peace of his heavenly Father.

His industry, temperance, and cleanliness, no doubt, contributed much to his health and comfort; so that he lived to be a very old man, with having but little sickness through the course of his life. His character being so remarkable for sobriety, honesty, and peace—that it induced some younger people to inquire by what means he had arrived to such a state, and attained such a standing in the neighbourhood where he lived. Ever willing to instruct, counsel, and admonish the youth, he could relate his own experience of the work of grace in his heart, which led him into such uprightness of life and conduct. For his memory did not appear to be much impaired by reason of old age.

To a friend who visited him in the eighty-sixth year of his age, he gave the following account of his early life, and religious experience. On being asked, whether he could remember in what way, and by what means, he was first brought to mind and follow *that,* which had been his guide and rule of faith and life, and which had led and preserved him so safely along through time? William answered as follows: "Oh! yes; that I can, right well. In the time of the old French war, my master (for I was a poor black boy, a slave) my master sent me to chop wood, on a hill-side, out of sight of any house; and there was a great forest of woods below me; and he told me to cut down all the trees on that hill-side. When I went home, in the evenings, I often heard them talking about the Indians killing and scalping people: and sometimes, some of the neighbours would come in, and they and my master's family talked of the Indians killing such and such,—nearer and nearer to us. And so, from time to time, I would hear them tell of the Indians killing, and scalping people, nearer and nearer: so that I began to think, like enough, by and by, they would kill me. And I thought more and more about it; and again would hear tell of their coming still nearer. At length, I thought, sure enough they will get so near, that they will hear the sound of my axe, and will come and kill me. Here is a great forest of woods below me, and no house in sight:—surely, I have not long to live. I expected every day would be my last;—that they would soon kill me, a poor black boy, here all alone."

"A thought then came into my mind, whether I was fit to die. It was showed me, and I saw plain enough, that I was not fit to die. Then it troubled me very much, that I was not fit to die; and I felt very desirous,—very anxious that I might be made fit to die. So I stood still, in great amazement; and it seemed as if a flaming sword passed through me. And when it passed over, and I recollected myself (for I stood so, some time) it was showed me how I should be made fit to die: and I was willing to do any thing, so I might be made fit to die.''

"Thus, I was brought to mind and follow *that,* that has been the guide and rule of my life,—*that within me,* that inclined me to good, and showed and condemned evil. Now I considered I had a new master—I had two masters; and it was showed me (in my mind) by my new Master, a certain tree on the hill-side, that I must not cut down. I knowed the tree well enough. I had not come to it yet. But I did not know what I *should* do; for my old master had told me to cut all the trees down, on that hill-side. My new Master forbids me to cut a certain one. So I thought a good deal about it. I cut on; and by and by I came to the tree. I cut on by it, and let it stand. But I expected, every day, my old master would come, and see that tree standing, and say, 'What did thee leave that tree standing for? Did not I tell thee to cut all the trees down, as thee went? Go, cut that tree down.' Then, I did'nt know what I *should* do. I cut on, and got some distance by it; and one day my old master brought out his axe, and cut the tree down himself; and never said, William why didn't thee cut that tree down? never said any thing to me about it. Then I thought, surely my new Master will make way for me, and take care of me, if I love him, and mind him, and am attentive to this my guide, and rule of life. And this seemed an evidence and proof of it, and strengthened me much in love, and confidence in my Guide.''

After the respectable and goodly old man, had given this interesting account of the way and manner in which he was brought to follow the guide of his life, the following question was put to him: "Well, William, has thee, from that time, till now, been so careful and attentive to thy guide, as never to say or do amiss?'' To which he replied, "Oh! no: I have missed it—I have several times missed it.'' He was then asked, "Well, William, in that case, how *did* thee get along?'' He answered, "Oh! when I missed it,—when I found I had said, or done wrong, I felt very sorry. I tried to be more careful, for time to come;—never to do so any more: and I believe I was forgiven.''

Another inquiry was made of William, how he and his old master got along together, after his change. He said, "Very well. Some time afterwards, one of the neighbours said to me, one day, 'William, thy master talks of setting thee free.' I did'nt think much about it—did'nt expect there was any thing in it; though I heard others say he talked of setting me free;—till, after some time, as my master was walking with me, going to my work, he said, 'William, would'nt thee like to be free?' I did'nt say any thing to it. I thought he might know I should like to be free. I did'nt make him any answer about it, but then I thought there was something in it. So after awhile, sure enough, he did set me free.''

There is no doubt his old master observed a great change in him; for his guide taught him to be dutiful, industrious and diligent in his business, careful in his words and actions, and sober, steady, and exemplary in all he said, and in all his conduct.

William Boen's guide, and rule of life and conduct, his *new Master,* as he called him, that did so much for him, and raised him from the state of a poor slave, to be a free man, in good esteem—thro' habits of temperance, sobriety, honest industry and integrity,—whereby he was enabled to become the respectable head of a family, and to acquire a house, and property of his own, sufficient for the comfortable accommodation of himself and family;—and who forsook him not when he became old, and grey-headed;—his new Master was the same Light that appears unto all; and it would guide every one in the right way, as it did him, if they would take it for their Master, and mind and obey it, as he did. It was the guide of his youth,—became his Lord and Master,—preserved him from evil,—and conducted him safely through the trials of life, to a good old age.

William Boen's new Master was, and is the same thing that the apostle Paul, in his Epistle to Titus, bears testimony to, in these words; "the grace of God, that bringeth salvation, hath appeared to all men;—teaching us, that, denying all ungodliness and worldly lusts, we should live soberly, righteously, and godly in this present world." Now, surely, if we don't take it for our master, and mind its teachings, we cannot *know* it to bring our salvation, or *save us* from *all ungodliness* and *worldly lusts,* as he did, and as all do, that are obedient to this grace of God, *the Light of Christ, within.*

In William Boen's simple account of the way and means, by which he was showed how he should be made fit to die;—that is, by minding and following *that within* him, which inclined him to good, and that showed and condemned him for evil,—the goodness, mercy, and condescending care of the Almighty Father, are strikingly manifest. How graciously he suits his dispensations to the weak and ignorant states of his children, who sincerely seek him, and inquire what they shall do to be saved! When William Boen thought of death, something showed him he was not fit to die. He "saw it plain enough," and was troubled. In his anxiety to be prepared to die, he became still and quiet—and then he felt condemnation, as a flaming sword, pass through him. When this had its effect to bring him to a state of humility and watchfulness, the Divine Light in his soul showed him the way in which he should walk, in order to become fit to die. He became willing to do any thing required of him: so, to prove his obedience, it was showed him, by his new Master, that he must leave a certain tree standing, where he was felling timber. He began to reason upon consequences, but resolved to obey his new Master, in preference to his old one. It was sufficient to test his faith and love; and though a simple circumstance, it was probably of great use to him ever after; as by it he was taught to be faithful in little things, and thus became ruler over more . . . .

3 SLAVES FOR SALE, 1743-81

White New Jerseyans bought, sold, and leased slaves much like livestock, real estate, or other forms of property. The following newspaper advertisements, dating from 1743 to 1781, provide an insight into the New Jersey slave trade. Although the stereotype of the lazy and dim-witted African persisted throughout the period, the advertisements reveal that blacks were prized as carpenters, blacksmiths, and miners—skilled workers and not just agricultural laborers.

New Jersey Archives, **ser. 1, 12: 186, 316, 339; 26: 88-90; 2, 1: 543; 5: 147, 223.**

TO BE LET,
For the Term of ten YEARS,

A PLANTATION SCITUATE IN THE TOWNSHIP of Greenwich, in the County of Gloucester, in New-Jersey, containing seven hundred Acres of Land, a considerable quantity of Land and good Meadow cleared, with a good Orchard, and new stone House and Kitchen. Also one half Part of a New Saw-Mill, adjoining to said Plantation, with nine hundred Acres of good Pines within a Mile of the said Mill; Likewise a likely young Negro Man, who understands Plantation or Saw-Mill business; to be Let with the said Plantation: As also there is to be sold a Negro Woman who understands Country business, and a likely young Negro Boy between 7 and 8 Years old, to be sold or put out for a Term of Years.

Any Person that is inclined to agree for any of the said Premises, may apply to the Subscriber, residing at Henry Wood's in Waterford in the said County, and agree on reasonable Terms with

MARY COLE.
—*The Pennsylvania Gazette, July* 14, 1743.

TO be Sold at publick Vendue, on *Friday* the 29th Instant, at the House of Mr. *Joseph Johnson,* in *Newark,* two Negro Men, whome understands Mining; as Also the Utencels belonging to the Mine, in *Kingsland's* Lands, with Pots and Kittles, &c. As also the remaining Part of the Leace of said Mine which being near two Years.—*The New-York Evening-Post, Aug.* 25, 1746.

To be SOLD,
TWO Likely Negro Men, one of them a Ship-Carpenter by Trade, and

the other understands a Team or Plantation-Work; Also a Negro Wench with two small Children; the Wench understands House-Work. Any Person inclining to purchase, may apply to Susannah Marsh, *Widow, at* Perth-Amboy, *who will dispose of them on reasonable Terms.—The New York Weekly Post Boy, March* 9, 1747.

To be LET, by William Kelly,

A very valuable Tract, of about 2000 Acres of Land, in the County of Morris, in East New-Jersey . . . The Title clear and indisputable, and will be warranted to the Purchaser. There is on it now, the largest and finest Breed of Cattle in America, imported from Holland, and as good Horses as any in the Province; all, or any of which, with about twenty Slaves, bred to farming and Country Work, (among which is a good Blacksmith, a Mason, and a Shoemaker,) will be sold, and Possession of the Whole immediately after given to the Tennant or a Purchaser. For further Particulars, enquire of John Berrian, Esq; near Prince-Town; Jonathan Hampton, and Abraham Clark, Jun., Esq; near Elizabeth-Town, or the Owner in New-York.—*The New York Gazette and Weekly Mercury, No.* 855, *March* 21, 1768.

TO BE SOLD.

Two Negro men, both under thirty, healthy and strong; one of them a valuable and compleat farmer in all its branches, to which he has been bred from a child, and is very stout. The other a genteel footman and waiter, understands the care of horses well, the management of a carriage, drives either on the box or as postilion, and in every respect suitable for a genteel family, or single Gentleman, and is fond of farming. Both have had the smallpox. Enquire of Mr. Coxe at Trenton, of Doctor Redman at Philadelphia. [1776]

To be SOLD cheap,
By the Subscriber,

A NEGRO MAN about thirty-two years of age, a negro woman about twenty-four, with a child of fifteen months, not for any fault, but want of employ. They being man and wife would make it most agreeable to sell them together; however a few miles separation will not prevent the sale. Any person inclining to purchase will receive satisfactory accounts of their characters by applying to

JOHN BRAY.

Raritan Landing, Dec. 11, 1780.

TO BE SOLD,
For any current Money,

A Negro Man and Woman with two Children, one a girl two years old; the other a boy on the breast. They will be sold cheap to any person who

will take the family. The only cause of selling them is the owner's want-
ing to lessen his family. For terms and particulars apply to Mr. Abraham
Hunt, Trenton, or the owner at Bowhill farm, Nottingham township,
Burlington county. [1781]

RANDLE MITCHELL.

---

4 TAKING THEIR FREEDOM, 1772–82

The following notices for fugitive slaves in New Jersey were
posted in New York, Pennsylvania, and New Jersey newspapers
between 1772 and 1782. Most of them appeared in the press of
neighboring states because New Jersey was without its own
newspaper until the *New-Jersey Gazette* commenced publication
in 1777. The appearance of such large numbers of notices is
evidence of the continuing desire of slaves for freedom and
testimony to their courage and cleverness. Without legal rights,
slaves could do little but hope for manumission, foment rebellion,
or run away.

In the face of potentially severe punishment if apprehended and
returned, black slaves ran away in significant numbers. It was a
problem troubling slaveholders across the colony. A sharp increase in the number of fugitives occurred during the Revolution
in large part because blacks sought to escape to areas held by the
Loyalist forces, in expectation of more favorable treatment, and
they realized that the disorderly conditions caused by the war
made their capture more difficult. [see chap. 3, doc. 6–8]

The sixteen runaway slaves mentioned in the following notices
were mostly black males, with an average age of twenty-five and
height of five feet and seven inches. Several were bilingual in
English and Dutch, German, or French. But others recently taken
from Africa were hardly able to communicate in their new environment. Blacks rarely ran away without taking along clothing,
food, other provisions, and occasionally firearms.

Smallpox was apparently a prevalent disease among slaves, as
evidenced by several references to the scars it left on the skin of
blacks. In a few cases a fugitive slave could be identified by whipping scars or work-related disabilities. Most of the fugitives made
their escape alone; but there are accounts of small groups abandoning the owner's premises. Fugitive slaves occasionally took

their small children with them. In seeking the return of their slaves, owners offered a wide range of financial rewards and threatened legal action against those who harbored them.

New Jersey Archives,
ser. 1, 28: 502-503, 342, 407, 547-48, 535-6, 503;
2, 1: 134; 5: 398, 180; 4: 121; 5: 157, 116.

Thirty Dollars Reward.

RUN-AWAY from the subscriber, living at Connecticut Farms, near Elizabeth-Town, New-Jersey, the 13th of March, a negro man named BRET: He is the same fellow the Salmons have had at Weyoming for three years past; is stout and well made, near 6 feet high, about 33 years old: Had on when he went away, a red great coat half worn, a blue coat, and a Kersey jacket of the same colour, with flat white metal buttons, buckskin breeches, and black and white stockings. He can read and write, and 'tis supposed will forge a pass. Whoever takes up and secures the said fellow in either Philadelphia or Easton goal so that his master may get him again, shall have the above reward, and all reasonable charges for bringing him to the subscriber. . . . 'Tis probable he may endeavour to get to the Mississippi; and in case taken there, and sent to New-York, the above reward will be paid by Hugh Gaine . . . . If apprehended, unless well secured, he will endeavour to make his escape, being strong and very artful. Those that harbour said fellow, may depend on being prosecuted by

JECAMIAH SMITH.

—*The New-York Gazette; and The Weekly Mercury, No.* 1124, *May* 10, 1773.

FIVE DOLLARS REWARD.

RUN-away from Samuel Ogden, of Boontown, in the County of Morris, and Province of New-Jersey, on Sunday the 18th of October last: A Negro Man named Mingo or Tim, he is about 30 Years of Age, has a Scar either on his Nose or on one of his Cheeks; is about 5 feet 7 or 8 Inches high, plays on the Violin, speaks good Dutch and English, and is much addicted to Strong drink: Had on when he went away a dark brown broad cloth Coat, with brass Philadelphia Buttons, a brown broad cloth waist-coat, with basket mohair Buttons, a Pair of red coating Trowsers, an ozenbrig Shirt and wool Hat. He was formerly the property of Isaac Wilkins, Esq; of West-Chester, about which Place it is not unlikely he may be lurking. Whoever apprehends said Negro and returns him to his Master, or secures him in any of his Majesty's goals, shall be paid the above Reward, and all reasonable Charges by

[1772]   SAMUEL OGDEN.

RUN-AWAY from the Subscriber, on Sunday Evening the 27th Day of December last, a Negro Man named JACK, about 33 Years old, a short spare Fellow: Had on when he went away, a brown double-breasted short Forrest Cloth Jacket, with plain Brass Buttons, lined with red Baze; a red Baze under Jacket, Leather Breeches, and Blue Yarn Stockings. He took with him a light Coat much wore of fine twilled Frize, the knap wore off, and a new blue Watch-coat of Coating, with white plated Buttons. He was purchased from Hendrick Emons, of Rockey-Hill in New Jersey, about 9 years ago, and it is supposed he is either gone that Way, where he has a Mother, or else to Anthony Ten Eyck's at Albany, where he has a Wife. . . . Any person that will take up said Negro and secure him, so that his Master may have him again, shall have Forty Shillings Reward, and all reasonable Charges, paid by

PETER KETELTAS.
—*New York Gazette and Weekly Mercury, No.* 1108, *January* 18, 1773.

FORTY SHILLINGS Reward.

RUN AWAY from the subscriber on Saturday last, the 26th instant, a Negro Man named Peter, about twenty years of age, about 5 feet high, a clumsey looking fellow, stoops a little in his walk. Had on and took with him, a light coloured wilton coatee, a red nap ditto, a clouded knit waistcoat, light coloured jean breeches with silk garters, black plush ditto, almost new shoes, clouded stockings, check shirt, plated buckles, an old beaver hat, and other articles. As he is a cunning artful fellow will endeavor to pass for a free man, he has a mother living in Trentown, a free woman named Violet, and it is likely he is gone that way. Whoever apprehends and secures said Negroe in any of his Majesty's goals so that his master may have him again, shall have the above reward, and reasonable charges if brought home, paid by

JOHN M'CALLA.
N.B. All masters of vessels and others are forbid to harbour or carry off said Negro at their peril.—*The Pennsylvania Gazette, No.* 2323, *June* 30, 1773.

THIRTY DOLLARS Reward.

RUN-AWAY from the subscribers, living in Hopewell township, Hunterdon county, and province of New Jersey, on Sunday evening last, the 13th inst. three Negro men, viz. BONTURAH, by trade a shoemaker, 27 years of age, and a well-set fellow: Had on and took with him, a suit of black clothes, a brown silk camblet coat, three linen shirts, good shoes and stockings. The second named JACK, 23 years old, and exceeds the others in stoutness: Had on and took with him, a yellowish brown close bodied coat, a vest, the fore parts calf-skin, with the hair on, new buckskin breeches, a new felt hat, good shoes and stockings. The third named FRANK, 19 years old: Had on and took with him, a green sagathy coat, a light coloured cut velvet vest, two striped Holland jackets, a brown coat, a red great coat, a pair of leather breeches, three shirts, the one ruffled, a pair of tow trowsers, a new castor hat, good shoes and stockings. They are all this country born, each near 5 feet 6 inches high, of the blackest kind, and as they can read, it is supposed they have passes, which the subscribers desire to have secured, with them. The one has a wife in Philadelphia. They took with them a fear-nought great coat. Whoever takes up and secures said Negroes in any of his Majesty's gaols, so that their masters may have them again, shall have the above reward, or TEN DOLLARS for either, and reasonable charges, paid by SAMUEL STOUT, sen. BENJAMIN STOUT, jun. and SAMUEL STOUT, jun. or by THOMAS SHIELDS, in Philadelphia.—*The Pennsylvania Journal, No.* 1593, *June* 16, 1773.

FORTY SHILLINGS REWARD.

RUN away from the subscriber, living at Great Egg Harbour, in Gloucester county, West New Jersey, on the 20th of March, a certain negroe man, called PERO, about 28 years old, five feet eight inches high, hobbles in his walk, his left foot having been froze, the great toe of which is considerably shorter than the other; had on and took with him, a blue duffil great coat, cotton striped under jacket, one pair of grey nap trowsers, and one pair of white swanskin ditto, much worn, speaks broken English. Whoever takes up said negroe and secures him in any of his Majesty's gaols, so that his master may have him again, shall receive the above reward, and reasonable charges, paid by

ELIJAH CLARK.

Newcastle Gaol, April 28, 1773.

Ten Dollars Reward.

RUN-away last Thursday from the Subscriber, at Newark, a certain Negro Fellow named Jack, about 25 years old, a square well-built Fellow, pretty black, Guiney born, and spoke bad English: He took with him several Sorts of Cloths, his Master's Gun, and a Grenadier's Sword, with Brass Mountings: He is supposed to have had on a good Beaver Hat cocked in the Fashion, a light coloured fine Cloth Jacket, without Sleeves, and may wear a Blanket Coat, he has a Scar right down his Forehead to his Nose, his country Mark, can handle a File, and understands the Brass Founder's Business. Whoever takes up the said Fellow, and delivers him to Mrs. Wilkins, near Ogden's Furnace, in Newark, shall have the above reward; or in New-York, to

JACOB WILKINS.

—*New York Gazette and Weekly Mercury, June* 25, 1776.

RUN AWAY a Negro man named Jack, about thirty-five years old, straight and well limbed, and about five feet ten inches high, very white even teeth, has holes in his ears, understands the coopers trade, and can talk French: had on a striped woollen shirt, a cloth-coloured jacket and waistcoat much worn and patched, a pair of buckskin breeches almost new and stained in the seat by riding bareback, grey stockings and shoes newly soaled; took with him homespon coat, buttons covered with the same, and lined with blue, a jacket and breeches of homespun dimity, a white linen shirt and pair of new shoes. Whoever apprehends the said Negro, and delivers him to the subscriber, or secures him in any gaol, so that he may be had again, shall be paid Three Pounds and reasonable charges by

JAMES PARKER.

Pitts-Town, Hunterdon county, March 9, 1782.

RAN AWAY,
From the subscribers last night,

A Negro Man named Joe, and a Negro Woman named Hester: The man is about five feet six or seven inches high, well set, full faced, of an open countenance, was formerly a servant to a British officer, speaks the German language well; had on and took with him a brown great coat badly dyed, white pewter buttons with the letters U.S.A. in a cypher, a green coat with red cuffs and cape and yellow buttons, white jacket and leather breeches, a pair of boots and a pair of shoes, two or three pair of stockings, and two or three shirts. The wench is small though well made, and has a lively eye, being bred in Carolina has the manners of the West-India slaves; she had on a red striped linsey short gown and petticoat, and took with her a dark brown cloak and sundry other clothes. Whoever takes up and secures the above Negroes shall receive Six Spanish milled dollars each, and reasonable charges.

ROBERT L. HOOPER,

Trenton, Jan. 8, 1781. ROBERT HOOPS.

Was taken up, and is now confined to Trenton gaol, by the subscriber, living in New-Germantown, Hunterdon County, State of New-Jersey, a young Negro Man, who says his name is Peter; he is nearly six feet high, of a slender make, speaks and understands very little English, and appears to have been but a short time in America, had scarce any cloathing. The owner is desired to apply, pay charges and take him away.

Dec. 2. GODFREY RHINEHEART

—*The Pennsylvania Packet January* 4, 1780.

Two Thousand Dollars Reward.
RAN AWAY,

On Sunday last from the subscriber, in Mendham township, Morris county.

A NEGRO MAN named JOE, about 30 years of age, five feet eight inches high, one leg a little shorter than the other, part of one of his great toes cut off, lost some foreteeth, and his back is much scarrified and in lumps by whipping.—Also a handsome NEGRO WENCH, 18 years of

age, with her Child about six weeks old, which from some of its clothes being found, she is supposed to have killed. The Negroes went off with one *Slight,* a soldier belonging to the 2d Pennsylvania regiment, and they stole, and took with them, a variety of clothes, and two horses, the one a bay, four years old, the other a grey, seven years old, and have switch tails. The soldier stole a written discharge, in the name of William Nelson, whom he will probably personate. Whoever takes up the said Negroes and horses, so that the owner may get them again, shall have the above reward, or Twelve Hundred dollars for the Negroes only, and Eight Hundred for the horses, or in proportion for any or either of them, and reasonable charges, paid by
Dec. 22, 1780   EBENEZER BLACKLY, jun.
—*N.J. Gazette, Vol.* IV, *No.* 157, *Dec.* 27, 1780.

One Thousand Dollars Reward.
RAN AWAY,

From the Subscriber, in Princeton, on Sunday evening, the 12th instant;
A NEGRO MAN, named Cæsar, about twenty-five years of age, about five feet eight inches high, marked with the small-pox, had on a blue camblet coat worn out at the elbows, a pair of new buck-skin breeches, straps without knee-buckles, old pumps with a hole in one of the toes or a new patch, a small felt hat lopt. Whoever apprehends the said Negro and delivers him to me, shall have the above reward, paid by
JOHN DENTON.

Princeton Nov. 14, 1780.
P.S. There is good reason to believe that he has been advised to go away, any substantial evidence who will discover the fact (if the plot be by a white person) on full conviction, shall have a reward of Six Thousand Dollars; if a black person, Five Hundred. As it is more than probable that there is more people goes to market to Staten-Island than ought; but if any person going there will please to call on Mr. Cubberly and enquire of his negro man Cæsar who it was that advised him to leave his master, and make a sufficient discovery whereby the subscriber may receive sufficient damage, shall have Ten Guineas or the exchange thereof in Continental money . . . .

5 SLAVES REBEL, 1734, 1737

The following two letters provide evidence of slave rebelliousness in New Jersey, a source of constant fear despite severe laws to discourage violence by slaves. The first letter, which appeared in the *New York Gazette* on March 25, 1734, was printed after an alleged slave uprising in Somerville, New Jersey. According to the anonymous writer, blacks there believed that enslavement was contrary to orders from King George II, and they planned to gain their freedom through a revolt in the spring of that year. Approximately thirty blacks were apprehended for complicity in the plot. One black was hanged, several had their ears cut off, and the authorities whipped others. The author of the letter urged colonists to "not be too careless of their own Safety, with respect of their Slaves," and he warned "how easie [*sic*] this Design might have been put in practice, if it had not been discovered. . . ." The second letter, appearing in the *Pennsylvania Gazette* between February 28 and March 7, 1737, concerned an alleged plot by two blacks to have a white slave owner poisoned. The plan was discovered and a confession was apparently obtained from the conspirators.

New Jersey Archives, ser. 1, 11: 335-37.

Mr. Bradford;

    THE Letter from *Burlington* printed in Franklin's Gazette, insinuating that the late rising of the Negroes in the *Eastern-Division* of *New Jersey,* was occasioned by the Papers lately published in the Neighbouring Province, the Authors of which he is very free with, I having been present at some of the Examinations of those Negroes, think it necessary to give the best account thereof I can, in order to warn all Masters of Negroes not to be too careless of their own Safety, with respect to their Slaves, which now begin to be Numerous, and in some of our Colonies too much indulged, and by some particular Persons rather encouraged in their Vices, than put under a due Regulation and Subjection. It appear'd upon Examination that Coll. *Thomas L____d* keeps at some Miles distance from his dwelling House, Negro-Quarters (as they are called) who provide for themselves, which Quarters have been a Randevouze for the Negroes, and proved a Pest to the Neighbourhood, by encouraging the Neighbours Negroes to steal from their Masters both Beef, Pork, Wheat, Fowles, &c., wherewith they feast and junket at those Quarters, and at times have met in great Companies. It was at one of these Meetings their design of Rising was agreed and some time since fully resolved on by some hundreds of them, but kept so private amongst themselves, that there was not the least appearance or suspicion of it, till the Negro of one *Hall* at *Rariton* having drank too much, accosted one *Renolds* on the Road, and told him, *The English-men were generally a pack of Villains, and kept the Negroes as Slaves, contrary to a positive Order from King* George, *sent to the* G[overnor] *of* New-York, *to set them all free, which*

the said G[overnor] *did intend to do, but was prevented by his* C[ouncil]
and A[ssembly] *and that was the reason there now subsisted so great a
difference between the* G[overnor] *and the People, &c. Rennels* was sur-
prized at the freedom and Independence of this Fellow, & told him, he
was a great Raskel to talk in that manner: The Negro answered, *That he
was as good a Man as himself, and that in a little Time he should be convinced of it.*

This was the first occasion of Suspicion of a Negro Plot. And upon
Rennel's Information of what this Fellow had said, he & another Negro
was taken up, Tryed, Condemned, and one Hang'd; *Hall's* Negro made
his escape, and is not yet taken. Upon this Examination and Tryal it appeared, that the Design of these Negroes was this, That so soon as the
Season was advanced that they could lie in the Woods, one certain Night
was agreed on, that every Negro in each Family was to Rise at Midnight,
cut the Throats of their Masters and Sons, but not meddle with the
Women, whom they intended to Plunder and Ravish the day following,
and then set all their Houses and Barns on Fire, Kill all the Draught
Horses, and secure the best Saddle Horses for their flight towards the
Indians in the *French* interest.

How easie this Design might have been put in Practice, if it had not
been discovered, I leave every one to judge, and how very necessary it is
for every Colony to make proper Laws and Ordinances for their own
Security, and against the Attemps of these barbarous Monsters (by some
so much indulged.) I would also have each and every one of us to
remember, and not forget the great Calamity and Disolation there was in
the City of *New-York* some years since, by the Negros rising there, and
murdering many good innocent People, and had it not been for his Majesty's Garrison there, that City (in all likelihood) had been reduced to
Ashes, and the greatest part of the Inhabitants Murdered. The late
Massacre perpetrated by the Negros in the Island of *St. John's,*[1] the very
great head they are come to in the Island of *Jamaica,*[2] and the general
Melancholy Apprehensions of his Majesty's Subjects in the *West-Indies,*
gives but too much room to fear there is some great Fatality attends the
English Dominion in *America,* from the too great Number of that unchristian and barbarous People being imported, and then by some too
much indulged in their Vices.—*The New-York Gazette, March* 25, 1734.

New Jersey Archives, ser. 1, 11: 523-24.

Philadelphia, March 7.

We hear from *Trenton,* That two Negroes were last Week imprison'd
on the following Occasion. 'Tis said that they were about to perswade
another Negroe to poison his Master; and to convince him of the Efficacy of the Drug which they presented him for that purpose, and the
Security of giving it, let him know that Mr. *Trent* and two of his Sons,

Mr. Lambert and two of his Wives, and sundry other Persons were remov'd by their Slaves in that Manner. This Discourse being overheard, they were apprehended, and 'tis said have made some Confession. But as the Persons above mention'd died apparently of common Distempers, it is not fully credited that any such Method was used to destroy them. The Drugs found on one of the Negroes, were Arsenick and an unknown kind of Root.—*The Pennsylvania Gazette, Feb.* 28 *to March* 7, 1737, 8.

---

1. On November 13, 1733 slaves on the island of St. John's, a Danish possession, revolted against the enforcement of harsh slave codes there. For six months they held the fort at Coral Bay.
2. Led by a fugitive slave named Cudjoe, Jamaican slaves revolted against the British settlers in 1734. The revolt ended with a negotiated settlement in 1739 which freed many of the slaves, gave them 1,500 acres of land, and pledged black assistance in the capture of any other runaways.

III

Bondage and the Revolution

THE American Revolution, in its emphasis on natural law and human rights, revitalized concern over black slavery and ultimately aided the abolitionist struggle. The era dramatized a powerful inconsistency between the colonists' libertarian beliefs and their enslavement of blacks, a contradiction so clear that it deeply troubled many Jerseymen. In the past, slavery had produced moral concern, but the war for independence made the institution appear all the more evil and pernicious. In the words of William Livingston (1723–90), the state's first governor, slavery was "utterly inconsistent with the principles of Christianity and humanity; and in Americans who have almost idolized liberty, peculiarly odious and disgraceful."[1]

During the Revolutionary as well as colonial periods, New Jersey's most outspoken advocates for emancipation came from the Quaker communities of Burlington, Gloucester, and Salem counties. In 1773 and 1774, Quaker petitioners urged the legislature to end the importation of slaves and adopt measures favorable to voluntary manumission. An appeal in 1775 from residents in Chesterfield, Burlington County, asked the Assembly to "take Slavekeeping into your most Serious Consideration, And pass an Act of freedom for them, that are now with us . . . ." [doc. 1]

Appeals on behalf of the slaves, however, were disputed at a time when the colonists were fighting for their independence. Although the state constitution of 1776 laid the basis for limited black civil rights, it did not outlaw slavery. When Governor Livingston proposed in 1778 that the Assembly manumit the slaves, he was rebuffed by that body. Slavery advocates used stereotypes to support their claim that blacks were unsuited for emancipation.

[doc. 2] Had not the economic dependence of free blacks upon local communities confirmed their inferiority? However distasteful, they argued, slavery was an essential supplement to the class of white laborers who were in short supply, especially during the war years. They feared that if abolitionists such as John Cooper (1729–85) of Burlington were successful in their efforts, the emancipated slaves would undoubtedly be enlisted by Loyalist forces. Pro-slavery spokesmen were unmoved by the humanitarian pleas to abolish slavery in the state, and they tolerated the incongruity of white men fighting for great principles while blacks remained in bondage. [doc. 3] Between 1774 and 1783 only one slave was manumitted in New Jersey, a glaring paradox in a society struggling to be free of imperial rule.[2]

Although the legislature postponed debate on slavery during the war, the issue nonetheless continued and actually was pursued more energetically in some communities. Few emancipation advocates were as eloquent or advanced as John Cooper, a precursor of the militant abolitionists of the 1830s and a man whose writings were influenced by the distinguished anti-slavery advocate, Anthony Benezet of Philadelphia. In 1780, Cooper called for the immediate emancipation of slaves. [doc. 4] After the publication of his views, an unusually large number of anti-slavery letters appeared in the local press.[3] Friends of the blacks were rightfully optimistic during this period. In 1780, after years of abolitionist agitation, Pennsylvania became the first mid-Atlantic state called to enact legislation abolishing slavery. The *New-Jersey Gazette* called the Pennsylvania law an "act of humanity, wisdom and justice."[4] New Jersey abolitionists were spurred to action, and the establishment of more newspapers in the state during the 1780s enabled them to disseminate their views more widely.

By their participation in the struggle against Great Britain, blacks contributed significantly to the emerging egalitarian spirit in New Jersey. The precedent for a black military role had been set during the colonial period when blacks had served in small numbers in the New Jersey militia. The Militia Act of 1777 continued the practice, permitting the enlistment of "all effective men between fifteen and fifty." This act was later amended to include "all able bodied men, not being slaves," but this restriction did not keep slaves out of the conflict.[5] Realizing that a display of patriotic zeal might enhance their prospects for manumission, slaves joined in the New Jersey theater of the war. A small number bore arms against the crown, while most drove wagons for the Continental Army or performed some other non-combatant service. Some slaves furnished the patriot militia with military intelligence. Certain blacks made outstanding contributions to the Revolution: Oliver Cromwell, a slave from Burlington County, served with distinction as a private in the New Jersey Continental Line; Jacob Francis served in the Hunterdon County militia between 1777 and 1781; and Prince Whipple, a free-born native African, was the bodyguard of Captain Abraham Whipple and crossed the Delaware with Washington on December 25–26, 1776. Samuel Sutphen, a slave from Somerset County, was also an active participant in the war. His detailed memoir is one of the best descriptions of the war in New Jersey from the viewpoint of the foot soldier.[6] [doc. 5]

Although many of the blacks fighting in New Jersey served in the state militia or the Continental Army, an undetermined number cast their lot with the Loyalist side. The role of these obscure men is a small but important aspect of early Afro-American history. Like their counterparts on the patriotic side, they generally joined the struggle to improve their condition and perhaps attain their freedom.[7] [doc. 6a, b, c] Blacks such as Samuel Sutphen, who fought with the rebels, faced the indignity of returning to bondage after the war, but others were manumitted because of their service. [doc. 7a, b] Jack Cudjo, a slave from Newark serving in the stead of his owner, Benjamin Coe, was manumitted and received an acre of ground on High Street in recognition of his service with the Continental Army.

Most of the slaves in New Jersey experienced little change in their status after the Revolution. Indeed, by the end of the war every northern state except New Jersey and New York adopted measures against slavery. Facing an uphill battle for complete abolition, New Jersey abolitionists concentrated on stopping the further importation of slaves into the state and improving their living conditions. A 1786 act achieved some of these objectives. [doc. 8] In 1789, legislation provided that slaves could not be removed from the state without their consent; masters were obliged to teach their slaves how to read and were not to abuse them. Blacks gained some voting rights in 1794 and legal residence two years later. Many forms of discrimination continued, but gains such as these seemed to offer the hope of slavery's eventual abolition.

After considerable public debate on slavery, the legislature defeated two emancipation bills between 1792 and 1794, the latter by one vote. The debates on these proposals revealed that slavery advocates had changed their views little since the end of the Revolutionary War. As in the past, free blacks were accused of notorious misconduct. The public was warned that abolition would be a dangerous undertaking, that freed slaves would be incapable of earning a living, and that abolition was tantamount to an unconstitutional confiscation of property. A petition, strangely enough from residents in nominally anti-slavery Salem County, warned that abolition would have a disastrous impact on the state's economy.

As the nineteenth century opened, slavery had been abolished in every northern state except for New Jersey. With slavery still practiced, New Jersey, as an incident in Egg Harbor in 1803 revealed, became unwittingly involved in the illegal trafficking of blacks to the South. [doc. 9] The efforts of New Jersey abolitionists were generally thwarted by strong opposition from the East Jersey counties, where slavery was most prevalent. Anti-slavery advocacy was also weakened by the predominantly rural character of the state, which made it difficult to organize support, and by the state's proximity to the South. In these discouraging conditions, abolitionists were forced to concede the improbability of complete and immediate emancipation.

With the assistance of Pennsylvania anti-slavery men, the New Jersey abolitionists formed the New Jersey Society for Promoting the Abolition of Slavery in 1793. As one of the last abolitionist organizations formed in a northern state, the Society's difficulties reflected the comparative weakness and disorganization of New Jersey's anti-slavery movement. Not until 1797 was the group able to circulate petitions requesting the legislature to abolish slavery. When the Society finally addressed the issue publicly, it favored gradual emancipation with compensation to slaveholders. In taking the middle ground between the Revolution's firm emphasis upon the rights of man and the importance placed on private property, the Society may have hastened abolition. In 1804 the Society, in an eloquent appeal to the legislature, advocated abolishing slavery for the unborn. This petition set the stage for the adoption of New Jersey's gradual emancipation law of 1804.[8] [doc. 10]

Against the background of New Jersey's traditional resistance to abolition, the passage of an Act for the Gradual Emancipation of Slavery was a remarkable achievement for the friends of blacks in the state. [doc. 11] For years pro-slavery legislators had successfully blocked attempts to bring New Jersey in line with other northern states which had legally abolished slavery. In order to make abolition acceptable to a decisive majority of legislators, anti-slavery lawmakers, like members of the Society for Promoting the Abolition of Slavery, offered as a compromise gradual emancipation and a thinly veiled form of compensation to slaveowners. The final vote on this act demonstrated that the compromise worked successfully. Members of both parties in the legislature supported it; fifteen Federalists and twenty-nine Republicans voted in favor of the law, while four Federalists and one Republican voted against it.[9] **[doc. 12]**

Despite an optimistic assessment by New Jersey abolitionists, gradual emancipation under the provisions of the law of 1804 was not without serious flaws. Bond labor was perpetuated for years by the partiality shown to slaveowners, who were permitted to hold the offspring of their slaves as servants for a legally specified time. Black children may have been viewed as legally free, but their young lives, and thus their future as adults, were still considerably determined by their white custodians. **[doc. 13]** Some owners violated the spirit of the measure by selling slaves to purchasers in the southern states. An act passed in 1812 permitted the export of slaves with their consent. **[doc. 14]** Slaveholders also abused the abandonment clause of the emancipation law and continued to benefit from an institution which many felt to be immoral.

1   CHESTERFIELD CITIZENS FOR MANUMISSION, 1775

The following petition from Quakers in Burlington County exhorts the House of Representatives and the General Assembly to enact legislation freeing slaves "now with us" and grant the eventual manumission of blacks "hereafter born amongst us." The Quakers believed that slavery was inconsistent with the Golden Rule and equitable principles, and they feared God's judgment on a society practicing such an immoral institution. The petition was tabled by the Assembly. Subsequent Quaker attempts to pass manumission bills were thwarted by pro-slavery representatives from East Jersey and overshadowed by the colonial struggle for independence.

**Inhabitants of Chesterfield Township to the
House of Representatives and General Assembly
of Province of New Jersey, Petition, 9 November 1775,
Manuscript Collection, Bureau of Archives and
History, New Jersey State Library.**

November 9th 1775

To the Honourable House of Representatives, and General Assembly for the Province of New Jersey, Gentlemen. We your humble Petitioners Inhabitants of Chesterfield Township County of Burlington and Province aforesaid Being justly alarmed with the present distressed situation of our County And truly thoughtful for ourselves and fellow Creatures, and Wishing to Avert the Judgment of God from our Heads, inveigh and act in our Power; And to do justice to ourselves and others, think it necessary and needful to do unto others, as we would they should do unto us. For we are taught to Judge not lest we should be Judged; For it is said, with what Judgment ye Judge ye shall be Judged And the Measure ye Mete to others shall be Measured to you again And that all things that ye would that Men should do unto you, even so ye should do unto them. We therefore your humble Petitioners Seeing Plainly the Evil Effects and bad Attendance of keeping Negroes in Slavery and how inconsistant it is with Equity. We therefore humbly Pray that you our Representatives Do take Slavekeeping into your most Serious Consideration, And pass an Act of freedom for them, that are now with us, as in your wisdom you shall think fit And for those unborn or that may hereafter be born amongst us to be free Males at Twenty-one and Females at Eighteen Years of Age. May you Gentlemen be the beginners of this Reformation, And may God Prosper it—And your Petitioners will ever Pray etc.

[51 signatures]

---

2   PERTH AMBOY CITIZENS DEFEND SLAVERY, 1774

In both slavery and freedom blacks "are a very dangerous people," claimed the petitioners in the following petition against manumission. They voiced white racial attitudes in Perth Amboy, where there was a distinct economic dependence on slavery. Not surprisingly, slavery was defended and blacks were disparaged when abolitionists called for manumission. This petition reached the legislature during debates on the voluntary manumission of slaves. For decades, Burlington County and other Quaker strongholds had urged lawmakers to revise prohibitive requirements for slaveholders who wished to free their slaves. (A law enacted in 1714 [chap. 1, doc. 5] forbade landholding among free blacks; owners had to pay twenty pounds per year for each slave they set free.) Perth Amboy residents feared that reforms in the law would endanger their security and perhaps threaten the entire slave system. New Jersey, they warned, was vulnerable to its large slave population, which was "most barbarous in human matters."

Inhabitants of Perth Amboy to William Franklin, Governor, and General Assembly, Petition, 12 January 1774, Manuscript Collection, Bureau of Archives and History, New Jersey State Library.

To his Exelencey William Franklin Esq. Governor the Honourable his Majasties Council and the Representatives of the Provence of New Jarsey in General Assembly met and Conveaned at Burlington.

The humble Petition of the inhabitance of the City of Perth Amboy sheweth that wee your Pettionors haveing been well informed that thair has Been A Number of Petitions Presented the Hous, this Preasent Session, for A Law for the more Equittible manumition of Slaves in this Provence, and that A Law for that Purpos is Braught in, and Likely to Pass . . . . therefore wee your Pettionors Humbly Beg Leave to mention to your Honours sum few Objections, of the many that might be made Against Entering into A Law of that nature, and in the first place wee humbly apprehend that the Law now in force is full as easey to those ownors who have A mind to set thair Slaves free, as the circumstances and cituation of our Province will admit of, with safety at Preasent . . . . and therefore needs no Amendmendment [sic]. Nevertheless if you in your wisdom should find it nesesary to Pass A Law wee Beg that you would not rush hastily into A Law which may be of the most Dismal Consequance, Perhaps, of any Law Ever yet Passed in this Provence and therefore surely Desarves the most Carefull inspection.

In the second place wee Do apprehend, from the Long Experiance wee have had, of Negros, both in slavery and freedom, that thay are A Very Daingerous People to have general freedom in any Province in his majasties Dominions, much more so, in so Defenceless A Provence as this of New Jarsey, that the Negros are very numerous Cannot be Denied, and that thay are the most Barberous in-human mastors to those un[der] them of any People in the world wee presume will not be Denied by any who have had any oppertunity of seeing any of them in that State. To keep them in Due subjection in A State of Slavery wee presume is very Deficult and will be much more so when generally set free, as thay will then have time to Consult any Plan thay Please to Lay, to invade the inhabitance and accomplish thair un-humen Designs, which wee have the strongest Reasons to beleave, would be noless then to Bring the White People into the same state thay the Negros now are in. Therefore wee humbly Beg that you will be very Careful to Presarve the Liberty of the White People of this Provence, Least in seting the Blacks free you Bring us into Bondage, which when once Dun will be Very Dificult to git rid off. Wee hold our selves to be free Born in this Provence, and tharefore slavery, and Especially to those Barberious Cretures, would be very Disagreable, which freedom thay Cannot Nead, Exsept in thair own Land, and therefore are more likely to set Easey under Slavery in A strange Land, then wee should in our own Country. Nevertheless if the Law should Pass wee your Petitionors Do humbly intreat your Carefull attention to the Aforesaid hints, and your Petitionors as in Duty Bound shall for Ever Pray.

City of Pirth Amboy 12th of januery of 1774.

[77 signatures]

---

3   PRO-SLAVERY LOGIC, 1781

The following letter from a self-proclaimed impartial citizen actually asserts a thinly veiled pro-slavery position. Slaves are viewed as legitimate property that may not be legally taken from their owners. Although the author grapples with the manifold legal and moral questions of slavery, he does not consider the relationship between white antipathy toward blacks and their lowly status. Rather, he employs racial stereotypes to show blacks unsuitable for manumission.

"Impartial" to the [Trenton] *New-Jersey Gazette*, 10 January 1781.

For The NEW-JERSEY GAZETTE.

AS the manumission of slaves has become a topick of general conversation, we beg permission to offer a few sentiments on the subject.

The merits of almost every case of litigation generally turns upon one or two points. In the present instance the question is, we conceive, Whether law, justice, and policy warrant the retaining our slaves in their present situation?

That we became legally possessed of them, or that they were introduced into this country agreeable to its laws, no one will presume to deny; and that we cannot constitutionally be divested of them by legislative authority, is, we humbly imagine, as evident as that white is not black, or that slavery is not freedom. Our most excellent constitution admits not the subject to be deprived of his life, liberty, or property but by a trial of a jury of his equals; and lest this inestimable privilege, the glory of freemen, should be infringed on, the constitution expressly requires that no member of the legislature shall possess a seat in the house, until he has solemnly sworn that he will maintain this immunity inviolate. It becomes therefore one of the unalterable particulars of our rights, and cannot be relinquished by the guardians of our liberties but at the expense of perfidy, and even of perjury itself. The liberation of our slaves therefore, without the concurrence of their possessors, we apprehend, is an object infinitely further distant from the legal attention of our Assembly than are the heavens above the earth.

Whether, as individuals, justice permits the detention of our Negroes, is next to be considered.—The Divine Saviour of men hath been pleased to give a summary of our duty towards each other in a single sentence, viz. "To do unto others as we would they should do to us"; or, "to love our neighbour as ourselves." As we profess to believe in a future judgment, that we shall one day give an account to the Supreme Governor of the world of our actions, it highly concerns us to be attentive that they be conformable to the heavenly law. That barbarity to our slaves is repugnant to this law, cannot be controverted; but whether the divine precept enjoins us to free them or not, is the dispute. Were we in their situation it is more than probable we should pant after freedom; and so does the poor debtor desire a release from his creditor, but the injunction, "to do unto others as we would be done to," does not oblige the latter to free the former of the debt, if it hath not been contracted by injustice. Nor can this command oblige us to liberate our slaves unless they were sinfully obtained, or are thus held in bondage. If the usages of the nations of Africa justify the foreign and domestick slavery of their captives, they can be purchased and retained without iniquity. But let us suppose our Negroes were stolen from their country; divested of that natural liberty given to them by heaven, and reduced to vassalage, it may be asked whether the whole of the guilt devolves not on the perpetrators of the deed? Whether any of the sin rests on those who have purchased of the posterity of the slaves, or inherit them by the gift or will of parents? The people of Africa were formerly and lawfully exposed here to sale as articles of commerce, and it may be queried if in conscience we were bound to enquire whether the Guinea-merchant became more rightfully possessed of his slaves than of his gold dust, or any other commodity of Africa? . . . It may be said, if our slaves were unjustly obtained it must be unjust to hold them in bondage. We readily grant it would be so for an unjust importer of them, or the heirs of the importer who received them without paying what is deemed an equivalent for the property; and we freely declare we would not retain a slave under these circumstances, or be instrumental in reducing a freeman to slavery for any consideration. But as the slaves are among us; as the sale of them among ourselves does not cause a farther importation of their countrymen, and if it is not disadvantageous to the slave, we are as free to declare we cannot comprehend why, without any injustice to him, he may not now be purchased and possessed.

Humanity, indeed, wishes they could enjoy liberty and happiness, consistent with justice to those who have honestly bought them, and we, in truth, consider our liberty as a prelude to their release from slavery. The love of freedom in due season, we trust, will be so predominant that either the individuals whose property they are, will, for their emancipation, disregard their cost; or the publick, by subscription or donation and not by law, (for we know of no just authority the legislature have to command the property of their constituents for this purpose without express permission) will chearfully defray it, and put them on an equal footing with ourselves . . . .

The other enquiry is, Whether the present is a proper period to effect so laudable a design.

That there is "a time for all things," is an indisputable truth . . . . That the present day would be improper for the execution of this business must, we think, appear evident to every one on the least reflection. Should our slaves be freed, they must either continue with us or inhabit some territory by themselves. If the freemen of the country find it difficult to support themselves and families at the present time, is it reasonable to suppose that our slaves, naturally indolent; unaccustomed to self-government; destitute of mechanical knowledge; unacquainted with letters; with a peculiar propensity to spirituous liquors; destitute of property, and without credit, would pay their taxes and provide for themselves, in the path of integrity, the necessaries and comforts of life? Is it not more rational to infer, from these considerations, that many of them would soon revert to their former state, more wretched than before; that great numbers would become pests to society; by plunder and rapine add to the horrors of war, and that dire necessity would compel us to deprive some of them not only of liberty but also of life? Their sloth alone might be sensibly felt by the community at this juncture, and on their arms, we are of opinion, for several obvious reasons, there could not be any just dependence. Our state of war forbids their removal to any exterior part of the country, not only in regard of safety, but also in other respects. Whenever they shall be emancipated, on mature deliberation perhaps it will be tho't, that small settlements of them in different parts of the continent, under proper regulations, will be most compatible with our safety and their felicity. They may thus become useful members of the body politick; enjoy the sunshine of freedom, together with the chearing rays of the light of the gospel . . . . Until this day shall arrive, it is to be hoped the possessors of slaves will revere the sacred precept, "to do as they would be done by"; mollify the hardness of slavery by acts of kindness; but above all, be particularly anxious to have them freed by instruction, admonition, and example from spiritual thraldom, and "brought into the glorious liberty of the children of God." The effecting of this will not only be paying a tribute to justice, but also an advancement of our temperal emolument; for experience will decide, that it will not be less politick and wise than humane and christian.

IMPARTIAL.

4   A PLEA FOR IMMEDIATE ABOLITION, 1780

With the following letter to the *New-Jersey Gazette,* John Cooper (1729–85) of Burlington sparked the unprecedented newspaper debates of the early 1780s. Few other commentators approached the problem of slavery with as much determination and intellectual fortitude. Cooper believed that slavery was clearly inconsistent with the goals of the Revolution, and he called upon Jerseymen to rid themselves of "the accursed thing." In contrast to most New Jersey abolitionists during this period, Cooper was opposed to gradual emancipation. "It would be," he warned, "plainly telling our slaves, we will not do justice unto you, but our posterity shall do justice to your posterity."

John Cooper, "To The Publick," [Trenton] *New-Jersey Gazette,* 20 September 1780.

Friends and Fellow-Citizens!

WHILST we are spilling our blood and exhausting our Treasure in defence of our own liberty, it would not perhaps be amiss to turn our eyes towards those of our fellow-men who are now groaning in bondage under us. We say "all men are equally entitled to liberty and the persuit of happiness"; but are we willing to grant this liberty to all men? The sentiment no doubt is just as well as generous; and must ever be read to our praise, provided our actions correspond therewith. But if after we have made such a declaration to the world, we continue to hold our fellow creatures in slavery, our words must rise up in judgement against us, and by the breath of our own mouths we shall stand condemned.

The war has already been prolonged far beyond what we once thought the abilities of Britain would admit of; and how much longer it may please Providence to suffer it to rage, or what the final event of it may be, is to us altogether unknown. The children of Israel, we find, could not conquer their enemies whilst they, the Israelites, had "the accursed things" amongst them. And as tyranny is the accursed thing against which we have waged war, how can we hope to prevail against our enemies whilst we ourselves are tyrants, holding thousands of our fellow creatures in slavery under us?

The Lord did not leave it a doubt with Joshua what was the reason they could not succeed; he told him in plain terms the reason was because they had also transgressed his covenant—they had "the accursed thing" among them. And if the Lord is still the same God, deciding the controversies amongst men upon the same principles, then although Britain may have transgressed his covenant* in endeavouring to enslave us, if we are not only also, but equally in the transgression, by holding the Africans and their posterity in slavery, how can we expect he will decide in our favour, unless we recede from such transgression? Unless we abolish tyranny, "the accursed thing," from amongst us, and do that justice to others which we ask of him for ourselves? . . . Can we imagine our prayers to Almighty God will meet with his approbation, or in the least degree tend to procure us relief from the hand of oppression, whilst the groans of our slaves are continually ascending mingled with them? I fear, indeed, that not only our prayers, but our publick fastings, are an abomination in his sight, and will so remain until we have washed our hands from tyranny, and the voice of a slave is not to be heard in our land.

. . . In our publick and most solemn declarations we say, we are resolved to die free;—that slavery is worse than death. He, therefore, who enslaves his fellow-creature must, in our esteem, be worse than he who takes his life; and yet, surprizing as it may seem, we hold thousands of our fellow-men in slavery, and slumber on under the dreadful load of guilt—Worse than murderers and yet at ease! A melancholy reflection indeed, that habit should be capable of reconciling the human mind to the greatest of all crimes—of lulling it to rest in the practice of that which, ere long, must cause it to tremble before the great, the awful tribunal; where all deception will be done away, and our transgressions appear in their fullest magnitude and greatest deformity! What shall we then think of the unlawful gain, we now derive from the labour of our innocent, tho' unfortunate slaves? myriads of whom perhaps we shall there behold smiling in the fullest fruition of peace, whilst their late lordly oppressors, conscious of their own guilt, trembling wait the awful sentence.

Let me now entreat us to pause a while, and examine our own hearts. Let us survey our ways with the impartial eye of reason and justice; and whatsoever shall appear to be out of order, that let us correct. Whilst we are making high pretentions and pompous declarations with regard to our own views and publick virtue, let us take care to act up to those pretentions and declarations; but above all things, let us candidly, in the sight of Heaven, do that justice to others which we ask for ourselves. This is the way for us to succeed in our present contest; this is the surest way that we can take to obtain PEACE, LIBERTY and SAFETY.

If we are determined not to emancipate our slaves, but to hold them still in bondage, let us alter our language upon the subject of tyranny; let us no longer speak of it as a thing in its own nature detestable, because in so doing, as hath been observed, we shall condemn ourselves. But let us rather declare to the world, that tyranny is a thing we are not principled against, but that we are resolved not to be slaves, because we ourselves mean to be tyrants. Such a declaration would certainly be more candid, or at least would better correspond with the conduct I have mentioned, than those we have usually made; though perhaps it might not be quite so pleasing, for justice is so lovely, and virtue so amiable, that we all love to be deemed their voteries, however estranged we may be from their ways.

Whatever colouring slavekeeping may receive from interested individuals who wish to keep it on foot, there is something in its nature so universally odious, that we meet with but few of the slavekeepers themselves that are willing to be thought tyrants; like unchaste women, they cannot bear to be deemed what they really are; for nothing is more clear, than that he who keeps a slave is a tyrant. Without tyranny, there can be no slavery in the sense here meant. And where slavekeeping is countenanced and upheld by any state or empire, the tyranny becomes national, and the iniquity also; and in such case a national scourge may very well be looked for. If, therefore, neither the love of justice, nor the feelings of humanity are sufficient to induce us to release our slaves from bondage, let the dread of divine retribution—of national calamities— induce us to do it . . . .

JOHN COOPER

As ye would that men should do to you, do ye also to them likewise. Luke vi.21.

---

5 SAMUEL SUTPHEN, SLAVE AND SOLDIER, ca. 1834

The participation of black men in the Revolutionary War challenged the old stereotype that blacks were unsuited for military service. Even though blacks had fought in the French and Indian War and at Lexington and Concord in April 1775, whites continued to question their military prowess. Despite legal and customary restrictions on black enlistment or recruitment, and General George Washington's warning against their use, some blacks fought on the patriot side. Samuel Sutphen (occasionally spelled Sutphin), who joined the war effort in place of his owner, Caspar Berger of Readington, saw service in New Jersey and New

York from 1776 to 1780. While blacks were usually relegated to non-military functions, Sutphen bore arms, drew guard duty, and served as a guide in Continental units. This war narrative was recorded by Dr. Lewis Condict (1773–1862) of Somerset County around 1834, when Sutphen was eighty-nine years old. As a tragic irony of his service during the Revolution, he labored as a slave for another twenty years before purchasing his freedom.

A. Van Doren Honeyman, ed.,
"The Revolutionary War Record of a Somerset County Slave,"
Somerset County Historical Quarterly
3 (1914): 186-90.

"At the beginning of the War was a slave to Guisbert Bogert of Somerset co. on the Raritan. Caspar Berger of Readington proposed to buy him of Bogert on condition of doing militia duty in Berger's stead during the War. I agreed to the terms, and Bogert sold me to Berger for £92,10, which I believe was paid. Berger had been out one month, and I afterward was to serve in his place. Capt. Matthias Lane commanded the militia co. and Col. Taylor the Regiment. This was the 6th year of the War. Berger brought me in the season of plane (?) seed sowing. Berger went out one month after I went to live with him, in Capt. Lane's Co. Immediately after I had finishing planting 4 acres corn, Co. was [classed?] and I took my turn with others; sometimes 12, sometimes 15 or 20 went at once. I believe Capt. Lane went on by 1st tour; marched thro' Boundbrook and Scotch Plains and Newark to Communipaw, where we were stationed 1 mo.; large militia force was there; a Regt. or more; built breastworks; Col Abm. Ten Eyck, Major Livin, Col. Hunt, Col. Schamp, Gen. Dickinson, Gen Blair (?). Staid a month in sight of New York—guard duty.

"Second tour in hay and harvest time. Capt. Jacob Ten Eyck stationed at Communipaw; 1 mo. guard duty. The Asia (?) was then in the harbor.[2] British fleet came into N. York harbor whilst on this tour. A large body of militia out. Frelinghuysen and Schamp were out.

"Third tour, l mo. Believes Capt. Lane commanded. Station and duty the same as before. British fleet came into the bay and harbor when on his 2nd tour. Large force of British was out. Was at the Long Island battle in Aug't; and Lane, and Col. Frelinghuysen. Lord Stirling had command of Jersey troops; our comp'y was in the heat of the battle. In the battle and after our defeat we were all dispersed. I found a colored man who took me from L.I. to Staten Isl'd in a skiff with two others of my Co., viz., Wm. Van Syckle and Jacob Johnson, a man of our age. The blk. man piloted us across Staten Isl'd to Eliz'town point, where we crossed to E.T.; came through this town and by Wheatsheaf and Short Hills, Quibbletown and Bound Brook, and so home in about 3 days after the battle. 2 of our co. were taken prisoners in this battle, viz., Peter Low and John Van Campen; they were exchanged some months after and got home.

"His 3rd tour now begins under Capt. Lane as before.

"4th tour under Capt. Ph. Van Arsdale toward Pluckemin in frosty weather, fall of the year. This was probably in October. Stationed at Commun'w and Bergen point.

"5th tour was in very cold weather; was marched up along the Millstone under Capt. Van Arsdale and Col. Schamp about New Year's holidays; out a month.

"Cornel's Lane of our Co. was shot through the hip the morning after the battle by the accidental discharge of a musket by one Todd. The ball passed in near the navel and came out near the back, as he was lying near a sapling. I assisted, with Thomas Oliver, to carry him home in a litter between 2 horses, made with poles and a bed thereon. Was out at this tour for 3 or 4 days. Went from Readington with the whole Co. by way of Milltown; escorted Col. Frelinghuysen to Princeton by Griggstown, and on Rocky Hill we heard the firing, and soon got into the heat of the battle. Believes Gen'l Washington marched with his army to Pluckemin into winter quarters.

"Some time in this same Winter a distinguished Tory named Christopher Vought, or Voke, led on a large body of Refugees and Tories from Lebanon in Hunterdon, said to be from 500 to 6 or 700, attempting to make their way to the headquarters of the army then at Brunswick. They were discovered by Dr. Jennings, and he made it known to Capt. Lane, and the Co. immediately called out with Capt. Jacob Ten Eyck's Comp'y to intercept them; fell in with them at the 2 Bridges, junction of the N. and S. branches of the Raritan; had a fight with them. Wm. Van Syckle of our Co. was wounded in the head; they ——— and ran to a fording place near Cornelius Van Derveer's mill on the N. Branch, where they crossed and made their way toward Brunswick. Ten Eyck's Co. took one prisoner, who was mounted, and Capt. Ten Eyck took his horse. In the night—toward last of winter.

"In the spring following, probably March, a party of the enemy from N.B. came out to Van Ess' mills on the Millstone. A party of militia under Lieut. Davis was stationed near the two bridges, when an express rider on a black horse from Col. Frelinghuysen gave tidings of the enemy at V. Ess' mills. I piloted Davis' Co. and as many others as we could assemble to a fording place over the S. branch, and hurried on to the mills. They had plundered the mill of grain and flour, and were on their way back to Brunswick, but had not got out of the lane leading from the mill to the great road. We headed them in the lane. The team laden with the flour was the first we fell in with; the lane, 100 yards, was filled with 4-horse teams. Davis ordered us to fire, and then we shot part of the 1st team, which stopped the whole drove. The drivers left their teams and run. A guard escorting the teams made their escape. We took, as was said, about 40 horses, and all the waggons, about 10, which were all sent off under an escort to Morristown.

"A party of Hessians, about 1 company (70), an escort for these teams from Brunswick, was discovered secreted behind a hedge with some 4 or 5 field pieces. They fired upon us and retreated. We followed on a piece, but Lt. Davis ordr'd us to retreat. Davis' Capt. Westcott from Cumberland had been left sick at Guysbert Bogert's, where he died, and was taken back to Cumberland Co. There was a large body of militia out, and Gen'l Dickinson commanded. The firing was principally across the river at the bridge. I was out on this alarm but one day. We mounted guard along the branch above the 2-bridges almost every night; nearly all this winter and spring on guard duty.

"About corn planting in the same year, as I think, my master was called on to go to the North. Capt. Isaiah Younglove and Lieut. Robt. Robertson were along the branch recruiting men for the northern service. Master Berger order'd me to go with Capt. Younglove for 9 months; this was the term of engagement for all his company. 3 men were furnished by each company for this expedition; 3 from our's, 3 from Ten Eyck's. David Seely from Cumberland Co. was Col. of this regim't. James Ray (?), a free mulatto man and Hendrick Johnson went from our Company. Our Reg't, under Col. Seely, assembled at Cornelius Slack's, Suckasunny plain, after corn planting, about last of May. Marched thro' Sussex Co., and Goshen to N. Windsor, Newburg. At Esopus we fell in with Domine Hardenburg, whom I knew at Somerset. Went to Westpoint first. A chain was fastened to a large rock and stretched across the river to prevent vessels from going up. Thence by Schenectady by Fort Schuyler, now Utica. Here we were for three days. Found here three children massacred by Indians, and had been brought here to repel the Indians who had massacred the whites. A massacre had also been made by the Indians at Cherry Valley, through which we passed on our way to Utica; also at Fort Montgomery. We pursued the Indians through the wilderness as far as Buffalo; had five ——— pieces. Gen'l Sullivan commanded. When we reached Buffalo it was husking corn time.

"It was a week after New Year's before we set out on our return march. The Indians retreated before us as we went onward. We got home about middle of January, returning by the same route, and were discharged after being home about a month. At Westpoint on our return we halted; and, standing sentry one cold night, snow knee deep, a party of Hessians and Highlanders, who had crossed the Hudson on the ice, came on us by surprise. After hailing the first one and he giving no answer, I fired and he fell. The whole guard came out, and all fired and killed sixteen. It was moonlight. The Light Horse soon rallied and came in their rear, and they surrendered prisoners (70). The Highlanders were dressed in woolen blue plaid trousers and armed with broad swords. As soon as I had fired, and repeated the fire twice or thrice, they returned my fire, and I fled till the guard came to my relief. I received a bullet upon the button of my gaiters, which drove the button and ball into my right leg just above the outer ankle bone. The ball and button were both cut out of the leg by Dr. Parrott, the surgeon of our Regiment, next morning. The fight was about at 10 at night. At the same time I received a wound in the tendon of the heel, just opposite the ankle, which seemed to be cut, and divided the large tendon almost through. [Note: Both wounds or scars yet visible and tangible]. Dr. Parrott attended me all this time. The Company and Regiment remained there all this time, but [I] hobbled along and kept up with the Regiment homeward. Capt. Younglove was wounded in the thigh this same night with a musket shot—fleshy part of the under side of the thigh. This was my last service.

"Henry Vroom, near the Burnt Mills, on the place of Brazer Beekman, was with me on guard at Cummunipaw under Capt. J. Ten Eyck. [Take this deposition, Enquire of Col Schamp by letter as to his recollection of Sutphin].

"After War ended applied and demanded my freedom of Berger. He sold me to Peter Ten Eyck for £110, a slave for life. Ten Eyck sold me to Rev. John Duryea for £92.10. I lived with him 2½ years, and [he] sold me to Peter Sutphen for the same money. Lived with him and his for two years as slave. Then lived with my mistress for one year. I agreed to pay him [Sutphen?] from the proceeds of my labor £92.10. I paid it and bought my freedom after the additional servitude of 20 years under different masters."

---

1. Extensive notes on this document are provided by Larry R. Gerlach, ed., *New Jersey in the American Revolution, 1763–1783: A Documentary History* (Trenton, N.J., 1975), pp. 354-60. "Although misinformation and distortions have crept into the account," according to Gerlach, "as the inevitable result of the passage of time, they are for the most part insignificant and do not detract from the overall reliability of the service record."
2. The *Asia* was a sixty-eight-gun British warship.

---

6 SLAVES AND THE WAR, 1777–80

Although the exigencies of war ultimately forced Americans to use slaves in state militias, the British wisely made an earlier bid for the military services of blacks. In 1775 the royal governor of Virginia, John Murray, earl of Dunmore, enraged slaveholders when he promised manumission to slaves who would help crush the insurrection against the crown. Such a tangible opportunity for freedom had never before been offered to blacks, and the decree influenced events in other colonies. Some New Jersey slaves fought on the Loyalist side. While the role of these blacks was not decisive, their exploits alarmed Jerseymen. On June 21, 1780 there was a raid at Conascung, Monmouth County, in which a contingent of refugee Tories, blacks, and Queen's Rangers pillaged the homes of some local residents and captured several slaves. The blacks were apparently under the command of an obscure black man named Ty, who led a motley contingent in raids on the Sandy Hook area. [doc. 6a]

On March 12, 1777, Reverend Alexander MacWhorter (1734–1807) described a British raid on Newark in which many atrocities were committed. The extent of black participation in this engagement is unclear, but blacks seem to have been no more respectful of the persons or property of the enemy than were the British troops.[doc. 6b]

As the struggle for independence continued, the number of runaway slaves in New Jersey and neighboring states rose dramatically. Some slaves, such as a woman called Maria of Philadelphia, sensed an opportunity for flight. [doc. 6c] Maria may have sought to return to family and friends in Flemington. The war made the policing of slaves more difficult, and in its destructive path it raised hopes for a successful escape to freedom.

a. Extract of a letter from Monmouth County, dated 22 June 1780. *New Jersey Archives,* ser. 2, 4:456-57.

"Yesterday morning a party of the enemy, consisting of Ty with 30 blacks, 36 Queen's Rangers, and 30 refugee tories, landed at Conascung. They by some means got in between our scouts undiscovered, and went up to Mr. James Mott's, sen. plundered his and several of the neighbours houses of almost everything in them; and carried off the following persons, viz. Mr. James Mott, sen. Jonathan Pearse, James Johnson, Joseph Dorset, William Blair, James Walling, jun. John Walling, son of Thomas, Philip Walling, James Wall, Matthew Griggs, also several Negroes, and a great deal of stock, but all the negroes, one excepted, and the horses, horned cattle and sheep, were, I believe, retaken by our people. We had wounded, Capt. Walling slightly, a Lieutenant Henderson had his arm broke, two privates supposed to be mortally, and a third slightly, in a skirmish we had with them on their retreat. The enemy acknowledge the loss of seven men, but we think it much more considerable." [—*New Jersey Gazette,* vol. 3, no. 131, 28 June 1780]

b. Reverend Alexander MacWhorter's letter, 12 March 1777. *New Jersey Archives,* ser. 2, 1:350-53.

"Great have been the ravages committed by the British troops in this part of the country, as to what has been done by them in Trenton, Princeton, &c. you have seen. Their footsteps with us are marked with desolation and ruin of every kind. I, with many others fled, from the town, and those that tarried behind suffered almost every manner of evil. The murder, robbery, ravishments, and insults, they were guilty of are dreadful. When I returned to the town, it looked more like a scene of ruin than a pleasant well cultivated village.

One Thomas Hayes, who lived about three miles out of town, as peaceable and inoffensive a man as in the state of New Jersey, was unprovokedly murdered by one of their Negroes, who run him through the body with his sword. He also cut and slashed his aged uncle in such a manner that he is not yet recovered of his wounds, though received about three months ago. The same fellow stabbed one Nathan Baldwin in the neighbourhood, who recovered. Three women were most horridly ravished by them, one of them an old woman near seventy years of age, whom they abused in a manner beyond description, another of them was a woman considerably advanced in her pregnancy, and the third was a young girl. Various others were assaulted by them, who, by the favorable interpositions of Providence, were preserved, that they did not accomplish upon them their base designs. Yea, not only common soldiers, but officers, even British officers, four or five, sometimes more sometimes less in a gang, went about the town by night, entering into houses and openly inquiring for women.

"Their plundering is so universal, and their robberies so atrocious, that I cannot fully describe their conduct, Whig and Tory were all treated in the same manner, except such who were happy enough to procure a sentinel to be placed as a guard at their door. There was one Nutman, who had always been a remarkable Tory, and who met the British troops with huzzas of joy, had his house plundered of almost everything; he himself had his shoes taken off his feet, and threatened to be hanged, so that with difficulty he escaped being murdered by them. It was diligently propagated by the Tories, before the enemy came, that all those who tarried in their houses would not be plundered, which induced some to stay, who otherwise would probably have saved many of their effects by removing them. But nothing was a greater deception or baser falsehood than this, as the event proved, for none were more robbed than those that tarried at home with their families. I shall only here mention a few names, John Ogden; Esq; an aged man, who had never done much in the controversy one way or another; they carried out of his house every thing they thought worth bearing away; they ripped open the feather beds, scattered the feathers in the air, and carried the ticks with them; broke his desk to pieces, and tore and destroyed a great number of important papers, deeds, wills, &c. belonging to himself and others, and they insulted and abused the old gentleman in the most outrageous manner, threatening sometimes to hang him, and sometimes to cut off his head. They hauled a sick son of his, whose life had been for some time despaired of, out of his bed, and grossly abused him, threatening him with death in a variety of forms.

"The next neighbour to this Ogden was one Benjamin Coe,[1] a very aged man, who, with his wife, was at home; they plundered and destroyed every thing in the house, and insulted them with such fury and rage, that the old people fled for fear of their lives; and then to shew the fulness of their malice, they burnt his house to ashes. Zophar Beach, Josiah Beach, Samuel Pennington, and others, who had large families, and were all at home, they robbed in so egregious a manner, that they were hardly left a rag of clothing, save what was on their backs. The mischief committed in the houses forsaken of their inhabitants, the destruction of fences, barns, stables, and other outhouses, the breaking of chests of drawers, desks, tables and other furniture, the burning and carrying away of carpenters and shoemakers tools are intirely beyond description.

"Now this is only a faint account of the justice and humanity of the British troops. They fully answer the character of the wicked, whose mercies are cruelty. For in addition to all, they imposed an oath of absolute submission to the British King, turning the declaration contained in Howe's proclamation into an oath, and causing the people solemnly to swear the same. Those who took the oath, and obtained what were falsely called protections, there are instances with us of these being robbed and plundered afterwards, but the most general way in which they obtained the effects of such people was by bargaining with them for their hay, cattle or corn, promising them pay, but none with us ever received any thing worth mentioning.

I might have observed, that it was not only the common soldiers that plundered and stole, but also their officers, and not merely low officers and subalterns, but some of high rank were aiding and abetting and reaped the profits of this business, no less a person than Gen. Erskine, who lodged at Daniel Baldwin's had his room furnished from a neighbouring house with mahogany chairs and tables, a considerable part of which was taken away with his baggage when he went to Elizabeth Town. Col. M'Donald who made his quarters at Alexander Robinson's had his room furnished in the same felonious manner, and the furniture was carried off, as though it had been part of his baggage. Another Colonel, whose name I have forget, sent his servants who took away a sick woman's bed, Mrs. Crane's, from under her for him to sleep upon. But there is no end of describing their inhuman conduct. And what they practised in this town seems, as far as I can hear, only a sample of their general treatment of the inhabitants wherever they came.''

ALEX. M'WHORTER.''

---

1. Benjamin Coe's slave, Jack Cudjo, fought with the Continental Army. Too old to fight against the British, Coe sent Cudjo as his replacement.

c. "One Thousand Dollars Reward," *New Jersey Archives,* ser. 2, 4:517.

RAN away this morning from the subscriber, a Negro Wench, named Maria, alias Amoritta; she is about 34 years of age, tall and well made, her face long, and features more regular than are common with her colour; she had on, or took with her, a pale blue and white short linsey gown and petticoat almost new, a petticoat of green baize, a pair of new high-heel'd leather shoes, good shifts of brown homespun linen, and aprons of the same. It is supposed she will endeavour to get into the Jersies, as she came from thence, and once lived with Mr. Thomas Lowrey, of Flemington, but it is suspected she is now lurking in this city,[1] or concealed by some free negroes. She also took her female child with her, named Jane, about 4 years old, well made, fat, round faced, and lively; had on or took with her, a brown homespun frock, also a blue and white linsey frock.

Whoever will deliver the said wench and child to the subscriber in Philadelphia, shall have the above reward.

July 10, 1780.   JOHN DUFFIELD.

N.B. All persons are forbid to harbour her at their peril.

---

1. Philadelphia.

---

7   FREEDOM FOR SOME, 1784, 1789

For a few blacks the Revolutionary War brought freedom. Such was the good fortune of Peter Williams and Negro Man Cato. Williams enlisted in the Continental Army after he escaped from his master, John Heard, a Loyalist of Woodbridge; and Cato, who also was the property of a Tory, David Fitz Randolph of Woodbridge, gave "essential services" to the rebellion. The legislature confiscated the property of the two slaveholders and manumitted Williams and Cato for their contributions to the struggle for independence. Other slaves achieved their freedom in this manner. But for a greater number, the war actually diminished the prospects for freedom, as many slaveowners sold their slaves to pay debts incurred during the Revolution.

a. An Act for setting free Peter Williams, a Negro, late the Property of John Heard, *New Jersey Laws,* 1 September 1784.

WHEREAS it appears upon Proof to the Legislature, that *John Heard,* of *Woodbridge,* in the County of *Middlesex,* joined the Enemies of the United States, by going into their Lines, and took with him a Negro Man, then his Property, named *Peter;* that said Negro Man came back from the Enemy in the Year One Thousand Seven Hundred and Eighty and served some Time with the Troops raised by this State for the Defence of the Frontiers; that he enlisted out of said Troops into the Continental Army, where he served faithfully until the End of the War; that said *John Heard's* Estate became confiscated, and consequently the said Negro Man, now known by the Name of *Peter Williams,* became the Property of this State; therefore, in Consideration of the faithful Services of the said *Peter,*

BE IT ENACTED *by the Council and General Assembly of this State, and it is hereby Enacted by the Authority of the same,* That the Negro Man named *Peter,* known and called by the Name of *Peter Williams,* late the Property of *John Heard,* shall be, and he, the said *Peter Williams,* is hereby declared to be manumitted and set free from Slavery and Servitude, as fully to all Intents and Purposes as though he had been free born and continued in such State of Freedom; any Law, Usage or Custom to the contrary notwithstanding.

A. *Passed at* New-Brunswick, September 1, 1784.

b. An Act for setting Free Negro Cato, *New Jersey Laws*, 25 November 1789.

WHEREAS it appears upon proof to the Legislature, that David Fitz Randolph of Woodbridge, in the County of Middlesex, joined the Enemies of the United States, by going into their Lines, whereby the whole of his Property became Forfeited to this State, and that the above named Negro Man Cato, was part thereof; and as it appears by sundry Vouchers, that the said Cato has rendered essential Services both to this State and the United States in the Time of the late War; therefore,

Sect. 1. BE IT ENACTED *by the Council and General Assembly of this State, and it is hereby Enacted by the Authority of the same,* That the Negro Man named Cato, who was late the Property of the above

named David Fitz Randolph, and now the Property of this State, shall, and the said Cato hereby is declared to be Manumitted and set free from Slavery and Servitude, as fully to all Intents and Purposes, as though he had been free-born, and continued in such State of Freedom, any Law, Usage or Custom to the contrary notwithstanding.
A. Passed at Perth-Amboy, November 25, 1789.

8   FIRST ABOLITIONIST VICTORY, 1786

The first important victory for New Jersey abolitionists after the Revolution occurred in 1786, when the legislature prohibited the importation of slaves and recognized the legality of voluntary manumissions. The act demonstrated two paradoxical attitudes toward slavery: the growing unpopularity of bond servitude in the new nation, which was eloquently stated in the act's preamble; and New Jersey's antipathy toward immediate abolition. The act's third section, for example, permitted owners to bring into the state slaves brought from Africa before 1776. Violators of the act faced weak penalties, and the slaves who were illegally imported into the state remained bond laborers. Notwithstanding the ideals which made the law possible, it was a conservative gesture toward emancipation.

An Act to Prevent the Importation of Slaves
Into the State of New-Jersey, and to Authorize the
Manumission of Them Under Certain Restrictions,
and to Prevent the Abuse of Slaves,
New Jersey Laws, **2 March 1786.**

WHEREAS the Principles of Justice and Humanity require, that the barbarous Custom of bringing the unoffending Africans from their native Country and Connections into a State of Slavery ought to be discountenanced, and as soon as possible prevented; and sound policy also requires, in order to afford ample Support to such of the Community as depend upon their Labour for their daily Subsistence, that the Importation of Slaves into this State from any other State or Country whatsoever, ought to be prohibited under certain Restrictions; and that such as are under Servitude in the State ought to be protected by Law from those Exercises of wanton Cruelty too often practised upon them; and that every unnecessary Obstruction in the Way of freeing Slaves should be removed; therefore,

Sect. 1. BE IT ENACTED *by the Council and General Assembly of this State, and it is hereby Enacted by the Authority of the same,* That, from and after the Publication of this Act, it shall not be lawful for any Person or Persons whatsoever to bring into this State, either for Sale or for Servitude, any Negro Slave brought from Africa since the Year Seventeen Hundred and Seventy-six; and every Person offending by bringing into this State any such Negro Slave shall, for each Slave, forfeit and Pay the Sum of Fifty Pounds, to be sued for and recovered with Costs by the Collector of the Township into which such Slave shall be brought, to be applied when recovered to the Use of the State.

2. *And be it further Enacted by the Authority aforesaid,* That if any Person shall either bring or procure to be brought into this State, any Negro or Mulatto Slave, who shall not have been born in or brought from Africa since the Year above-mentioned, and either sell or buy, or cause such Negro or Mulatto Slave to be sold, or to remain in this State, for the Space of six Months, every such Person, so bringing or procuring to be brought or selling or purchasing such Slave, not born in or brought from Africa since the Year aforesaid, shall, for every such Slave, forfeit and pay the Sum of Twenty Pounds, to be sued for and recovered with Costs by the Collector of the Township into which such Slave shall be brought or remain after the Time limited for that Purpose, the Forfeiture to be applied to the Use of the State as aforesaid.

3. *Provided always, and be it further Enacted by the Authority aforesaid,* That Nothing in this Act contained shall be construed to prevent any Person who shall remove into the State, to take a settled Residence here, from bringing all his or her Slaves without incurring the Penalties aforesaid, excepting such Slaves as shall have been brought from Africa since the Year first above-mentioned, or to prevent any Foreigners or others having only a temporary Residence in this State, for the Purpose of transacting any particular Business, or on their Travels, from bringing and employing such Slaves as Servants, during the Time of his or her Stay here, provided such Slave shall not be sold or disposed of in this State.

4. *And be it further Enacted by the Authority aforesaid,* That all the Forfeitures which may be recovered as aforesaid shall, by the Collector recovering the same, be paid into the Treasury; and if any Collector shall be put to any necessary Expence in prosecuting as aforesaid, he shall be credited for the same out of the publick Money in his Hands; and in case any Collector shall neglect or refuse to prosecute to Effect, for any Fine or Forfeiture incurred as aforesaid, he shall, for every such Neglect or Refusal, forfeit and pay the Sum which he ought to have recovered, which, together with the Sums recovered by any Collector upon Non-Payment thereof, shall be sued for and recovered with Costs, by the

Treasurer of this State for the Time being, to be applied to the Use of the State.

5. *And be it further Enacted by the Authority aforesaid,* That it shall and may be lawful for any Owner, Master or Mistress of any Negro or Mulatto Slave, to manumit and set free such Slave by executing a Writing under Hand and Seal, certifying such Manumission, and also obtaining a Certificate, signed by two of the Overseers of the Poor of the Township, and any two Justices of the Peace of the County wherein the said Master or Mistress may reside . . . .

A. Passed at Trenton, March 2, 1786.

9   KIDNAPPING AT EGG HARBOR, 1803

As slavery came to an end in the northern states, unscrupulous whites occasionally attempted to take advantage of the dubious legal rights of the freedmen by kidnapping and selling them into bondage in the South. This problem is brought to light in the following document on the activities of Reuben Pitcher of Martha's Vineyard, Massachusetts, and the ill-fated voyage of the Sloop *Nancy.* In April 1803 this small vessel embarked from Boston with four freedmen. Three of the blacks had been obtained from jail, where they had been confined for debt; another was apparently deluded by Pitcher's promise of gainful employment. After a short stay at Pitcher's farm on Martha's Vineyard, the sloop, with the four freedmen, Pitcher, and Captain Nicholas Booker, set a course for Savannah, Georgia. When the vessel anchored at Egg Harbor in Burlington County, New Jersey, however, the blacks escaped, fearing they would be sold into slavery. Although their recapture was assisted by some local whites, the kidnapping scheme began to unravel when Captain Booker refused to participate further, and when a Captain Clark, whose services Pitcher had sought, exposed the plot to local authorities. The vessel was soon seized and the four blacks were extended the protection of habeas corpus. Later, they were set free and permitted to "hire themselves where they pleasd . . . ." This resolution suggests that in the twilight of New Jersey slavery, the rights of free blacks could be upheld in a community where individuals of conscience steadfastly defended democratic principles.

Rough Statement of Sloop *Nancy,* 1803, Manuscript Collection, Burlington County Historical Society.

About the latter end of the 5 mo. last, a small Sloop calld Nancy having on board 4 blk People was siezd at Eggharbour On an Information that She was engaged in the transportation of Blacks to the Southern States—One of the Captains Nicholas Boaker gave the followg acct. that the owner Reuben Pitcher had shipd him at Boston under promise to give him one half the neat Profits or if he would stay with him Six Mos. or a year that he would put $1000 Dols. in his Pocket—that he was going to the Southward with as many blacks as he could pick up—for which purpose he designed to touch at many Ports where he had connections in said Business. Of the 4 Blacks he then had, three of them he had purchased out of Boston Jail where they were confind for Small Debts & which, with the Expences were pd by Pitcher & Indentures taken on them for 6 to 12 mos. the other he met in Boston Street & persuaded him to go with him to his Farm at Marthas Vineyard & Drive his Coach clean his Boots &c—Pitcher accordingly took them all to Martha's Vineyard, & after a short stay there, embarkd in his intended voyage—they made several small stops & finally put into Eggharbour to refit—here, the Blacks having taken the alarm that they were going to be sold, got on shore & ran away—on which Pitcher interested the People of Eggharbour & took them again—this excited enquiry & Captain Boaker & he havg Disagreed on the Passage had concluded to Separate, on which Pitcher engagd Capt Clark, to whom he also imparted his Design to take said Blacks & as many more as they could get to Savanna & offerd him a share in the Profits, or a very handsome sum if he would stay with & assist him in the prosecution of his said scheme—Capt Clark appeard to disapprove in Principle the Diabolical Project, & turnd informer against Pitcher who seemd alarmd & very desirous to get off, but the Corroner with the Assistance of Eli Mathis & some others made a seizure of the Vessel & Stores & sent an acct. thereof to the Acting Com.—who took such Measures as appeard to them best—A Habeus Corpus was servd on acct of the blacks, who were bro. to Burln. with the two Captains Boaker & Clark—the blacks were permitted to go & hire themselves where they pleasd & the Evidence of the Captains was taken before Thos. Adams Esq—at the Court in the 8th Mo. the Vessel was condemnd—Pitcher not appearg to make any Defence—Griffith, the Attorney says he designs giving orders to the Marshall to sell said Vessel, & he must report that She is not to be found, for the Corronor, W. Crammer, made a pretended appraissmt and she was valued at $70—whereupon said Crammer took security of Pitcher for that sum & let him go off with the Sloop Stores &c—The Expences in this Business already paid amount to upward of 40 Dols & in all probability considerably more will accrue.

10   A CALL FOR GRADUAL ABOLITION OF SLAVERY, 1804

The following petition was probably submitted to the legislature in February 1804, contributing to the ongoing legislative debate on the abolition of slavery. It is one of the most important statements against slavery made in the early-nineteenth-century New Jersey. Drawing upon the ideals of the Enlightenment and the American Revolution, the New Jersey Society for Promoting the Abolition of Slavery declared slavery to be indefensible in a free society devoted to reason and humanity.

The Society did not contest the right of slaveholders to keep their slaves, because it believed that a general emancipation would violate the sanctity of property. This position may also have resulted from anxiety over the economic impact of general emancipation and the fear of a large free black population. The right to own slaves did not, however, sanction the enslavement of the unborn, who "at some given age should be free-men and free-women, and their children wholly." The call for gradual abolition was a practical alternative to more extreme measures which the legislature surely would have rejected. This moderate approach helped win public and legislative acceptance for the idea of emancipation.

William Griffith, et al.,
To the Legislative-Council and General Assembly
of the State of New-Jersey **(np, nd), broadside.**

THE New-Jersey Society for promoting the gradual Abolition of Slavery, request leave, through us the underwritten members thereof, to present before the Legislature their earnest entreaty and testimony in favor of the law now depending for the gradual extinction of Slavery in this state.

The principle of hereditary bondage can no longer be defended in a land of freedom, and by a people distinguished for reason and humanity; and few, very few, at this day, we should hope, will plead for it on the ground of private property. Even those who hold by purchase, and reason only on the basis of trafic, cannot in candor but acknowledge, that to enslave children to the latest posterity for the cost of the parent, and that too after the Father and Mother have worn out their lives in servitude for the price paid, is a satisfaction vastly disproportionate!

It is alleged, that to emancipate those now living, generally, would be to violate private rights in possession, and productive of many public evils. But as respects those who may *in future be born,* this objection does not apply: And we trust that the time has arrived when the united voice of reason and policy require that they should be admitted to the common blessings of Liberty; and not come into existence only to labor for others . . . to be bought and sold . . . and to transmit the same wretched inheritance in their posterity. The obvious way to effect this great and necessary end will be to declare, that all born after the passage of the law shall at some given age be free-men and free-women, and their children wholly free.

Surely years and years of servitude will compensate sufficiently the master for the cares and expences of childhood. How little indeed is really expended upon the first period of their infancy? Nurtured by the mother in the recesses of labor; uneducated, and almost unheeded, they arrive at the age of usefulness at an imperceptible cost. Few of them but at seven and ten years old begin to earn their subsistence . . . and will not servitude until twenty one fully repay the expenses of infancy? It may be alleged that cases of particular hardship will happen: Some parents may have proved a burthern, and some children from accident or disease continue so for many years; but these instances will be rare, and the inequality be greatly overballanced in the general operation of the liberal term of twenty one years service. What extensive regulation ever takes place without producing some individual losses? Legislators must often act without respect to these on the wide scale of public utility; . . . they indeed will cease to act at all, if a few possible or probable disadvantages of a private nature, must deter them from the execution of measures calculated for the good of the whole.

If then the principle is admitted that perpetual slavery is politically wrong, and morally a departure from the great laws of nature and humanity, certainly this question of profit and loss may be adjusted. Shall that forever stand in the way of emancipation? Will nothing short of the *servitude of children to the end of time satisfy the owner for the price paid for, or the value of the Parent?* . . . The value given for slaves is commonly settled with reference to personal capacity for labor, and not regulated by any views to the service of their after born issue; and all the owners of slaves in possession, whether held by immediate purchase or by descent, will in general be thereby paid for the consideration advanced. We ask you, fellow-citizens and Legislators, for no *law* to touch property *in possession* however acquired; neither for the disannulling of that by which Twelve Thousand human beings are doomed to die as they were born . . . . *Vassals in a land of Freedom!* We suplicate you for the *unborn;* these have *not been bought,* and when they come into possession let a *fair equivalent in personal service satisfy the possessor for the care and cost of their infancy.* A period will then be fixed after which it may be said that IN NEW-JERSEY NO MAN IS BORN A SLAVE!

It is not credible that prejudice or personal interest can much longer hold out against a claim like this . . . a claim advocated by the natural feelings of the human heart, and acknowledged by Americans in their act of Independence, as among the most undeniable rights of man. Why then should this just and necessary measure be any longer delayed? We cannot but indulge the hope that the propitious moment has come, when the voice of humanity, intreating for the opressed, will be heard . . . when an assembly of enlightened Legislators, acting on the principles of Eternal Justice, and in conformity with their Christian Characters; will resolve *"to bind up the broken hearted, to proclaim liberty"* to the captives, *and the opening of the prison to them that are bound."* Thus will it be your praise to have blotted from your country perhaps its greatest crime, and to have restored to an unhappy race of men, that long lost charter from which we ourselves derive so many blessings,—THE CHARTER OF MAN's LIBERTY!

William Griffith, Richard Hartshorne, Thomas Redman, William Newbold, Gershom Craft, David Wright, Samuel Clement, Committee.

11 GRADUAL ABOLITION IS ENACTED, 1804

On February 15, 1804, New Jersey adopted legislation for the gradual abolition of slavery, years after the other northern states had moved to eradicate slavery. The law grew out of the Revolution's emphasis on the equality of men, but there were other forces working against the "peculiar institution." Unlike the southern states, where blacks were a significant part of the population, the 12,422 slaves in New Jersey accounted for only 5.8 percent of the population in 1800. It was thus much easier for Jerseymen to accept the emancipation of blacks, whose contact with whites was generally less than in the southern states. The lawmakers may have realized that the continued practice of slavery would inevitably increase the number of blacks in the state's population. In addition, while slavery remained profitable in many sections of East Jersey, the state's economy grew increasingly committed to the use of free labor. By the early nineteenth century, moreover, many whites viewed slavery as an unfortunate legacy of the colonial period.

The law provided that children born of slaves after July 4, 1804 were to be free, with such offspring becoming servants of the owner of the mother until the age of twenty-five for males and twenty-one for females. According to the abandonment clause (section 3), the owner was required to maintain the child for one year, after which he could abandon the child to the local overseer of the poor; this was a form of compensated emancipation, which was an obvious boon to slaveholders. Owners were allowed to release and maintain at public expense the offspring of their slaves. Before its repeal in 1811, the abandonment clause led to considerable fraud. By 1808 the costs of maintaining abandoned children accounted for nearly thirty percent of the total state budget.

Slavery died a slow death in New Jersey with the passage of this act in 1804, as well as subsequent legislation in 1820 designed to codify the state's abolition laws, and a law passed in 1846 which substituted apprenticeship for bondage. By 1810, there were 10,851 slaves (4.4 percent), and in 1820 there were 7,557 (2.7 percent). In the thirty years before the Civil War a dramatic decrease in the number of slaves occurred. In 1860 there were still eighteen slaves in the state who labored as "apprentices" for life. Not until the adoption of the Thirteenth Amendment in 1865 did all remnants of slavery disappear in New Jersey.

An Act for the Gradual Abolition of Slavery, *New Jersey Laws,* 15 February 1804.

Sec. 1. *BE it enacted by the Council and General Assembly of this State, and it is hereby enacted by the authority of the same,* That every child born of a slave within this state, after the fourth day of July next, shall be free; but shall remain the servant of the owner of his or her mother, and the executors, administrators or assigns of such owner, in the same manner as if such child had been bound to service by the trustees or overseers of the poor, and shall continue in such service, if a male, until the age of twenty-five years, and if a female until the age of twenty-one years.

2. *And be it enacted,* That every person being an inhabitant of this state, who shall be entitled to the service of a child born as aforesaid, after the said fourth day of July next, shall within nine months after the birth of such child, cause to be delivered to the clerk of the county whereof such person shall be an inhabitant, a certificate in writing, containing the name and addition of such person, and the name, age, and sex of the child so born; which certificate, whether the same be delivered

before or after the said nine months, shall be by the said clerk recorded in a book to be by him provided for that purpose; and such record thereof shall be good evidence of the age of such child, and the clerk of such county shall receive from said person twelve cents for every child so registered; and if any person shall neglect to deliver such certificate to the said clerk within said nine months, such person shall forfeit and pay for every such offence, five dollars, and the further sum of one dollar for every month such person shall neglect to deliver the same, to be sued for and recovered by any person who will sue for the same, the one half to the use of such prosecutor, and the residue to the use of the poor of the township in which such delinquent shall reside.

3. *And be it enacted,* That the person entitled to the service of any child born as aforesaid, may, nevertheless within one year after the birth of such child, elect to abandon such right; in which case a notification of such abandonment, under the hand of such person, shall be filed with the clerk of the township, or where there may be a county poor-house established then with the clerk of the board of trustees of said poor-house of the county in which such person shall reside; but every child so abandoned shall be maintained by such person until such child arrives to the age of one year, and thereafter shall be considered as a pauper of such township or county, and liable to be bound out by the trustees or overseers of the poor in the same manner as other poor children are directed to be bound out until, if a male, the age of twenty-five, and if a female, the age of twenty-one; and such child, while such pauper, until it shall be bound out, shall be maintained by the trustees or overseers of the poor of such county or township, as the case may be, at the expence of this state; and for that purpose the director of the board of chosen freeholders of the county is hereby required from time to time, to draw his warrant on the treasurer in favor of such trustees or overseers for the amount of such expence, not exceeding the rate of three dollars per month, provided the accounts for the same be first certified and approved by such board of trustees, or the town committee of such township; and every person who shall omit to notify such abandonment as aforesaid, shall be considered as having elected to retain the service of such child, and be liable for its maintenance until the period to which its servitude is limited as aforesaid.

A. Passed at Trenton, Feb. 15, 1804.

12 SUPPORT FOR THE ACT OF 1804

The public debate which followed the passage of the gradual abolition law in New Jersey centered on two conflicting questions: was the act in violation of the property rights of slaveowners; or, was it partial to the financial interests of that group? In the following letter to the *True American,* an anonymous observer claimed that the act was a sensible and equitable approach to the difficult task of ending slavery in the state. Like many other opinions on the issue published after the law was enacted, it revealed that Jerseymen were fundamentally divided over the Revolution's emphasis on human rights and the sanctity of property. It is clear that in this case more weight was given to the latter. Readers are reminded that the law did not interfere with slaves bound to their owners; they were, he said, to be "set free by that great days-man, Death." Moreover, the author did not foresee the abuses which ultimately resulted from the abandonment clause, and he did not consider that gradual abolition, in promising eventual freedom for the offspring of slaves, conflicted with the inviolable truths expressed in the Declaration of Independence.

A Citizen, "For the True American," Trenton *True American,* 30 April 1804.

Messrs Printers,

I have been not a little surprised to find that some of our fellow citizens are dissatisfied with the law which lately passed the Legislature of this state for the gradual Abolition of Slavery; and my surprise is encreased on reflecting that tho' the measure has been long contemplated; tho' at the last fall's sitting the bill was brought forward, was postponed to the next sitting, and meantime published for general information by order of the Legislature, that their Constituents might have an opportunity of expressing their sentiments upon it before it became a law—yet not a single petition was presented to the Legislature against it, though numbers were in favor of it—not a paragraph in opposition to it appeared in any paper, though several powerful pieces were published in support of it. Surely, if the law was so objectionable, the time and mode to have pointed out its evils, and its follies would have been while it was pending, by petitions or remonstrances. From hearing not a voice in opposition to it, while many plead loudly and warmly in its favor, the Legislature might rationally conclude that it would be universally agreeable.

But I am inclined to believe that the evils feared from this law are mostly imaginary. It cannot be expected to lay the axe at the roots of such a deep and intricate system, without suffering some inconveniences; but I believe the present law will be found as free from evil consequences as any that could have been enacted on the subject.

The Legislature have not interfered with any Slaves in existence. They are left to serve their masters till set free by that great days-man, Death. The Legislature have only provided that those children who are born of slaves after the fourth of July next, shall be enlarged from servitude, as soon as they arrive at ages when they will probably have fully repaid their masters for the expence of bringing them up, and when they will likely be able to earn a decent livelihood for themselves. Or in case the owner of any slave should not wish to raise the children of such slave born after the time aforesaid, he shall be at liberty to throw them upon the State for maintenance.

The foregoing provisions show such a just respect for the interests, and such an anxious desire to meet the wishes, of those who possess Slaves, that I think no Slaveholder can with either justice or generosity find fault with the law, or condemn the Legislature for passing it.

It has been apprehended by some, that the clause authorizing owners of slaves to abandon the children of such slaves, would prove pernicious and burthernsome to the state. I think time and experience will prove that this fear is unfounded. This clause was introduced in order to leave the owners of slaves an alternative, either to raise the children of the slaves, or get rid of them at a year old. And the provision that the state should support such abandoned children, was inserted, in order that those counties who had no slaves in them, might assist the counties in which slavery still existed in gradually getting rid of it also—It was an honorable, a humane, a generous concession of those counties who have no Slaves, to those who have; and may the magnanimous measure draw down the blessings of Heaven on the heads of its adopters and supporters!—But tho' this concession was praiseworthy, and salutary in securing the passage of the law, yet it will not throw that burthen on the State that some have feared. The clause was copied from the Abolition-Law of the State of New York, which has been in operation for a number of years; and the children which have been abandoned in that state, if I am rightly informed, have been so very few as never to make any sensible addition to the taxes of the State. Nor do I believe that the maintenance of those children of Slaves who will be abandoned by their masters in this state, will ever amount to a cent a year for each taxable inhabitant of the State!

With regard to this law being a party measure, nothing need be said more than to observe, that both parties in the Legislature went hand in hand in forming and passing the Law—that the voters in Assembly were thirty four for it, to four against it, Mr. Blanch of Bergen being out-of-doors—and that the votes in Council were all in favor of it but one.

For my own part, I am fully persuaded that the more the law is considered and discussed, the less objectionable it will seem; and this is all the apology I have to offer, for troubling you with these remarks.

A CITIZEN.

13   THE INDENTURE OF SUSAN, 1810

After the Act for the Gradual Abolition of Slavery was enacted in 1804, the character of the institution was dramatically and forever changed. The law, despite its flaws, culminated years of ameliorative efforts on the part of anti-slavery men; and despite violations of the act, the lives of bondsmen and women and their offspring generally improved as efforts were made to prepare them for the challenges of freedom. The following indenture concerns the future of the girl, Susan. After the death of her mother's owner, John Cox of Bridgewater, Somerset County, the overseers of the poor, Peter D. Vroom and Henry Brokaw of Hillsborough, provided that the child be taken by Edward Dayle and to be apprenticed to him until she reached the age of eighteen years. For her "master" Dayle, Susan was to "serve in all lawful business" and "honestly, orderly and obediently demean and behave herself." The indenture also provided that Susan be taught to read, trained in housewifery, and given clothing at the end of her apprenticeship. Like most indentures penned after the 1804 law, the overseers were primarily concerned that freed blacks not become a burden to the white population.

Indenture of Susan, 30 October 1810,
Miscellaneous Manuscripts (MG 25),
Manuscript Collections, The New Jersey Historical Society.

This Indenture witnesseth that Peter D. Vroom and Henry Brokaw, overseers of the poor of the township of Hillsborough in the county of Somerset have and by these presents, do put and place a negro girl named Susan of the age of four years on the 29th day of July last past, born of the body of a female slave late the property of John Cox dec'd of the township of Bridgwater and county aforesaid apprntice to Edward Dayle of the township of Riding and county of Hunterdon, his heirs and assigns, with him to dwell and serve from the date hereof, until the said appentice shall accomplish the full age of eighteen years which will be on the 29th day of July 1824. during all which time the said apprntice her said master faithfilly shall serve in all lawful businesses and shall honestly, orderly and obediently demean and behave herself towards her said master and all his, and the said master for himself, his executors and administrators doth covenant and agree to and with the said overseers of the poor and their successors for the time being, that he the said Edward Dayle, the apprentice shall and will teach or cause to be taught to read and housewifery and during all said term, find and provide all things necessary for an apprentice so that she be not chargable to the said township, and at the experation of said term, the said master shall give the said apprentice good every day waring apperel and also a sunday suit fitting for such an apprentice—

In witness whereof the said parties have hereunto interchangably set their hands and seals the thirtyth day of october in the year of our Lord eighteen hundrend and ten 1810—

Sealed and delivered)   Nichl. Williamson
in the presents of)   Nathan Allen
                          Edward Dalley
                          Peter D. Vroom
                          Henry Brokaw

14 REMOVAL TO THE SOUTH, 1818

The weak safeguards against violations of the spirit of the 1804 gradual abolition law placed many slaves in a precarious situation. In the years after the law was enacted, unscrupulous owners sold an undetermined number of blacks to slave traders in the southern states. In 1812 the legislature passed a law designed to discourage the practice but allowed slaves to be voluntarily removed from New Jersey. Not surprisingly, the provision was flouted since owners, exploiting the ignorance of their slaves, promised them short-term service in the South while, in fact, dooming them to a life of perpetual bondage in a region where slavery was much harsher. The following document acknowledges the willingness of Harvey, and eighteen-year-old slave from Middlesex County, "to remove and go out of this State to Point Coupee [Parish] in the State of Louisiana."

Removal, 22 April 1818, Middlesex County,
New Jersey Records, 2 (Manumission of Slaves): 257,
Special Collections, Alexander Library, Rutgers University.

REMOVAL HAREY   ss:

State of New Jersey
Middlesex County

Be it remembered that on this twenty second day of April in the year of our Lord one thousand eight hundred and eighteen Nicholas VanWickle of the county of Middlesex in New Jersey, brought before us Jacob Van-Wickle and John Outcalt Esquires, two of the Judges of the Court of Common Pleas of the county and State aforesaid, his male slave named Harey aged Eighteen years and the said Harey having no parents in this said State, being by us examined separate and apart from his said master, declared that he was willing, and that he freely consented to remove and go out of this State to Point Coupee in the State of Louisiana and there to serve Colonel Charl's Morgan and Nicholas Vanwickle or either of them their heirs or assigns jointly or severally.—In testimony whereof, we have hereunto set our hands, the day and year first above written.—

Jb. VanWickle

Jn. Outcalt   Judges

Received June 15th. 1818 & recorded by [William Phillips] Deare, Clerk

IV

Twilight of Slavery

THE American Revolution kindled a new spirit of human freedom, but Jerseymen continued to shoulder the great moral and spiritual burden of slavery and racial inequality. Gradual abolition after 1804 left freedmen and their posterity politically disenfranchised and economically subservient. Freedom under these conditions was of dubious value. A growing African colonization movement encouraged efforts to remove as many free blacks as possible to Africa. The repugnant image of freedmen had its origins in colonial history and continued in the nineteenth century. Whites feared that total emancipation would endanger their racial and economic superiority, threaten to undermine racial purity, place white workers in precarious competition with black laborers, and hamper the maintenance of law and order. White Jerseymen conducted themselves in such a way as to deny the promise of American democracy to blacks.

The resistance of New Jersey to black equality during the first half of the nineteenth century was in part the product of local demographic patterns. Late-eighteenth-century New Jersey had more blacks than any other northern state. In counties with large black populations, the anxiety over emancipation rose inevitably as more blacks became free under the provisions of the 1804 act. By 1810 there were approximately two freedmen for every slave in the state. On the eve of the Civil War, the black population, which numbered 25,336 in a total population of 646,699, was proportionally twice as large as that in any other free state.[1]

Even among friends of the blacks, the gradual emancipation of slaves was a terrifying challenge. In 1821 the Sabbath School for Coloured People in the Newark Academy, boasting that "no section of our Country affords greater means of instruction for the

people of Colour than this Town,'' was distressed that perhaps in
no other place is ''the benevolence of whites less esteemed by
those who ought to appreciate it as one of their greatest blessings.'' At a time when the city's population was becoming larger
and more diversified, Newark's streets, according to the Department,

> . . . are overrun with ignorance and profanity; and often the Sab-
> bath is made a Season of all most ungovernable excess of noise and
> confusion, especially the evenings when boys of all description and
> color lurking along our walks intrude upon the peaceful abodes of
> those who live on our public streets and like the heathen manifest a
> want of that decorum which distinguishes a land of light from a land
> of Heathenish darkness.[2]

Concern grew after about 1810 that emancipation, though
preferable to slavery, had produced a wretched mass of humanity
having little hope of social improvement. Some reasoned that the
colonization of free blacks in Africa afforded a practical and
moral resolution to these problems. [doc. 1] ''New Jersey men,''
historian Marion Thompson Wright observed, ''were among the
original sponsors of this effort.'' In 1816 the Reverend Robert
Finley, a Presbyterian minister from Basking Ridge, published a
pamphlet entitled *Thoughts on the Colonization of Free Blacks*,
which stated the ideals of the colonization movement in the
United States. The voluntary removal of free blacks was
desirable, Finley argued, because they would never be accorded
racial equality in the United States. Colonization offered a moral
restitution by whites who had committed the crime of enslaving
their fellow men, and it was a missionary movement to take Christianity to the pagan African continent. To fulfill his vision of a
Christian Africa pioneered by freedmen from the New World,
Finley helped to form the American Colonization Society in
Washington, D.C. in 1816.[3]

The American Colonization Society won many supporters in
New Jersey. Perhaps no other free state was so enthusiastic for
the expatriation of Afro-Americans. During the ante-bellum
years, the legislature received several petitions in support of the
Society's efforts. The lawmakers responded to these appeals with
an annual appropriation of $1,000 between 1852 and 1859 to
remove free blacks from New Jersey to colonies in West Africa. In
1838 funds were collected by the New Jersey Colonization Society
to establish a town on the west coast of Africa to be named New

Jersey.[4] The advocacy of black uplift through the return of free blacks to Africa was appealing because it involved both expediency and the Christian missionary spirit. The programs of the Society assuaged the guilt many whites in the northern states felt toward slavery. In 1816, this desire to purge oneself of complicity in human bondage found concrete expression in the formation of the African School in Parsippany, which trained freedmen for missionary work in Africa. [doc. 2] The efforts of the American Colonization Society and its state auxiliary convinced very few blacks to leave New Jersey; however, no other movement relating to blacks enlisted as much support in the state's white population. [doc. 3]

Aware of the threat which the American Colonization Society posed to their desire for equality, free blacks in New Jersey sought to discredit the organization and vigorously fought against its programs. In the early 1840s, anti-colonization petitions to the legislature were received from blacks in Westfield, Rahway, Elizabeth, Paterson, Newark, Trenton, Princeton, and New Brunswick. They denounced the Society as an instrument of the southern slave system which sought to rid the country of its free black population. That view was stated in 1840 by Samuel E. Cornish, a Presbyterian minister in Newark, and Theodore S. Wright, a graduate of the Princeton Theological Seminary. [doc. 4] Their treatise on the colonization scheme was a significant contribution to early Afro-American protest, marking the beginning of an articulate race leadership in the state at a time when white public opinion had taken on a disquietingly racist character.[5]

The opposition of black abolitionists to African colonization encouraged white anti-slavery advocates to reassess their support of the scheme. In the early nineteenth century, white abolitionists envisioned colonization as the fulfillment of their Christian duty, but by the ante-bellum period, many of them were convinced of the movement's moral inconsistency and its thinly veiled hostility toward free black Americans. As in the past, abolitionism in New Jersey was an unpopular movement. There were, however, anti-slavery strongholds in New Brunswick and Belleville, where, in 1840, the well-known abolitionists Theodore Dwight Weld, Angelina Grimké Weld, and Sarah M. Grimké settled. Sympathetic voices continued to be heard from Salem and Burlington counties. Perhaps the most strident criticism of slavery, however, came from Essex County because of the efforts of the Essex

County Anti-Slavery Society, which in 1840 helped to form the New Jersey Anti-Slavery Society. The abolitionists' moral indictment of slavery and dedication to racial equality, nevertheless, earned very little support in nineteenth-century New Jersey. [doc. 5]

The legal status of blacks in New Jersey deteriorated during much of the century. In 1807 free black men, along with women, were stripped of the franchise despite having enjoyed it since the Revolutionary era.[6] The pressure to restrict the franchise to white men mounted during the Jacksonian era and culminated in the ratification of a new constitution in 1844. The constitution was a symbol of expanding democracy in New Jersey; for example, voters no longer had to meet a property qualification. But the document was also the instrument of popular feelings against black residents, restricting the franchise to white male citizens.[7]

Although the denial of the vote was their greatest legal disability, free blacks in New Jersey endured other forms of discrimination which subordinated them to the white population. Under the provisions of a law passed in 1778, New Jersey courts accepted the testimony of a black in a criminal trial only when it was against another black. If free blacks became paupers, they could be removed to the town where they had last been slaves and the former owners forced to provide for them. In public schools blacks were not legally segregated, but the custom of separate schools was well established by the Civil War. New Jersey law was unclear on the legality of slavery prior to the ratification of the Thirteenth Amendment to the U.S. Constitution.[8]

In an effort to ameliorate their condition, blacks formed institutions devoted to group uplift and agitation against slavery and colonization. The most important of these groups was the church. In the three decades before the Civil War, black churches were formed in New Brunswick, Newark, Burlington, Trenton, and other communities. Little is known of the early history of these institutions, but it may be safely stated that the African Methodist Episcopal, Presbyterian, and Baptist churches served as social, cultural, and religious outlets for their congregations. Black churches helped to instill group identity among the freedmen and, through their ministers, protested against colonization and racial discrimination.[9]

In keeping with the emerging ethos of group uplift, free blacks in New Jersey also formed organizations devoted to intellectual pursuits. Literary societies were started in some of the larger towns, and classes were conducted by some churches. Voluntary efforts such as these, however, were insufficient, prompting black leaders to turn to public support. Newark officials appropriated $100 to maintain a Colored School for the city's black children.[10]

As the conflict over slavery intensified in the nation during the 1840s and 1850s, blacks in New Jersey kept up the pressure for the elevation of their legal status. They did not have to rely solely on white abolitionists since articulate black leaders had risen in a generation of freedom. In 1849 blacks from Salem and Gloucester counties petitioned the legislature to remove voting disabilities against them. [doc. 6] When their appeal was rejected, sixteen leaders convened in Trenton in August 1849 for the first Negro Convention in the history of New Jersey. Unlike the petitioners who had appealed to an unsympathetic legislature, the delegates in Trenton resolved to solicit the people of New Jersey to end the inequitable qualifications for the franchise. Reverends Joshua Woodlin of Burlington, W.T. Catto of Trenton, and Ishmael Locke of Camden were authorized to submit "An Address to the Citizens of New Jersey." [doc. 7]

The Convention was followed by a flurry of pro-franchise petitions to the legislature from blacks in Gloucester, Cumberland, Mercer, Middlesex, Monmouth, and Salem counties. Suffrage had become a conspicuous issue in the state largely as a result of the urgency it was given by blacks. Early in 1850, John S. Rock of Salem invoked the ideals expressed in the Convention's "Address" and made a personal appeal to the conscience of the state.[11] [doc. 8] Unfortunately, calls for the enfranchisement of black men came during the ascendancy of the pro-South Democratic Party in state government. Under those conditions black men were not granted the right to vote until the adoption of the Fifteenth Amendment to the U.S. Constitution in 1870. It was not until the ratification of the Nineteenth Amendment in 1920 that black women gained that right.

While free blacks in New Jersey struggled for equality, hundreds of escaping slaves from Maryland, Delaware, and the more distant slave states sought their help in the Underground Railroad. It followed three principal courses in New Jersey: along the Delaware from Camden to Burlington; from Salem through Woodbury, Mount Laurel, and Burlington to Princeton; and through Greenwich, with stations at Swedesboro, Mount Holly, and Burlington directing the runaways to the Camden route. The existence of slavery in Delaware and on Maryland's eastern shore also brought slaves to southern New Jersey who were escaping across the Delaware Bay to Cape May.[12]

One of the most notable anti-slavery activists in New Jersey and neighboring Delaware was Harriet Tubman (ca. 1821–1913), a fearless conductor of the Underground Railroad during the 1850s. In the summer of 1852, Tubman worked as a cook in a Cape May hotel. It is possible that from this strategic location she helped slaves from Maryland and Delaware escape across the Delaware Bay to Cape May and on to safer northern havens. Tubman, who in 1849 escaped slavery in Maryland, may have helped more than 300 slaves escape to free states. During the Civil War she went to South Carolina, where she worked as a cook, laundress, nurse, and occasionally as a guide and spy for the Union Army.[13]

In spite of the assistance given by blacks and sympathetic whites, New Jersey was not a prime haven for escaped slaves. An act passed by the legislature in 1826 provided for the return of fugitive slaves in New Jersey to their owners. It was amended in 1837 to allow for a review by three justices and the privilege of a jury trial in such cases. On account of the state's pro-South sentiments, escaped slaves could never be certain of a successful flight through New Jersey. [doc. 9] "Our State," the anti-slavery *New Jersey Freeman* observed in 1846, "still continues to be the hunting ground of the kidnapper, and some of our inhabitants have during the past year been dragged away without even the forms of law, into hopeless Slavery."[14]

The emerging sectional conflict and the Civil War inflamed the pro-South sentiments of New Jersey. It was the only northern state to vote against Abraham Lincoln in the presidential elections of both 1860 and 1864. Lincoln's conduct of the war was bitterly denounced by the Democrats, who were in control of the legislature. The Emancipation Proclamation was viewed contemptuously as a usurpation of the constitutional right to property. Democrats argued that it would produce a bloody upheaval of blacks in the South. Some southern sympathizers in New Jersey sought to show a connection between the Union war effort and an abolitionist plot to subvert white racial purity.[15] "Not satisfied with violating the Constitution for the negro's sake," wrote David Naar as editor of the Trenton *Daily True American,* "not content with demanding his political and social equality, these abolition radicals are now found openly advocating amalgamation."[16]
[doc. 10]

Against the background of war and anxiety over emancipated blacks, New Jersey lawmakers considered extraordinary measures to prevent an anticipated migration of freedmen from the South. Soon after the Emancipation Proclamation was formally issued on January 1, 1863, an Act to Prevent the Immigration of Negroes and to Define the Standing of the Negro Race in the State of New Jersey was submitted. The Assembly's Judiciary Committee did not act on the bill; but another measure, an Act to Prevent the Immigration of Negroes and Mulattoes, was passed by the Assembly by a vote of thirty-three to twenty. It provided that blacks entering New Jersey would be transported to Liberia or to the West Indies, suggesting the continued support given to the colonization of free blacks. When the act was brought before the Senate it was allowed to die after two readings. Other attempts to preserve the racial status quo and resist the Emancipation Proclamation took the form of petitions against the influx of freedmen to New Jersey and the so-called Peace Resolutions, which advocated an immediate peace with the Confederacy and objected to the emancipation of slaves as unconstitutional. There were also efforts to keep New Jersey blacks out of the Union Army and prevent racial intermixing.

The anti-black rhetoric of the New Jersey press and the antagonism of the legislature did not diminish efforts by black men to aid the Union. [doc. 11] There was an added incentive in the Civil War, because blacks saw in the war a crusade for their own freedom. A total of 2,909 men (including thirty-seven white officers) in the United States Colored Troops were credited to New Jersey, although an undetermined number of these probably lived outside of the state. The Union Army pay structure discriminated against blacks. Congress enacted the Enlistment Act of July 17, 1862, which mandated that white soldiers holding the rank of private should be paid $13 a month and $3.50 for clothing, while blacks were accorded $7 and $3 allocations. Moreover, the persistent stereotype that blacks were unsuited to the rigors of war caused many of them to be relegated to non-combatant functions. But this indignity and inequities in pay were removed toward the end of the conflict. New Jersey black soldiers saw combat at Fort Wagner, Chapins Farm, Petersburg, and other campaigns.[17] Their participation in the crusade for their brothers' and sisters' freedom strengthened the resolve that their future was in the United States rather than on foreign soil. [doc. 12]

---

1   AFRICAN COLONIZATION IS PROPOSED, 1816

In the following petition, 107 citizens requested the legislature to encourage the establishment of a colony for free blacks on the coast of Africa or elsewhere. The petitioners viewed such expatriation as a solution to the social and economic crisis associated with their emancipation. Although they were alarmed by the degraded condition of the freedmen, the petitioners and, indeed, most proponents of colonization did not champion an improvement in the legal status of freedmen.

John Neilson, et al.,
To the Honourable the Legislature of New-Jersey
(New Brunswick, N.J., 1816), broadside.

The Memorial and Petition of the subscribers, inhabitants of New-Jersey, showeth: That they have viewed with great interest and concern the present condition and future prospects of the free people of colour in this and our sister States. While the love of liberty, and the feelings of humanity have produced the emancipation of a great number of these people, and are gradually effecting the freedom of the rest; it is with much regret that your Petitioners observe the degraded situation in which those who have been freed from slavery remain; and from a variety of considerations will probably remain while they continue among the whites.

To enable them to rise to that condition to which they are entitled by the laws of God and nature, it appears desirable, and even necessary, to separate them from their former masters, and place them in some favourable situation by themselves, perhaps in Africa, the land of their fathers. It is therefore respectfully requested of the Legislature to instruct, by Resolution or otherwise, the Senators and Representatives from the State of New-Jersey, to lay before the Congress at their next meeting, as a subject of consideration, The expediency of forming a colony on the coast of Africa, or elsewhere, where such of the people of colour as are now free, or may be hereafter set free, may with their own consent be removed: And your petitioners will, as in duty bound, ever pray.

New Brunswick, December 4th 1816

[107 signatures]

2   A SCHOOL FOR YOUNG BLACK MEN, 1816

The formal education of blacks in New Jersey began somewhat haphazardly in the late eighteenth century when masters were required by law to teach their slaves to read and write. By 1801 white-run schools for blacks had opened in Burlington, Salem, and Trenton. Another school, the Sabbath School for Coloured People in the Newark Academy, enrolled females as students (ca. 1819–21), teaching them to read the Bible; this somewhat rudimentary education was notable in comparison with the contemporary emphasis on housewifery for women.

A more ambitious educational institution was begun in Parsippany by the Presbyterian Synod of New York and New Jersey; for Presbyterians, the African School was an unprecedented commitment to black uplift, but it stemmed largely from the Synod's advocacy of African colonization. Robert Finley and other outspoken colonization advocates served on the school's board of directors. The Synod envisioned that the end of slavery and paganism in Africa would be fostered by the work of black Christians educated in the New World. It called upon its parishioners to renounce the notion of irreversible black ignorance. The view of Africa expressed here reflects contemporary ignorance of the continent: "Africa has no science to communicate; Africa has no religion to impart." The Synod's support of missionary work in Africa incorrectly presumed the willingness of the native population to receive Christianity.

Presbyterian Church in the U.S.A.
Synod of New York and New Jersey,
An Address to the Public on the Subject of the
African School **(New York, 1816), pp. 3-8.**

The Synod of New-York and New-Jersey, at their meeting in the city of New-York, October 1816, unanimously resolved to appoint a Board of Directors to establish and superintend an African School, for the purpose of educating young men of colour, to be teachers and preachers to people of colour within these States and elsewhere. The following persons were elected members of the Board for the present year.

MINISTERS.	LAYMEN.
Dr. Jas. Richards,	Hon. Aaron Ogden, L.L.D.
Dr. Edw. D. Griffin,	Saml. Bayard, Esq.
Dr. John B. Romeyn,	Joseph C. Hornblower, Esq.
Mr. Robert Finley,	Mr. John E. Caldwell,
Mr. John McDowell,	Mr. Zechariah Lewis,
Mr. Gardiner Spring.	Mr. Rensselaer Havens.

The Board thus appointed beg leave to submit to the public the following thoughts on the subject of preparing for the great negro-world teachers of their own race.

By computations founded on the latest information, there are in Africa and its islands twenty millions of the proper negro race, besides thirty millions who differ from them more or less in complexion and features. There are supposed to be a million and a half of the same people in the United States; and a million and a half more may be reckoned for the Floridas, Mexico, South America, and the West India Islands, to say nothing of New-Guinea. Here then is a vast world of twenty-three millions of souls, (besides the thirty millions before mentioned;) a population equal to that of the United States, Great Britain, Ireland, Sweden, and Denmark united.

Though we are fully persuaded that to the end of the world there will remain different orders in Society, it cannot be supposed that so considerable a portion of the human race, consisting of so many independent nations, and occupying the greater part of one of the four quarters of the globe, are always to be regarded as made only for slaves, or are to be excluded from the blessings of Christianity and civilization during the approaching period of the millennium. In those days which are yet to come, and which are even now at the door, the descendants of Ham,[1] we are bound to believe, will attain to an elevation and dignity which will do away the memory of their past disgrace, and give them a rank among the polished nations of Europe and America. Africa will yet boast of her poets and orators. Eloquence will play on the tumid lips of her sons, and sable hands will strike the lyre, and weave the silken web. On the Niger as on the Thames, temples will arise to the living God; and perhaps the arid sands will find the curse of barrenness repealed by the same Power that will turn Palestine into a fruitful field.

If Africa is to stand forth in the glory of Christianity and civilization, her own sons, and not the sons of strangers, must be the instructers of her youth, and her ministers of religion. No nation will ever advance far in any improvement but by the instrumentality of her own children. Strangers may make a beginning, but strangers cannot continue to support her schools and her churches. To sustain such a weight at arm's length, would exhaust both patience and power. History presents no instance of the kind. Apostles and missionaries may pass over a country, but native teachers must finish the work. So it was in primitive times. So it was in every country of Europe when it received the Christian faith. So it is in India at the present day. The debilitated and jetty Hindoos prolong and extend the order which European missionaries have established.

To say that Africans are not competent to become teachers and preachers, is therefore to say that one quarter of the world is never to support a Christian Church. And why is this said? Are not the coloured people of these States as competent for such offices as Hottentots, many of whom are now proclaiming to their countrymen the unsearchable riches of Christ? We are not to judge of the power of the lion from what we see of him incaged and enchained. Let us not first debase and then libel. If we would judge of the sleeping energies of African minds, let us peruse some portions of modern history, over which for obvious reasons we must here cast a vail; let us look to the progress made in our Sunday Schools, and in the African Seminary recently established in one of our cities.

If Africa must have African teachers and preachers, who shall prepare them but the Christian world? Africa has no science to communicate; Africa has no religion to impart. For the present, and for a considerable time to come, she must be a passive receiver, and Christian nations must convey to her the light and grace. If any of her children are taught, and made competent to instruct their countrymen, European or American benevolence must teach them. We must begin the series of a Gospel ministry that shall perpetuate itself among the tribes of that vast continent.

This work plainly devolves on America rather than Europe, for two reasons. First, the great mass of the transported Africans are here. Allowing that there are thirty thousand dispersed through the different nations of Europe, the number in the United States alone, compared to that in all Europe, is as fifty to one. Here this vast mass is concentrated; there the small number are thinly scattered over different countries, and lost in an overwhelming population. Our advantages to make selections are to those enjoyed by any nation in Europe as two or three hundred to one. And our chances to find proper subjects are still greater. Here special attentions may be easily directed to form the African character; there the attempt is almost impossible. Perhaps in no district of Europe could an African school or congregation be collected; either of these might be done in almost any neighbourhood South of New-England, and even in the large towns of that part of the Union. No spot on earth is so well fitted for the sublime and holy effort, as that on which we dwell. Secondly, no portion of the world is so deeply indebted to Africa as this Western continent and its islands. This is the prison which has received all her captive sons. America is the only civilized country in which slavery is allowed. Though some of the Christian nations of Europe tolerate it in their American colonies, not one of them, it is believed, admit it in the parent state. This land of freedom is the only enlightened land of slaves. On the principle of slavery we have nothing to say. We only affirm that

America is the great receptable which has received the streams that Africa has discharged. And for this we owe her large arrears.

The Board are aware of the many difficulties which attend this undertaking, and of the disappointments which they must expect to meet; but in the name of the Lord they will go forward. They are not unmindful of the existing state of things in their own country, and of the duties thence resulting. Should an opening be made for any of their young men within these States, and should this Board be authorized to send them forth, they will select only the most faithful and discreet, and give them peremptory instructions to inculcate subordination according to the apostolic example. The whole wisdom and dignity of the Synod, under whose direction the Board act, are a guarantee to the public for the caution and prudence of their proceedings.

The Board at present have no funds, and for these they cast themselves on the charity of a compassionate public, making their appeal especially to those whose hearts are penetrated with the love of Christ. The tears of Africa will not plead in vain. The injunctions of a Saviour will not be heard in vain. They only add, that any donations conveyed to their Treasurer, Joseph C. Hornblower, Esq. of Newark, will be gratefully acknowledged.

The Board hope to be ready to receive applications from young men without delay, and will be thankful for notices of proper characters from any part of the Union. Applicants must possess respectable talents, sound discretion, undoubted piety, be able to read and write, and come well recommended. Correspondents will please direct their letters, except those which contain donations, to the Secretary of the Board.

By order of the Board,

JAMES RICHARDS, *President.*
EDWARD D. GRIFFIN, *Secretary.*

Newark, (N.J.)
Oct. 29, 1816.

---

1.   Christian societies believed that Africans descended from one of Ham's four sons, Canaan. The origins of the story are found in the book of Genesis, chapters 9 and 10. After Ham looked upon the nakedness of his father, Noah, Canaan was cursed by Noah with the exclamation that he would be a "servant of servants" unto his brothers. Europeans and American whites employed the curse as a rationale for the enslavement of blacks. A probing discussion of the use of this story in colonial society is made by Winthrop D. Jordan, *White Over Black,* passim.

3   IN DEFENSE OF COLONIZATION, 1824

In the following speech, James S. Green (1792–1862), a prominent supporter of the colonization movement, drew a disturbing
picture of the state's bi-racial character. In Green's judgement,
New Jersey's ever-increasing free black population was a "mass
of ignorance, misery, and depravity." The black laborer, he
warned, "secretly and cordially hates and despises the hand that
feeds and maintains him." But Green was not an apologist for the
white man's treatment of blacks: "You make them free," he
admonished his audience, "but you make them worthless." He
argued that further increases in the free black population of New
Jersey would compound the race's misery. In time blacks would
seek an improvement in their legal status; and, like the patriots of
the Revolutionary era, they would resist taxation without
representation through armed struggle. Green's defense of colonization reveals that the emancipation of blacks in the state
prompted fears of violent racial confrontation.

*Proceedings of a Meeting Held at Princeton, New-Jersey,
July 14, 1824, To Form a Society in the State of New-Jersey,
to Cooperate With the American Colonization Society*
(Princeton, N.J., 1824), pp. 12-20.

I RISE, Sir, to move, that the Constitution just read be adopted; and I
cannot suffer the opportunity to pass without expressing my warmest approbation of a Plan, embracing in it many manifest and important advantages both to our State and our Country. I do not expect to throw any
new light on a subject, rendered already luminous by the most brilliant
talents of the nation. I do not expect to add another thrill to feelings
already warmed and excited by the most powerful appeals; but you will
indulge me, while I attempt simply to discharge what I conceive to be a
duty, obligatory upon me on this occasion, as a citizen of New-Jersey
and of the United States.

We all agree in one position—that Slavery can be defended on no rational ground whatever; that it involves a violation of every law, human
and divine; that it is at war with all the best feelings of our hearts; that
the barbarities which have been inflicted upon the degraded sons and
daughters of Africa, are an outrage upon the dignity and character of a
human being. . . .

We all agree too, that we owe much to the children of Africa in the way of remuneration or recompense. Our fathers have contracted a great—an enormous *moral* debt—a debt that now incumbers and embarrasses our whole country; a debt that like a mighty incubus, is pressing to death the energies of the nation. Relief must be had; a discharge of this debt must be effected, or consequences absolutely ruinous will ensue. It is believed to be yet practicable to escape these consequences, if we exert ourselves with energy, and without delay. But it is high time to be up and doing; to examine into our situation; to call forth our best exertions in united efforts to avert the ruin that otherwise threatens us.

And now, Sir, I am prepared to say that the plan of colonization, on which we are met to deliberate, appears to me to offer the most eligible,—and indeed, so far as I can see—the only effectual mode of relief. The adoption of this plan will, I think, enable us in time to pay what we owe. It will form a sinking fund, by the gradual operation of which, this debt will be ultimately discharged, and we be released forever from its burden. You already perceive that the view which I take of this subject has regard, as much to our own interest as to the interest of the blacks. Such is the fact. The excellence of the plan proposed is, that it unites these interests; it makes them one and the same. I have no hesitation in saying that, for one, I would not advocate this plan, did I think that we were adding another mite to the debt already contracted, or another cruelty to that long and disgusting catalogue of wrongs, at which the eye of the philanthropist weeps, and the heart of the benevolent sickens. I would not raise my voice in its praise, did I not believe, that the plan recommends itself by every consideration, consistent at once with the calls of humanity and the suggestions of policy; by the advancement of the black man's rights, and the white man's interest and easement. Let us, for a moment, bring this matter as near as we can to ourselves. Let us consider how New-Jersey is interested in this plan of colonization.—Will its adoption improve our situation? For unless we can demonstrate this, we shall, I fear, persuade but few to lend us their aid. To the State of New-Jersey, then, inquiring how her interests are concerned in this business, I will endeavour to give an impartial and candid answer.

We find by the Census of 1810, that her Slaves are numbered at more than ten thousand, and her free blacks at more than seven thousand. This number has increased since that period, and we find by the Census of 1820, that the black population of New-Jersey is more than twenty thousand. What a mass of ignorance, misery and depravity, is here mingled with every portion of our population, and threatening the whole with a moral and political pestilence. My answer then to the State of New-Jersey is, that this enormous mass of revolting wretchedness and deadly pollution will, it is believed, be ultimately taken out of her territory, if the plan of the Colonization Society be adopted. This is the special concern—and who will say it is not a most interesting concern—which the State of New-Jersey has in this great national affair.

Have you, Sir, ever looked at this domestic evil in the detail of its certain and deleterious consequences?—did you ever count the number, one by one, to ascertain and feel the danger, with which we are surrounded? Here is a host of individuals, shut out by education or prejudice, from all social intercourse with the whites; entertaining no natural feelings of sympathy or kindness towards us; utter outcasts from all the highest privileges of freemen, and as to most of them, from all the decencies of civilization. No ray of joy lights up their countenance, no throb of delight heaves their bosoms, in view of the growing prosperity and importance of our country. It is no concern of theirs. It brings no advantage to them. It affords nothing to them that is cheering. As to those who are yet in Slavery, when the cloud of misfortune lowers upon the affairs of their masters, no distress is manifested—nay, I might rather say, that oftentimes a feeling of delight is created; and the thought crosses their discontented minds that the judgments of Heaven have revenged their wrongs; that the God of all the earth hath at last punished their oppressors.

Such is the character, I do not say of every individual, but yet certainly of the great majority of your black population. And are we, Sir, entirely safe, while we breathe the same atmosphere with this powerful and discontented horde? If intelligence should reach you, that three thousand men had landed on your shores, with the avowed intention of marching to this place, to burn your buildings, to murder the inhabitants, to plunder your property, what stir, what anxiety, what exertion would every where mark the village, and neighbourhood, and State; every man would be at his post, and the words "coward," and "traitor," would be marked in burning characters on the forehead of every one, who should refuse to join in the resistance. But for myself, I do verily believe, we have a more dangerous foe than this to contend with; a foe under the disguise of slave or servant; one who is admitted without reserve into the bosom of our families; one to whom we often commit the custody of our dwellings; one to whom we frequently confide the care of our children, and yet one who secretly and cordially hates and despises the hand that feeds and maintains him. We all know that a foe in disguise is more dangerous than an open enemy. Against the last we can march, meet, face, and conquer him. The other is silent; his approach is unobserved; and the first notice that we may receive of his hostile intention may be cries and dying groans, or the midnight-conflagration of our dwellings.

But it may be asked—is there not a prospect—that by education, and an increase of the immunities which the blacks already enjoy, their habits, and feelings may be improved? Alas, Sir, I am most unwillingly compelled to say, in reply, that every day's observation and experience teach us, that, with a few honourable exceptions, they degenerate in proportion as they are indulged. You may make them free, but you make them worthless.

By some this is thought singular, and not susceptible of an explanation. To me, the explanation seems easy. By the policy and habits of the country, the blacks are completely excluded from every post of honour and profit; they are denied all alliance with the whites, either in business or by marriage; they are almost shut out from every employment of a liberal character; in a word, they are hopelessly precluded from ever becoming distinguished in church or state. Now, by such means you destroy all the usual incentives to industry and emulation, and provident foresight, and even to virtue. The slave is a mere animal, robbed of all the nobler feelings of our nature, unmoved by the calls of ambition or the suggestions of prudence, and a freed negro, who must always be a proscribed individual, is really but little better. He is sunk below the level of the community around him and he becomes the creature of the moment. You have left him no wish, but that of the present hour, to be gratified. If the day is past with him, and he has had meat and drink and cloathing; this is his all. Hence you find, with an exception here and there, that negroes are improvident, and careless; if free, working but little during the summer, and living by plunder and begging during the winter;—if slaves, no way attentive to the interests of their owners, and working more from the fear of correction, than the impulse of duty. It is not wonderful—it must be apparent—that the circumstances I have mentioned, must have a natural, unavoidable, powerful, and pernicious effect upon the whole of our black population.

How is it that a freeman—I speak now of a man who is truly and entirely free; the man who is admitted to all the rights and privileges of the citizen—how is it that such a man, with small capital, with little to begin with, amasses in a few years, sufficient property to place him above want? Why Sir, he rises early and sits up late; he works hard; and the money he earns he lays by, or employs it with prudence and caution in the business he has embarked in. He is encouraged to all this by the hope and wish, that his family may be placed on vantage ground; that his children may be educated; that plenty may smile around him; and that the evening of his days may not be overcast with the clouds of poverty and distress. Here is the obvious cause, why he so often rises from the plainness of mediocrity to the splendour of affluence. *He works for himself and saves for himself.* But the exact reverse of all this takes place with the slave; and in a great measure with him, who, while he is called a free man, is yet more than half a slave in reality. *He works for another and consumes for himself.* He has no motive to save. He is to derive no essential benefit from it. All he can receive is the support of animal existence; and of this he thinks he is certain. It is the interest of his master to secure him this. In a word, slavery is a soil in which industry, and generosity, and ambition, necessarily wither and die; and this takes place in every state which approaches slavery, just in proportion to the degree of approximation.

We have upon our statute book a law, which by a slow but certain process, is ultimately to emancipate the whole black population of our State. I allude to that law which declares every child born of a slave within this State, after the 4th July 1804, free,—completely emancipated; reserving to the owner of the mother an interest in its services for a limited period. This law has been in force for twenty years, and its silent but powerful operation may be observed by all, by comparing the Census of 1810 with the Census of 1820. By the first, the slaves of New-Jersey are numbered at 10,851, by the second at 7,557, exhibiting a decrease of 2,294 in ten years. The free blacks are estimated at 7,843 in 1810, and at 12,460 in 1820, making an increase of 4,617 in ten years.—Look abroad through the State, and but few, very few ancient negroes meet the eye. The most, if not the whole of them, have descended to the grave; and its silence has hushed forever their lamentations. But extend your view into futurity; look forward for twenty years to come, and recollect that your black population will then all be free—no longer the chains of slavery; completely independant; with no other restraint than the law. Yes, and you will then have, without exaggeration, a black population amounting to at least twenty-five thousand individuals, and every one of them excluded by your laws from all participation in the government— made to bear a portion of its burdens, and yet allowed no part in the election of those who impose these burdens. This, it may be recollected, was the very ground of our complaint against Great Britain, which brought on the war of Independence. There is intelligence enough among the blacks to be fully apprised of this fact, and at the period comtemplated it will not fail to be urged. Yet the plea will not be admitted—and what will be the consequence? Refusal will beget resentment, and resentment will produce resistance to taxation, and resistance to taxation will bring in the civil authority to enforce the law, and the civil authority will eventually be resisted with arms by the blacks, and arms will be repelled with arms by the whites. Here is the natural process, by which we may be involved in all the evils of a civil and servile war—And if such a war shall take place, it ought to be remembered that it will be with "a foe, whom no recollections of former kindness will soften, and whom the remembrance of severity will goad to phrenzy." You will not understand me as saying that this issue of things is *certain*, even if no measures are taken with a view to prevent it. But I declare to you, Sir, that I think it more *probable*, than many occurrences in which the negroes have actually been concerned within the memory of us all.

But perhaps there are those,—and there are I believe a few such in the State, who will reply to all this by saying, that they would remove the whole of these objections and obstacles at once, by admitting the blacks to a full and perfect participation of all the immunities, privileges, and honours, of the white population. This may be said, Sir, but I seriously doubt, whether there are three white persons in the State, who would really and truly act upon this plan. Nay, I seriously doubt, whether there is one white father or mother in New-Jersey, who would be willing, that a son or daughter should contract marriage with the best educated negro, male or female, that now exists. And what do you think, Sir, of a black Governor, a black Chief Justice, a black member of Congress, a black member of the Legislature, a black Justice of the Peace, or even a black Lawyer. I appeal to you, and to every individual in this Assembly, whether the very naming of these things, does not excite feelings which demonstrate that they could not, at least for a long time to come, be realized among us. No Sir, they cannot.—Call it folly, to be frightened by the word *black*; prejudice to hate a black skin; the mere effect of education to seperate this race so widely from ourselves. I admit it all. But still the fact is so, and you cannot help it. You must put the blacks by *themselves* and they must make a society of their own, if they are to be real freemen. Humanity, as well as justice, calls for this. For among the whites of this country, they will be treated for some generations to come, if not forever, as inferior beings. . . .

4   FREEMEN PROTEST COLONIZATION, 1840

The Reverend Samuel E. Cornish (1796–1858) was a pivotal figure in the fight against the American Colonization Society and a leading thinker on the question of the black man's identity in American society. In 1827, Cornish and John Russwurm formed a powerful new weapon in the race's quest for equality, *Freedom's Journal.* It was the first black newspaper in the United States. Two years later, after an ideological split with Russwurm over the African colonization movement, Cornish became the sole editor of the *Rights of All,* which succeeded *Freedom's Journal.* Cornish's opposition to colonization was based on his conviction that democracy was the birthright of both American blacks and whites. He believed that efforts to remove free blacks to Africa were in concert with pro-slavery interests, for without the determined abolitionist pressure of free blacks, the institution of slavery would continue. He was also an early advocate of black economic nationalism, urging his brethren to acquire land in the northern states. To mark the race's identity in American society, Cornish coined the term "Colored American." In 1840 he helped to form the American and Foreign Anti-Slavery Society.

Cornish left New York for Belleville, New Jersey in June 1838. He called the idyllic village, perhaps prematurely, "an agrarian Eden where a man was man, his color of no consequence." After encountering racial discrimination there, he moved to Newark and became pastor of the First Presbyterian Church on Plane Street. In collaboration with Theodore S. Wright, a black Presbyterian minister in New York City, he soon published the following seminal statement against the colonization scheme.

The document posits several compelling criticisms of African colonization. Cornish and Wright rejected the popular assumption that the free colored people "yearned in their hearts for Africa." Actually, according to the authors, free blacks had long protested the work of the American Colonization Society. The degraded condition of the race in the United States, according to Cornish and Wright, resulted from the force or guile of slave-owners. Advocates of colonization were discredited for their opposition to the educational and legal improvement of the race. The authors appealed to whites to allow the race to prove itself, a plea often echoed in the advocacy literature of nineteenth-century black Americans.

Samuel E. Cornish and Theodore S. Wright,
The Colonization Scheme Considered,
in Its Rejection by the Colored People . . .
(Newark, N.J., 1840), pp. 3-7, 9-10, 12-13, 20-21, 26.

TO THE
HON. THEODORE FRELINGHUYSEN[1]
AND THE
HON. BENJAMIN F. BUTLER:[2]

New York, April 1, 1840.

Gentlemen:—

The undersigned, Colored citizens and Ministers of the Gospel, have not been inattentive to the course of the Colonization meetings, which you have either been active in getting up in this city, during the winter, or in the proceedings of which you have shared. As the sole object of these meetings was to act on the interests of the colored people, it is a matter of course, that we should feel, in a good degree, anxious about their results. And this the more especially, as none of that class were invited to take part in them, and they have been carried on without any reference whatever to their wishes or opinions. Shut out from these meetings, where, it would seem altogether essential, that our views should be fully known, our natural recourse is to the press. The fitness of resorting to the press in matters of high public concernment, such as you have, again and again, in the most formal and impressive manner, represented the colonization scheme to be, is sanctioned by every day's use of it in the discussion of such matters. The propriety of addressing ourselves to YOU, who stand out before the community among the most distinguished of its advocates, no one will question—any more than you will our *right* to do so.

But we have another and a stronger reason for addressing to YOU what we have to say on the present occasion. If, among those who are earnestly urging forward Colonization, there be any, who, it may be supposed, will weigh our arguments and judge of our facts *fairly*—any, who can be brought to sympathize with those who are still suffering the inconveniences, the harrassings, the afflictions, the perils, which that inexorable scheme ceases not to bring on them—such will most probably be found among the learned and intelligent and liberal of the *Christian* community. Such you are represented to us to be. Viewing you in this light, we say not a word against your sincerity, when you profess to have in view only the promotion of our happiness—however fully we may be convinced, that you have mistaken the channel in which your beneficence should be made to flow.

It is not our intention, at this time, to enter on the relations of the Colonization scheme to the multiplied interests of our country. We propose limiting ourselves, mainly to a few of the subjects discussed in your addresses delivered at the meetings before referred to;—to the effect of the scheme on the colored people of the free States;—and its probable influence in civilizing and christianizing Africa, and putting an end to the slave trade.

I. Mr.Butler asserted, that the Colonization project was received with great delight by the colored people, for whom it was set on foot, and that they *"yearned in their hearts for Africa."* If this had been said of *southern slaves*—if it had been asserted that *they* "yearned for Africa," or indeed, for any other part of the world, even more inhospitable and unhappy, where they might be free from their masters, there would probably have been no one to dissent from the opinion. But so far as it was intended to apply to the free colored people of the South, and to the colored inhabitants of the free States, we cannot—even after making liberal allowance for the poetic coloring with which it was found expedient to invest what ought to have been a plain business matter—we cannot, we say, find sufficient grounds for excusing, much less justifying Mr. Butler for saying, "the free colored people have hearts which *yearn* for Africa." A few undeniable facts will justify us in this judgment—while they serve to correct the error of Mr. B., and save him from falling into it on any future occasion.

The Colonization society was scarcely known to have been organized, before its object was protested against, in a public meeting of the free colored people of Richmond, Va. Not long afterward, (in August, 1817),

the largest meeting ever yet held of the colored people of the free States—
the number being computed at 3000—came together in Philadelphia, to
consider the Colonization scheme. Mr. James Forten, a man distinguished not only for his wealth and successful industry, but for his sufferings in the Revolutionary war, presided at its deliberations. After ample time allowed for duly considering every benefit which Colonization
held out to the colored people, there was not a single voice in that vast
assembly which was not raised for its decisive, thorough condemnation.

Meetings of a similar kind were held in Washington City, in Baltimore,
New York, Providence, Boston,—indeed all the cities, and in most of the
large towns, throughout the free States. The abhorrence which was
generally expressed of the whole scheme proved, that those to whose acceptance it was offered regarded it but as little more merciful than *death*.
From the earliest period of those public meetings up to this time, we
fearlessly assert, that no credible testimony can be adduced, showing,
that there has been any abatement in the repugnance of the colored people to colonization. . . .

Besides the uniform testimony furnished by large meetings throughout
the free States,—and in the Slave States, too, whilst they were permitted
to be held—there is the additional fact, that the colored people have entirely ceased emigrating from the former. The poetic machinery by which
the scheme was urged, at first beguiled *some*, and they went to Liberia,
but to lie down in their graves. The fate of the forty emigrants who went
out in the Brig Vine, which sailed from Boston at an early period of the
enterprize, bears mournful testimony to the reality of the delusion. They
perished in a short time—the pestilence not leaving *one*, it is believed, to
communicate to their friends in this country the story of their disappointment and death.

Now, gentlemen, had you known the foregoing facts, we do not
believe you would have asserted, that the "free colored people had hearts
which *yearned* for Africa." *Why* you did not know them, important as
they are, and accessible too; why you hazarded an assertion so pernicious
to your colored fellow citizens, without first ascertaining whether it was
true or not, is for you, not us, to explain.

II. The Colonization scheme was set on foot, and is yet maintained by
Slaveholders, with the view as they have not been backward to declare,
of perpetuating their system of Slavery, *undisturbed*. From the first, no
very high expectations seem to have been entertained, that an enterprize,
so unnecessary, so unnatural, so condemned by the most elemental
truths of political economy, so profitless, so perilous, bearing about it so
little of hope, so much of despair, would commend itself strongly to that
class of the community to which it purported solely to be addressed. But
little reliance appears to have been placed on obtaining their *voluntary*
consent to exchange for the fens and morasses of barbarous and heathen
Africa, this, the country of their fathers for generations, and of their

own nativity—where land was abundant and cheap—where labor was in demand and its rewards sure—where education *could* be obtained, albeit, for the most part, with difficulty—where the common ordinances of religion, as well as its higher institutions were established—where every interest had the promise of advancement—and where, notwithstanding they were called to suffer many ills brought on them by others, they might yet live in hope, that the dark cloud of Slavery which had so long obscured the free principles asserted by our governments, would one day pass away and permit these principles to shine in all their warmth and effulgence, if *not on themselves*, on no very distant generation of their descendants. The benefits (?) proposed to the free colored people by a removal, which involved the necessity to a great extent, of breaking up their domestic relations—relations singularly dear to them, because of the sweet and (*we* speak from *experience*) enduring consolations they afforded in seasons of persecution and distress;—of exposing their lives to the death-damps of Africa under an equatorial sun—their own morals, and those of their children, to the influences and temptations of the most treacherous and sin-sunken heathen that live, and of the demons called *Christians*, by whose teaching and example these same heathen have been raised to their eminence in vice and crime;—all these benefits, we say, were unheeded, notwithstanding they were dressed out on the gaudy and gorgeous drapery of the poet, recommended by the adroitness of the rhetorician—passed by the eloquence of the orator, and, what is more, sanctified by a standing proclamation of the Priesthood, both religious and political, investing each emigrant, irrespective of character or conduct, with the solemn office and standing of a Christian Missionary to the heathen. But every appeal was ineffectual and so far as the Society depended on the *voluntary* consent of the colored people, it might as well have been dissolved.

Whatever individual exceptions there may exist among Slave-holders on the score of *goodness and gentleness*, (that there may be such we will not here stop to enquire) as an *embodied interest*, they know no retiring ebb when moving upon objects connected with their atrocious system. The political history of the country, from the time when South Carolina and Georgia refused to enter the Union, unless the traffic in human flesh should be secured to them for twenty years, proves this. Their fierce onset—guilefully laid aside, not abandoned—to add Texas to our territory, with the audaciously avowed purpose of strengthening and perpetuating the slave-system, proves this . . . .

PREJUDICE! What is it? Lexicographers tell us, it a decision of the mind formed without due examination of the facts or arguments which are necessary to a just and impartial determination. And *prejudice against* COLOR! What does this mean? Yor are both sensible—nay, learned men. Pray, instruct us in this mystery of slave-holding philosophy—scarcely spoken of in Britain, wholly unknown and unfelt among the learned, the wise, the refined of France and other nations of

Europe. Can prejudice exist against that which has in it nothing of the moral or the intellectual? Is it a down right absurdity to say of men, that they are prejudiced against *sound* or *sight*—against the *earth*, or the *sea*, or the *air*, or *light*? And is it a less one to say, that they are prejudiced against *color*? If not, how is it, gentlemen, that you can connect your names and give your influence to a great National movement, (one which it pleased you to say, we were more indebted to for the integrity of the Union than to any other cause since its commencement) resting for support on a *philosophical absurdity*? . . .

To say of a community, that it is laboring under a present, an existing prejudice, offers no disparagement to the power of truth; but to say, that it is laboring under a prejudice which is *irremovable*, is to pronounce, that error is an overmatch for truth, and to despair of the improvement of the world. To assert of a people, that they will always be guided by prejudice in relation to *any* interest, is to declare, that they are hopelessly stupid and besotted. That such a notion should be entertained by minds that reflect but a little, ought not to be expected; but that it should be cherished and inculcated by gentlemen who, from the nature of their pursuits, may be regarded as *professional* investigators of truth—by gentlemen who can testify to the efficacy of that agent in exterminating deep-set prejudices from their own hearts; and who, beholding its mighty powers, contemplate them with awe, and look to them for the expulsion of all error, the casting out of all wrong, and the renovation of the world;—this, we say, seems passing strange.

But you may say, that, *seeing the colored people cannot, as a class, "rise" to an equality with the community around them, much less to honors and distinctions, and that they cannot be happy here, we merely act on the popular prejudice with a SINGLE VIEW TO THEIR HAPPINESS.* Whilst we by no means draw in question the sincerity of this declaration, we yet beg leave to say, that the body of the colored people of this country who are free, are not *minors*; or, if they are so considered by others, they have not yet been divested of the common law right of choosing their guardians; that this they have not as yet done, but have considered—as in the case of other men—that their happiness has been committed to their own keeping; and that, as a class, they deem themselves reasonably well qualified, on the score of intelligence, to judge what will most promote it. After mature consideration, they decided against the Colonization scheme, as eminently hostile to their happiness. The working of the scheme for twenty years has served but to confirm them in the soundness of their decision. All this time, they have been suffering under malignant influences, which, if they were not engendered by that scheme, were greatly aggravated by it. They have remonstrated as strongly as they could; they have entreated as earnestly as they could. But, thus far, it has all been of no avail . . . .

III. But the colonizationist finds, in the CHRISTIANIZATION OF AFRICA, and the BREAKING UP OF THE SLAVE-TRADE, enough to justify him for the ills he is bringing on us. Were it even certain, that these benefits would ensue, it would, in no wise, be a warrant for the *wrongs* he inflicts; for to *"do evil that good may come"* is not sounder in morals now, than it was a hundred years ago, not less indefensible in Protestants than in Catholics. But we shall attempt to show that, the expectation of these benefits is delusive—not without the hope, that, should we succeed, but to a reasonable degree of probability, it may have its influence on your minds.

We do not propose to rest our success on a comparison of the multitudinous and contradictory testimonies that have reached this country, of the ill or good success which has, thus far, attended the Liberian colony in christianizing the aborigines and breaking up the slave-trade. We shall omit all argument from them; first, because they *are* contradictory; second, because these testimonies, together with the comparisons of them, and the inferences, are, already to a considerable extent, before the public. To these we shall make no reference where they admit of the least dispute. We wish to have the questions before us decided, not on insulated facts, nor by accidental or transitory occurrences, but on those broad and comprehensive and permanent principles, which are known to operate with unbroken uniformity, on man in a social state, wherever, and under whatever form, that social state exists.

We call your attention, then, to the colonization of heathen countries in modern times, conducted solely by colonists from christian countries. Samples only of this we shall give. In 1492, when Hispaniola was discovered it contained a *million* of people, described by Columbus as the most "affectionate, tractable and peaceable" that he had ever seen. Sixteen years afterward, when the Governor (Albuquerque) made an enumeration, there were but 14,000 left. They had been reduced to this remnant, by severe labor, insufficient rest and food, and other hardships, notwithstanding all the efforts of the Spanish Crown to protect them from the cruelty and rapacity of the colonists. Spain was then, as she is now considered, one of the most *religious* nations in Europe.

The Indians have disappeared before the Pilgrim Fathers of New England,—and this, too, without any perceptible amelioration of their moral condition! No community has better merited the title of *religious* than the settlers of New England.

So did the Indians in Pennsylvania, and disappear before the colonists of William Penn, the brightest example on record of a Christian statesman.

Throughout our southern States similar unhappy results have taken place. This generation is witness to the total extinction of some of the mighty tribes that once bore sway on the soil where we inhabit—to the wasting away of others—to the transfer of their remnants from our midst to the wilderness, on the ground that *separation from us* is the only way in which they can be civilized, or even preserved from extinction—to the hunting down with blood-hounds such of them as we have been unable to subdue in customary warfare, and who refuse to become exiles from the land of their fathers, and commit themselves to our broken faith. This is a melancholy picture, but it is one that is presented by a people who would be unwilling to have their *christianity* disparagingly compared with that of any other people on the globe.

The fact, that christian colonization has either uniformly wrought the extermination of the aborigines, or that it *tends* to do so, except where the Colonists themselves lapse into barbarism—as was the case with the Portuguese settlements on the western coast of Africa—has not unfrequently been adduced, to prove the ill success that will *probably* attend all similar efforts for the christianization of the heathen; but nowhere have we seen a sufficient ground-work laid, to show, *why* these results have been so uniform heretofore, and why they may, *to a moral certainty*, be expected to exhibit the same uniformity hereafter. Colonizationists generally seem satisfied with attributing these remarkable phenomena to the accidental difference of *color*. This easy, off-hand solution owes its birth, if we mistake not, to the colonization-school. It was not dreamed of, till this project was set on foot by the slave-holders to secure a more quiet existence to their "system," and it has always kept close company with its parent—being found useful in reconciling honest and conscientious persons to the indirect compulsion it was found necessary to resort to, to wring from the colored people their "consent" to be exiled. But is it convincing, gentlemen, to a philosophical enquirer—does it satisfy *your* minds? If so, how do you dispose of the fact, that, in the whole history of colonization by the white race among the colored, from the time of Vasco de Gama till now, no mention is made of *color*, as offering an obstacle to aboriginal christianization? Or, of the fact, that, in all the records of missions, since their earliest institution, there is not an occurrence, direct or incidental, serving to show, that a white missionary has been any the less useful among the colored heathen of every shade, even the deepest, because he differed from them in complexion? Go to the Islands of the Pacific—of the Indian ocean—to our own aborigines—to the black—yes, the *black* natives of Northern India—to the negroes of Eastern Africa—of Western Africa—and you never once hear it whispered, that the missionary would be more acceptable, were he of a darker hue . . . .

IV. We will next examine whether the likelihood of the slave trade being broken up by the colonies, is as encouraging as the christianizing of the aborigines by the same instrumentality.

Without intending, in any way, to countenance the loathsome character given of the emigrant class by the colonizationists, we may safely hazard the opinion, that their moral restraints from engaging in the slave trade are not, in any way, *stronger* than those of the *whites* in this country. Now, although *kidnapping*, by the laws of (perhaps) all the States, is visited with severe punishment; and although public sentiment gives its support to the laws; yet, kidnapping persons from the free

States, and selling them for slaves at the south, is a business which is carried on by white persons among us, to by no means an inconsiderable extent, nor without a due regard to *system*. From all the free States bordering on the slave, and even from some of the farming slaveholding States, scores of persons, born undeniably free, are every year trepanned by kidnappers, and beguiled, or hurried forcibly away, into the planting South, where they are sold as slaves, with but little chance of regaining their liberty. Three young men, whose free birth admits of no question, were inveigled in this city, not very long ago, and taken to New Orleans, where they were sold as slaves, by the captain of the vessel with whom they sailed as hands. One of them has succeeded in getting back; all traces of the others are lost, and the kidnapper is unpunished. Nor was it very long since, that three men, apparently confederates, were apprehended in Cincinnati, on suspicion of having kidnapped, and taken away, several colored people, who were suddenly missed from their dwellings. On examining the party, ropes, cords, and straps with slip-knots, &c., and ingenious contrivances of various kinds for quickly and securely binding human victims, were found on them. And it was but the other day, that two citizens of Massachusetts were convicted of kidnapping, and selling as a slave in Virginia, a lad, the son of one of their neighbors. In ferreting out this case, another of the same kind was discovered. If now, with all these appliances and means of restraint—early education, public opinion, the danger of detection, disgrace, and punishment;—if all these prove ineffectual on the *whites*, for breaking down the slave trade in its most odious form *here among us*, ought it to be expected of the colonists, that they will *surpass* the whites, and not only refrain from engaging in the trade themselves, and reaping its large profits, but that they will outstrip their teachers in being *officious* to break it up?—and this too, in a part of the world where it is as much *the* great business, as the raising and selling of cotton is the great business of the planting South? Neither philosophy nor experience warrants such calculations . . . .

And are there no such influences operating on the colored people of the free States? Who is it that is most caressed among us? *The slaveholder.* Who is it that is most honorably treated by the most honorable in the free states? *The slaveholder.* To whom do the Legislatures of the free states grant peculiar privileges—to whom give *carte blanche* to dishonor their free principles and displace their free institutions, wherever he may travel in their confines, by suffering him to introduce among them, at pleasure, troops of slaves, with all the usages of a slaveholding country and constitution? To the *southern slaveholder, and no one else.* Is a political meeting to be harangued in New York, or Boston, or Philadelphia—who is so sought after to do it as a Kentucky, or a Tennessee, or a South Carolina slaveholder? Is one of our wealthy and fashionable congregations to be preached to? What minister more sure of acceptance than he who visits the North, to sell his five hundred or thousand cotton bales, raised by the unpaid labor of his scores of slaves? Who so certain as he to hear, "welcome, brother"!—while he that would rebuke him is repelled with, "begone, fanatic"! . . .

We have thus, gentlemen, furnished you with facts that bear especially on such parts of the Colonization scheme, as have of late been almost exclusively held up before the public wherewith to win its favor. With these facts we think you have not before been made acquainted. We have also, presented you with the reasonings which they have given rise to in our minds. With these, it is not to be supposed, that you are familiar.

Having now done what we could, we ask you in view of the whole case, whether you ought longer to take advantage of our weakness to press on us an enterprise that we have unremittingly rejected from the first? Whether you ought to persist in a scheme which nourishes an unreasonable and unchristian prejudice—which persuades legislators to continue their unjust enactments against us in all their rigor—which exposes us to the persecution of the proud and profligate—which cuts us off from employment, and straitens our means of subsistence—which afflicts us with the feeling, that our condition is unstable, and prevents us from making systematic effort for our improvement, or for the advancement of our own usefulness and happiness and that of our families.

We ask for an answer. May it be such as shall give peace to your own consciences, and be approved of God in "the judgment of the great day."

With Christian regard, we are, gentlemen, respectfully yours,
SAMUEL E. CORNISH,
THEODORE S. WRIGHT.

---

1. Theodore Frelinghuysen (1787–1862) of Newark was the vice president of the American Colonization Society. He served as U.S. Senator from New Jersey, 1829–35 and mayor of Newark, 1837–38.

2. Benjamin F. Butler (1795–1858) was a distinguished attorney and politician who served as U.S. attorney general from 1833 to 1838 under Andrew Jackson and Martin Van Buren. At the time this letter was addressed to him, Butler was serving as U.S. attorney for the Southern District of New York.

---

5 MILITANT ABOLITIONISM GROWS, 1841

Despite the ascendancy of the American Colonization Society, friends of the blacks struggled to keep abolitionism alive in New Jersey. By the late 1830s, New Jersey anti-slavery advocates, like the emerging new breed of abolitionists, bitterly attacked the institution of slavery and denounced those who gave it support. The

New Jersey State Anti-Slavery Society, which was formed in 1840, symbolized the militant character of abolitionism during the antebellum years. At its second annual meeting on January 13, 1841, the Society branded as "outrageously unjust and infamous in its character" a resolution of the general committee of the national Methodist Episcopal Church which reinforced racial inequities in state laws. It also criticized the Presbyterian Church for actions unsympathetic to the abolitionist cause. Of particular interest here is the third resolution of the Society, which stated the accomplishments of the abolitionists, and the resolution recommending that the legislature improve the legal status of free blacks in New Jersey.

The New Jersey State Anti-Slavery Society, Record Book (MG 134), Manuscript Collections, The New Jersey Historical Society.

At 3 oclock P.M. the Business Committee presented the following Resolutions which were discussed and passed unanimously.

Resolv'd 1st. That the following Resolution passed by the general Committee of the Methodist Episcopal Church in May 1840 is outrageously unjust and infamous in its character,—"Resolv'd that it is inexpedient and unjustifiable for any preacher to permit Colored persons to give testimony against white persons, in any state, where they are denied that priviledge by law.

Resolv'd 2nd. That the New School General Assembly of the Presbyterian Church bowed the knee to the dark spirit of Slavery, when it requested certain Presbyteries to rescind their resolutions against Slavery and in favour of Anti Slavery principles.

Resolv'd 3. That to the question "what have the Abolitionist done" this is our answer—They have kept Texas out of the Union. They have influenc'd Legislatures to pass resolutions in favour of the Abolition of Slavery in the District of Columbia to pass Laws granting trial by jury to alledged fugitives from slavery—They have rescued from slavery hundreds of kidnapped freeman; they have defended the A[r]mistad Captives;[1] they have helped on their way to Canada thousands of slaves, who had taken their own bodies into their own possession; they have unmasked that greatest of all humbugs the Colonization Society; they have defined, discussed, and enforced the foundation principles of our Government; and given them a far stronger hold upon hundreds of thousands than they ever had before. They have secured a homage to the dignity and sacredness of human rights more profound than has ever been rendered to them in this republic. They have settled legal, constitutional and biblical questions fundamental to human rights; they have got hundreds of Ministers to preach against slavery, and thousands of Christians to pray against it, and hundreds of thousands of men and women to petition against it; they have abolished the "Negro Seat" in many churches; they have given to thousands of colored children the means of education; they have entirely uprooted "prejudice against colour" from many minds, and greatly weakened it in tens of thousands more; they have produced a great change in public sentiment in the free States on the subject of slavery, and excited in multitudes an abhorrence of slavery that will never die.

Resolv'd 4. That we hail with peculiar pleasure the movement and resolutions of various religious bodies in favour of the abolition of slavery—

Resolv'd 5. That we regard with satisfaction the high stand taken by the Riply Presbytery of Ohio, and several Methodist and Baptist bodies to remove the evils of slavery and to advance the Civil Moral and religious condition of the Color'd population of our land.

Resolv'd That we cordially approve of the spirit and doings of the Worlds Convention held in London last June to abolish Slavery, throughout the world and heartily welcome the kind suggestions, and recommendations, made to the President and Governors of the different States of the Union.

Resolv'd That we welcome with great pleasure the stand taken by John A. James, Doct. Wardlow and other British Abolitionists and cheerfully acquiesce in their kind and fatherly admonitions and reproofs, and hope they may be received with a right spirit and improved to the honour of religion and benefit of the Colored race.

Resolv'd That we recommend to our honorable legislature the condition of the colored people of our state that they may have equal priviledges in the rights of suffrage, the holding of real estate and all other abilities, as free Citizens of New Jersey.

Resolv'd That it be recommended to the Abolitionists of New Jersey to open subscription lists for the benefit of the A[r]mistad Captives.

Resolv'd That we adjourn to meet in Burlington on the 2nd Tuesday in August next.

> J. H. Payne, Pres.
> C. Breese, Sec'y.

---

1. A case of extraordinary importance to the abolitionist cause in 1840 and 1841, involving the right of fifty-four captured Africans to return to their homeland. It was eventually brought before the U.S. Supreme Court, where former President John Quincy Adams successfully defended them on March 8, 1841. The *Armistad* captives later returned to their native land, Sierra Leone.

6 FREE BLACKS PROTEST DISENFRANCHISEMENT, 1849

After the adoption of the New Jersey Constitution of 1844, free blacks organized to resist the racial qualification for voting which it imposed. In 1849 petitioners in Salem and Gloucester counties asked the legislature to remove the voting disability against them. Drawing upon American democratic ideals, they appealed for the franchise on the basis that free blacks were taxpayers, loyal to their country and dedicated to self-improvement. Conscious of the nativist sentiments of many legislators, the petitioners further substantiated their appeal by drawing attention to "foreigners," who voted while native-born blacks were denied the right.[1] The disenfranchisement of free blacks was considered contrary to both divine and human law. The Senate Judiciary Committee reported unfavorably on this petition, and it was not acted on by the legislature.

**"To the Senate and House Assembly of the State
of New Jersey, at Trenton Assembled,"
Rochester, New York *North Star,* 7 April 1849.**

Gentlemen:

We, the undersigned petitioners of the State of New Jersey, being free colored citizens of the above-mentioned state, have for a long time felt grieved, that we are, by a provision in the laws of this our state, deprived of the elective franchise; and therefore do most respectfully petition and earnestly pray your honorable body to take the subject into consideration at your present session, and use your influence to have the laws so altered in respect to us, as to remove the disability and grant us the right of elective franchise, in common with, and under the same provisions of other free citizens of this state.

And we are induced respectfully to ask this right, upon the following considerations:

First. Because we are taxed in common and equally with other citizens, which tax we have paid, and are willing so to do without complaining.

Second. We ask it because our ancestors were among the pioneers of our country, and we are native born citizens, and have never by insurrection, mobs, or tumults, committed any act whereby the public peace or safety was endangered.

Third. Because we are now making as rapid improvements in moral, intellectual and political science as any other portion of the laboring class in the state, by maintaining churches, schools, temperance and beneficial societies, giving support to the general diffusion of knowledge by contributions to support the press in the expenditure of several thousand dollars annually throughout the state, for newspapers, periodicals, etc.

Fourth. Because it is a right granted to foreigners of the same class who have been in the country from two to five years, and whose situations and prejudices in favor of the land of their nativity do not permit them to be as well acquainted with republican institutions as we, the native born citizens of this state.[1]

Fifth. Because it is contrary to the genius and prosperity of any republican country to oppress her own home born sons; it being a law in the universal government of God, that he who doeth a wrong to his neighbor shall receive an evil to himself, and inasmuch as true republicanism is based upon the laws of universal suffrage, it is a violation of this law, and consequently pernicious to the fundamental principles of republican institutions to withhold a common right from any class or portion of an unoffending people.

Sixth. Because it is unconstitutional; the framers of the constitution having pledged their honor, lives, and property never to submit to taxation without representation, having carefully guarded this right by an article prohibiting any state in the union from making it legal to disqualify any of her tax-paying citizens for the exercise of the right to choose their representatives.

Seventh. And lastly, we ask it from a full conviction that the improvements of the age, the philanthropy of the state, and the good sense of our rulers have all looked forward for such a movement and were waiting for those most concerned therein, to enter upon the measure, and the work would be accomplished. All of which we most respectfully submit to the wisdom, justice and truthfulness of your honorable body, and we shall most sincerely pray, God save the commonwealth.

------

1. John S. Rock [see below, doc. 8] makes a similar argument.

------

7 CONVENTION AFFIRMS EQUALITY, 1849

Beginning in Philadelphia in 1830 and continuing until the 1870s in various cities, the Negro Convention Movement fostered considerable agitation on behalf of blacks. It dramatized the free blacks' abhorrence of the American Colonization Society and was instrumental in the development of an articulate black leadership during the Civil War and Reconstruction. The most reputable conventions attracted black leaders from many cities to consider anti-slavery measures and foster support for black educational and economic uplift. Many conventions, though, drew only local leaders in an effort to improve conditions within an individual state. Such was the purpose of the Coloured Convention which met in Trenton in August 1849. The following address from that meeting is one of the most compelling affirmations of black equality made in nineteenth-century New Jersey. Although a brief document, it contains essential elements of early Afro-American protest: a reverence for the principles articulated in the Declaration of Independence; an appeal to the conscience of whites; and an implicit faith that American democracy was committed to the full attainment of human rights for its citizens.

**"An Address from the Coloured Convention,
Assembled at Trenton, on the 21st and 22nd Days
of August, 1849." Quoted in Marion Thompson Wright,
"Negro Suffrage in New Jersey, 1776–1875,"
Journal of Negro History 33 (1948): 188-89.**

We, the undersigned, on behalf of the aforesaid Convention, do make and promulgate this appeal to all the people in common throughout this our native State:—

Being endowed, under the blessings of a beneficent Providence and favourable circumstances, with the same rationality, knowledge and feelings, in common with the better and more favoured portions of civilized mankind, we would no longer deride you and ourselves by exhibiting the gross inconsistency, and by so far belying the universal law and the great prompting of our nature; cultivated as we claim to be, as to have you longer suppose that we are ignorant of the important and undeniable fact that we are indeed *men* like unto yourselves.

Knowing then, that these things are so, you will naturally be led to suppose that the same kind of teaching, and under the same influences, we should necessarily have the same kind of feeling and the same general ideas in common with yourselves.

And inasmuch as you have declared, and we have learned the fact— that all men are by nature free and independent, and have certain natural and inalienable rights, among which are those of enjoying and defending life and liberty, acquiring, possessing, and protecting property, and of pursuing and obtaining safety and happiness.

And that all political power is inherent in the people; and that they have the right at all times to alter or reform the same, whenever the public good may require it.

Therefore we now appeal to you in the face of your assertions, and in respect of your justice, your patriotism, your intelligence, your honesty and love of liberty—and in remembrance of your accountability to Him from whom cometh every good and perfect gift—requesting that you will use your influence, each for himself, in assisting us in this our purpose of obtaining for ourselves and our posterity, the blessings and perquisites of liberty in the exercise of the elective franchise, or right of suffrage; which we respectfully ask as a right belonging to us in the character of *men*; but heretofore withheld as an attache of color, in the conservative spirit of some, and the ignorance, envy and prejudice of others.

In conclusion, we would only say that, with our knowledge of the eminent standing of the highest virtues of which humanity is capable—the religion, morality, intelligence, jurisprudence and good citizenship, generally evinced in this our native State—we confidently expect a majority of your signatures to our petitions wherever presented; and we verily believe that the day is not far distant when New Jersey shall be hailed as the first consistent reformer of human rights in the Western World.

Signed,   Rev. Woodlin, of Burlington
        ''   W. T. Catto, of Trenton
        ''   I. Locke, of Camden
On Behalf of the Convention

8 JOHN S. ROCK ARGUES FOR ENFRANCHISEMENT, 1850

The denial of suffrage to free blacks was so repugnant to democratic principles that the most articulate and influential Afro-Americans spoke out against it. Not surprisingly, ministers constituted the majority of the leadership because blacks had been virtually excluded from other learned pursuits. John S. Rock of Salem was an exception to this pattern. He completed studies in dentistry in 1849, and was graduated from the American Medical College in Philadelphia three years later. He later practiced medicine and dentistry in Boston. After a severe illness prevented him from continuing his medical practice, he studied law and in 1861 was admitted to the bar in Massachusetts. In 1865 he became the first black attorney accredited to practice in the U.S. Supreme Court. During his extraordinary career, Rock was an advocate of many humanitarian concerns, particularly the abolition of slavery and the eradication of racial intolerance. His address to the citizens of New Jersey supported the enfranchisement of black men in the state and attacked the "enemies" who favored the expatriation of free blacks to Africa. Consistent with nineteenth-century black advocacy, Rock called on the whites of New Jersey to treat blacks as humans.

Rochester, New York *North Star*, 8 February 1850.

Citizens, in addressing you in favor of a disfranchised portion of the *legal* tax-payers of New Jersey, I feel, from the success our enterprise has already been crowned with, that intelligence, humanity and justice, may be styled characteristics of the citizens of this State.

Knowing, then, that I am speaking to an intelligent and human people, who believe in that noble sentiment set forth in the Declaration of Independence, that "all men are created free and equal," etc. I take the liberty of speaking freely to you, being one of the disfranchised, and I do not believe your hearts are so callous as not to listen to the voice of the oppressed.

Although the above Declaration declares that "all men are created free and equal," those noble words, in their common acceptation, do not and cannot apply to the disfranchised people I am now speaking of; because, indirectly, you deny the disfranchised are men. You say that all men are created free and equal, and at the same time, you *deny* that equality, which is nothing more nor less than denying our manhood. If we are not free and equal, (according to the Declaration of Independence), we are not men, because *"all* men are created free and equal."

We confess there is something about this we never could understand. We are denied our rights as men, at the same time are taxed in common with yourselves, and obliged to support the government in her denunciations. If we are not men, why are we dealt with as such when we do not pay our taxes, or when we infringe the laws? Whenever we become delinquent in the one, or a transgressor in the other, there is then no question about our manhood; we are treated as men, to all intents and purposes. If we are men, when our taxes are due, and men when we transgress the laws, we are men when our taxes are not due, and when we do not transgress the laws.

There are many reasons why colored men should be enfranchised. We have been reared in this State, and are acquainted with her institutions. Our fidelity to this country has never been questioned. We have done nothing to cause our disfranchisement; on the contrary, we have done all a people could do to entitle them to be enfranchised.

It is said, "there is not sufficient intelligence amongst us to warrant the restoration of those rights," and that we are not sufficiently acquainted with the government, etc.; but they do not say we do not have sufficient intelligence and knowledge of the government, to warrant us to pay our taxes, because we cannot thoroughly understand how the money goes!

If we, who have always been with you, do not understand something of the regulations of this country, how miserably ignorant are the thousands of voters who arrive in this country annually, who know nothing of this government, and but little of any government! There is no just plea, and apology for you to shut every avenue to elevation, and then complain of degradation; what else can be expected, while we are looked upon as *things,* and treated worse than unthinking animals?

In the Revolution, Colored soldiers fought side by side with you in your struggles for liberty; and there is not a battle-field from Maine to Georgia, which has not been crimsoned by our blood, and whitened by our bones. In 1814, a Bill passed the Legislature of New York, accepting the services of 2,000 colored volunteers. In the battle on Lake Erie, Commodore Perry's fleet was manned chiefly by colored seamen. Many black sailors served under Commodore McDonough when he conquered Lake Champlain. Many were in the battles of Plattsburgh and Sackett's Harbor. Gen. Jackson called out colored troops from Louisiana and Alabama, and in solemn proclamation attested to their fidelity and courage.

But some of our enemies say, we "had better go to Africa." We ask, Why? They say, we "cannot rise in this country, the prejudices are too strong to overcome;" that we had better be "kings among beggars, than beggars among kings." As neither of the positions is enviable, we will not quarrel about the beggarly or kingly conditions. We think these titular philanthropists who try to make the people believe we can never rise in this country, and that money must be raised, by appropriation or otherwise, to expatriate us, would do well to hold their peace—give their extra change to the poor, emigrate to the country of their forefathers as quickly as possible, and take their incendiary reports along with them.

They say, "this is not our country." We would ask, Whom does it belong to? If this country is yours, and was gained by conquest, then we are *particeps criminis,*[1] and are equally entitled to the spoil.

Africa is urged upon us as the country of our forefathers! If this is good sophistry—and we think it will pass—then it follows that all men must go to the country of their forefathers: in this case, the blacks will go to Africa, and the whites to Europe; and where will the mixed races go? We suppose, in such an event, they would occupy the inter-medium— that is, the Mediterranean Sea! What would become of the Indians? Would they go to the country of their forefathers? If so, where is it?

This sophistry is not designed to aggrandize any but the descendants of the European nations: Africa is the country for the Africans, their descendants and mongrels of various colors; Asia the country of the Asiatics; the East Indies the place for Malays; Patagonia the country for the Indian; and *any place the white man chooses to go.* HIS country! . . .

---

1. Latin for a party to the crime.

9 A FUGITIVE SLAVE FINDS FREEDOM, 1824

New Jersey's proximity to Maryland and Delaware enabled hundreds of slaves to make a journey to freedom which was precarious and often unsuccessful. Daniel Clark, an escaped slave from Delaware, was more fortunate than many runaways. In 1824 he was befriended by sympathizers in Gloucester County, who raised $140 for his manumission, thus ending what must have been many days of anxiety over the threat of recapture and return to bondage.

N.J. Historical Records Survey Project,
Transcriptions of Early County Records of New Jersey,
Gloucester County Series, Slave Documents
(Newark, N.J., 1940), p. 46.

Certificates of Manumissions
Know all Men by these Presents, That Whereas Daniel Clark otherwise called Benjamin Clark a black man Slave born in the county of Kent in the State of Delaware in the month of November in the year of our Lord one thousand Seven hundred and Eighty one the Slave of Jenifer Taylor: and by him given & delivered to me the Subscriber sometime about the year of our Lord one thousand eight hundred and ten absconded from me, and is now residing in the Township of Newton in the County of Gloucester and State of New Jersey—And Whereas divers benevolent persons have contributed the Sum of one hundred and forty dollars for the purpose of affecting his Manumission—Now therefore know ye That I Ignatius Taylor of the County of Kent in said State of Delaware in consideration of the Said Sum of one hundred and forty dollars to me in hand paid the receipt whereof is hereby acknowledged, and of the further Sum of one hundred and Sixty dollars agreed to be paid by the said Daniel Clark otherwise called Benjamin Clark, and for which I acknowledge the receipt of his bond in Satisfaction of, Do hereby on this sixteenth day of June in the year of our Lord one thousand eight hundred and twenty four Manumit liberate and Set free And by these Presents have manumitted, liberated and set free, the said Daniel Clark otherwise called Benjamin Clark and do hereby fully discharge and acquit the Said Daniel Clark otherwise called Benjamin from all services or demand of Services hereafter to be claimed by me or any person claiming under me—And I do hereby for myself my heirs executors & administrators cavenant and agree to & with the said Daniel Clark otherwise called Ben-

jamin Clark that I have not Sold or conveyed him to any person Whatever and that I have full and perfect authority to Manumit him from Slavery—In Witness Whereof I have hereto set my hand and Seal the day and year above written—

Sealed and Delivered ⎫   Ign. Taylor
in presence of   ⎬
                       ⎭
Interlineations and erasures made before Syning
Jenifer Taylor
J H Sloan

Be it remembered that on the Sixteenth day of June in the year of our Lord one thousand eight hundred and twenty four personaly appeared before me the subscriber one of the Masters of the court of Chancery of the State of New Jersey Ignatius Taylor the grantor named in the foregoing manumission I being Satisfied he is the grantor therein named and having first made known to him the contents thereof who acknowledged that he Syned Sealed and delivered the Same as his voluntary act and deed for the uses and purposes therein named

J H Sloan M.C.

Manumission of
Benjn Clark
Received July 1 1824 and Recorded in the Clerks Office of Gloucester County at Woodbury In Liber A of Manumissions folio 20 &c

J J Foster Clk.

10   OPPOSITION TO EMANCIPATION, 1863

Although most Peace Democrats (called Copperheads by their detractors) were unsympathetic to blacks, David Naar of Trenton was particularly racist. As editor of the Trenton *Daily True American*, he expressed the position of the Democratic Party during the ante-bellum and Civil War years. But he went much further than the party's traditional opposition to abolitionism and its support of state's rights, achieving notoriety for his racist diatribes. The Afro-American, in his opinion, was to be feared economically and socially since he was "by nature treacherous, . . . worthless and imbecilic." He supported legislation to prevent the migration of freedmen to New Jersey, reasoning that there were already too many blacks in the state. When President Lincoln issued the Emancipation Proclamation on January 1, 1863, Naar envisioned the North virtually invaded by undesirable blacks, a prospect set down in the following anonymous poem reprinted from the Cincinnati *Enquirer*. The poem clearly supports Naar's racist editorial policy.

Anonymous poem,
Trenton *Daily True American*,
13 January 1863.

They come, they come, in multitudes,
    Along Ohio's tide;
The "shucking tramp" of their brogans,
    By Susquehanna's side.
They feel the winter's icy breath,
    The dreary way along;
They are coming, Father Abraham,
    About four millions strong.

They come, a nation's guests, to share
    Our firesides and our bread;
They'll live without the grammar,
    But they'll die unless they're fed.
We'd rather pray, it's cheaper, and
    We'll pray both loud and long;
They are coming, Father Abraham,
    About four millions strong.

Come all ye brave philanthropists,
    Philanthropesses fair;
Turn out your seedy hats and coats,
    And shirts the worse for wear;
Hymn books and musty bacon; bring
    The reeking store along.
They are coming, Father Abraham,
    About four millions strong.

And though the country may be poor,
    And labor be oppressed,
And white men starved and die in want,
    You surely will be blessed;
For fools, in ages yet to come,
    Will sing your praises long:
They are coming, Father Abraham,
    About four millions strong.

Then take them to your arms, my braves;
　　Don't bid them stay away;
The good time's surely coming now,—
　　The long expected day;
Let brother Beecher raise aloft
　　The banner and the song;
They are coming, Father Abraham,
　　About four millions strong.

11   JOINING THE UNION ARMY, 1863

Not surprisingly, the desire to fight against the South was strong among blacks in the northern states, most of whom regarded slavery as the pivotal issue in the Civil War. In the following letter, L.D. Sims, an obscure resident of Newark, refuses to let severe illness minimize his enthusiasm for the Union cause. Marcus L. Ward (1812–84), to whom Sims's letter is addressed, was a prominent Newark businessman and philanthropist and governor of New Jersey, 1866–69. During the Civil War he earned the, sobriquet "The Soldier's Friend" and established the Marcus L. Ward Office for Soldier's Business to aid and serve enlisted men and their families. Though New Jersey did not itself organize any regiments of Colored Troops, black New Jersey recruits and substitutes were assigned to regiments elsewhere and credited to New Jersey. Most of the nearly 2,900 black New Jersey soldiers served in infantry regiments, though a few served in cavalry units, and 469 died in service.

L. D. Sims to Marcus L. Ward,
11 June 1863, Marcus L. Ward Papers (MG 28),
Manuscript Collections, The New Jersey Historical Society.

Newark NJ
June 11, 1863

Dear Sir.

Two weeks ago when you interested yourself to get me a position in a Color'd Regiment I had good reason for believing myself physically fit for active service—I had been free from Rheumatism for months.

Since then without any apparant cause I have been laid up three days by my old foe—and am now going to see the Surgeon of the Enrolling

Board with a view of getting into the Invalid Corps.—If I get into the latter, I could do effective garrison duty, and when fit, get transfer'd to field duty.

I have the papers required by the Provost Marshal-General—except the Surgeons Certificate—and merely state the fact of my late attack to account for this application to the Enrolling Board in case its President Capt Miller should speak to you about me.

very respectfully
L D Sims.

---

12 LINCOLN'S PRO-COLONIZATION POSITION DISPUTED, 1862

Alfred P. Smith (1832–1901), a black journalist from Saddle River, addressed the following open letter to President Abraham Lincoln during the critical year of 1862, when the military role of black men and the future of slavery in the South were still unresolved issues. Like many white Americans, Lincoln resisted the introduction of black soldiers, fearing that they were too servile and cowardly to make good soldiers. He also faced another problem in the adverse reaction of the border states to the use of black soldiers, and the possibility that such a policy would intensify Confederate resistance. In keeping with his pragmatic approach to the conduct of the war, Lincoln countermanded attempts by Union generals to recruit free blacks and postponed their induction until a propitious turn in the struggle. Meanwhile, he espoused a pessimistic view of the race's future in the United States and supported the voluntary colonization of blacks in the Caribbean or Central America. During the Congressional session of 1861–62 federal lawmakers appropriated $600,000 to assist the expatriation of blacks freed by the District of Columbia Emancipation Act and the Second Confiscation Act.

Smith's tongue-in-cheek disputation of Lincoln's pro-colonization position draws upon the common themes in nineteenth-century black thought. He directs Lincoln's attention to the role of blacks in the settlement of the American colonies and their patriotism during the Revolution. Like earlier spokesmen, Smith claimed that colonization was contemptuous of the Afro-Americans' attachment to the land of their birth. Rather than send them abroad, he asks Lincoln to purge the South of traitors and make it the home of "the loyal, emancipated blacks."

Smith, who was a cripple since his boyhood, reported for the Paterson *Guardian* when he wrote the following letter. During the 1880s and 1890s he was the publisher and editor of the *Landscape: A Country Newspaper.*

A. P. Smith, "A Black Man's Talk to the President," from the Paterson *Guardian*, reprinted in the New York *National Anti-Slavery Standard*, 6 September 1862.

To the President of the United States.

HONORED SIR: As you are awaiting a reply from the negroes of the country to your recent Colonization proposition, you will not, I trust, think it strange that an humble person like myself should venture to address you. Not long since I was highly gratified by the assurance you, sir, are reported to have given President Geffrard,[1] that you will not tear your shirt even if he does send a negro to Washington. This assurance is also very encouraging to me at the present time, as I am unable to see why a Native American Negro should be more objectionable to you than one belonging to a foreign country. Should I, however, manifest extraordinary stupidity in my remarks, please, sir, to extend your gracious pardon and be kind enough to attribute all my perversity to the tightness of my hair, which perhaps may render my cranium impervious to your most cogent reasoning.

In the outset, good Mr. President, permit me to congratulate you on your good fortune in having a sum of money placed at your disposal in times like these. In this respect, sir (especially if it is in specie), you are highly favored above ordinary mortals. Could you now but, also, enjoy the luxury of spending it, for the benefit of those philanthropic coal speculators you refer to, I can well believe that you might feel yourself raised to the highest pinnacle of human happiness.

The simplicity, good sir, with which you assume that colored Americans should be expatriated, colonized in some foreign country, is decidedly rich—cool and refreshing as the breezes of "Egypt," or the verdure of your prairie home. The assertions, however, you do make in favor of your assumption, are worthy of a passing notice. If admitted, they would make sad havoc with the doctrines that have been cherished by the good and great of all ages. Different races, indeed! Let me tell you, sir, President though you are, there is but one race of men on the face of the earth: One Lord, one faith, one baptism, one God and Father of all, who is above all, and through all, and in all. Physical differences no doubt there are; no two persons on earth are exactly alike in this respect; but what of that? In physical conformation, you, Mr. President, may differ somewhat from the negro, and also from the majority of white men; you may even, as you intimate, feel this difference on your part to be very disadvantageous to you; but does it follow that therefore you should be removed to a foreign country? Must you and I and Vice-President Hamlin[2] and all of us submit to a microscopic examination of our hair, to determine whether the United States or Central America shall be our future home?

Pardon me, sir, if I say you betray a lamentable ignorance of a large portion of the country over which, doubtless for some wise purpose, you have been called to preside. You forget Massachusetts, Maine, Rhode Island—States that are the brightest exemplars of progress on earth—where all men are equal before the law, black and white living together in peace and harmony.

But were all you say on this point true, must I crush out my cherished hopes and aspirations, abandon my home, and become a pander to the mean and selfish spirit that oppresses me?

Pray tell us, is our right to a home in this country less than your own, Mr. Lincoln? Read history, if you please, and you will learn that more than two centuries ago Mr. White-man and Mr. Black-man settled in this country together. The negro, sir, was here in the infancy of the nation; he was here during its growth, and we are here to-day. If, through all these years of sorrow and affliction, there is one thing for which we have been noted more than all else, it is our love of country—our patriotism. In peace, the country has been blessed with our humble labor, nor have we ever been found wanting in the times that have tried the souls of men. We were with Warren on Bunker Hill, with Washington at Morristown and Valley Forge, with Lafayette at Yorktown, with Perry, Decatur and McDonough, in their cruisings, and with Jackson at New Orleans, battling side by side with the white man for nationality, national rights, and national glory. And when the history of the present atrocious insurrection is written, the historian will record, "Whoever was false, the blacks were true." Would you, then, in truckling subserviency to the sympathizers with this bloody rebellion, remove the purest patriotism the country affords? If you would, let me tell you, sir, you cannot do it. Neither fraud nor force can succeed, but by the fatal ruin of the country. Are you an American? So are we. Are you a patriot? So are we. Would you spurn all absurd, meddlesome, impudent propositions for colonization in a foreign country? So do we.

I trust, good Mr. President, you will not rend your garments when I tell you that the question of colonization, so persistently thrust upon us by the heartless traders in the woes of a bleeding people, has long been settled by a unanimous determination to remain, and survive or perish, rise or fall with the country of our birth. In our conventions, conferences, etc., again and again, in the most emphatic language, we have declared our utter detestation of this colonization scheme, whatever form it may assume.

In holy horror, disinterested sir, you may hold up your hands at what you choose to denominate the "selfishness" of the unalterable resolution; but, pray tell us, is it any more selfish than your own determination to remain here, instead of emigrating to some pretty foreign country; and is it as selfish as the desire to exclude us from a country where there is room enough for ten times the present population? Or is it, think you, as selfish as the coal traders and the swarms of contractors, agents, etc., for whose benefit you are so anxious to spend some of the money our liberal Congress has placed at your disposal? If it is selfishness, please, sir, to remember your own plea for the coal speculations, etc., viz; all persons look to their self-interest.

But pray, good Mr. President, why should we, why should anybody swelter, digging coal, if there be any, in Central America? In that country, where the sun blazes with a fervor unknown in these high latitudes—where a broad-brimmed Panama, a cigar and a pair of spurs is considered a comfortable costume for the natives—why should we, why should anybody dig coal? Do tell. Might we not just as well dig ice on the coast of Labrador? But say you, "Coal land is the best thing I know of to begin an enterprise." Astounding discovery! Worthy to be recorded in golden letters, like the Lunar Cycle in the Temple of Minerva. "Coal land, sir!" Pardon, Mr. President, if my African risibilities get the better of me—if I do show my ivories whenever I read that sentence! Coal land, sir! If you please, sir, give McClellan some, give Halleck some, and, by all means, save a little strip for yourself. Coal land, sir!

Twenty-five negroes digging coal in Central America! Mighty plan! Equal to about twenty-five negroes splitting rails in Sangamon!

It was my intention to have shown you, sir, the necessity of retaining the labor of the negroes in the South, as freemen, but space will not permit. According to theory, white men can't stand it, can't live *honestly* in the South; we can. Henceforth, then, let this be the motto: "The Gulf States, purged of traitors, the home of the loyal, emancipated blacks!" And then, good sir, if you have any nearer friends than we are, let them have that coal-digging job.

Yours, respectfully,   A.P. SMITH.

Saddle River, N.J.

---

1. Nicholas Fabre Geffrard (1806–79), president of Haiti, 1859–67.
2. Hannibal Hamlin (1809–91), U.S. vice president, 1861–65.

V

Quest for Racial Identity

O N November 19, 1863, President Abraham Lincoln participated in dedication services for the Gettysburg Cemetery
in Pennsylvania. Eulogizing the dead there, he hoped that they
should not have died in vain and "that this nation, under God,
shall have a new birth of freedom," an increasingly elusive ideal
for black Americans in the remaining years of the nineteenth century. Southern freedmen were soon debased by a social and
economic system barely distinguishable from slavery. National
leaders turned their attention to the problems of industrialization,
ultimately abandoning their commitment to racial reforms in the
South. Blacks in the northern states fared somewhat better during
those years. Yet, like the freedmen, they had few friends in the
white population. By the turn of the century, the Afro-American's
crusade for freedom appeared to have been defeated, and the
race's future seemed dependent on its own untested resources.

The prospects for blacks in New Jersey immediately after the
Civil War were especially doubtful. [doc. 1] In the past, New
Jersey had exhibited little sympathy for black aspirations. While
most northern states viewed slavery as morally indefensible, and
upon that premise had fought the Confederacy, New Jersey had
not held that view. The popular outlook on the war among
Jerseymen was "the Constitution as it is, the Nation as it was."
This unsympathetic judgment persisted after the conflict. The
Democrat-controlled legislature refused to ratify the Thirteenth
and Fifteenth Amendments to the U.S. Constitution, upon which
the hopes of racial equality rested. When the Republican Party
won control of the legislature in 1868, the Fourteenth Amendment
was ratified. The Democrats, however, rescinded the measure as
soon as they were returned to power.[1]

Despite the reception accorded the Reconstruction amendments by New Jersey lawmakers, the measures gained sufficient backing in the nation. The civil rights momentum of the northern states and the establishment of Reconstruction governments in the South intensified the struggle for equality in New Jersey. "Class and caste," argued one black Jerseyman, "are utterly at war with republican institutions. Exclusive rights for none, equal rights for all, is the grand central idea which the Declaration of Independence and the United States Constitution set forth."[2] On March 31, 1870, Thomas Mundy Peterson of Perth Amboy became the first black in the nation to vote under protection of the Fifteenth Amendment. The amendment's passage also occasioned a huge celebration by blacks in New Brunswick on May 26, 1870. [doc. 2] Within a year, the first black juror in New Jersey's history served in West Milford. Gains were also made on other fronts. In 1872, Newark opened all of its public schools to black children. Three years later the legislature struck the word "white" from the state constitution. The most important development in the struggle for legal equality came with the passage of the state's Civil Rights Act in 1884. [doc. 3] Just before this extraordinary measure was enacted, the Reverend Jeremiah H. Pierce of Burlington drew upon the egalitarian spirit of the period and successfully challenged school segregation in a landmark case before the Supreme Court of New Jersey. [doc. 4]

Those gains, however, were impeded as the creed of white supremacy reasserted itself across the country. By the 1890s blacks were forced into an inferior status in American society. Rayford W. Logan has called the period from about 1877 to the end of World War I the low point in American race relations, an era in which the nation's political leaders and the courts betrayed the civil rights of blacks. In the South violence against blacks was widespread and the Fifteenth Amendment was systematically violated, leaving black voters largely disenfranchised by the turn of the century. These reversals corresponded with the Republican Party's indifference to further civil rights gains for freedmen.[3] The old abolitionist spirit also suffered in New Jersey. Symbolic of the period's broken promises and its implicit anti-black mood, the Civil Rights Act of 1884 and the New Jersey Supreme Court's mandate in the Pierce decision were flouted in many parts of the state.

As a result of the decline in civil rights and the contemporary popularity of the gospel of work in industrial America, black leaders increasingly emphasized race uplift rather than appeals for desegregation and equality. They supported programs for educational improvement, economic development, the building of a sound moral character, and race pride.[4] The affirmation of black nationalism was an expression of race pride and chauvinism espoused by religious organizations, intellectuals, and business leaders. Historians John H. Bracey, Jr., August Meier, and Elliott Rudwick have noted that black nationalism "has been used in American history to describe a body of social thought, attitudes, and actions ranging from the simplest expression of ethnocentrism and racial solidarity to the comprehensive and sophisticated ideologies of Pan-Negroism or Pan Africanism." The origins of Afro-American nationalism are obscure, but blacks clearly shared a belief in their own common historical experience and destiny by the time of the American Revolution. Black nationalist spokesmen differed in their approach and in their interpretation of history, but generally, racial solidarity was the nucleus of nationalist ideologies and programs.[5]

From the early nineteenth century, varied forms of nationalist expression became pronounced during periods of exceptional racial tension and disillusionment. After Reconstruction, nationalist expression inevitably rose in reaction to the resurgence of white supremacy in the South, the establishment of racial segregation in many parts of the United States, and the emphasis given to racial theories on the human condition. Some nationalists, such as Bishop Henry McNeal Turner of the African Methodist Episcopal Church, believed that harmonious race relations were impossible in America and advocated emigration to Africa.[6] But most leaders saw nationalist programs as a means to develop the economic, political, and cultural institutions of the race in America, and eventually to gain racial equality. This implicit paradox in the ideals of nationalism was given eloquent recognition by W.E.B. DuBois in 1897 when he observed that "one ever feels his two-ness—an American, a Negro; two souls, two thoughts, two unreconciled strivings; two warring ideals in one dark body, whose dogged strength alone keeps it from being torn asunder."[7] In 1877 the black physician, Dr. James Still of Burlington County, enunciated many of the essential elements of nationalism in his autobiography, *Early Recollections and Life of Dr. James Still,* a work which also revealed the "two-ness" felt by its author. [doc. 5]

The most formidable spokesman of nationalism at the time was

Booker T. Washington, the principal of Tuskegee Institute in Alabama. Washington addressed his program of race uplift primarily to southern blacks barely a generation out of slavery. His was a program of modest achievements wrought by the initiative of blacks and financed largely by white business interests. It accommodated itself to the disenfranchisement of black voters and racial segregation in the South.[8] Washington's faith in educational uplift and economic development, which he underscored in his famous Atlanta Exposition Address of 1895, was shared by many black spokesmen in New Jersey, particularly the ministerial leadership. In 1887, Reverend Junius C. Ayler of Princeton expressed concerns resembling Washington's. [doc. 6] The Tuskegeean's philosophy of race uplift was also supported by the Reverend A. P. Miller of St. Mark's African Methodist Episcopal Zion Church in Jersey City. [doc. 7] This denomination was especially sensitive to the nationalist persuasion at the time. Although some ministers were influenced by the visions of economic development popularized by Booker T. Washington, the New Jersey Conference of the African Methodist Episcopal Church took a more militant stance. At its annual meeting in 1886 the Conference associated itself with the Pan-Africanism of Bishop Henry McNeal Turner. [doc. 8]

Probably the clearest manifestation of black nationalism in New Jersey was the formation of several predominantly black communities. They were formed not only because of white racial hostilities, but also because their inhabitants desired to live apart from whites and maintain their customs, family ties, land holdings, and, in some cases, social isolation. One of the oldest and best known of these settlements was Gouldtown, which was located in Fairfield Township, Cumberland County. Its inhabitants claimed to be descendants of Benjamin Gould, a black man, and his wife, Elizabeth Adams, the granddaughter of John Fenwick (1618–83), the proprietor of West Jersey from 1671. By 1900 five generations of Goulds had lived in the settlement, which a contemporary observer characterized as a farming community of light-skinned blacks. In addition, Gouldtown contained several members of the Pierce family who were also racially mixed. In the twentieth century the settlement decreased in number because of the out-migration of Goulds and Pierces to Philadelphia, Pittsburgh, New York, Boston, and Chicago. In 1907 approximately fifty families remained. They held over 3,000 acres valued at $102,460 and personal property worth $9,100.[9]

Ten miles south of Gouldtown another black settlement was located in Springtown, Greenwich Township. The inhabitants there, descendants of slaves who had escaped from Delaware and Maryland, were much darker in complexion than the Gould-towners, and a tacitly drawn color line seems to have separated the social life of the two communities. By the early twentieth century the community was declining because of the emigration of families to industrial cities.[10]

The lure of the city in the twentieth century also decreased the population in the predominantly black town of Snowhill (later called Free Haven and Lawnside) in Camden County. Blacks first settled there in the late eighteenth century. During the ante-bellum years it became a refuge for fugitive slaves from the southern states. Another settlement in Whitesboro, Cape May County, was composed of blacks who had fled the racial violence in Wilmington, North Carolina, in 1898.[11]

The provincialism of these communities created conditions favorable to the attainment of group integrity. Local residents started small businesses and churches. Public school segregation in South Jersey provided some opportunities for black teachers in predominantly black areas. Social and mutual aid organizations were established. Interestingly enough, some of the settlements perceived the desegregation of public schools as a possible threat to their teachers and administrators, a view which contributed to the survival of a dual school system in many parts of Atlantic, Cape May, and Camden counties in the twentieth century.[12]

In New Jersey municipalities where blacks were a minority, it was naturally more difficult to maintain independence from white society. Nonetheless, blacks in the late nineteenth century often lived in tightly knit communities having a remarkable degree of self-sufficiency. Prior to the great migration of World War I, which brought thousands of southern blacks into the state, black communities in many areas were cohesive. The Negro church, still the paramount institution at the time, stressed Christian respectability. Religious and secular leaders emphasized the work ethic. Responsibility to family and community seems to have been the central idea among older families.[13] This was the social and intellectual background of Paul Robeson (1898–1976) of Princeton, one of the state's most gifted and accomplished native sons and an important figure in American culture and social protest in the twentieth century. In 1958, Robeson published his autobiography, *Here I Stand,* in which he recalled the profound influence of his parents on his life and principles and on race relations in the town of Princeton.[14] [doc. 9]

Advocates of race solidarity and uplift emerged, too, from the ranks of black entrepreneurs, educators, and journalists in New Jersey. By the turn of the century blacks had founded twelve weekly newspapers in the state, but most of them did not last more than a short time. Of all the papers started during the last two decades of the nineteenth century, only two were in existence by 1900, and none of the weeklies begun in 1900 lasted more than a decade.[15] Nonetheless, the black press was an essential part of the civil rights movement during the period. Newspapers were symbols of community growth, carrying information of interest to blacks while articulating grievances to the larger population. [doc. 10] The establishment of the Bordentown School in 1886 by the Reverend W.A. Rice represented the most successful transplantation of Washingtonian plans to New Jersey, and it was often referred to as the Tuskegee of the North. In 1894 the state assumed control of the institution and it became the Manual Training and Industrial School for Colored Youth. [doc. 11]

Politically, black voters in New Jersey remained loyal to the Republican Party—the party of Lincoln and ostensibly the protector of the political rights of freedmen. By the early twentieth century, however, the party was under attack for abandoning the ideals of its founders, and some leaders urged blacks to become politically independent and to support candidates sympathetic to their concerns. This view was espoused notably by W.E.B. DuBois, the brilliant young scholar and antagonist of Booker T. Washington; T. Thomas Fortune, editor of the *New York Age;* and William Monroe Trotter, the Boston *Guardian*'s militant editor. The prospects for a new political alliance seemed brightest in New Jersey, where a crusade against privilege, big business, and corruption was kindled by the meteoric political rise of Woodrow Wilson, who was elected governor in 1910. Wilson's personal integrity and belief that American democracy entrusted civil society with a moral duty to combat social inequities won the enthusiastic support of national black leaders. In August 1910 the National Independent Political League, an organization of black leaders which sought to promote the Democratic Party among black voters, met in Atlantic City. At a subsequent meeting in Washington in October, Wilson's gubernatorial candidacy was endorsed by the organization. He was also supported by influential blacks when he became the Democratic standard-bearer in the 1912 presidential election.

But blacks in the nation were soon to learn, as some in New Jersey had foreseen, that Wilson was not a champion of racial justice. The racial policies of his administration were marked by the further segregation of federal offices and a poor record in appointing blacks to positions within the government. These actions were consistent with Wilson's racial views at the beginning of his public career in New Jersey.[16] **[doc. 12a,b]**

Blacks in New Jersey formed several organizations devoted to race uplift at the turn of the century, but this effort is largely obscured by the unavailability of documentary sources. The increase in the black population from 25,336 to 69,844 between 1860 and 1900 fostered the development of remarkably strong churches, professional interest groups, social work organizations, and protest groups. In spite of the setbacks encountered during the period, blacks in New Jersey established the social, economic, and intellectual bases for future progress.

1 EQUAL RIGHTS LEAGUE ATTACKS SEGREGATION, 1865

The State Convention of Colored Men reflected the impetus which the Civil War gave to civil rights appeals. It assembled thirty-one prominent blacks in New Jersey, and, in response to the growing influence of women in the civil rights movement, seated several females as non-voting delegates. In accordance with the agenda established by the National Convention of Colored Men in Syracuse, New York, in 1864, the State Convention's primary purpose was to launch the Equal Rights League in New Jersey. The new organization was probably the first statewide body of blacks to attack segregation and disenfranchisement. This ambitious undertaking began with a census of the black population designed to ascertain its social and economic status. The League also hoped to arouse the state's conscience, claiming that racial discrimination retarded the progress and elevation of black residents. New Jersey residents were reminded of the race's respect for the law and patriotism "in the hour of the nation's peril." Like appeals for racial justice made during the ante-bellum period, the League's resolutions articulated moral principles which were inherent in the American Revolution and sanctioned by natural law. After 1865 the history of the Equal Rights League is obscure, and apparently the Negro Convention Movement in New Jersey came to an end.

Samuel G. Gould, "Address Issued to the people of New Jersey, by The Equal Right's League of New Jersey," *Proceedings of the State Convention of Colored Men of the State of New Jersey* (Bridgeton, N.J., 1865), pp. 14-15.

WHEREAS, We, the colored people of the State of New Jersey have been for a long time deprived of our political rights, and have thereby labored under many disadvantages, and suffered many wrongs, the influence of which has retarded our progress and elevation; therefore, we must respectfully appeal to the citizens of New Jersey, and the friends of humanity, to restore to us all the rights of *Loyal Citizens.* We ask it as our right

First, Because we are law-abiding, loyal people, and always have been.

Second, Because in the hour of the nation's peril, *when called,* we rallied to the rescue, and thereby gave our influence, our money and our lives, for the restoration of her government.

Third, We ask it in the name of the Declaration of Independence, which declares *all* men to be free and equal born, and "endowed with certain inalienable rights among which are life, liberty, and the pursuit of happiness," and without the acknowledgement of our *political* rights, these cannot be enjoyed.

Fourth, We ask it in the name of God of our holy religion, who declares that he has no respect of persons, and also declares that He "hath made of one blood all nations of men to dwell on the face of the earth, and hath determined the times before appointed, and the bounds of their habitations" (Acts xvii, 26).

2   CELEBRATING THE FIFTEENTH AMENDMENT, 1870

With the exception of the Emancipation Proclamation, blacks in northern states viewed the Fifteenth Amendment to the U.S. Constitution as their most significant victory in the struggle for human dignity and equal rights. Not surprisingly, in New Jersey, where blacks had been denied suffrage since the early part of the century, the amendment was greeted with considerable enthusiasm. The following is a newspaper account of the celebration by blacks in New Brunswick of the newly acquired voting rights of black men. It was an event of extraordinary symbolic importance. Hundreds of Afro-Americans from New Brunswick, Bound Brook, Newark, Flemington, and Elizabeth participated in this dramatic demonstration, probably the first large-scale parade by black citizens in the state's history.

Of the many black leaders at the celebration, William Whipper no doubt drew the greatest attention. In 1870, Whipper was a seasoned veteran of the abolitionist movement. He formed the American Moral Reform Society in 1835, which, as an outgrowth of the early national Negro Conventions, was devoted to the encouragement of Christian morality and the Protestant virtues of thrift, temperance, and hard work among blacks. In his early years as a race leader, Whipper sought to deemphasize the importance of racial solidarity in the fight for freedom and civil rights. But, by 1870, as his resolution at the celebration showed, race pride and accomplishment had become important to him. The resolution, like most appeals by black Jerseymen in the nineteenth century, stressed the role which blacks played in the preservation of American freedom. More importantly, it reflected black assertiveness during Reconstruction, acknowledging the sacrifices which Denmark Vesey, David Walker, Nat Turner, François Dominique Toussaint L'Ouverture, and John Brown had made to the cause of liberty.

"Grand Celebration of the Fifteenth Amendment," *New Brunswick Weekly Fredonian*, 27 May 1870.

. . . The procession was a very creditable one, and made a very fine display. It was about one quarter of a mile in length. The sidewalks along the route were thronged with people, white and colored, and no disturbance occurred to mar the proceedings, or attempts to interfere with the colored people in their festivities were made so far as we were able to learn. The procession marched over the grounds in front of the residence of Hon. LEVI D. JARRARD, on George-street, and gave cheers for Mr. J. and the flag which he had raised in honor of the occasion.

As the procession passed through Dennis-street rousing cheers were given for the FREDONIAN and its flag. The banners carried in the procession were severally inscribed as follows: "John Brown, a Martyr for

Liberty"; "Grant and Education"; "In God we Trust"; "Our Star Shines"; "Liberty for all"; "The Fifteenth Amendment," &c., &c.

The following persons were appointed special police officers by Mayor JANEWAY, for the purpose of keeping order on the streets during the day and evening: John M. Downie, Captain, with Andrew Brower, Wallace Labone, William Gray, Millard Stevens, George Holman, Charles Garretson, Nathaniel Cunningham, Jacob Burbank and Charles Weller.

After the procession a party of gentlemen, consisting of the speakers of the day, and the officers of the Halsey Club, of Newark, namely WM. R. COE, President, P.A. TREADWELL, Captain, and E.S. HAZZARD, Secretary, and also a few of its members, were handsomely entertained by the Vice-President, Mr. THOMAS MARSH. Then followed toasts, speeches, &c., after which the party separated.

THE MEETING

At three o'clock P.M. a public meeting was held in the Court House Square. A large platform was constructed on the easterly side of the Court House, which was occupied by the speaker and officers of the meeting, the Excelsior (colored) Cornet Band and citizens generally. There was a promiscuous gathering of white and colored people of both sexes to hear the speeches, and the meeting was one of the most enthusiastic as well as one of the largest ever held in this City, thousands of people being in attendance.

After music by the Band, Rev. WM. E. WALKER, of Trenton, called the meeting to order and nominated the following persons as the officers of the meeting:

President—WM. WHIPPER, Esq., of New-Brunswick.

Vice-Presidents—Rev. STEPHEN SMITH, of Philadelphia, Rev. WM. E. WALKER, of Trenton, and Rev. JAMES V. PIERCE, THOMAS MARSH, JOHN F. BABCOCK, Prof G.W. ATHERTON and WOODBRIDGE STRONG, of New-Brunswick.

The nominations were unanimously confirmed. Rev. Mr. WALKER then read the following preamble and resolutions, which had been prepared by the President, WM. WHIPPER, of this City:

WHEREAS, A century ago the institutions that formed the scourge of this virgin wilderness were founded on the doctrine of the divine right of kings, and the divine right of complexion, to govern and control the civil destiny of nations;

And Whereas, The inauguration of the rebellion in 1775, and the issuing of the Declaration of American Independence, and the war which followed, swept Colonial vassalage from the soil; and the rebellion of 1861, and the subsequent legislation that succeeded it, has eradicated the latter from the civil institutions of our country;

And Whereas, The great living principles of our National Creed has now, after a protracted struggle of 94 years, become the ever glorious preamble to the constitution of 1870; it therefore becomes us who are the immediate recipients of these blessings to celebrate this illustrious event with a pomp and splendor becoming American freemen, and transmit to future ages the heroic virtues of CRISPUS ATTUCKS, our kinsman by the ties of race, of suffering and wrong, the first martyr to civil liberty who fell in Massachusetts in defense of American revolution;

And Whereas, We have great cause for rejoicing that the spirit of liberty has penetrated American soil deeper down than the Magna Charter of King John, and culminated in producing the extraordinary fact of a nation triumphing over itself; therefore let us pledge ourselves that so far as in us lies we will aid in transmitting to future generations the great principles of freedom conferred on us by the Constitution of the United States to the latest period of time.

Therefore, be it Resolved, That our homage and reverence is due to Almighty God, the great disposer of human events, for His chastening influence on the spirit of civil and religious liberty in all lands, and more especially our own, and that our thanks are also due to the living and dead compatriots who were willing and active laborers, without distinction of caste, color, or condition in this great centurion struggle for freedom, justice and right.

Resolved, That in the history of races, and great struggles for the promotion of civil and religious liberty, it is established law of Providence that great leaders will be thrown to the surface; and while we honor and adore the illustrious names of the Adamses, Otises, and Henrys of revolutionary fame, we will not fail to enumerate in the same catalogue the Veseys, the Walkers, the Turners, Touissant L'Overtures and John Browns as distinguished coadjutors in the same sacred cause. Our distinguished laborers in this field of progressive reform have not been surpassed in devotion and efficiency in any former age or generation. We have had our Lundys, Garrisons, Douglas's, Phillips, Sumners, and Stephens, to compare with the Sharpes, Clarksons, Wilberforce and O'Connells of the British Empire, and in our own generation the representative men of our race in the field, the camp and forum, have challenged the admiration of millions.

Resolved, that we recognize in this revolution of freedom and progress the existence of a mysterious cause that has induced the abettors of slavery to voluntarily contribute to its overthrow, and thus aid in the deliverance of captives by hastening the prophetic period when "a nation shall be born in a day," and demonstrate to succeeding generations that "righteousness exalteth a nation, and sin is a reproach to any people."

Resolved, That the future historian may enquire why in the decrees of an All Wise Providence the State of Virginia, blest with the finest climate in the world, the nursing mother of patriots, warriors, and statesmen, and the first to receive the footprints of an American slave, should become the theatre on which two rebellions terminated in favor of liberty, and that the swords of such illustrious Generals as Cornwallis and Lee should have been surrendered to such patriotic and liberty-loving Generals as Washington and Grant.

Resolved, That as our national enfranchisement is due to the untiring labors of the Republican party, let us prove our appreciation of the rich boon, and the time will not be distant when the whole nation will rejoice at the event.

The resolutions were unanimously adopted . . . .

3 CIVIL RIGHTS ACT PASSED, 1884

In 1884 the New Jersey legislature enacted the state's first major civil rights act after the Civil War. This extraordinary measure guaranteed equal access to public accommodations for all New Jersey citizens. Under its provisions persons violating the civil rights of an individual were fined and required to pay damages to the aggrieved party. Discrimination based on race or previous condition of servitude was also prohibited in the selection of jurors. Blacks in New Jersey had never witnessed such a high-sounding defense of their civil equality by the state government. But the law failed to end many of the forms of discrimination faced by blacks in their daily lives. It was openly violated, especially in the matter of public accommodations. Throughout the state, white resistance to desegregation and racial equality proved stronger than legal guarantees. In 1917 the act was revised so as to weaken its impact on racial injustice. Much like the U.S. Supreme Court, which between 1873 and 1898 undermined the Reconstruction amendments and civil rights laws, New Jersey lawmakers ultimately narrowed the scope of legal reforms beneficial to blacks. As late as the 1940s blacks in Newark, the state's largest city, were forced to sit in segregated balconies in the downtown theaters.

An Act to Protect All Citizens in Their Civil and Legal Rights, *New Jersey Laws,* 10 May 1884.

1. BE IT ENACTED *by the Senate and General Assembly of the State of New Jersey,* That all persons within the jurisdiction of the state of New Jersey shall be entitled to the full and equal enjoyment of the accommodations, advantages, facilities and privileges of inns, public conveyances on land or water, theatres and other places of public amuse-

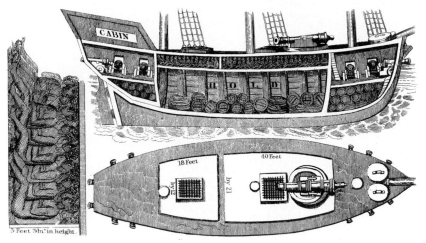

Fig. 1: Diagram of a slave ship showing the stowing of slaves, included in the annual report of the American Colonization Society in 1849. **Fig. 2:** Detail from the logbook of the ship *Catherine* recording some of the nineteen slave deaths on board. During a voyage between September 1732 and July 1733, the *Catherine* brought 238 slaves as cargo from the western coast of Africa. Sailing from New York and Perth Amboy, the *Catherine* was one of the many vessels importing slaves to East Jersey and New York in the colonial period.

20 DOLLARS REWARD.

RAN-away from the subscribers at Pompton, on Monday the 13th inst. two negroes, the oldest named JACK, about 5 feet 7 or 8 inches high, 28 years of age, of a tawney complexion, pretty large eyes, speaks Dutch and English, makes himself very free with strangers ; had on when he went away a deep blue short coat, lined with light colored shaloon, a light swansdown vest, and a claret colored homespun cloth trowsers. The other named JOE, about 20 years old, between 5 feet 4 or 5 inches high, dark complexion, speaks also Dutch and English, and of a bashful disposition ; had on when he went away a gray linsey woolsey short coat, with trowsers of the same, and dark swansdown vest, his hair something strait like an indian ; they were both seen at the Jersey races, and are supposed to have gone into New-york, or to Tappan, near the north river, with some other blacks attending the races from that quarter. The above reward, with reasonable charges will be given for both, or ten dollars for each, by us

Henry R. Van Ness, _Jacob J. Van Ness._
May 25, 1807. 56-3wp

Fig. 3: Runaway notice from the Newark _Sentinel of Freedom,_ 26 August 1807. Local newspapers frequently included notices for the return of runaway slaves. **[chap. 2, doc. 4]** Such notices gave information the owner felt would identify the fugitives, such as personality traits, clothing and possessions, and physical characteristics. **Fig. 4:** Slave quarters were as much a part of many large New Jersey farms as of southern plantations. The quarters at Morven, the Princeton estate of Richard Stockton (1730–81) built, ca. 1754–55, housed male and female slaves separately.

Fig. 3

Fig. 4

Fig. 5

Fig. 5: Prince Whipple, *second from right,* shown crossing the Delaware with George Washington prior to the Battle of Trenton on Christmas Day, 1776 (Engraving by J. N. Gimbrede after a painting by Thomas Sully). Whipple was one of several black New Jerseyans who made notable contributions during the Revolutionary War. A free-born native African, he was the bodyguard of Captain Abraham Whipple. Jack Cudjo, a slave, served in the Continental Army in the place of his owner, Benjamin Coe of Newark. Cudjo was manumitted in recognition of his service and was given an acre of ground on High Street in Newark. **Fig. 6:** The Coe homestead (1866), built during the Revolutionary era, stood at the corner of Court and Washington streets in Newark. **[see chap. 3, doc. 6b]**   **Fig. 6**

Fig. 7: John Woolman, a Quaker tailor and storekeeper from Mount Holly, Burlington County, wrote one of the earliest attacks on slavery. His treatise, *Some Considerations on the Keeping of Negroes,* published in 1754, stressed the common humanity of blacks and whites, and examined racial prejudice in colonial America. **[chap. 1, doc. 6]** This likeness of Woolman was drawn by his contemporary, Robert Smith III. Woolman's anti-slavery speeches and essays impressed many of his contemporaries, but it was not until 1786 that anti-slavery supporters succeeded in stopping the importation of slaves to New Jersey. **Fig. 8:** In 1793 the New Jersey Society for Promoting the Abolition of Slavery was formed. This engraving appeared on the Society's membership certificate. **[chap. 3, doc. 10]**

Fig. 8

Fig. 7

ISAIAH LVIII. 6.

ISAIAH LXI. I.

HE CAME TO PROCLAIM LIBERTY
TO THE CAPTIVE, AND THE
OPENING OF THE PRISON
TO THEM THAT ARE BOUND.

Am not I a Man and a Brother?

Fig. 9

New Jersey provided a major route of escape for fugitive slaves traveling from the South along the Underground Railroad. Some fugitives attempted escape across the Delaware Bay, while others fled by foot or public conveyance. **Fig. 9:** Four young fugitive slaves chose the water route from Lewes, Delaware. "A fierce gale was blowing, and the waves were running fearfully high; not daunted . . ., they reached their much desired haven, the Jersey shore." **Fig. 10:** Jane Johnson escaped with her two sons with the aid of abolitionists. She left her master as they were boarding the ferry to Camden on a journey from Philadelphia to New York, probably via the Camden and Amboy Railroad. These incidents were recorded by William Still, younger brother of Dr. James Still of Medford Township, in his book *The Underground Rail Road*.

Fig. 10

Fig. 11

Fig. 13

Fig. 12

Fig. 11: The Butler Medal, named after General Benjamin F. Butler (1818–93), was awarded to U.S. Colored Troops "Distinguished for Courage" during the campaign before Richmond in 1864, in which several hundred New Jerseyans served. Black military service to the Union provided a strong argument for the enfranchisement of black men, as Thomas Nast illustrated in his cartoon. **Fig. 12:** "Franchise. And Not This Man?" by Thomas Nast, from *Harper's Weekly,* 5 August 1865. Nast was a one-time resident of Morristown and a spokesman for racial justice. **Fig. 13:** Thomas Mundy Peterson was the first black voter in the United States to vote under the guarantees of the Fifteenth Amendment. Peterson here wears a medal awarded him by the citizens of Perth Amboy in honor of his historic vote cast in that city on March 31, 1870.

Fig. 14

Fig. 14: Dr. James Still, the son of slaves, built an impressive reputation around his practice of herbal medicine which he advocated instead of the "heroic" techniques typical of medical practice in his time. He also articulated a race philosophy strikingly similar to that later espoused by Booker T. Washington. [chap. 5, doc. 5] Fig. 15: The Still home and office in Medford Township was rebuilt by Still in 1869 "with all the modern improvements."

Fig. 15

Fig. 16

Fig. 17

Fig. 18

Fig. 19

While embracing the work ethic and a belief in self-reliance, most free blacks in the nineteenth century found their work opportunities limited to menial jobs. **Fig. 16:** Peter Lee (1804–1902) was freed by the New Jersey law of 1804 but spent his life as a servant for the Stevens family of Hoboken. **Fig. 17:** Benjamin Jackson (1820–86) developed a successful trade as a porter at the Camden and Amboy Railroad terminal in Burlington. At the turn of the century the Wood family of West Orange included a carpenter, a waiter, laborers, and a doorman. **Fig. 18:** John Wood, *right,* at a New York office building. **Fig. 19:** Mrs. Sophronia Wood.

Fig. 20

The growth of civic and fraternal organizations during the late nineteenth and early twentieth centuries was especially important to the identity and solidarity of black communities. **Fig. 20:** Alpha Company No. 1, Knights of Pythias, Atlantic City, ca. 1915. **Fig. 21:** Colored Branch, YMCA, Central Place, Orange, New Jersey, 1901.

Fig. 21

Fig. 22

Black men gave distinguished military service during World War I. Though segregated into "colored troops" and usually assigned to support duties, blacks enlisted in large numbers and served in nearly every branch of the Army. Pressure by activists resulted in the introduction of training facilities for black officers. **Fig. 22:** Signal training for black troops at Camp Dix in New Jersey. **Fig. 23:** Non-commissioned officers of the Second Support Company of the New Jersey State Militia.

Fig. 23

Fig. 24

Several independent black communities were formed in New Jersey over the years, partly in reaction to white hostility, but also as an expression of black nationalism. Gouldtown, Cumberland County, was one of the oldest of these towns. Its inhabitants traced their lineage to Benjamin Gould, a black man, and Elizabeth Adams, a granddaughter of John Fenwick, the proprietor of West Jersey from 1671. **Fig. 24:** School children outside the Gouldtown school in 1924. Most of these children were members of the Gould and Pierce families. **Fig. 25:** The Lawnside Volunteer Fire Department in 1968. Lawnside, Camden County, was settled in the late eighteenth century, becoming a refuge for southern fugitive slaves in the ante-bellum period.

Fig. 25

Fig. 26

Major migration from the South and restrictive housing practices had created large black ghettos in many New Jersey cities by the 1930s. These communities were especially hard hit by the Depression. New Deal programs served to bring some jobs to blacks and supported hopes for equal opportunity in the future. **Fig. 26:** A Newark street in the 1930s. **Fig. 27:** Newark actors and actresses rehearsing for a production of a minstrel show, "Brother Mose," under a WPA Federal Theatre Project in 1936.

Fig. 27

Fig. 28

In the 1930s blacks stood at the crossroads between centuries of menial labor in stereotypical occupations and a possible future free of racial barriers in the professional and industrial workplace. **Fig. 28:** Trenton road workers, 1930s. Integrated road crews such as this not only improved local transportation but also helped erode discriminatory practices keeping white and black workers apart. **Fig. 29:** Aides in the Household Training Project, Newark, ca. 1938–39. Women in this WPA program were trained to be professional housekeepers and were placed by the WPA for varying lengths of time in needy or distressed homes.

Fig. 29

Fig. 30   **Fig. 31**

Fig. 32   **Fig. 33**

Fig. 30: James D. Carr, the first black graduate of Rutgers University. A member of the class of 1892, Carr became an attorney and assistant corporation counsel to the City of New York. **Fig. 31:** Paul Robeson, Rutgers, class of 1919, became an internationally known actor, vocal artist, and human rights advocate. **[chap. 5, doc. 9] Fig. 32:** Marion Thompson Wright was a social worker for the Newark Department of Welfare in the 1930s. She earned her Ph.D. from Teachers College, Columbia University in 1940 and taught at Howard University until 1962. Her extensive research and publication during the 1940s and 1950s earned her preeminence as the historian of Afro-Americans in New Jersey. **Fig. 33:** Harold A. Lett, leading advocate of interracial cooperation, was the executive secretary of the New Jersey Urban League from 1934 to 1945. **[chap. 6, doc. 6].**

Fig. 34

Fig. 34: Anna Monroe, *center,* with members of the Bethany Baptist Church, Newark, 1947. Monroe was one of the early black community workers in Newark and a member of the Bethany congregation. Throughout the twentieth century the older, institutional Afro-American churches remained a vital force for racial justice and black self-help. From such congregations came many of the early twentieth-century black leaders in education, social service, business, and civil rights.

In 1951 many of the state's civil rights organizations, labor unions, and radical groups supported the cause of the Trenton Six. **[chap. 7, doc. 6] Fig. 35:** Pickets at the State House, Trenton. William L. Patterson of the Civil Rights Congress, *second from left.*

Fig. 35

Fig. 36

In the 1960s violent civil disorders erupted in several New Jersey cities as a result of increasingly adverse urban economic conditions and frustration with municipal failure to deal with problems facing black neighborhoods. [**chap. 7, doc. 9**] **Fig. 36:** National Guardsmen positioned along Springfield Avenue, Newark on July 15, 1967. The Newark disorders lasted nearly a week; they resulted in the loss of twenty-three lives and over $10,000,000 in property damage.

ment; subject only to the conditions and limitations established by law, and applicable alike to citizens of every race and color, regardless of any previous condition of servitude.

2. *And be it enacted,* That any person who shall violate the foregoing section by denying to any citizen, except for reasons by law applicable to citizens of every race and color, and regardless of any previous condition of servitude, the full enjoyment of any of the accommodations, advantages, facilities or privileges in said section enumerated, or by aiding or inciting such denial, shall, for every such offense, forfeit and pay the sum of five hundred dollars to the person aggrieved thereby, to be recovered in an action of debt, with full costs, and shall also, for every such offense, be deemed guilty of a misdemeanor, and upon conviction thereof shall be fined not less than five hundred nor more than one thousand dollars, or shall be imprisoned not less than thirty days nor more than one year.

3. *And be it enacted,* That no citizen possessing all other qualifications which are or may be prescribed by law shall be disqualified for service as grand or petit juror in any court of this state, on account of race, color or previous condition of servitude, and any officer or other person charged with any duty in the selection or summoning of jurors who shall exclude or fail to summon any citizen for the cause aforesaid shall, on conviction thereof, be deemed guilty of a misdemeanor, and be fined not more than five thousand dollars.

4. *And be It enacted,* That this act shall take effect immediately.
Approved May 10, 1884.

4   SCHOOL SEGREGATION OUTLAWED, 1884

On June 13, 1883 the Reverend Jeremiah H. Pierce went before the Supreme Court in Trenton to argue that his four children should be admitted to the segregated white schools in Burlington City. He based his case on New Jersey's 1881 school law and 1844 Constitution and desegregation precedents then being set around the nation. The court's decision in Pierce's favor marked one of the most important civil rights gains in the state's history, although its impact on racial segregation in public education was not immediate. The Supreme Court's decision of February 21, 1884 held that the denial of admission to Pierce's children was in violation of the New Jersey School Law of 1881. Like the 1884 Civil Rights Act, the effect of the Pierce decision was weakened by the prevailing racial customs and by the failure of public officials to enforce the law. Many school districts in the southern part of the state continued to practice segregation in classrooms and teacher assignments until the 1940s. Burlington maintained a separate school for blacks until 1948.

Jeremiah H. Pierce, *A Brief Statement of the Public School Contest . . . Together With a Brief of the Relator's Early Life and Experience* (Philadelphia, 1884), pp. i-iv, 28-31.

We desire in this little brief to give to the public the benefit of reading some of our efforts in behalf of the despised race of people in New Jersey.

I was born in the township of Bridgeton, in the county of Cumberland, and state above named. My parents were of pious principles, and done their part in training their children in the way they should go (whether the training has been well followed or not), and, being engaged in the business of farming, there was always something to employ our time, and the principles in industry, self-respect and general economy were always set before us. After I had finished my time with my parents, I then started to go through for myself on my own responsibility, and started out on the principle that I would give to every man his due as far as able, and also demand the same in return as far as was consistent.

The first ten years of my married life were nearly all spent in the business of farming, but at length I saw that there was some special work that demanded my attention in the interest of humanity, and I felt resolved to leave all and follow the impression that was made on my mind.

Though I had been engaged in the services of the Master for some years, yet I resolved to go in obedience to the call to lift up the fallen and care for the dying as far as was in my power so to do. Feeling an evidence of divine commission, I took with me the Law and the Gospel, with the object of administering to every one such things as would add to their benefit in any way possible, either morally, intellectually or civilly, temporally or spiritually. And, in order to be properly introduced to the work, I was received into the Philadelphia Annual Conference of the African M.E. Church on Monday, May 10th. 1875, in the city of Harrisburg, by Bishop James A. Shorter, and right then the Bishop asked me if I was prepared to go wherever I might be sent. My answer was that I wished to keep within the reach of good schools, and the consolation from the Bishop was: "There will not be much trouble about that, for public school houses are quite numerous almost everywhere now-a-days." And, of course, I thought they were for the benefit of my children as well as any one else.

I was then transferred to the New Jersey Conference, and appointed to Milford circuit, but did not take my family that year from their former home, but the following year I was appointed to Elizabeth station, and then I moved my family to that city and found, so far as the white friends were concerned, everything was all right; first class schools and free access regardless of color, just as it is in all the well-arranged and most enterprising cities of the state. But when I left there I returned my family back to their former home, where I should have said before a mixed school existed.

I was next appointed to the Yorktown circuit, but did not take my family with me the first year, but on my second appointment to that charge I moved my family into the village of Woodstown, Salem county, and so marvelous was the circumstance that we were published in the papers as being the first colored family that had ever lived in said town; but nevertheless we were there, and found many warm-hearted white friends in that town who dared to be friends.

On moving to that town I was asked by my own people where I expected to send my children to school. My answer was positive: "I will send them to the public school in the town wherever I reside." I saw they doubted, but time proved the fact.

On making application, some of the trustees attempted to insult and bluff me off, but when they saw that I meant business, they were wise enough to step aside and let me pass, and yet did obstruct the rights of other children for some time, but the time came at length when they yielded, and I am told that all races can mix in said school now. And though my children were the first black spots in that school, to the credit of the teachers in Woodstown I can say much pain was taken with them, and they learned very fast.

On leaving Woodstown I moved to Allentown, N.J. There we had no difficulty, because the people of that vicinity had before I reached there concluded to be loyal, and to acknowledge a man to be a man, and to care for humanity generally. We remained in that peaceful village for three years, and then left many warm-hearted friends, regardless of color or condition. To be friendly was their aim.

Next, at the annual conference convened at Bridgeton, in April, 1883, I was appointed to Burlington station, and after taking charge, as soon as was convenient I moved my family into said city and located at 136 East Pearl Street, which brought us up to the 10th of May, and, strange to say, before we got our goods in the house the principal of the public school was there numbering the children.

After getting a little settled in our new home, I then went to one trustee and asked for a permit to enter my children into school, and, without asking any questions as to how many children or what their grade was, he soon had a single permit written. I then inquired what school he was directing me to, and was informed that there was but one school in Burlington where colored children could go, and that was especially set apart for them; the rest were all for white children, and, it being against the rules to permit colored children to enter said schools, he was not disposed to break the rule.

"I suppose if my children were white you would give me permits and at once?"

"O, yes," was the reply; "but as it is I cannot. I admit that it is your right if you choose to contend for it, but I think you will have some trouble before you succeed."

I then called on another. He expressed his willingness, but realized that he would be alone in the effort. I then called on the third, and he could not seem to realize that I belonged to the human race, and positively declared that no colored child would ever get into the white schools in Burlington by his vote, and, further, that he would be very sorry to see the day when colored children can go to school with the white in this city, "for," said he "I have a little boy of my own that I shall want to send to school some of these days, and should be very sorry to have him go with colored children. I am a good Republican, too," was his remark; but he is a real estate agent—more proper, his name is Joshua Taylor. I expressed my opinion to the gentleman quite freely, and then left. I then wrote an application to the trustee board, and placed it in the hands of one of its members to be presented to the board, which was done, and yet it was treated with silent contempt. At length I went to seek legal advice, and the first counselor that I called upon was Mr. A. S. Appelget, of Hightstown. I related to him the circumstances, and told him that I wanted a lawyer who was both able and willing to handle the case. Mr. Appelget was not inclined to boast of his ability, but assured me that so far as the will was concerned he was the man I was looking for; and, therefore, in view of his former success (for I had some knowledge of his ability), together with the assurance he gave me, I resolved to engage his services in the present case,—and that he did his part nobly and proved his will and ability by going straight forward with the matter may be seen by the dates of the procedure and the arguments in the case, as did also the court before whom he presented the case.

Mr. Appelget is a lawyer who can be trusted by his client every time with perfect safety, and what he says may be relied upon and promptly performed, and in this very act he should never be forgotten by the people whom he so nobly defended in their public rights. I mean especially the people of color, and the particulars of the same will be learned by carefully reading this little book further on.

Now, while I have been taking this course through the country from place to place, there have been various opinions and expressions about the matter. Some have been favorable to ostracism, could they have had their way. Some have taken the chance to try and make the impression that it was because of self-exultation that led me thus to act, because I felt myself to be superior to my race of people, and that I thought more of my children. I will admit that I think too much of my children to sacrifice them to the diabolical wishes of ungodly and inhuman characters. And, regardless of frowns or smiles, I am responsible for their training in early life. But while this is a fact, it is also true as stated in the beginning that I have a general interest in the defence of my race, and, had I no children of my own, I would take the same stand against this color line, for with me color is nothing, but quality is a great deal, and cultivation improves the quality in man, beast or vegetation. And to enable us to get at that, the laws of this country have been made plain to defend every citizen in his rights, but for want of moral courage, O how many fall back and allow themselves to be deprived of that which would do them good and add greatly to their comfort—I mean their God-given rights. But, thanks be to God that all men are not alike; we have a few who have become fools that wisdom may spring up.

And now, as may be seen in this little volume, what is decided by law for one, becomes law for all, so far as civil rights are concerned. And as I have connected in this book some articles that have been written in the papers by myself and others, I need not proceed to repeat my sentiments in full again, but will say that hope and trust that by the time this difficulty is finally settled, all men will know me well enough to allow me to enjoy my civil rights in this free country, and then we will go on peacefully.

I do not feel to boast of anything, for I have only done my duty through God's help, and what I have is the favor of the Lord. And though some of my people throughout the state may not appreciate the course taken, yet it is nevertheless true that it is to their best interest to mix the schools, and give their little ones a fair education, as that exceeds all other favors we can do for our children.

I would furthermore say that all ministers and teachers, in my opinion, ought to do their part in leading the less-enlightened people onward in the road to success, and though sometimes the clouds may seem thick and heavy, "go through" is my motto; and if an institution or organization is not established on the right basis, go at it, make or break.

We must make sacrifices for the interest of our fellows, and now my prayer is that our people throughout the whole world, as far as this volume may be extended and read, will resolve to be united in one another's interest, and help to build each other up, and in so doing we shall rise above all the opposing powers, and be a people in deed in truth.

Yours, very respectfully, for the cause of humanity,

REV. J.H. PIERCE.

Burlington, N.J., March 17th, 1884.

NEW JERSEY SUPREME COURT, February Term, 1884.

State
    Ex rel.   *Jeremiah H. Pierce*
                      vs.   *Mandamus.*
        The Union District Trustees.

The supplement to "An Act to establish a system of public instruction," approved March 23, 1881 (P.L. 1881 p. 186) makes it unlawful for school trustees to exclude children from any public school on the ground that they are of the negro race.

On rule to show cause why a mandamus should not issue commanding the respondents, the trustees of public school in the city of Burlington, to meet together and by resolution order, direct and instruct the teachers of the several public schools in said city to receive Gertrude Pierce, Rufus Pierce, Gilbert A. Pierce and Hannah Pierce, children of the relator, into said schools for the purposes of instruction, without any denial or abridgement of their rights and privileges on account of race or color, and subject only to such legal restrictions and requirements as all other persons, over five and under eighteen years of age, residing within said city, are required to conform to, pupils attending said schools.

Argued November Term 1883 before Justices Knapp, Magie and Dixon.

Mr. A.S. Appelget, for relator.
Mr. M.H. Stratton, for respondents.

The opinion of the Court was delivered by Nixon, J. The relator is a citizen of New Jersey, and since the tenth day of May last has resided with his wife and children in the city of Burlington. Four of his children named in the rule are within the school age, and were included in the census of school children in said city taken last May according to law. On May 23 last the relator applied to the respondents for the admission of each of these children into one of the two public schools nearest his residence, and, they having refused to grant the requisite permits, each of the children sought admission directly from the principles of these schools, which was likewise refused. Thereupon the relator, on behalf of himself and his children, instituted these proceedings to enforce their right.

The Constitution of the State (Art. IV. Sec. VII, paragraph 6) declares that the legislature shall provide for the maintenance and support of a thorough and efficient system of free public schools for the instruction of all the children in the state between the ages of five and eighteen years. Our school law (Rev. p. 1070, Sec. 94) provides that all public schools in this State shall be free to all persons over five and under eighteen years of age residing within the school district. The city of Burlington contains four public schools, but constitute a single school district under the government of the respondents. Hence there can be no doubt of the legal right of those children to enter one of those schools for free instruction. So, too, I think it is equally clear that the respondents may make reasonable by-laws, not incompatible with the laws of the United States or of this state (P.L. 1848, p. 10) and not in conflict with the general regulations of the State Board of Education (Rev. p. 1076, Sec. 39) for determining into which of the schools these children shall be admitted. But by the case laid before us, it does not appear that any by-law was referred to or any reason given as warranting the refusal to receive these children when they asked admission into the schools specified, nor now is any such rule or reason shown except one which will presently be noticed. Under these circumstances it was not necessary that application should be made unsuccessfully at every public school in the city, before it could become evident that the legal rights of the relator were infringed. Such a requirement enforced in our large cities would entail very great inconvenience upon private citizens without any corresponding advantage. The relator was, I think, entitled to have his children educated in the public school nearest his residence, unless there was some just reason for sending them elsewhere.

The ground of their exclusion in the present instance is manifested by the state of the case agreed upon under the rule to show cause. Of the four public schools in Burlington, one is for colored children, and three are exclusively for white children; and it was into schools of the latter sort that the relator's children sought entrance. He is a mulatto, and therefore his children were excluded. Is exclusion upon that ground permissable?

We need not consider this question in the broad aspects presented by counsel. The power of the legislature to enact the law which has been promulgated on the subject is indubitable, and the law itself is unmistakably explicit. It is "that no child between the age of five and eighteen years of age, shall be excluded from any public school in this state on account of his or her religion, nationality or color." (P.L. 1881, p. 186). This statute made the respondents' refusal illegal.

Counsel for the respondents contend that it does not appear but what the refusal may have been founded on the fact that the schools selected by the relator were full of the grade of instruction there such as his children were incapable of. No doubt, a refusal so supported would be legal; but no such ground can be discovered in the evidence. *Prima facie* the children were entitled to admission, and according to the proof their exclusion was because the relator was a mulatto, or it was without any reason at all. In either case it was unlawful.

Counsel further urges that, since under the rule of the trustees an Italian (for example) as dark as the relator's children would have been admitted, the exclusion was therefore owing not to "color," but to race, which the status does not prohibit. But I think the term "color" as applied to persons in this country has had too distinct a history to leave possible such an interpretation of the law. Both in the statute and in the regulations of the respondents persons of color are persons of the negro race.

The rule to show cause should be made absolute and a peremptory mandamus be awarded.

---

5   DR. JAMES STILL ADVISES HIS PEOPLE, 1877

Dr. James Still (1812–85), the older brother of the famous abolitionist William Still (1821–1902) of Philadelphia, was a practitioner of folk remedies, rather than a formally educated physician. Through personal sacrifice and his close association with whites in the pinelands of Burlington County, he rose from the poverty of his slave parentage to become one of the most celebrated black men in nineteenth-century New Jersey. In 1877, James Still published his autobiography, from which the following chapter is taken. The most striking feature of his advice to blacks is its similarity to the philosophy of Booker T. Washington. Nearly twenty years before Washington was to deliver his Atlanta Address, Still urged the race to adopt the Protestant work ethic and criticized blacks for their shortcomings. These concerns would later become associated with the Tuskegeean. Dr. Still also expressed support for black economic development and displayed a suspicion that city life adversely affected the race. Yet, there were differences between the two leaders. Washington accepted racial segregation in education, but Still argued that it was contrary to the best interests of both races.

Early Recollections and Life of Dr. James Still
(Philadelphia, 1877), pp. 228-41.

It has long been my opinion that the colored people as a race have much to blame in themselves for their present condition.

True, we have been in bondage all or most of our lives, and thus shut out from advantages social and educational. Of the few who were redeemed years ago by the great labor and personal sacrifice, and sometimes at the cost of human life, only a part of them appreciate their altered condition. Some have made their freedom a by-word and a jest.

The race is too much addicted to indolence and self-pride. Each would like to be the leader or orator of the race. They would like to occupy positions of ease, but are unwilling to pursue the path of labor, which only brings peace, and comfort, and success. They are too much delighted with parties, festivals, and all places of amusement, from which they reap no reward. The husbands love personal comfort, and are outraged if wives are not general attendants at washing-places during the week. They think it too much to maintain a wife at home, or to hold sacred any obligation to children, and hold that they can break the conjugal or parental relation at will.

Many of these are church members, and seemingly happy in their way of devotion. They hold long meetings, make long prayers, and use odd gestures, enter the meeting at any time during service, and go out at will. Christ denounced such worship as this, as did he also inculcate truth. Punctuality is a part of sincere worship, yet this is a great fault among colored people. The hour appointed for worship is the hour to be there, but they manifest great carelessness with regard to their word, and continue to come in from the beginning to the end of the meeting. Perhaps they will be accountable for untruthfulness.

There is also much said by our people about the prejudice between the two races. I admit there is too much; but how can it be otherwise than manifested when a white and colored man meet each other and both are full of prejudice against each other? Therefore it is hard to tell which has the most. But when white and colored Christians meet in the true freedom of their Lord there is no prejudice, for all things have become new.

My colored friends, should you conduct yourselves on true moral principles, not gaudy in manners nor boisterous in talk, your ways calm and decisive, your word so sacred that 'tis never violated, your promises fulfilled, your debts paid, modest in all things and meddlesome in none, you shall find the monster Prejudice only a thing to be talked about. Merit alone will promote you to respect. You will also see the prejudice between the whites of the higher and lower classes. It is not expected that the rich and refined should mingle with the poor and low. It is no matter what color they are, my experience for the last thirty years is that man is man according to merit. Where truth and prosperity are in the ascending, prejudice is in the descending, scale. Many a colored man supposes, and so does many a white one, that when he is making money his neighbors will estimate him by the show he makes. He does not seem to understand that humility should dwell with frailty, and atone for ignorance, error, and imperfection. In all my practice I have ever found that prejudice would skulk when confronted by common sense. I cannot see but that I have had a full share of practice. I have been treated with all due respect. Every color and class has its preferences, for reasons inherent in one's very being; to account for certain predilections would be simply impossible.

Thus we see also among the learned and great men as a proof, say, there is to be a man elected to some high office of the State or nation. He is not run singly, but with opposition. Two are nominated, all things con-

sidered, of equal ability. Their propensities for good or bad are proclaimed aloud. Persons are prejudiced on both sides. Some choose one
and some the other, and the two parties become regular combatants.
Money on each side is freely lavished, even though those who lavish it
will only be the losers. Here we see prejudice in its might with no good
reason therefor. One or the other must win the race. There is a prejudice
used for an accommodation between white and colored people; for instance, a white and a colored person are ever so familiar for a long time,
they eat and drink with each other, they share each other's pleasures,
what belongs to one is common stock to both, they could not enjoy each
other more were they of the same color.

Peradventure, each one's business calls him from home to the same
place. Then they meet numerous people from different sections. The
white and the colored meet each other. They are not the same jovial
friends that they were at home. The white man will give his colored
friend an askance look by way of recognition and to show the company
that he holds himself higher than a colored man. They both feel the sting,
but this is prejudice for accommodation.

Perhaps we, the colored people, are somewhat to blame for this treatment. Let us ask ourselves why it is so. The answer is, we are not
possessors of lands and stocks, etc. We have been content to be waiters
and coachmen, and would be happy to sit down in our leisure moments
and tell about the fine coach and horses committed to our charge. This
we could do with considerable flourish, and with as much pride as
though they were ours. This did not require much manual labor, of
which we never were fond.

Cities have been the places of our choice. It is dignifying to be called a
citizen, and sight-seeing was a great thing to us. Besides, if a man lived in
the country and labored in the fields, he was not considered sane, even
though he possessed more than twenty citizens of the colored race. I am
sorry that this state of things exists. It is nevertheless true, and all complain of prejudice and hard times. It is what they have worked for, and
they are now receiving their pay, richly but reluctantly.

To every colored man who wishes to rise, to kill a prejudice that rests
in his path, I say leave the city and go to the country, where land is
cheap; purchase what you can and go to work; raise your own bread and
butter; be frugal; bring up your children yourselves, and teach them to
labor; teach them that the farmer holds the keys of the storehouses of the
nations. Through them comes the staff of life; through them merchants
live and indolent gentlemen loll at jovial boards. Men of equal ability are
just the same as two ten-pound weights; one placed in a balance cannot
weigh the other down, as there will be no choice, for there will be ten
pounds on each side. It is ten pounds and no more.

As I write, a colored man steps into my office. After the common salu-
tation, I remark, "I have not seen you for a long time; where have you
been?" "Well, I was at a watering-place all summer, and after that went

to wait upon a doctor." "Were wages good?" I asked. "No; nothing." "You did not work for nothing, did you?" "As good as nothing," he replied; "only twelve dollars per month." "But that is better than nothing; your work was not heavy and your board was included."

"Oh, I had rather beg than work at that price!" he said. "My wife was there too, and she got only two dollars per week."

"You must consider that these are hard times," I argued. "If you and your wife had continued for four months you would have had eighty dollars coming to you, beside your board, fuel, and rent. I consider that would have been quite an item in these times."

"Oh, there's plenty of money in the country, but they do not want to pay a man for his labor."

"Well, I admit there is plenty of money in the hands of those who have saved it, but there is nothing doing to cause it to circulate. When I was a young man, we thought eight or ten dollars a month good wages for men, and seventy-five cents a week good wages for women, and all seemed satisfied."

"Yes, but everything was lower than," he continued.

"Yes," said I, "and persons not so vain and foolish. I think the colored people much at fault for living as they do. If they would leave the towns and move into the forest, where land is cheap, buy, and go to work and raise their living and become landholders, how much better it would show for them."

He admitted this, but added that the wives of colored men were too proud for that.

I then told him of a man who came from the old country, who told me that on arriving at Burlington, New Jersey, he had but six cents, and that he gave for a glass of whiskey, and that he knew another who had done the same thing, and was now owner of two or three farms.

"I am sorry," I said, "that the colored people want their good things as they go along, and rags and poverty in their old age. As to begging or stealing, I should be ashamed. I do not think there is much honor in either, even in old age, if one has had his health in his young days."

I have always been opposed to separate colored churches and schools, for several reasons. "God is love," and we are commanded to love one another, "not as Cain, who was of the wicked one." Also, "Whosoever hateth his brother is a murderer." Further, "Beloved, let us love one another, for love is to God." "If God so loved us, we ought also to love one another." "He that dwelleth in love, dwelleth in God and God in him." "There is no fear in love, but perfect love casteth out fear, because fear hath torment." "He that feareth is not made perfect in love." "Whosoever believeth that Jesus is the Christ is born of God, and every one that loveth Him that begat, loveth Him also that is begotten of Him."

I am not able to understand how we are to be the possessors of these beatifical blessings, and at the same time entertain in our hearts a malignity which forbids us to worship together the Holy God of love. I have always believed the separation of the churches a trick of the devil to keep open the chasm between Christians, into which I fear many shall fall and be lost to all eternity. I believe Christianity would have been far advanced to-day had not the churches separated. When an army goes into the field to fight its enemy it were best to confront it with a whole army, and confide for succor in the chief commander, God. I do not think that it was intended by the Almighty that separate worship and separate heavens were for the different colors of mankind. Unity of worship would have promoted morality, sociableness, and helped to break down the middle wall of existing prejudice. It would clearly have demonstrated to the world that we were sons of God, because we lived together in love.

I think it would have been an advantage to my own race, by making us more guarded in expression, and saved us from the ridicule which sometimes we receive justly for eccentricities in worship. I have myself been caused to laugh at the sermons delivered by colored preachers; at the same time, they were a shame to the Christianity in both the white and the colored races.

But some of my colored friends will say, "If we had not withdrawn from the white congregations we would have had no liberties in the church, we could not have become preachers and leaders." To any friend who may entertain this sentiment, I say, "If you were called of God to preach or to lead, if God had a message to deliver to the world through you, not all the powers of darkness could have prevailed against you." "If God be for us, who shall be against us?" He is more than all that could be against us. "But we have to take back seats," one says. If you are one of God's soldiers one would be able to chase a thousand, and two to put ten thousand to flight. "When we get happy, we cannot shout," some one else will say; "the white members look upon us frowningly." Perhaps the white brethren are like myself, in that I was looking to see their light shining daily. They look for truth, continency, love of virtue, all of which if we practice we shall do well.

I think every person should read Christ's Sermon on the Mount for instruction. There the Lord says that we should not be as the hypocrites, who love to pray standing in the synagogues and in the corners of the streets that they may be seen of men, but He recommends closet prayer as that which shall bring the open reward. And says again, that except your righteousness shall exceed the righteousness of the scribes and Pharisees, ye shall in no case enter into the kingdom of heaven.

I do not know from whom we could have received better instruction. Again, by separation we become strangers to each other, white and colored, and when we meet it is in that inimical manner in which we are more like heathens than like Christian friends, thus making the moments when we are together tedious and barren. This exhibition is at once a strong blow against Christianity before a sinful world of mankind.

I have been opposed to colored schools wholly because they were against the principles of Christian fellowship. I think that co-education would be beneficial to each race. First, it would establish Christian unity. It would elevate the colored race by a sort of refinement in their expression. It would make them believe that they were a part and parcel of mankind. It would arouse in them the desire to be cleanly and as refined as their class-mates. It would stimulate them to love education, and to appreciate it. It would dispel that horrible idea that they were esteemed nothing above the beast. It would make them feel justice to be a reality and not a sham.

Separate schools are debasing to the manners of each, whilst it causes the one to imbibe imbecility and the other superiority, thus fixing a great gulf between them, which shall be impassable. It plants the seed of hate in their youthful hearts, and there it is watered from the streams of strife until it becomes so deeply rooted that it grows to a large tree, whose branches spread over the whole land and become the habitation of every unclean and hateful bird, and its fruit is poisonous to the nation. Separation causes in the colored child hate, and unbecoming behavior, and habitual idleness with indelible slovenliness; for all of which, I fear, a Christian republic will have to render an account.

I have sometimes thought it strange that Christians in our enlightened land manifest such zeal for the poor heathen of other lands as to send ministers and money for their civilization, when at their own doors thousands are compelled to wallow all their days, from the cradle to the grave, among the most dispiteous of mankind, and are the recipients of cold rebuke from those they have known all their lives. I can only say, with Jefferson, that I tremble for my country when I reflect that God is just, and that his justice cannot sleep forever.

It seems to me that unity and hate are a part of Christian civilization, because it is taught to the little children in the schools that to do justice and righteousness to the colored children is a flagrant wrong. Thus it becomes a part of their early education. I am sorry to say that such are the facts with few exceptions, and the more the shame to Christendom . . . .

6   EDUCATION AND ECONOMIC ADVANCEMENT, 1887

The Reverend Junius C. Ayler of Princeton called the following address "a stepping stone to Negro development and race recognition." It was included in a book of lectures he published in 1887 at a time when the prevailing theories of race and civilizations claimed that blacks were inferior to Anglo-Saxons. Such an argument tended to rationalize the debasement of blacks in Western societies, particularly the United States and Great Britain, which were becoming interested in imperial conquests of non-white populations. Ayler, in addition to his religious duties, was an etymologist and the editor and publisher of the *Trumpet* (1888–95), a weekly newspaper in Princeton. In this lecture he attempted to show that blacks were not innately inferior. He argued that the race's lowly condition resulted from slavery and the ignorance and poverty which the institution imposed upon blacks. Ayler was concerned with the proper name for blacks. He claimed that they were Negroes, with emphasis on the capital "N." During this period, and for many years thereafter, Negro Americans were not accorded this sign of dignity. Ayler, like Booker T. Washington and other race leaders, also urged blacks to acquire education and accumulate capital.

Junius C. Ayler, "Solution of the Negro Problem," *Guide Lights. Lectures* (Princeton, N.J., 1887), pp. 20-32.

An attempt to solve the Negro Problem may be regarded by some as a conceited effort. But conceit is an evidence of genious. Furthermore, the idea of conceit cannot reasonably enter into an attempt to solve the solvable, but only into an irrational effort to solve the insolvable. The former would be sense, the latter nonsense. The very term Problem implies, not a profound enigma, but a solution; the former draws out the uninspired imaginative powers of the mind, while the latter calls for mathematical and scientific rules, as well as logical deductions.

The frequent discussions and elaborate newspaper articles on the Negro Problem have probably led thousands to regard it as a subject of mysticism. But not so. The Negro Problem is a race question for solution. It is not only a question for solution but it is time that some energetic mind, guided by the light of reason, had performed the task. The first question to be answered bearing on this subject is the

RACE NAME.

What is our name? Are we Negroes or colored people? On one hand I hear a thousand answers coming from east, west, north and south: *"We are colored people, we are not Negroes."* On the other hand I hear a few thinkers answer in rather a feeble tone, "we are negroes." The latter are right, but not right enough, because they are weak on the idea, and spell it with a small "n." From another quarter I hear a few men of fine sense, fertile brain, and race pride, say in a strong tone of voice, "we are Negroes." They are more right, in fact, they are absolutely right, because they spell it with a capital "N." The term Negro is a race title, and therefore good sense; while the word colored as applied to us is a sham title, and therefore nonsense. The former is linguistic, and will stand the fiery test of etymological criticism; Negro coming either directly from the Latin *niger,* or indirectly through a Spanish word having the same meaning, both signifying *black.* The word color, the sham-title, is of an artificial signification, which implies on application a change in our inherent nature. *Objection:* But you said the word colored is nonsense. Yes, because it is in the first place non-linguistic—it is not bad language, but no language. Secondly, it does not apply to us. While it does apply to men, it does not apply to us exceptionally to all other men.

When we speak of races of men from a standpoint of color, Thompson says, "there are five: the White, the Yellow, the Brown, the Red, and the Black." The term Black is last not because it is least, but because it is strongest in composition; it is in this connection synonymous with the term Negro, hence, you see, if the term colored (for it is a term in this connection) is generic in its racial signification, it can not be applied to us. It is not a distinctive term.

But you are proving to us to be Black, says one. Yes, that is my aim. Black is our original color, hence, the divine color, in application to our race; if divine, then providential; while the variations are purely accidental by being in this country. We were black when we were brought to this country, and *ought* to be now; but we have been changed somewhat by an illegal and non-ethical accident.

Prove that we were originally black, says one. While the word Ham in the Hebrew signifies hot, Plutarch discovered in the Coptic tongue the idea of blackness as well. While I have endeavored to prove that we are or ought to be black, my chief aim is to prove that we are Negroes.

While the color has accidentally changed, the name Negro has not; for the term *niger,* which signifies black, existed prior to its meaning. The term Negro is the term for me, and for every other Africo-American. Let us stick to the name and make it what it *ought to be,* by rejecting the slang use of it.

The name is absolutely pure in the abstract, but like the music of a violin in a Christian church, makes the old veterans disgusted; not because of immortality in the instrument, or in the performer, but because of its association. The slang use of the term Negro has almost embittered many of us against our own name. Let me say to "my brother in black," stand by your name. It sounds badly for one to disown his name. Having chalked out the color line, I secondly call attention to *the true cause of existing prejudice against the Negro.*

The first important question that presents itself to my mind is, does prejudice exist against us as a race?

That the finger of Prejudice points at the Negro throughout the South, and in the North more or less, is evident. It is admitted by the white man and known by the Negro. But the true cause of this prejudice is a question upon which much has been said—some tracing it to color, and others to condition. While I do not wish to be dogmatic in reference to a question of such vital import, and upon which such able men have written and spoken *pro* and *con,* yet, I say (with some degree of reverence) that the cause of the existing prejudice against us as a race is not color, in the popular sense, but condition. I do not say this to open a field for discussion, nor to make any anthropological display, but from solid conviction, and an honest heart, to correct in the minds of some what I claim to be an error.

To establish the affirmative I proceed negatively to show *(a) that it is not color.* How long has prejudice existed against the Negro? While others may think differently, it doutless co-existed *ab initio* with Slavery. Then if it began with slavery, it seems almost self-evident that Slavery is the cause, not color.

The Negro was disrecognized when he was subordinated, enslaved and made property by a law that was both non-ethical and inequitable. If prejudice began with slavery, there were thousands of years (between the origin of Negro Color and that of Negro Slavery), when prejudice did not exist.

If color be the cause, why not the cause during those centuries?

That we are Hamitic in stock, no anthropologist will deny, and that Ham was a black man no one will deny but he who favors discussion. Yet he was not disrespected because of his color. Furthermore, we are told by the ethnologist of the A.M.E. Church that three distinct colors were in the Ark; Red, White and Black—Martin R. Delaney.

(b) *If color is the cause of prejudice, why not exist against other races of a dark hue?* Why not exist against the Indian from a racial standpoint? Why not against the Australian, or the Hottentot, with their various tints, deep hues and dark shades of color, each falling below the white?

Admitting (for argument's sake) that we are the blackest of races, and that blackness is the cause of prejudice, why does not prejudice exist against the above named races in proportion to their color? If color in the superlative is the cause of prejudice in the superlative, why not color in the comparative be the cause of prejudice in the comparative? Yes, but it is not so; every tint, hue, shade and color are held in a higher scale socially, legally, politically, and even religiously, than the Negro; hence, as a race, other colored people are recognized as men *ought* to be and we are not; therefore color is not the cause.

If color were the cause, it would stand as a bar to the recognition extended to other races of similar color. Consequently color is not the mother of prejudice, but condition. As a matter of course we are not, or should not be held accountable for our condition, for we have in twenty-three years advanced a century. Nevertheless the condition exists. Those in whom is the spirit of caste, and from whom we receive the high hand of prejudice are at fault; as I heard a representative from the Theological Seminary of Alexandria, Va., say at Princeton to the Inter-Seminary

Alliance in 1885, "We are responsible for the condition of the colored man," true, for our condition was born of Slavery, out of which grew *(a) illiteracy.* I never shall forget a remark made at New Brunswick, N.J., by Rev. Henry Ward Beecher in his popular lecture entitled, "The Reign of the common people." He said, well might the Southern white man keep the Negro in ignorance, to educate him was to set him free. Any man will sprout if you give him a chance. I am not certain that I quote the Rev. Gentleman verbatim, but I do in substance. He simply meant to say to give the Negro a book was to give him a chance. Hence we see that illiteracy is the eldest son of slavery, the influence of which still impedes Negro progress, or in other words it serves as a check-rein to hold him back, but ere long with God in the front, an iron grip and rapid strides, we shall break through opposition, burst the check-rein asunder and go to the top of the intellectual mountain.

That education, is the first essential force that turns the great wheel of human success, no sane mind will deny, or that it is the data upon which other essentials rest.

Show me an educated people, irrespective of color, with other requisites and I will show you a people held in high distinction in the court, school and church. Hence I say *educate!* EDUCATE!! Not only one man out of ten, but six out of ten, then we can realize the beauty of the phrase, *vox populi, vox Dei.* Having considered the first, we pass on to the second son of slavery, *Poverty,* which is a necessary consequence of ignorance.

Show me a people senseless and I will show you a people moneyless—a people who don't know how to earn much money, don't know how to save it; don't know how to invest it. Therefore I urge and encourage the attainment of education, and the acquisition of capital co-ordinately by the Negro race.

The combination of the two will remove our condition—which is to remove the cause of existing prejudice. When we become able to run our own factories, steam and sail ships, and become sharers in railroad companies, (which will doubtless in time take place,) prejudice will actually pass away—and color practically will not be seen. And

3rd, In further proof of our argument, let us compare (our) the prejudice of to-day (1887) with that of the emancipation (1863). Is prejudice as evident now as then? Why no; a blind man can't see, but he can realize the difference. Whereas the Negro was set free penniless and ignorant, (which was his condition) with the keen blade of prejudice ready to cut him down, (which was the result of slavery), he is now a citizen, and in accordance with the progress made in intellectual development and acquisition of property, he is a farmer, a mechanic, a merchant, a preacher, a teacher, a lawyer, and a physician. Why all this change? Our color has not changed. We are just as black to-day as when emancipated, and consequently we can very readily see that a change of condition (not color) has broken down to some extent the high hand of prejudice.

4th. *We notice probable objections.* To prove that color is the cause of prejudice against the Negro, some men of color have been rejected, who compared favorably in both brain and means, *e.g.,* Bishops Campbell and Payne,[1] not long since were ejected from trains in Southern states. *Reply;* this objection is rather difficult to meet. Permit me to say that color is not the real cause of the outrages perpetrated upon these men; but let us look beneath the surface. They represent a race that have been, and are to some extent in unfavorable circumstances, and it is from the representative standpoint that I speak.

It requires a majority to rule—hence educate and finance six men of our race out of ten, instead of four out of ten, and we will see a difference—an advance to the astonishment of friend and foe. No. It is not color, but the colored man, who is in a certain condition, and is known by his color to belong to that people who have been humiliated. Not only known by his color, but is also known to have not as yet been thoroughly redeemed or redeemed himself from that condition. Why are not the Negro scholar and the Negro capitalist more generally recognized? Why because he is indirectly and unintentionally held back by the majority of his race who have not had the privilege of drinking from the fountain of learning, and of unlocking the chest of wealth.

As a part of, and friend to my race, let me tell you as there is no "royal road to learning," let us not stop to pick flowers by the way, but "go hunting with books."

5th. *The immovableness of color.* It is evident that if color is the cause of this prejudice, we are in a terrible fix, and in a hopeless condition, for I am sure if color is the cause, the cause is immovable—hence our destiny is fixed, our attempted progress a farce, and the highest standard of social, political and legal recognition is reached, which is a very sad thought, but I thank God that no such immovable and unchangeable thing as color is the cause of disrecognition—while our condition is unfavorable it is hopeful, for our future is bright. Negro progress is not only evident on the golden shores of America, the land of the free, and the home of the brave, but in Africa, the land of Ham, celebrated for her antiquity, science and architecture, though for centuries shrouded in superstition and idolatry, is to-day represented as the rising star—by way of the Congo the light of the Gospel is breaking through the outskirts, finding its way into the interior.

An objector may produce the theory that we are returning gradually to the original Adamite color. I say theory, because that is all it is; and admitting its possibility, (for it is not probable) it is an exceedingly slow process of attaining recognition, for we are turning white very slowly. I doubt the probability of this theory on Scriptural grounds. In the language of Jeremiah I ask, "Can the Ehtiopian change his skin, or the leopard his spots?" The inference drawn from this question is negative. That is, the development of the Ethiopian skin into red, or the leopard-spots into some other hue, is very improbable if not impossible. Without dwelling on details, I say it is clear to every logical mind, that if color is the cause of prejudice our limits in that respect are fixed, as is seen by the above passage.

He who holds that color is the cause, looks on the dark side of the picture *(a)* for it is poor argument to hold up to the children. They would naturally ask is my color changeable, which question demands a negative answer. Well then we might as well stop, for we can only develop into recognition as fast as we turn white, which is not at all. Hence the children are led by this kind of talk into despondency.

(b) It is poor argument to meet our enemies with. To tell them when they insult us by ejecting us from first-class rail road coaches, with first-class tickets in our hand or hat, by refusing us admission into hotels, etc., that you do this because I am *black,* is poor argument I think. This kind of talk throws the burden of censure on a very different Being from those committing the outrage, whereas it would be far stronger argument to say to them 'You maltreat me on account of race-condition, and you are the cause of that condition—subject me to slavery, ignorance and poverty, and then maltreat me, and disrecognize my manhood for it,' an argument that our opponents cannot meet. But in conclusion.

Let us aim at the right mark—condition—not color. Let us make rapid strides to remove the real cause of caste, not so much by thundering from a political rostrum into the ears of uncultured people, as by intellectual development, and money-making and money-saving.

Money and brain are recognized by both Church and State, especially in the latter, for in the White-House money is demanded to turn the great political wheel, and the educated man is the one who manipulates, regulates and shapes our government. Thus we might come from the White-House down to municipal wire-pulling. Hence I say *educate, educate, make money, make money.* Send the Negro into science, art, and literature. Literature of the best sort. Literature that will impregnate his mind with beautiful gems of thought. Send him into languages, tongues, mathematics, trades and business, and hypothetically speaking black men will turn white, kinky hair will become straight. Men will be known by their manhood, and not by their color. What will education do for a people, for a nation? What has it done for Japan? Why the introduction of common schools opened up the way for church and pulpit. Japan has a territory of 170,000 square miles, with 40,000,000 of inhabitants, who were hood-winked by the blackness of heathenism, and held down by the intrigues of other anti-christians, but when the day broke and the light of intelligence burst forth with sacred dawn therein, it was a sunlight rising in a "Sun-rise-Kingdom," or a little bird floating in the breeze singing the sweet song educate! educate!! carrying the sacred gems of christianity, and the pearl of great price under her wings. Hence the utility of the common school. It was to christianity what John was to

Christ—opening up the way—working out a change of thought and speech—actuating Japanese to lean on the bosom of Christ, and to be fostered by the Church.

----

1. African Methodist Episcopal Bishops Jabez P. Campbell and Daniel A. Payne.

7   BLACK SELF-RELIANCE, ca. 1900

In asking his brethren to "depend more upon our own strong arms, our own common sense and exertions to change conditions, North as well as South, that hamper and militate against us," Reverend A. P. Miller, pastor of St. Mark's African Methodist Episcopal Zion Church in Jersey City, enunciated the doctrine of black self-reliance around the turn of the century. Miller's views coincided with the philosophy of Booker T. Washington, the period's most influential black leader. Like the Tuskegeean, Miller asserted that ignorance was the greatest burden of his people, and he advised blacks to develop themselves morally. The principal difference between the two men was in their view of the political status of the race. Washington's public statements belittled the importance of the vote for southern blacks. As an Afro-American leader in New Jersey, Miller realized that the intelligent use of the vote was essential to group progress. He claimed that blacks, in their subservience to the Republican Party, were responsible for their own political impotence, a view which was shared by other black leaders in the North.

Rev. A. P. Miller, "Internal Burdens Which We as a Race Must Throw Off," *Black Man's Burdens or the Two Sides of The Negro Problem* (Jersey City, 190- or 191-), pp. 9-15.

We have discussed, thus far, certain external conditions, not of our own creation, which have been our burdens as a race in the past in this country. Let us now turn our attention to internal conditions which we can and must master and throw off if we are ultimately to rise to a higher plane in the intellectual, industrial, moral, political, and religious world round about us.

We are living in an age that is intense, earnest, and aggressively materialistic, and we must keep up with the onmoving procession or be crowded out of the race. In this great struggle for the ascendency the weak and unenergetic go down, while the strong and persevering rush on and succeed. Here, in this great contest in the industrial world, the law of the survival of the fittest is the law of human action and conduct, and not the law of love. In this matter-of-fact world of ours, where sentiment counts for but little, energy, might, tact, and success are everything—an uncrowned king. The onlooking crowd applauds the man who succeeds, no matter what the color of his skin or his race identity.

We must accept things in this struggle as they really are. We must know our own shortcomings and weaknesses, burdens which encumber us which we are in a position to remove; for before we can rise, as a race, we must first realize that our future, our ultimate salvation, in our American industrial and political struggle, is in our own hands. This is the law of race as well as individual evolution, and from it there is no escape.

The first burden that greets us as we approach this problem is that of ignorance, growing out of the past, with its slave antecedents. As a people our progress during the past thirty-six years of freedom has been phenomenal, considering the obstacles from within as well as from without, and yet there are more ignorant colored people in this country to-day than there were in 1863, when we numbered only four million. The rank and file of our people, notwithstanding the grand work done by public and private schools and various other institutions established and maintained in the South for our education since the war, are, comparatively speaking, ignorant. This at present is our great burden, as ignorance is always at a disadvantage, no matter where and in whom found.

This to us is one of the unfortunate legacies of slavery, and we must get rid of it, as a class, else continue to march in the rear of America's progressive, ever-advancing column. It is said, "Time and tide wait for no man." Neither does civilization. It is our duty not only to get a common school education, but an academic, if possible, and we should keep ourselves generally informed as to the most important current movements of the day. We should keep abreast with the times, and as far as possible understand the most important events of the past and the imperative needs of the present. Such a class of persons, no matter what the color of their skin, with energy and tact, cannot long be considered an unimportant factor in the community, State, and nation.

What we most need, as a starter, is a more general intelligence amongst us—more culture. We need not only more knowledge of books, but also of men and affairs in general. In the business and industrial activities of the nation we are terribly hampered, as a race, not only by our ignorance, but also by a lack of energy and "stick-to-it-iveness." We tire too soon in the presence of difficulties, forgetting the old adage, "There is no royal road to success" or wealth.

In politics we are the slaves of a certain party whose policy is to keep us in line by calling our attention constantly to what the *grand old party* did for our race thirty-six years ago. Hence we slavishly hold on to an old shell year after year, while even janitorships, in many Northern States, held by colored men, are painfully few. And yet in Connecticut, New York, New Jersey, Rhode Island, and Massachusetts the black man holds the balance of power. What is it worth to him as a citizen and voter? Practically nothing. Who is to blame? Ourselves. Our ignorance, jealousies, and stupidity prevent our marshaling our forces so as to secure that political recognition which is our due as citizens and voters. We must educate ourselves in matters of diplomacy, in the use of the forces at our command, and find a way by which to get there, and thus, through the medium of politics, lift ourselves to a higher level in the State and nation. Here ignorance is the great burden that keeps us down. How long shall such be the case?

Slavery not only left us a legacy of ignorance, but also one of poverty. When a people are both ignorant and poor the struggle upward is doubly difficult, and progress made is painfully slow. Our lack of cash to insure us a place in the industrial and business world is not only a burden, but a source of weakness, and when we add to this *inexperience,* the rock upon which many a fortune has been hopelessly wrecked, we have the situation in a nutshell.

While many amongst us are meeting with a measurable degree of success in the securing of homes and launching out into independent enterprises, the masses are poor and shiftless, living a "from-pillar-to-post life." They huddle together in large centers, where work is scarce, rents are dear, though in inferior localities, which places become breeders of idleness, vice, and crime. Many who live in such places, in idleness and sin, do not want work, and yet they are not only one of the race's greatest burdens and drawbacks, but become a menace to society, the State, and nation.

More of us, as laborers, should seek employment and homes in the country, where opportunities are presented not only for the acquiring of good, industrious habits, but also to save our money, purchase small country homesteads, and thus become, in families, potent factors in the body politic. Thousands of Northern farmers would gladly employ colored help, and here we have an opening for that vast idle, unemployed class amongst us who hang around saloons, are ofttimes vicious and insulting, and constitute our criminals. Here we have an outlet for that surplus population in Southern States, where many of our people are working on starvation wages, and where all conditions for a better state of things are cruelly against us.

CHATTANOOGA CONVENTION.

A thinning-out process in these densely populated districts in the South, a course which common sense suggests to us as the most practicable scheme, has in it a practical solution for our sociological, industrial, and political problems in that section of our common country. It will lessen race antipathies, antagonisms, and crimes among both races in that section, where almost daily some inoffensive Negro is murdered, many times because he has in him the elements of a successful competitor and business man. *All Negroes who are lynched in the South are not criminals,* and common sense dictates that where men cannot live in peace, secure in the enjoyment of their civil and political rights and the fruits of their labor, they should quietly move out.

In this great struggle to secure a sure footing in this American republic, for the establishment and preservation of whose institutions the Negro has labored, fought, bled, and died, *a passive faith in God and in the Republican Party will avail us nothing. We must depend more upon our own strong arms, our own common sense and exertions to change conditions, North as well as South, that hamper and militate against us.* If we would have a voice in ruling this country we must have a hand in owning it. The more we own the better. Men who have *nothing* in citizenship *except the ballot* are a weak and dangerous element when temptations are so strong to play into the hands of demagogues.

The loud and imperative call now is for the universal practice of a *more rigid economy,* to live more within our means, and to be given less to display, cultivating more and more a spirit of race pride and loyalty. Ignorance and poverty are phases of our race—hindrances which are within the province of our own control. We can strive for a larger range of knowledge and intellectual vision. We can by the practice of a more rigid economy lay down for ourselves and our children a broader and stronger material foundation upon which to rest in the future.

In conclusion, you will permit me to call your attention to another great burden under which the black man labors at present in this country, in the lack of that *force of character* which never fails, in course of time, to give prominence and power to its possessor, regardless of race or color. It is not always a disgrace to be ignorant and poor. Conditions may excuse men and women for being hampered by these, as, for instance, when four million of our people came up out of the house of bondage in 1863 in ignorance and poverty. No one ever thought of taunting them because of wearing these badges of slavery. And yet, even as slaves, our fathers and mothers knew that character in this world was the pearl of great price, in comparison with which the wealth and learning of all ages were as nothing.

Therefore, during the dark days of slavery, when ignorance, wretchedness, and woe were the black man's lot, and the only joy he had came right down from heaven, born of a regenerated heart—to which white folks generally were strangers in that section of our country—how often could these plaintive notes be heard, night and day: "You may have all this world, but give me Jesus!" What a wealth of meaning is found in these words, in the light of eternity and human destiny, in our relation to

God and our fellow-men, here and hereafter! The black man realized in the gloomiest hours of his enslavement is this country that he could have, with every other blessing of an earthly sort withheld from him, the priceless blessing of an undying hope in Christ—and *a character* which should continue to shine on and on through the countless ages of eternity.

In this he was wise. It was the possession of this hope which reaches out into the sphere of the unknown, the eternal, untraversed by naked reason, that give him a character which plucked from his bosom a spirit of vindictiveness and revenge, and made him patiently wait upon God until the time of his deliverance came. The black man's Christian character enabled him to pray for his oppressors, "Father, forgive them, for they know not what they do."

It is better, infinitely safer in the end, to be weak while trusting in God and the right, than to be seemingly strong while trusting in self and the wrong. The civilizations of Babylon, Egypt, Greece, and Rome were all materially strong, rich in art and literature, but they lacked a moral basis; they stood upon sand, and when the supreme crisis came went down, and now live only in story and song. Their civilization lacked love, character—the permanent element. They made burdens for men; did not carry them for them in their weakness, and thus brought upon themselves sure and swift destruction.

In the eternal word it is said, "The nation and kingdom that will not serve Thee shall perish." Will America learn a lesson from the civilizations and effete kingdoms of the past? A nation or government that would long endure must do right, and not make burdens for weaker races to carry. It is better, more divine, to suffer wrongs than to inflict them upon others, whoever they may be. An element of weakness in a nation or individual is the tendency to do wrong.

Let us, as a race, in this country, accept conditions as they really are, trust in God, and do the right at all times and under all circumstances, ever casting our burdens upon Him who has cared for us in all our trying past, and we may rest assured that He will sustain and comfort us in all the future. We have more to fear from burdens and ills that come from within than from all that man may contrive against us. Our greatest foes lurk within—*our own ignorance, poverty, and immoralities.* Right moral character will make us good husbands and wives, fathers and mothers, citizens and neighbors. Right moral character, culture, and cash, elements in our American civilization quite within our reach, will within a few generations give us that status in this American republic which can no longer be questioned. There is set before us in freedom an open door to culture, character, and wealth. The possession of these essentials in civilization invariably leads to influence, honor, and preeminence. Before they can be attained there must be amongst us a more general recognition of this fact in human experience, that each race or class, as

well as each man, regardless of color or clime, must work out his own
salvation.

Our burdens God will carry
 If true to Him we be;
Our hearts need ne'er grow weary
 While serving faithfully;
The cause of truth will triumph
 Where wrong seems now enthroned;
The evil shall be vanquished,
 The earth by Christ be owned.

8 THE CHURCH CHAMPIONS RACE PRIDE, 1886

As the largest black religious body in New Jersey, the African
Methodist Episcopal Church embodied hopes for improvement in
the race's condition. Formed in 1816, the Church was one of the
first black agencies devoted to moral activism in the United
States. Indeed, African Methodist Episcopal churches in New
Jersey contributed much to early agitation against colonization,
slavery, and the disenfranchisement of free blacks. By the late
nineteenth century the Church gave expression to the contemporary emphasis on black nationalism. It championed race pride
and solidarity, and, through Sunday schools and institutions for
the clergy, promoted educational advancement. These concerns
are reflected in the following "Report on Education." Of particular interest here is the reverence to Africa, "the Fatherland."
There was a general increase in the Church's interest in Africa
during the late nineteenth century, largely as the result of Bishop
Henry McNeal Turner's advocacy of emigration to the continent.
Although Turner's Back-to-Africa vision is not mentioned here,
the "Report" acknowledges the influence of R.H. Cain, bishop
of the New Jersey Conference, who believed that a future generation of Afro-Americans would return to the "promised land."
Not surprisingly, Cain was a protégé of Bishop Turner.

J. P. Sampson, et al., "Report on Education,"
Proceedings of the New Jersey Annual Conference of
the African Methodist Episcopal Church **(np, 1886), pp. 45-46.**

. . . Never before since South Carolina fired upon our country's flag;
never before since the organization of our church, nor since the forma-

tion of the government, has there been a greater impetus to lead out, to lift up, and to educate the masses than now; and this is being done, not only through the schools, or such acquirements as are being made within the walls of school rooms, academies, colleges and universities, but in all the practical walks of civilized life. As an evidence of this, it may be observed that the time was when kings and queens received the greatest consideration, but to-day, the humblest citizen, however obscure, discoverers in science, and public benefactors, or the writer of some good book for the betterment of society, awaken our enthusiasm.

With regard to the immediate subject matter of our report, touching the educational progress of the church and the entire race, inspired by our standard, it will be noticed that there is a continual decrease of illiteracy, every year, not only in all the churches within the bounds of our Conference, but in all the churches throughout the Connection, and this fact is more clearly exhibited by the improved and correct responsive reading by the pews, as well as by the pulpit; by the less emotional or more intelligent methods of worship by the members and congregations; by the various temperance and literary societies connected with our Churches; by the more systematic and simple manner of teaching the Scriptures and conducting the service on the part of our pastors, and finally, by the better knowledge which is being evidenced every day by the local officers, stewards and trustees with regard to their duties and relations to the church as a connection, and its jurisdiction over them as officiaries under its management.

We have noticed with satisfaction the readiness with which the New Jersey Conference, in annual meeting assembled, have seconded every measure put forth by the educational department to advance the cause of education throughout the connection; and we further pledge ourselves to do all in our power to make endowment day a grand success everywhere throughout the borders of our Conference; and we would further and again recommend to every minister and member of our churches to subscribe at once to the *Christian Recorder,* our church paper, and the *A.M.E. Church Review,* our church magazine, also the *Budget,* an important statistical publication, and the church text books, written by our members, all educating forces, and at the same time furnishing valuable historical information with regard to the growth and progress of the church.

This Conference is by no means indifferent to the great work that is being accomplished by our adult collegiate schools, Wilberforce, Raccoe and other similar church seminaries and theological institutions. We would again advise our young men preparing for the ministry, to stand on their merit and Christian character, as ministers of the Lord Jesus Christ, instead of playing upon the passions and credulity of the people as a passport to preferment and position in the church, for we are commanded to study in order to show ourselves workmen approved of God. Then abide your time, and you will find that true merit will increase, while everything like appeals to passions instead of reason and good sense, will decrease.

There was a time, not long ago, when the bare mention of the Father land, the dark and far away continent, awakened not only our prejudice, but a spirit of resentment and almost contempt; but now, inspired by the missionary spirit of our beloved Bishop, with his sweet missionary song, "Over the Ocean," sung with the most inspiring zest by himself and con= gregation at the close of our Conference, and in the auditorium to thousands at Ocean Grove last summer, that name has a sweeter sound, the distance is shorter and our Conference looks anxiously to the day when, under his guidance, we shall have all the coast of Africa dotted with our churches; when at the tap of the drum and the unfurling of our banner, millions in heathen lands shall be marshalled at the altars of God, redeemed and disenthralled, and when all shall know the Lord, from the rivers to the ends of the earth.

J. P. SAMPSON
A. H. NEWTON
W. H. YEOCUM
J. T. DIGGS
Educational Committee

9 PAUL ROBESON OF PRINCETON, 1898–1919

Our nation has produced few figures as internationally acclaimed as was Paul Robeson (1898–1976) during his career as a singer, actor, and social activist. Robeson's importance and contributions are evident in many fields, and his life was deeply influenced by the emergence of blacks in the mainstream of world history in the twentieth century. In recent years any mystery shrouding Robeson's achievements and uncompromising opposition to racism has given way to a revived interest in his life and thought.

The first of the two selections below is taken from the prologue to Robeson's autobiography, *Here I Stand.* Published in 1958, this work is a compelling account of his life and the development of his political and social views. It is a personal history of considerable importance in American literature and the emergence of black protest. In this selection, Robeson recalled his boyhood in Princeton, where he was born in 1898 and lived until he was nine years old; later his family lived in Westfield and Somerville. Of particular interest in the following selection is Robeson's tribute to his father, the Reverend William Drew Robeson. From his father, Paul acquired strong personal convictions, dedication to the work ethic, respect for the elocution of black ministers, and a love of music. These were influences of enduring importance in Robeson's life. They provide an insight into the strength in some of the families like the Robesons, headed by former slaves. Robeson also paid tribute to his mother, Maria Louisa Bustill Robeson, who died when he was six years old.

The second document is a letter from James D. Carr, who in 1892 became the first black graduate of Rutgers College. In 1919, Carr, then assistant corporation counsel to New York City, wrote Rutgers President William H.S. Demarest to protest a racial incident in October 1916 while Robeson was on the school's football team. Scheduled to play against Washington and Lee University in Virginia, Robeson was barred from the game after the southern school objected to playing against a black man. Carr's letter was dated nearly three years after the incident, apparently because during the interim he was uncertain over the reason why Robeson's name was not on the players' roster.

Paul Robeson entered Rutgers after he placed first in a statewide academic scholarship examination. Only two black students had attended the school since its founding in 1766. He was greeted with a harsh, often-times cruel display of racial prejudice. A heavily drawn color line barred him from traveling with the Rutgers Glee Club, and he was the target of abuse by his teammates on the football team. By the time he graduated in 1919, however, Robeson had gained the respect and admiration of the Rutgers community. In his junior year (1918), he was inducted into the prestigious honor society, Phi Beta Kappa. Walter Camp named him to the All-American football team in 1917 and 1918, the first athlete at Rutgers to be selected. Robeson was also the recipient of fifteen athletic letters, and he was elected to the Cap and Skull honor fraternity in his senior year. The class prophecy of that year predicted Robeson was destined to become governor of New Jersey.

After graduation from Rutgers, Robeson attended the Columbia University School of Law, which, aside from further sharpening his intellect, placed him near the dynamic black community emerging in Harlem. In 1925, in New York, he performed his first concert devoted entirely to Negro music. By the 1930s the reputation of this proud and extremely talented young man had reached far beyond New Jersey, and he had become a leading international concert singer.

a.   Paul Robeson, "A Home in That Rock," *Here I Stand* (Boston, 1958; reprint ed., 1971), pp. 6-16.

The glory of my boyhood years was my father. I loved him like no one in all the world. His people, among whom he moved as a patriarch for many years before I was born, loved him, too. And the white folks— even the most lordly of aristocratic Princeton—had to respect him.

Born a plantation slave in Martin County, North Carolina, my father escaped at the age of fifteen, in 1860, and made his way North on the Underground Railroad. In 1876, after working his way through Lincoln University, he married my mother, Maria Louisa Bustill, a school teacher in nearby Philadelphia. Following a brief pastorate in Wilkes-Barre, Pennsylvania, he was called to be pastor of the Witherspoon Street Presbyterian Church in Princeton, New Jersey, where I was born on April 9, 1898.

I was the youngest of Reverend Robeson's children, and there were four others living at the time of my birth: William D., Jr., age 17; Reeve, 12: Benjamin, 6; and Marion, my only sister, who was 4.

In later years my father was pastor of A.M.E. Zion churches in the nearby towns of Westfield and Somerville, until his death in 1918, at the age of seventy-three. An editorial in the Somerville newspaper made this comment at the time:

> "The death of Rev. W. D. Robeson takes from this community one who has done a quiet but successful work among his own people for the past eight years. Mr. Robeson was a man of strong character . . . he was very familiar with the characteristics of his race and was always interested in their welfare. He quickly resented any attempt to belittle them or to interfere with their rights. He had the temperament which has produced so many orators in the South and he held his people together in the church here with a fine discernment of their needs. He has left his impress on the colored race throughout the State and he will be greatly missed here."

Go today to the towns in that part of New Jersey and your will find his memory still warm in the communities he served. As you drive down on the highway past New Brunswick you may see the William D. Robeson Houses, a government project named for him. In Princeton, the Witherspoon Street Presbyterian Church still stands, with one of the stained-glass windows glowing "In Loving Remembrance of Sabra Robeson" who was my father's slave mother on the Carolina plantation. Many of the older church members and other long-time residents you might meet on the shady lanes of the Negro community nearby—Green Street, Hulfish Street, Quarry, Jackson, Birch, John—will tell you with quiet pride of my father's devoted labors, his wisdom, his dignity. And they will tell you, too, about my mother, Maria Louisa: how she moved, so strong and tender, in their midst—comforting the sick, mothering the orphaned, collecting food and clothing for the hungry and ragged, opening to many the wonders of book learning.

I cannot say that I remember her, though my memory of other things goes back before her tragic death. I was six years old when she, a near-blind invalid at the time, was fatally burned in a household accident. I remember her lying in the coffin, and the funeral, and the relatives who came, but it must be that the pain and shock of her death blotted out all other personal recollections. Others have told me of her remarkable intellect, her strength of character and spirit which contributed so much to my father's development and work. She was a companion to him in his studies; she helped compose his sermons; she was his right hand in all his community work.

Maria Louisa Robeson, born on November 8, 1853, in Philadelphia, was a member of the noted Bustill family. The history of the Bustills, who are of mixed Negro, Indian and white Quaker stock, goes back to the earliest days of America. My great-great-grandfather, Cyrus Bustill, who baked bread for Washington's troops, became a leader of the Negroes in Philadelphia; and in 1787 he was a founder of the Free African Society, first mutual aid organization of American Negroes. Through the years the Bustills produced many teachers, artists and scholars, and, in the Quaker tradition, took part in running the Underground Railroad by which so many, like my father, escaped from bondage.

I don't know if the custom is still observed, but when I was a boy the Bustill Family Association held annual reunions to which all of the relatives from far and near would come. I find in my college scrapbook a printed program of the reunion of 1918, held at Maple Grove in Philadelphia. My aunt, Gertrude Bustill Mossell, is listed as vice-president of the association; and on the program of the day was a reading of the family history by my cousin, Annie Bustill Smith, and speeches by various other members, including an address by "Mr. Paul Roberson." (Though this spelling of my name was a printer's error, it is likely that "Roberson" was the ancestral name of the slave-holding Robesons from whom my father got his name. The county seat of his birthplace, Martin County, N.C., is Robersonville; and one of the earliest Negro freedom petitions on record is that of a slave, Ned Griffin, who, in 1784, from Edgecombe County which adjoins Martin County, urged the state government to grant him the freedom that was promised for his services in the Revolutionary Army and which was being denied him by his owner, one Abner *Robeson*.)

I cannot recall anything I said in my speech on that occasion, though I did jot down in my scrapbook its title—"Loyalty to Convictions." That I chose this topic was not accidental, for that was the text of my father's life—loyalty to one's convictions. Unbending. Despite anything. From my youngest days I was imbued with that concept. This bedrock idea of integrity was taught by Reverend Robeson to his children not so much by preachment (for by nature Pop was restrained of speech, often silent at home, and among us Robesons the deepest feelings are largely unexpressed in words) but, rather, by the daily example of his life and work.

Though my father was a man of ordinary height, he was very broad of shoulder and his physical bearing reflected the rock-like strength and dignity of his character. He had the greatest speaking voice I have ever heard. It was a deep, sonorous basso, richly melodic and refined, vibrant with the love and compassion which filled him. How proudly, as a boy, I walked at his side, my hand in his, as he moved among the people! There was a wide gap in years between us—he was fifty-three when I was born, near sixty when my mother died—but during many of his years as a widower I was the only child at home and his devoted care and attention bound us closely together. It was not like him to be demonstrative in his love, nor was he quick to praise. Doing the right thing—well, that was something to be taken for granted in his children. I knew what I must do—when to come home from play, my duties in the household, my time for study—and I readily yielded to his quiet discipline. Only once did I disobey him.

I was ten years old at the time, and we were then living in Westfield. My father told me to do something and I didn't do it. "Come here," he said; but I ran away. He ran after me. I darted across the road. He followed, stumbled and fell. I was horrified. I hurried back, helped Pop to his feet. He had knocked out one of his teeth. I have never forgotten the emotions—the sense of horror, shame, ingratitude, selfishness—that overwhelmed me. I adored him, would have given my life for him in a flash—and here I had hurt him, disobeyed him! Never did he have to admonish me again; and this incident became a source of tremendous discipline which has lasted through the years.

I have said that the white families who dominated Princeton recognized my father's dignity and accorded him respect. How remarkable that was, and what a tribute to his character, can be appreciated fully only when one recalls that the Princeton of my boyhood (and I don't think it has changed much since then) was for all the world like any small town in the deep South. Less than fifty miles from New York, and even closer to Philadelphia, Princeton was spiritually located in Dixie. Traditionally the great university—which is practically all there is in the town—has drawn a large part of its student body and faculty from below the Mason-Dixon Line, and along with these sons of the Bourbons came the most rigid social and economic patterns of White Supremacy. And like the South to which its heart belonged, Princeton's controlling mind was in Wall Street. Bourbon and Banker were one in Princeton, and there the decaying smell of the plantation Big House was blended with the crisper smell of the Countinghouse. The theology was Calvin: the religion—cash.

Rich Princeton was white; the Negroes were there to do the work. An aristocracy must have its retainers, and so the people of our small Negro community were, for the most part, a servant class—domestics in the homes of the wealthy, serving as cooks, waiters and caretakers at the university, coachmen for the town and laborers at the nearby farms and brickyards. I had the closest of ties with these workers since many of my father's relatives—Uncle Ben and Uncle John and Cousin Carraway and Cousin Chance and others—had come to this town and found employment at such jobs.

Princeton was Jim Crow: the grade school that I attended was segregated and Negroes were not permitted in any high school. My oldest brother, Bill, had to travel to Trenton—eleven miles away—to attend high school, and I would have had to do the same had we not moved to another town. No Negro students were admitted to the university, although one or two were allowed to attend the divinity school.

Under the caste system in Princeton the Negro, restricted to menial jobs at low pay and lacking any semblance of political rights or bargaining power, could hope not for justice but for charity. The stern hearts and tight purses of the master class could on occasion be opened by appeals from the "deserving poor," and then philanthropy, in the form of donations, small loans or cast-off clothing might be looked for. The Negro church, center of community life, was the main avenue through which such boons were sought and received, and, in fact, the Witherspoon Street Presbyterian Church was itself largely built by white philanthropy. The pastor was a sort of bridge between the Have-nots and the Haves, and he served his flock in many worldly ways—seeking work for the jobless, money for the needy, mercy from the Law.

In performing these Christian duties my father came to know and be known by all of the so-called "Best People" of the town. But though the door of the university president might be open to him, Reverend Robeson could not push open the doors of that school for his son, when Bill was ready for college. The pious president, a fellow Presbyterian, said: No, it is quite impossible. That was Woodrow Wilson—Virginian, graduate of Princeton, professor there for a decade, college president from 1902 to 1910, then Governor of New Jersey, elected President of the United States in 1912, reelected in 1916 because "he kept us out of the war" into which he led the nation one month after his second inaugural, Nobel Peace Prize winner, apostle of the New Liberalism, advocate of democracy for the world and Jim Crow for America!

He who comes hat-in-hand is expected to bow and bend, and so i marvel that there was no hint of servility in my father's make-up. Just as in youth he had refused to remain a slave, so in all the years of his manhood he disdained to be an Uncle Tom. From him we learned, and never doubted it, that the Negro was in every way the equal of the white man. And we fiercely resolved to prove it.

That a so-called lowly station in life was no bar to a man's assertion of his full human dignity was heroically demonstrated by my father in the face of a grievous blow that came to him when I was still a baby. After more than two decades of honored leadership in his church, a factional dispute among the members removed him as pastor. Adding to the pain was the fact that some of his closest kin were part of the ousting faction. A gentle scholar and teacher all his adult life, my father, then past middle age, with an invalid wife and dependent children at home, was forced to begin life anew. He got a horse and a wagon, and began to earn his living hauling ashes for the townsfolk. This was his work at the time I first remember him and I recall the growing mound of dusty ashes dumped into our backyard at 13 Green Street. A fond memory remains of our horse, a mare named Bess, whom I grew to love and who loved me. My father also went into the hack business, and as a coachman drove the gay young students around town and on trips to the seashore.

Ash-man, coachman, he was still the dignified Reverend Robeson to the community, and no man carried himself with greater pride. Not once did I hear him complain of the poverty and misfortune of those years. Not one word of bitterness ever came from him. Serene, undaunted, he struggled to earn a livelihood and see to our education. Soon after the tragedy that took his wife from him, Pop sent my brother Ben away to prep school and Biddle University (now Johnson C. Smith) in North Carolina, and my sister Marion to Scotia Seminary, a school for colored girls in the same state. Bill, the oldest, was then at Lincoln University—the school my father had attended—and for a time Reeve (or Reed, as we called him) was at home, working as a hack driver.

Some might say that Reed did not turn out as well as the other Robeson children, and it is a fact that my father was sorely disappointed in this son and disapproved of his carefree and undisciplined ways. Yet I admired this rough older brother and I learned from him a quick militancy against racial insults and abuse. Many was the time that Reed, resenting some remark by a Southern gentleman-student, would leap down from his coachman's seat, drag out the offender and punish him with his fists. He always carried for protection a bag of small, jagged rocks—a weapon he used with reckless abandon whenever the occasion called for action.

Inevitably there were brushes with the Law, and then my father, troubled in heart, would don his grave frock-coat and go down to get Reed out of trouble again. But this happened once too often, and one day I stood sadly and silently by as Pop told Reed he would have to leave—he must live his life elsewhere because his example was a dangerous one for his young brother Paul.

Reed is dead now. He won no honors in classroom, pulpit or platform. Yet I remember him with love. Restless, rebellious, scoffing at conventions, defiant of the white man's law—I've known many Negroes like Reed. I see them every day. Blindly, in their own reckless manner, they seek a way out for themselves; alone, they pound with their fists and fury against walls that only the shoulders of the many can topple. "Don't ever take low," was the lesson Reed taught me. "Stand up to them and hit back harder than they hit you!" When the many have learned that lesson, everything will be different and then the fiery ones like Reed will be able to live out their lives in peace and no one will have cause to frown on them.

Because I was younger, my own days in Princeton were happier ones. Mostly I played. There were the vacant lots for ball games, and the wonderful moments when Bill, vacationing from college where he played on the team, would teach me how to play football. He was my first coach, and over and over again on a weed-grown lot he would put me through the paces—how to tackle a man so he stayed tackled, how to run with the ball. Then there were the winter evenings at home with Pop: he loved to play checkers and so we two would sit for hours in the parlor, engrossed in our game, not speaking much but wonderfully happy together.

My father never talked with us about his early years as a slave or about his parents, Benjamin and Sabra, though long afterward I learned from others that before his mother died, Pop made at least one, and possibly two, dangerous trips back to the plantation to see her. I'm sure that had he ever spoken about this part of his life it would have been utterly impossible for me as a boy to grasp the idea that a noble human being like my father had actually been owned by another man—to be bought and sold, used and abused at will.

(I might mention here, in passing, that many years later in New York I met one of the family that had held my father in bondage. I had gone to a downtown night club to hear a friend who was singing in the place, and there I was accosted by a man who introduced himself as one of the Robesons of North Carolina. He said he was sure that I'd be pleased to hear that his mother was quite proud of my accomplishments in life, and that she had carefully kept a scrapbook on the various honors that I had won for the family name. Then the stranger went on to say that he would like to get together with me for a chat some day soon. "You see," he confided proudly, "your father used to work for my grandfather." As politely as was possible under the circumstances I assured the Southern gentleman that it was undoubtedly true that the Negroes who had come by his family's name had added a bit more distinction to it than did any of the original owners or their descendants. "You say my father 'used to work' for your grandfather. Let's put it the way it was: *Your grandfather exploited my father as a slave!*"—That ended it; and *this* Robeson never did have a chummy get-together with *that* one.)

Not old enough to work for them, I had very little connection with the white people of Princeton; but there were some white children among my playmates. One of these was a boy, about my age, whose father owned the neighborhood grocery a few doors from our house. We could not go to school together, of course, but during the long summer days we were inseparable companions at play. Once—and I don't remember why—the two of us got into a small-boy fight. After much crouching and circling and menacing gestures, we each got up enough courage to land a blow on the other's nose and then, wailing loudly, we ran away to our homes. Next day we were friends again.

There must have been moments when I felt the sorrows of a motherless child, but what I most remember from my youngest days was an abiding sense of comfort and security. I got plenty of mothering, not only from Pop and my brothers and sister when they were home, but from the whole of our close-knit community. Across the street and down each block were all my aunts and uncles and cousins—including some who were not actual relatives at all. So, if I were to try to put down the names of all the folks who helped raise me, it would read like a roster of Negro Princeton. In a way I was "adopted" by all these good people, and there was always a place at their tables and a place in a bed (often with two or three other young ones) for Reverend Robeson's boy when my father was away on one of his trips to the seashore or attending a church conference.

Hard-working people, and poor, most of them, in worldly goods—but how rich in compassion! How filled with the goodness of humanity and the spiritual steel forged by centuries of oppression! There was the honest joy of laughter in these homes, folk-wit and story, hearty appetites for life as for the nourishing greens and black-eyed peas and cornmeal bread they shared with me. Here in this little hemmed-in world where home must be theatre and concert hall and social center, there was a warmth of song. Songs of love and longing, songs of trials and triumphs, deep-flowing rivers and rollicking brooks, hymn-song and ragtime ballad, gospels and blues, and the healing comfort to be found in the illimitable sorrow of the spirituals.

Yes, I heard my people singing!—in the glow of parlor coalstove and on summer porches sweet with lilac air, from choir loft and Sunday morning pews— and my soul was filled with their harmonies. Then, too, I heard these songs in the very sermons of my father, for in the Negro's speech there is much of the phrasing and rhythms of folk-song. The great, soaring gospels we love are merely sermons that are sung; and as we thrill to such gifted gospel singers as Mahalia Jackson, we hear the rhythmic eloquence of our preachers, so many of whom, like my father, are masters of poetic speech.

There was something else, too, that I remember from Princeton. Something strange, perhaps, and not easy to describe. I early became conscious—I don't quite know how—of a special feeling of the Negro community for me. I was no different from the other kids of the neighborhood—playing our games of Follow the Leader and Run Sheep Run, saying "yes ma'am" and never sassing our elders, fearing to cross the nearby cemetery because of the "ghosts," coming reluctant and new-scrubbed to Sunday School. And yet, like my father, the people claimed to see something special about me. Whatever it was, and no one really said, they felt I was fated for great things to come. Somehow they were sure of it, and because of that belief they added an extra measure to the affection they lavished on their preacher's motherless child.

I didn't know what I was supposed to be when I grew up. A minister like my father? A teacher like my mother? Maybe. But whatever the vocation might be, I must grow up to be a "credit to the race," as they said. "You got something, boy, something deep down inside, that will take you to the top. You'll see—sure as I'm sitting here!" I wondered at times about this notion that I was some kind of child of destiny and that my future would be linked with the longed-for better days to come, but I didn't worry about it. Being grown up was a million years ahead. Now was the time for play.

Though we moved away from Princeton in 1907, when I was nine, I was back and forth between the other towns and this community until I finished college at twenty-one. Visiting Princeton was always being at home . . . .

b.   James D. Carr to William H. S. Demarest, 6 June 1919, Rutgers University Archives.

June 6, 1919.

President William H. S. Demarest, LL.D.,
Rutgers College,
New Brunswick, N.J.

Dear Sir:-

During the celebration of the one hundred and fiftieth anniversary of Rutgers College, a statement appeared in the public press that Washington and Lee University, scheduled for a football game with Rutgers, had protested the playing of Paul Robeson, a regular member of the Rutgers team, because of his color. In reading an account of the game, I saw that Robeson's name was not among the players. My suspicions were immediately aroused. After a considerable lapse of time, I learned that Washington and Lee's protest had been honored, and that Robeson, either by covert suggestion, or official athletic authority, had been excluded from the game.

You may imagine my deep chagrin and bitterness at the thought that my Alma Mater, ever proud of her glorious traditions, her unsullied honor, her high ideals, and her spiritual mission, prostituted her sacred principles, when they were brazenly challenged, and laid her convictions upon the altar of compromise.

Is it possible that the honor of Rutgers is virile only when untested and unchallenged? Shall men, whose progenitors tried to destroy this Union, be permitted to make a mockery of our democratic ideals by robbing a youth, whose progenitors helped to save the Union, of that equality of opportunity and privilege that should be the crowning glory of our institutions of learning?

I am deeply moved at the injustice done to a student of Rutgers, in good and regular standing, of good moral character and splendid mental equipment,—one of the best athletes ever developed at Rutgers,—who, because guilty of a skin not colored as their own, was excluded from the honorable field of athletic encounter, as one inferior, and from those lists in which so many competitors for glory were engaged, in which he had formerly been, and into which, with a humiliating tardiness, he was afterwards admitted. He was robbed of the honor and glory of contending in an athletic contest for his college before an assembled multitude composed of representative men and women, of various avocations, from all the corners of the earth. Not only he, individually, but his race as well, was deprived of the opportunity of showing its athletic ability, and, perhaps, its athletic superiority. His achievements on that day may have been handed down as traditions not only to honor his Alma Mater, but, also, to honor himself, individually, and his race, collectively. What an awful spectacle one of Rutgers' premier athletes on the side lines because of his color! Can you imagine his thoughts and feelings when, in contemplative mood, he reflects in the years to come that his Alma Mater faltered and quailed when the test came, and that she preferred the holding of an athletic contest to the maintenance of her honor and principles?

I am provoked to this protest by a similar action of the University of Pennsylvania, heralded in the public press less than two weeks ago. Annapolis protested the playing of the Captain of one of the athletic teams of the University of Pennsylvania, a Colored man. Almost unanimously his fellow athletes decided to withdraw from the field and cancel the contest. In this, however, they were overruled by the athletic manager, who ordered the games to proceed. One of the University's premier athletes on the side lines because of his color! Such prostitution of principle must cease, or the hypocrisy must be exposed.

The Trustees and Faculty of Rutgers College should disavow the action of an athletic manager who dishonored her ancient traditions by denying to one of her students, solely on account of his Color, equality of opportunity and privilege. If they consider an athletic contest more than the maintenance of a principle, then they should disavow the ideals, the spiritual mission and the lofty purposes which the sons of Rutgers have ever believed that they cherished as the crowning glory of her existence. May we ever fervently pray that the Sun of Righteousness may shine upon our beloved Alma Mater, now growing and blossoming into the full fruition of her hopes.

Very respectfully yours,

Rutgers '92   /s/ James D. Carr

10   EVIDENCE OF PROGRESS, 1880

"Although not yet up to the world's standard of civilization and enlightenment," observed the *Sentinel* in 1880, [the Negro] "is advancing toward it with giant strides." This optimistic outlook was often expressed by black newspapers and other publications reflecting the views of black businessmen and professionals. The newspaper's editor, R. Henri Hubert (1857–1909), was a lifelong Trentonian. Before he founded the *Sentinel* (originally called the *Expositor*) in 1880, Hubert was a reporter for the *Plainfield State Republican* and two Trenton papers, the *Daily State Sentinel* and the *Daily Free Press*. He also taught in the Trenton public school system, was doorkeeper of the New Jersey Senate, and in 1884 served as secretary to the former black Senator from Mississippi, Blanche K. Bruce. In 1886, Hubert became associated with Martin J. Lehman, a local white businessman, in the manufacture of cigars. The *Sentinel,* which was a four-page weekly, lasted only two years (1880–82) and is one of the few black newspapers preserved from that period.

Trenton *Sentinel,* 26 June 1880.

. . . The history of the world records no more gratifying evidence of advancement under the most disadvantageous circumstances than is shown by the Negro in America during the past 15 years. Starting from a depth of ignorance and poverty, smarting under centuries of oppression and injustice and harassed and hampered by a cruel and bitter prejudice such as no people ever suffered, every respectable avocation barred, every avenue for advancement closed to him, the progress which the Negro has made in spite of these almost insurmountable obstacles is something wonderful . . . . No black man can look upon it without pride and confidence in the ultimate future of his race. The Negro is advancing. Although not yet up to the world's standard of civilization and enlightenment, he is advancing toward it with giant strides. And as a quickened sense of justice and a proper enforcement of the law break down the barriers which are now imposed and open the opportunities which are now closed to him, his advancement will be rapid and irresistible. . . .

11 BORDENTOWN SCHOOL, TUSKEGEE OF THE NORTH, 1920-25

During the late nineteenth century, industrial training for blacks gained widespread acceptance in the United States largely as a result of the remarkable career of Booker T. Washington of Tuskegee Institute in Alabama. Civil rights advocates, though, viewed this kind of education as an effort to maintain racial segregation and inferiority. Though a chorus of protest emerged against the emphasis on industrial education and the leadership of Booker T. Washington, the Bordentown School was founded in 1886 and continued to flourish. According to the following publication by the school, Bordentown provided its students with basic skills for employment in New Jersey industry and agriculture. Character building was another important objective in Bordentown's strict system of training.

The Bordentown School was only marginally successful in improving the industrial opportunities of blacks. Although scores of its graduates obtained employment, racial discrimination kept most of them in the menial capacities. Moreover, the school's curriculum, like that of Tuskegee Institute, was years behind the industrial sector it claimed to serve. In the first half of the twentieth century, Bordentown had little success in forming a class of black managers and skilled workers.

Following the explanation of Bordentown's purpose and program is an assessment of the school by Booker T. Washington. Of particular interest here is Washington's implicit acceptance of a subordinate status for black workers in New Jersey, a view that attracted fewer adherents as the twentieth century wore on. By the 1940s black civil rights leaders called for substantial improvements in the school's facilities and the admission of white students. Although some reforms were made, the school could not survive the growing opposition to industrial education. In 1955 the Tuskegee of the North was closed.

a. New Jersey Manual Training and Industrial School for Colored Youth, *Bordentown and Its Training* (Bordentown, N.J., [1926]), pp. 3-10.

BORDENTOWN'S HISTORY
The visitor finds it hard, on entering the beautiful gateway which New Jersey's colored citizens have presented to Bordentown, to remember in

the imposing campus the old Ironsides School that existed thirty years ago. Established in 1886 by the Reverend W.A. Rice, a minister of the African Methodist Episcopal Church, Ironsides, as the school was then called, was supported by voluntary public contributions. As this rather precarious means of support proved unsatisfactory, the State was asked first to aid, and then to take over control of the school, which was done on May 24, 1894. By act of the Legislature on February 19, 1900, the school was placed under the control and supervision of the State Board of Education and has remained under the guidance of that body since then. At the same time the school's course of study was changed from a purely normal one to a combination of industrial and academic work. Its location was also changed, and leaving the two frame buildings in the center of the town it founded its new home on the old Parnell estate just outside of town. Here on the banks of the Delaware on a high bluff overlooking a curve of the river, has been established the new Bordentown which is fulfilling the promise of the old Ironsides, and which has become a source of pride to the citizens of New Jersey. The late James R. Gregory succeeded Mr. Rice as principal after the State took control, and he served in this position for about eighteen years. In 1915, William R. Valentine, a native of Montclair and at that time supervising principal in the colored schools of Indianapolis, was appointed to the principalship and is still in charge of the school.

Recognizing the fact that vocational training is always the most expensive branch of education in actual money outlay on equipment, New Jersey has put the student at Bordentown under thoroughly modern conditions of study. Modern brick buildings for the training and housing of students, a lovely campus of green lawns and ancient towering trees, equipment installed by experts, all this goes to make up a plant valued at close to one million dollars and devoted to vocational training of New Jersey's colored youth. The beautiful assembly building with spacious dining hall, auditorium, and gymnasium, and the imposing administration building with well-lighted and ventilated classrooms are examples of the nearly ideal conditions under which students at Bordentown work.

COURSE OF STUDY

It must be emphasized that Bordentown is a vocational school and that its aim is primarily to prepare students for the pursuit of a trade. No attempt is made blindly to copy the courses of a public high school but rather are those subjects selected which will be of most service to the man or woman entering a trade, and students are not encouraged to attend who are not interested in the vocational side of the school's course. Bordentown's academic work very closely parallels the regular public school curriculum from the sixth grade up through the second year of high school, and the student graduating from Bordentown receives two years of credit in the general course in any New Jersey public high school, according to the recent certification granted by the State Board of Education. Students expecting to enter college are advised to attend one of the regular public high schools.

Bordentown's school day is equally divided between trade and academic work, the morning period being spent on one branch, and the afternoon on the other. Girls are instructed industrially in plain sewing, and domestic science. Those who show special aptitude in sewing are carried further through a course in dressmaking. Boys have a wider range of choice, and courses are offered in printing, wood-working, agriculture, auto mechanics, plumbing, and general mechanics. The teaching staff in both the academic and trade branches is of particularly high quality, and its members hold degrees from the leading colleges, normal schools and technical schools of the East.

TRADE INSTRUCTION

Trade instruction is not confined to simple shop practice and theory, but the whole school plant is utilized to supplement the class room. Boys in the carpentry shop learn there the use of tools, whereupon they are assigned to the general repair work of the grounds, putting their instruction to practical test. Meanwhile work in the shop goes on through cabinet-making, reading of blue prints and rough construction work. Graduates of the wood-working department are not finished carpenters, but have learned enough to enter them in the trade as apprentice craftsmen. The same is true of the mechanics department. Rough wiring and electrical repair is done by students; firing of boilers is done by students under the supervision of the mechanics instructor as part of their practical training; every auto on the school grounds is under the care of a senior student in the auto-mechanics department who is responsible for its repair and upkeep.

Trade instruction at Bordentown, in short, is adapted to the difficulties which the colored boy or girl will face in seeking work after graduation. A student is not permitted to become merely a specialist along one line, but gains experience in several related lines of work, so that he or she may easily fit into any one of several lines of employment. The general mechanics department best illustrates this. Of five recent graduates from that department, one is an electrical contractor of Montclair, one fires boilers in Atlantic City, one is employed as plumber by the school, and two more are machinists in factories. Graduates from the girls' dressmaking department have no difficulty in establishing profitable independent businesses wherever they go. A recent report of the extension department showed that sixty-eight per cent of Bordentown's graduates are following the trade which they learned at school or are in some related line of work. Nor does the influence of the school stop with its graduates. Hundreds of boys and girls who failed to complete the courses are nevertheless profiting by what training they did get and are making good at their trades. Others have gone further in school and are enrolled in business, in teaching, in the professions. Mechanics, carpenters, printers, faithful employees and progressive business owners, efficient wives and devoted husbands, they are making good in their chosen fields, and are bearing daily testimony to the fact that Bordentown training pays.

Admission to Bordentown is made by regular application to the principal. Each applicant is investigated to determine whether his character, mentality and physical development warrant the expense which his admission to Bordentown means to the State. An applicant must be over fourteen years of age, must have completed the fifth grade, must be a resident of New Jersey, and must be physically strong enough to stand the rigorous system of Bordentown training. An applicant must also prove good character. The school is able to accommodate two hundred boys and one hundred and forty girls. This is made possible by the completion of a new boy's dormitory. The student body is representative of every section of the State, and in the registration for 1924–1925, sixty cities and eighteen counties were represented.

From the standpoint of the healthy-minded, active boy or girl, life at Bordentown is by no means simply a daily round of classes and shop study, though the student's daily program is full. Beginning with a six-thirty breakfast, the boys and girls go through a schedule which keeps them occupied until "taps" at nine-thirty, and yet which is so varied and full of interest that few students feel themselves over-worked or driven. Class time, meal time, play time, work time, all are intermingled in such a manner that the day's routine never become monotonous nor the youthful energy over-taxed. Athletics have come to play an important part in school life, and the name Bordentown has come to stand for clean and vigorous sport among followers of school-boy competition. Football, baseball, basketball, and track are all regularly organized sports and Bordentown teams are known from New York to Washington.

Nor are the girls neglected in this respect. Basketball, hiking, and calisthenics in the fall and winter, with baseball, track and field sports in the spring insure their being in the open air frequently and leading an active life. Physical directors for both boys and girls are members of the faculty, and athletics are conducted in accordance with the rules of hygiene. For the boys and girls without athletic ability, there are clubs and other organizations to encourage social talents. Literary clubs, social clubs, a student YMCA and a YWCA have enthusiastic members. A glee club and a boys' band give opportunities to the musically inclined. In addition to these activities, the school sets aside each Friday night for recreation. A motion picture, a program by a well-known artist, or a student play may be presented in the auditorium, or perhaps a social gathering may be held in the school gymnasium to vary the routine of campus life. Here, as in trade instruction, every advantage is taken of the beautiful campus to make student life at Bordentown as pleasant as possible.

Military training is required of every boy. There are three companies under the command of student officers, who are supervised by the Commandant. Military uniform is worn and the fundamentals of military courtesy and discipline are stressed deeply. This training is as important as any received at the school, although its benefits cannot be estimated by any set standards. Imagine the benefit which a boy receives who comes to Bordentown perhaps from the city, perhaps from the country, raw, untrained, undisciplined, who learns in his military training to take instruction and orders from those more experienced than he and to give instruction and orders to those less experienced than he. Imagine that boy or girl learning organization methods in the class and club activities of the school, acquiring a social finish in the parties and entertainments given by the students, learning how to meet people and get along with them, and amid all this, daily perfecting himself in the fundamentals of some trade that will carry the student out into the world, fitted to meet the competition of modern industrial life. Bordentown, to sum up a description, trains boys and girls for life by giving them a taste of life.

b.   "Dr. Booker T. Washington's Report on Bordentown," *Weekly Letter of the Manual Training and Industrial School* 2 (28 December 1920).

About seven years ago Dr. C.N. Kendall, Commissioner of Education and the State Board of Education of New Jersey, invited the late Dr. Booker T. Washington, founder of the Tuskegee Institute, to visit the Bordentown School. Following is a letter to Commissioner Kendall from Dr. Washington under date of August 1913, in which he outlines briefly the results of his observations and suggestions for making of the school a strong and useful institution:

"The location of the Bordentown School is one of the best and most attractive of any school in the country and from that point of view I think presents a good opportunity for the building up of a good, strong, useful institution.

"I find that there are in the State of New Jersey not far from 90,000 colored people. In order to make this school of the greatest assistance to these people I would suggest that a rough inexpensive survey be made with the view of finding out just what the prevailing occupations are among the colored people. After getting this information I think the occupations in which the majority of them are now employed would serve as a pretty safe basis as to the kind of instruction that ought to be most emphasized at Bordentown.

"My own feeling is that the school can be of high service to our people in that State. Just now, by getting hold of the farming classes, I think an examination would show that there are quite a number of people in certain communities of New Jersey who are engaged in farming, and I am quite sure that the proper kind of teaching at Bordentown can lead an increased number to go into farming, in some of its branches.

FARMING, GARDENING AND FARM MECHANICS

"I believe that farming, including the growing of ordinary farm products, truck gardening, dairying, fruit growing, poultry raising, ought to constitute the basis for the principal industrial work.

"Based on these farming operations, of course there ought to follow lessons in farm mechanics, such as any ordinary farmer would be called upon to use. In connection with this theoretical and practical lessons ought to be given in proper methods of marketing farm products.

"In observing the occupations of the colored people of New Jersey, I have noted that an unusually large number of men and boys are employed in taking care of lawns, gardens, etc. I think that a simple course in landscape gardening, including the care of lawns and gardens, might prove practical and valuable.

DOMESTIC SCIENCE, CHILD NURSING, SEWING

"I think an examination will show that a very large number of colored women and girls in New Jersey are engaged in some line of household work either in the hire of somebody else or for themselves. This kind of work, for the most part, embraces cooking, table serving, laundering, care of bedrooms and child nursing. Since this is true, I think these industries for the women, in connection with sewing, possibly millinery work and dressmaking, ought to be especially emphasized.

ACADEMIC WORK NOT TO BE NEGLECTED

"Now, in connection with what I have already suggested, I think one ought to be very careful not to give the people the impression that the academic or mental training is going to be discarded or pushed aside, but I do think that the industrial occupations to which I have referred together with others that I shall name later ought to constitute largely the basis for much of the work in mathematics, grammar, composition, physics, etc.

"Academic work, dovetailed into these practical industries, gives a more severe mental training than is true, in my opinion, of the old-form abstract book education.

"If it could possibly be done, I should urge whenever there is money appropriated by the State Legislature for any permanent improvement in connection with the institution that a way be provided by which the pupils, under careful supervision of instructors, could do the work whenever this is possible; in this way the building trades could be taught.

BUILDING TRADES AND AUTO MECHANICS

"I note a growing demand in every part of the country for colored chauffeurs, and I am wondering whether or not it would be a good thing to introduce a course in automobile repairing and in running automobiles. I have noted, too, that the young colored men who serve as chauffeurs, for the main part, seem to be a fine set of fellows. I think this idea would add a good deal of strength and popularity to the school.

EXTENSION WORK

"In order to give the school real standing, influence and popularity among the people of the State, I think the work of the teachers, especially the principal, ought not to be confined to the four walls of the schoolroom, but a large part of his duty ought to be in the direction of getting out among the colored people in the large centres of population, in such centres as Jersey City, Newark, the Oranges, as well as in the farming districts; and he should, through a systematic canvass and course of addresses, make the people know just what the school is doing and what it stands for.

"As far as possible I think the school ought to have extension courses whereby night school work could be carried on in large centres of population, so that every young person could feel that he would have an opportunity to connect himself with the Bordentown school, even though he or she might not be able to attend it on the grounds.

STUDENTS OUT OF THE STATE

"I think that restricting the attendance of pupils to persons within the State of New Jersey tends to isolate the school. I think it would be helped very much if the law could be changed so that the students from anywhere might attend.

"This would place the institution in competition with other institutions, and in that way give it new strength. If the State of New Jersey does not care to pay for the education of outside people, the counter-argument might be made to the effect that other States are now educating New Jersey colored people—for example, we are doing it here at Tuskegee.

FARMERS' CONFERENCES AND SHORT COURSES

"I would also suggest that a farmers' conference, that would meet at least once a year, be organized as soon as possible, that the leading and successful farmers be invited to come to Bordentown and tell how they have succeeded. I believe that this conference would grow from year to year in power and strength.

"I should also strongly urge that as soon as possible a short winter course in farming be introduced. I think the school ought also be responsible for a series of farmers' institutes conducted in different parts of the State wherever there are any considerable number of colored farmers.

12   WILSON'S VIEWS ON RACE ARE QUESTIONED, 1910, 1911

Although Woodrow Wilson's gubernatorial candidacy received the support of influential blacks in New Jersey and other northern states, there was concern over his racial views and the racial practices of Princeton University while he was its president. In **doc. 12a** Charles N. Grandison, a former president of Bennet College in Greensboro, North Carolina, and pastor of Ezion Methodist Church in Wilmington, Delaware, questioned an allegation that under Wilson's leadership, Princeton refused to admit blacks to the student body. Grandison's doubt over the validity of the charge suggests that he was uninformed about Wilson's role at the University.

Wilson became the president of Princeton in 1902 after a brilliant career as a political scientist and historian. Under his leadership, Princeton was recognized as one of the leading institutions of higher learning in the nation. Yet, Wilson maintained a racist admissions policy against blacks. Black applicants were informed that they were not accepted to the University because of their race.

Such a policy was not only a reflection of the social mores of the town of Princeton, which historically had links with the planter aristocracy of the South. It was also a manifestation of Wilson's own racial views. Born and reared in the South, Wilson accepted that region's views on race throughout his life. Although he rejected the most blatant forms of white supremacy, he believed that whites were the natural guardians of blacks, and he defended segregation as being in the best interests of both races. In the speeches he delivered as the Democratic gubernatorial candidate, Wilson often used a derogatory and stereotypical joke involving a "darky." On several occasions when he attacked the protectionist Aldrich-Payne Tariff, he warned that a close inspection would find "a nigger" (or, more properly, some troublesome restriction) was concealed by the law. In **doc. 12b,** a letter from William Hunter Maxwell, a black jeweler from Newark and president of the Newark Negro Council and the Negro Progressive Republican League, Governor-elect Wilson was asked to make a statement of friendliness toward blacks in his inaugural address. The new governor did not follow this suggestion.

a.   Charles N. Grandison to Woodrow Wilson, 26 September 1910, Arthur Link, ed., *The Papers of Woodrow Wilson* 21 (Princeton, N.J., 1976), pp. 171-72.

Atlantic City, N.J. Sept. 26, 1910.

Dear Sir:

I trust you will pardon the liberty I take of addressing you, and I beg to assure you that nothing but a sincere interest in you and the cause you represent and an earnest desire for the triumph of righteousness and civil decency could induce me to obtrude myself upon your notice.

Speaking one day last week to an influential colored man of this city, a man of my own race, about the coming election in this State this fall, I remarked to him that I intended to give my public and private support to the ticket which you so worthily head. He replied by saying that Princeton University would not admit to its academic department a Negro student and that you, being a Southern man, was in sympathy with the policy of excluding Negroes from the academic department of that institution, and had so expressed yourself. I told him I could not believe that statement, unless it came from one less partisan in his views than he. I can not bring myself to believe that a man of your breadth of vision and of your high moral ideals would be willing to close the door of opportunity in the face of any aspiring human being, whatever his race or nationality; and I write imploring that I may have direct from you, in brief but unequivocal terms, your attitude on the race question as it manifests itself in this country.

It may interest you to know that I was in the great fight in Philadelphia five years ago against the Durham ring and in the interest of the City Party, and it is said that my services contributed considerably to the defeat of the "gang." Hoping an early and favorable reply, I am

Yours truly, (Rev.) C.N. Grandison.

b.   William Hunter Maxwell to Woodrow Wilson, 2 January 1911, Arthur Link, ed., *The Papers of Woodrow Wilson* 22 (Princeton, N.J., 1976), p. 290.

Newark, N.J., Jan. 2, 1911.

Honorable Sir:

In what I am about to say I do not wish to appear as audacious or insolent in the least, and I honestly hope that you will not take it in that light.

To my personal knowledge a number of colored people hereabout and in New Jersey seem always to be a little scrupulous as to their rights etc. when a southern man and a democrat holds office which administers over them. As for myself I am not one of these colored persons. As for yourself, I have believed in you since I first learned of you and I voted for you.

What I wish to suggest is this, since this feeling prevails to some extent, do you not think that it would be well to make some statement in your inaugural address, that will tend to assure the colored people of New Jersey of your utter and entire friendliness towards them.

I regret very deeply to have to even hint of any separateness in the matter of human beings and their relations the one with the other. But the fact remains and has to be met.

I know that you intend to use all persons right, according to the standard of the true spirit of America. But of course that is a bit too general for some of our people of this day and time who have suffered from various and un-American discriminations, and that more than many of the other races. I hope that what I have said will appear to you as it does to me, I am not intimating anything special for one more than the other. Justice and unselfish purpose in life is what all men should strive to. A life of pure and unselfish service in the only life worth living.

Very Truly Your's, Wm. H. Maxwell.

VI

Newcomers
Between the Wars

O N October 16, 1901, President Theodore Roosevelt and
Booker T. Washington dined together at the White House
in a widely reported meeting that suggested the possibility of
federal commitment to better American race relations. Actually,
the affair was little more than symbolic recognition of the
Tuskegeean's pre-eminence among black leaders. The racial
hostilities of the late nineteenth century continued with seemingly
undiminished fervor. In 1901 more than 100 blacks were lynched,
and during the next few years there was a rise in racial violence
against blacks. The most shocking outbreak occurred in August
1908 in Springfield, Illinois, home of Abraham Lincoln, where
whites lynched two black men and drove many families from their
homes. By the time order was restored six persons had died and
more than seventy had been injured as a result of the violence.
Two years later in Asbury Park, New Jersey, a black man believed
to be the murderer of a ten-year-old white girl was nearly attacked
by a mob of whites while he was in police custody. [doc. 1] In 1911
the National Association for the Advancement of Colored People
fought for the release of a black man unjustly accused of the
murder of a white woman in Lakewood, New Jersey. Afterwards,
the NAACP's magazine, the *Crisis,* claimed: "New Jersey seems
lately to have changed the phrase 'Look for the criminal' to 'Look
for the Negro.' " In 1926 several blacks were beaten and a Negro
church was burned by a mob of whites in Carteret after a black
man was arrested for the murder of a white boxer.[1] Although
these were extreme instances of anti-black behavior in New
Jersey, their meaning was unmistakable—the color line was to be
preserved, and extra-legal police practices and violence against

blacks were a potential means to that end. Black leaders protested against the violence, but their pleas for toleration and protection evoked little official response.

The deterioration of race relations in the early years of the century, and frustration with Booker T. Washington's conservative leadership, united black civil rights advocates in the northern states. In 1905 a group of them, led by the young social scientist, W.E.B. DuBois, met at Niagara Falls, Canada, to found the Niagara Movement. As the first protest group in the nation devoted to equal citizenship rights for blacks, the Niagara Movement revived the abolitionist spirit of the Civil War and Reconstruction years. The group challenged Washington's leadership and his philosophy of race uplift through industrial education and accommodation to white supremacy. After the Movement was formed, Washington's influence among blacks and liberal whites in the North declined, as seen in the founding of the National Association for the Advancement of Colored People in 1910. When the Tuskegeean died in 1915, his program for race redemption had been largely rejected.

The prevalent violence against blacks in the South, their poverty there, and the resurgence of protest in the North, influenced the history of Afro-Americans in New Jersey between the two world wars. Blacks in the southern states, realizing the hopelessness of race relations there, sought to improve their condition through an exodus, a massive migration to the northern states. They came to New Jersey in greater numbers than to any other northern state. Between 1890 and 1900 the black population in New Jersey increased from 47,638 to 69,844, an increase of 46.6 percent. Between 1910 and 1930 it grew from 89,760 to 208,828, an increase of 132.6 percent. The growth rate slowed over the next ten years as a result of a decline in the number of southern migrants. In 1940 there were 226,973 blacks in the state, an increase of 8.6 percent from 1930.[2]

Although racial violence in the South was an important stimulus for the migration, that region's economic backwardness was the primary cause. Around the turn of the century, local industries employed black workers in a variety of unskilled capacities, but the availability of white immigrant labor and the opposition of white workers to the use of blacks kept their numbers small. In 1903 the Bureau of Statistics of Labor and Industries of New Jersey reported on the employment of black men and the low esteem in which they were held by white workers. [doc. 2] In the next few years resistance to the employment of blacks in New Jersey's industries was overshadowed by the World War I labor crisis. The war interrupted European immigration to the United States and forced factory owners to find another source of cheap labor. Industrialists in New Jersey and other northern states sent agents to the South to convince agricultural workers there of the economic and social advantages of the North. These appeals, the hostility of race relations in the South, and the poverty of black families there brought a tide of newcomers to New Jersey. In a few years black workers, including an increasing number of black women, heretofore confined to domestic and agricultural jobs, entered industrial and commercial establishments buoyed up by the war economy.

The migrants obtained employment in New Jersey's industrial towns during the war, but the skilled trades remained virtually closed to them. Generally, they lacked experience in industrial labor, a disability which forced them into the least desirable and lowest-paying jobs. Racial prejudice also worked powerfully against an improvement in their condition. In the working class districts of urban New Jersey there had always been suspicion of outsiders. This was especially prevalent in the case of blacks because of the low esteem in which they were held in American society, and because blacks, it was believed, would undersell their labor. Under these conditions black laborers were barred from most labor unions, they were not able to rise above menial employment in New Jersey industries, and the labor community remained sharply split along racial lines.[3]

Employers also sought to keep black workers in lowly positions, but for other reasons. Industrialists were acutely aware that the employment of blacks in jobs above the menial level constituted a potentially explosive labor issue. Keeping them at the bottom of the occupational ladder was a practical labor policy. In most industries a rigid color line had been established which forced blacks into jobs for which employers thought they were peculiarly suited. In 1932 a statewide study of black life by the New Jersey Conference of Social Work found that the majority of employers questioned believed "that Negroes have proved most satisfactory as janitors, laborers, drivers, cleaners, elevator operators, molders, furnace men; while working under high temperature as well as under low temperature; in loading and unloading materials . . . ." According to most employers, black workers "proved least satisfactory where speed was important, where responsibility is required, in jobs requiring thought and careful workmanship, where continuous work is essential, on night shifts, as supervisors, outside in the winter, on jobs requiring intellect, and 'where common sense is required.' "[4] These stereotypes of black workers persisted during the inter-war years, and they contributed to a pessimistic view of New Jersey by the newcomers. By the 1930s blacks referred to the state as "the Georgia of the North."[5]

Despite the racial barriers of New Jersey, the migrants came there in ever-increasing numbers. Significantly, the state was readily accessible to potential migrants. The larger cities—Camden, Trenton, Atlantic City, Elizabeth, Paterson, Jersey City, and Newark—were reached by railroad and located close to Philadelphia or New York, where thousands more blacks settled during the migration years. Between 1910 and 1920, Essex, Union, Camden, and Atlantic counties experienced the greatest influx of newcomers. In the next ten years the migration dispersed to Hudson, Monmouth, Atlantic, Bergen, Passaic, and Mercer counties. Dramatic increases in the number of blacks occurred in Paterson, Passaic, Atlantic City, Camden, Elizabeth, and Newark.[6]

Newark, the most populous city in New Jersey as well as the industrial and financial center of the state, attracted more migrants than any other municipality. During World War I, Newark bustled with activity. Political leaders called it "the city of opportunity," a boast which was first made during the city's golden age in the late nineteenth century. Race relations there were peaceful and remained so during the war. The public schools were desegregated and there was little evidence of white resistance to the increased enrollment of black children during the early years of the migration. Newark was attractive, too, because it had one of the state's most developed black communities. Migrants found established leadership, churches, social service agencies, and other black organizations.[7]

But the established black community and the public officials in Newark were unable to assist the thousands of migrants who came in search of work. "We have found," said William M. Ashby, the executive secretary of the Newark Urban League in 1919, "that we have usually been pushed into the worst part of the locality, physically and morally. Malaria, tuberculosis, factories with their odors and often immoral houses, whose sight we cannot escape, impress their stamp upon our wives, sisters, and children . . . ."[8] Helen Pendleton, also a member of the League, gave a poignant description of the difficulties of black settlement in Newark during the war in which she showed the migrants to be victims of widespread exploitation in housing and employment. [doc. 3]

After World War I the migration increased and efforts were made by property owners and real estate interests to restrict black settlement to the old working class districts of New Jersey's cities. It became increasingly difficult for most families to escape the demeaning life of the ghetto because of racial discrimination and declining employment opportunities in the state's old industrial towns. Several years before the Great Depression forced hundreds of thousands of people out of work in New Jersey, joblessness was a chronic condition for blacks. By 1930 most black city dwellers lived in distinct ghettos, notorious for their bad housing, poor health standards, social deterioration, and poverty. The adverse effects of the ghetto and racial discrimination on black health conditions in New Jersey were described in a 1932 study by two social workers, Beatrice Myers and Ira De A. Reid. [doc. 4]

As the black ghettos expanded in size and population, many organizations and institutions were formed which were essential to the survival and integrity of the community. Most of these groups were started by the migrants themselves. They catered almost exclusively to blacks and were important symbols of race accomplishment. The greatest institutional growth occurred among the religious groups which proliferated during the interwar years. Churches formed during these years were mostly small, independent bodies that were housed in the shoddy structures of the ghetto. In many cities they constituted an essential moral authority in the ghetto, and they represented the only social and cultural outlet in the community.

The most successful independent church in this period was headed by Father Divine, the self-styled god and leader of the Kingdom of Peace. The sect attracted several thousand black and white followers in the northern states. Father Divine's ministry stressed peace and brotherhood, concerns which were appealing to newcomers in the strange and often hostile northern cities. In New Jersey he was especially influential in Newark, where three missions of the Kingdom were established in addition to a large building on Central Avenue and the impressive eight-story, 250-

room Divine Riviera Hotel on Clinton Avenue and High Street. The sect also owned the Fairmont Hotel on Bergen Avenue in Jersey City. Many of the properties owned by the Kingdom were used for business as well as religious purposes.

Like many of the religious leaders of the black urban poor of the period, Father Divine exhibited a keen understanding of the social and psychological trauma experienced by the newcomers in northern cities, and his ministry sought to reduce their alienation. During the Depression years, when large numbers of blacks were out of work, Divine's missions provided food, clothing, and shelter to the indigent. He denounced racism, called on blacks to reject the evils of alcohol, tobacco, and sexual promiscuity, and was a dramatic personification of the black man as a god-like hero. "Independence of white control," as E.U. Essien-Udom, a Nigerian historian, has observed, "rejection of the traditional Christian concept of God, denial of the power of the dominant society, and differentiation of his followers from the Negro subculture and society are policies which Father Divine shares with the black nationalists."[9]

Another sect in New Jersey was headed by Noble Drew Ali, a migrant from North Carolina, who proclaimed himself a prophet of Islam. Much like Father Divine, Ali drew his followers from among the newcomers in Newark's black ghetto. In 1913 he founded the Moorish-American Science Temple, an Islamic sect which appealed to blacks dissatisfied with the Christian church. Twelve years later he moved the headquarters of his sect to Chicago, from which it spread to other northern cities. When the Temple split in 1930, part of its membership continued to follow the teachings of Ali, while another faction preceded the emergence of the Nation of Islam under the leadership of Elijah Muhammad. The sects headed by Father Divine and Noble Drew Ali were larger than most of the independent religious bodies, and, unlike the other groups, both had business concerns operated by their constituents. Usually such bodies reflected the poverty of their followers and were inexperienced in the management of business interests.

Older black churches, supported by long-time residents, had a somewhat different community role than independent churches and sects. They were more socially prestigious and affluent than the churches formed by migrants. In cities where black churches had been formed in the nineteenth century, these older churches contained the leading citizens of the black community, and their ministers were commonly active in civic affairs. [doc. 5]

Working through church organizations and the secular groups formed during the migration years, the black professionals, businessmen and women, and members of prestigious families sought to assist and express the interests of the less fortunate. Among the organizations involved in statewide activities on behalf of the race were the State Federation of Colored Women's Clubs, the "colored" Young Women's and Men's Christian Association, the Urban League, the Commonwealth Dental Association, the Essex County Negro Business League, the North Jersey Medical Society, the Modern Beauticians Association, political groups, fraternal organizations, and alumni groups. Much like the articulate spokesmen of the nineteenth century who challenged slavery and disenfranchisement, the small group of upwardly mobile blacks in New Jersey between the wars brought the question of racial inequality and civil rights to wider public attention. At the same time, these blacks pursued goals of racial liberation for those less fortunate. Their advocacy of civil rights was inextricably linked to a belief in racial pride and a commitment to black uplift. [doc. 6]

The protest against racial injustice in New Jersey during this period was greatly stimulated by the growth in the number of black newspapers. Between 1900 and 1940 the number of newspapers founded by blacks rose from twelve to approximately thirty-five. The growth was largely the result of the development of a receptive market in black communities, as well as the ambition, economic resources, talent, and aggressiveness of black publishers. Newark and Atlantic City, with large black populations and comparatively stronger economic bases than other communities, had the greatest number of black newspapers.[10] As in the past, the Afro-American press expressed the concerns of the community and the black business interests from which it received its financial support.

The state's most widely circulated black weekly, the *New Jersey Herald News* (later the *Newark Herald News*) symbolized the contributory role of the press in the growth of protest. The paper reported on discriminatory practices in the state, and it addressed these problems in its editorials. It gave comfort to militant organizations working for race betterment and equality, and it championed black businesses. In banner headlines which suggested the urgency of black concerns, the *Herald News* proclaimed: "Dixie W.P.A. Workers Get Pay Raise, Negroes to Get

Slice of U.S. Cash, See Roosevelt's Hand in Making Funds Available"; "Negro Must Use Politics to Win Rights"; "Negroes Shun 'Jim Crow' "; "Poor Housing Conditions Are Assailed in Englewood"; "Suit Filed Against Elizabeth Theater for Jim Crow"; "Store With All Negro Staff Successful"; and "Race Unity."[11] [doc. 7, 8, 9] Had not the black press in New Jersey dramatized the grievances and aspirations of the race, civil rights activities would probably have been substantially reduced, and blacks would have been without a powerful voice on behalf of their movement.

The Depression gave considerable impetus to Afro-American demands for full equality in New Jersey. Blacks had been unemployed in proportionally greater numbers than whites for many years before the economic collapse, but the 1930s were especially difficult for them. As in other parts of the nation, blacks lost their livelihoods earlier than white workers, and they usually remained on the welfare rolls longer. By 1936 blacks accounted for 23.5 percent of the relief population in New Jersey, although they represented only 5 percent of the total population in 1930. In 1937 blacks in the eight largest cities of the state were disproportionately on relief—three to six times their actual numbers in the population.[12] Their joblessness was compounded by the exclusionary practices of most trade unions in New Jersey, a condition that was revealed in 1932 by the Interracial Committee of the New Jersey Conference of Social Work. [see doc. 5] The Committee's comprehensive study, *The Negro in New Jersey*, reported that of the forty-one organized labor groups in the state only 268 of their total membership of 18,019, or 1.5 percent, were blacks.

The Negro in New Jersey revealed a great deal about the peculiar economic status of blacks in the state. It found that black workers were employed in the lowest paying jobs; fifty-seven percent of the employers questioned said that qualified black workers were excluded from better jobs; and blacks were the most economically depressed group in New Jersey. Because of these inequities, blacks were virtually trapped in the deteriorating central cities. Most residential communities were closed to black families, except for domestic laborers in white households. In those cities where housing opportunities existed for blacks, poverty virtually precluded moving to better neighborhoods. The most distressing observation made by the Interracial Committee's study, and one which was expressed by a number of studies on the race's condition in New Jersey during the Depression, was that the prevalence of racial discrimination denied black residents opportunities and liberties commonly extended to white ethnic groups.

As the Depression exposed many of the long-standing problems of blacks in New Jersey, it dramatized the need to solve the causes of social inequity. The New Deal administration of President Franklin D. Roosevelt broke sharply with the conservative Republican administrations of the 1920s. It called for an end to special privileges for the traditional power groups in American society, and it held out the promise that blacks would be accorded the same treatment by the federal government as whites. Although the remaining vestiges of racial discrimination undermined that promise, the New Deal was, nonetheless, more receptive to civil rights appeals than any previous administration since Reconstruction. Blacks received relief and jobs under federal programs, and Roosevelt expressed the belief that all Americans were entitled to equality of opportunity.[13]

Blacks were attracted to the Democratic Party by the egalitarian philosophy of the New Deal, and beginning in 1932 they increasingly discarded their traditional allegiance to the Republican Party. [see doc. 5] By 1936 blacks made a dramatic reversal in their voting pattern as a plurality of their numbers supported Roosevelt's reelection. Blacks also voted for local Democrats in large numbers. In 1937, New Jersey elected its first black Democratic assemblyman, Guy Moorehead of Newark. (In 1921, Walter G. Alexander, a Republican from Orange, had become the first black to serve in that capacity.)

The growing numbers of black voters strengthened their role in New Jersey politics. Assemblyman Walter Hargrave, a Democrat from Essex County, sponsored a bill in 1938 to establish the New Jersey State Temporary Commission on the Condition of the Urban Colored Population. This agency advanced racial equality in public employment, housing, and education, and it was the first state agency devoted to the improvement of blacks in New Jersey. Unfortunately, the emerging political power of the race was exploited in some cities by white politicians, as Lester B. Granger of the National Urban League observed in a study of the Jersey City Democratic machine of Mayor Frank Hague. [doc. 10]

Demands for racial equality and civil rights intensified with American involvement in World War II. Since the Revolutionary War, blacks from New Jersey had participated in all of the nation's major military conflicts. Black soldiers had been organized during World War I in a separate company of the New Jersey

State Militia and assigned guard duty at vital installations; another group served overseas in the 371st and 372nd Infantry. After the war, Company A, the black unit of the State Militia, was organized by William D. Nabors, a career soldier; Robert Trott, a veteran of the Spanish-American War; John S. Brown of Orange; attorney J. Mercer Burrell of Newark; and John H. Lindsey of Newark. Efforts to sustain black involvement in the State Militia were made in Atlantic City, Camden, and Trenton, where Companies B, C, and D were formed respectively. On March 10, 1941 these companies, which constituted the First Battalion of the 372nd Infantry of the New Jersey National Guard, were ordered into federal service.[14]

The struggle against fascism in Europe during World War II reinforced the black American's struggle for equality. In both struggles, the attention of the world community was directed against the dangers of racism and group subjugation. As early as 1935, when Italian soldiers invaded Ethiopia, blacks were among the first to protest the evils of fascism. That aggressive action by an industrialized European power against an impoverished, but proud, African nation compelled blacks to become more aware of international developments and to organize against their adversaries. In several American cities and in New Jersey, the defense of Ethiopia's national integrity became a major concern of blacks. Funds were raised on behalf of the African nation, and stories about Emperor Haile Selassie of Ethiopia appeared frequently in black newspapers.[15]

American blacks were also early opponents of National Socialism in Germany. The racist views of Adolph Hitler were manifested in his contemptuous treatment of two black Olympic athletes, Jesse Owens and Ralph Metcalf, at the Berlin Games in 1936. When the United States entered the war against the Axis powers, many blacks claimed that there was a disturbing inconsistency between their participation in the struggle for democracy abroad and their mistreatment in America. They resolved, however, to fight against injustices on both fronts. In February 1939 the *Newark Herald News* raised the question, "Shall We Fight?" [doc. 11] Most blacks answered affirmatively.[16]

As the United States developed its military capabilities, industrial growth increased. Rising industrial production ended the Depression and raised the economic status of white families; blacks, however, were excluded from firms producing war matériel. In an effort to put an end to such forms of discrimination, A. Philip Randolph, president of the Brotherhood of Sleeping Car Porters, called in January 1941 for a march of between 50,000 and 100,000 blacks on the nation's capital. The March on Washington Movement was enthusiastically supported by black organizations in New Jersey. As it gained momentum, raising the specter of thousands of dissatisfied blacks rallying against the inequities of American society, President Roosevelt issued Executive Order 8802 on June 25, 1941, prohibiting racial discrimination in defense employment. It was the most important action on behalf of racial equality taken by the government since Reconstruction. In spite of the widespread violation of the order in the southern states and in parts of the North, Roosevelt's action succeeded in breaking the color line in scores of industries. When the United States entered the war on December 8, 1941, a profound change in American race relations was well under way and the stage was set for the civil rights movement of the second half of the twentieth century.

During the war, blacks in New Jersey gained employment opportunities that had been denied them just a few years before. Prospects for better housing improved for some families, and black leaders increased the pressure for constitutional guarantees against racial discrimination. These gains resulted largely from the urgency given to the concerns of blacks by the great migration between 1919 and 1941. The increasing number of newcomers who had survived the difficult years of adjustment in New Jersey kept alive and gave deeper meaning to the struggle for equality.

1 A RACIAL INCIDENT AT ASBURY PARK, 1910

In New Jersey during the early years of the twentieth century there was considerable uncertainty over the prospects for better race relations. In some communities, ethnic tensions erupted when the color line was threatened or when a black man was suspected of a hideous crime against a white person. Such was the case in Asbury Park, which had experienced a sharp increase in its black population from 273 in 1900 to 1,973 in 1910. On November 13, 1910 a ten-year-old white girl, Marie Smith, was found dead, apparently murdered, after she had been missing for four days.

The police searched the black community for Thomas Williams, a drifter who had been employed by the dead girl's great aunt. After Williams' arrest, a mob of whites gathered at the police station on November 13 and 14 but were prevented from seizing the suspect. Fearing that another attempt to wrest Williams from the jail might be successful, the police took him to the Monmouth County jail at Freehold. The incident drew attention throughout the state and in other communities. William Monroe Trotter, an outspoken civil rights advocate and editor of the Boston *Guardian,* wrote Governor Woodrow Wilson soon after the mob attacked the jail in Perth Amboy and urged him to "speak out against the threat of lynching an untried Colored man in the state of New Jersey." Soon afterward the NAACP questioned the right of the police to hold Williams, who throughout the ordeal maintained his innocence, and it obtained his release. The following description of the incident appeared in the NAACP's magazine, the *Crisis.*

"The Old Story," *Crisis* 1 (January 1911): 20.

There is without doubt a large criminal and semi-criminal class among colored people. This is but another way of saying that the social uplift of a group of freedmen is a serious task. But it is also true, and painfully true, that the crime imputed carelessly and recklessly against colored people gives an impression of far greater criminality than the facts warrant.

Take, for instance, a typical case: A little innocent school-girl is brutally murdered in New Jersey. A Negro vagabond is arrested. Immediately the news is heralded from East to West, from North to South, in Europe and Asia, of the crime of this black murderer. Immediately a frenzied, hysterical mob gathers and attempts to lynch the poor wretch. He is spirited away and the public is almost sorry that he has escaped summary justice. Without counsel or friends, the man is shut up in prison and tortured to make him confess. "They did pretty near everything to me except kill me," whispered the wretched man to the first friend he saw.

Finally, after the whole black race in America had suffered aspersion for several weeks, sense begins to dawn in Jersey. After all, what proof was there against this man? He was lazy, he had been in jail for alleged theft from gypsies, he was good natured, and he drank whiskey. That was all. Yet he stayed in jail under no charge and under universal censure. The coroner's jury found no evidence to indict him. Still he lay in jail. Finally the National Association for the Advancement of Colored People stepped in and said, "What are you holding this man for?" The

Public Prosecutor got red in the face and vociferated. Then he went downtown, and when the *habeas corpus* proceedings came and the judge asked again: "Why are you holding this man?" the prosecutor said chirpily, "For violating election laws," and brought a mass of testimony. Then the judge discharged the prisoner from the murder charge and congratulated the National Association for the Advancement of Colored People—but the man is still in jail.

Such justice is outrageous and such methods disgraceful. Black folk are willing to shoulder their own sins, but the difference between a vagabond and a murderer is too tremendous to be lightly ignored.

2   DISCRIMINATION IN THE INDUSTRIAL WORKPLACE, 1903

Only grudgingly did New Jersey factories employ blacks as industrial workers around the turn of the century. Despite the race's emphasis on uplift and industrial work, the traditional stereotype of blacks as lazy, undependable, and incapable laborers persisted. In the following report by New Jersey's Bureau of Statistics of Labor and Industries, these views were shown to have been extensive and a formidable barrier to the employment of black men in the skilled trades. Out of the 398 manufacturing establishments which participated in the Bureau's survey, for example, blacks were employed in only eighty-three, and in those firms blacks usually were relegated to lowly positions. The Bureau also found that most labor unions in the state practiced racial discrimination or exclusion.

The report took a decidedly paternalistic approach to the problems of black workers in a predominantly white labor market, and it underrated the impact of racism on the opportunities available to blacks. Certain parts of the report are fallacious, particularly the assertion that distinctions were not made in the education of black and white children in New Jersey. [see chap. 5, doc. 4] Equally erroneous was the statement that "the less energetic of the race were those who came to the northern and eastern States . . . ." Nonetheless, the report is of historical value. It is the first known official examination of black workers in the industrial life of New Jersey.

Twenty-Sixth Annual Report of the Bureau of
Statistics of Labor and Industries of New Jersey
(Somerville, N.J., 1904), pp. 163-68, 183, 188-91, 205-210.

For some years back the minds of thoughtful people have been drawn to a contemplation of the negro problem, particularly that phase of it which relates to the industrial outlook for the race, and the degree of success that has attended the efforts of its individual members to make a place for themselves in the great fundamental activities of life by the pursuit of which only, all races have succeeded in elevating themselves.

So important is this subject that a general conviction is growing everywhere in the nation, that a careful study of the conditions and needs of the negro population, a study absolutely removed from race prejudice and partisan bias, is necessary to the highest interests of both negroes and whites.

The twelfth census of the United States shows that the negro race is not dying out as many predicted it would, but that it is indeed increasing as fast as the white native born, and will continue to do so in the future so far as any hindrance to its growth now in view is concerned.

The nearly nine millions which forms the present negro population of the country, added to by the natural increase of nearly one hundred and fifty thousand a year, the gain shown to have taken place between 1890 and 1900 is, apparently, destined to be a part of the nation for all time.

The conditions surrounding this great number of human beings comprising about twelve per cent of our total population, who are backward in, or utterly ignorant of, the arts and sciences which are the groundwork and main support of our civilization, is a matter that should not be guessed at, but investigated with a view to ascertaining all the facts, and, guided by the knowledge thus acquired, public interests demand that their development should be assisted in every possible way.

There is certainly a noticeable absence of negroes in the trades requiring skill, and as it is from the ranks of workmen engaged in such labor that most, if not all, the successful organizers of great industrial enterprises are drawn, it would seem from their failure to obtain a footing in these advanced branches of labor, that the negro race has reached the limit of its capacity in the coarse and comparatively ill-paid work requiring only bodily strength, at which it is now almost universally employed.

This exclusion from advanced and gainful occupations, whether due to incapacity inherent in the race or to prejudice on the part of white workmen, or in part to both causes, is, while it continues, an effectual barrier to the negro's moral and industrial development.

Excellence in labor, industry, skill, perseverance, intelligence, thrift, ambition, and self-denial, are the means by which in a country of free opportunities like ours, men are constantly passing from the lowest to the highest strata of labor, and from the most restricted to the widest spheres of activity in the social and industrial life of the nation.

To inspire an individual or a race with the ambition that leads to high achievement, there must be an incentive in the form of prospective rewards and a clear course open in the path that leads upwards. If these are wanting, hope and ambition die and effort ceases to be directed to anything higher or more far-reaching than obtaining merely the things necessary to sustain life on the lowest animal plane.

The State has not neglected its duty to the negro race; since the emancipation it has provided liberally for their education, making no distinction in this respect between their children and those of the whites. Indeed, in many places special educational efforts directed toward meeting the peculiar requirements of negro children have been made, and although these extend backward over a full generation, it cannot as yet be said that the results reached satisfy the hopeful anticipations of their friends, or are commensurate with the efforts made on their behalf.

It may be said that with equal educational facilities enjoyed for so many years the negroes should make a better showing in the superior lines of employment, and that their failure to do so is due to racial incapacity for anything higher than the commonest forms of labor; that if they possessed the necessary mental qualifications, ambition to advance and a capacity for something better than the menial work, they would, through their own exertions, have succeeded in establishing themselves at least to some extent, in the superior grades of labor. But such reasoning would be superficial; it should be borne in mind that servile labor in its most extreme form—slavery, has been the lot of the negro race from the settlement of the continent up to forty years ago . . . .

The Negro race forms a very important constituent group in the nation, and what they are able to make of themselves is a matter of profound importance to all. If they are to advance to the level of the general citizenship of the country it is necessary that they should first of all earn a living; to do this they must have the ability and will to labor effectively, and should receive enough for that labor to live decently and rear their children.

The future of the negro depends on his being naturally capable of qualifying himself to meet these requirements. If he can do so, the future is assured to him; although it may take a long time to bring about the change, the practice of industry, thrift, self-restraint and the development of the moral qualities that grow from an advancing and hopeful life, will finally remove such prejudice as may now be entertained toward him. But if he cannot rise, and that by his own efforts, then, indeed, is he apparently destined to be in freedom as in slavery, a being to whom the paths leading to high achievement are forever closed.

The question is one of the highest importance not only to the negro race, but to the entire nation. If the blacks are incapable of advancement, and cannot take a place in the currents which flow through the industrial and social life of the nation, if so large an element of our population is destined to remain permanently in the lowest strata of labor without a hope that the lot of the son will ever be better than that of the father, we shall be confronted with a problem in social and political economy far more difficult of solution than any that has thus far confronted us since the beginning of our national life.

If the negro is capable of advancement it is in the highest degree a matter of interest to both races that no impediment be placed in his way. The workingmen should be especially concerned in seeing that he be given a free field and fair play; for the depth to which he may descend or be forced downward must ultimately become the same for the white laborer who competes with him . . . .

This great accession of colored people is, of course, not due to natural increase, but to immigration from the South, the exodus of negroes from that section to the western, northern and eastern States having been from a variety of causes, particularly great during the past ten years. The increase of negro population from 1890 to 1900 shows a higher percentage in New Jersey than elsewhere, except in the far western and northwestern States or territories, to which places a relatively greater number have gone, attracted by the opportunities offered for farming or for employment as agricultural laborers. The less energetic of the race were those who came to the northern and eastern States, tempted to do so, probably, by the prospects of in some way making an easy living in the cities. At least that would seem to be the case in New Jersey, the foregoing table showing the abnormal increase of the negro population has been in the counties having the largest towns, while in the agricultural counties that do not show a decrease only a slight gain, very much below that of the whites has taken place.

The negro's preference for the cities is natural because of the advantage which life in them offers compared with the agricultural districts. Many come because there are better schools to which they can send their children for a longer period of time in the year than they could do in the country; their churches, too, and other forms of social association are attractive, and for many there is the alluring prospect of being able to obtain some kind of employment that will be easier and more remunerative than the drudgery of plantation or farm life. But, on the whole, his predilection is productive of unfortunate consequences. Without the ability to perform any kind of labor for which there is a demand, the negro soon loses such ambition as he had and becomes a competitor with others of his race for such chance jobs as most of them depend upon to eke out a scanty and precarious livelihood . . . .

To ascertain what foothold the negroes have at present in factory and other forms of skilled employment, a blank containing the following questions was sent to a selected number of representative establishments engaged in each of the chief industries carried on in the State:

1. Total number of employees.
2. Total number of negroes employed, if any.
3. How many of the negroes are skilled or semi-skilled workmen?

4. What kind of skilled work is done by negroes?
5. What wages do negro workmen receive per week?
6. Are negroes paid the same wages as white men for the same kind of work?
7. How do negroes compare in efficiency with white men on the same kind of work?
8. Do negroes improve in efficiency?
9. Have the negro workmen received any education or are they totally illiterate?
10. Shall you continue to employ negro workmen? . . .

The opinions expressed by owners and managers of industrial establishments on the subject of negro labor which follow, are interesting and important; reflecting as they do the impressions of broad minded men of affairs, based on experience in organizing and managing large forces of labor. Almost without exception it will be found that the spirit running through these communications is tolerent and kindly, showing no trace of prejudice and advancing only such objections to the negro workman as are entirely in his power to overcome.

One firm of cornice and skylight manufacturers who formerly employed negroes says of them as workmen:

"We do not care for them, because they are not reliable; at least that has been our experience. We had quite a number in our employ at one time; they can be trained to do good work, but they cannot be depended upon. At least, that is the conclusion we have come to after having had many of them in our employ for several years."

A firm of food canners writes of negro labor as follows: "We do not employ negroes in our factory but have some of them on a farm where they are paid the same wages as whites, viz: $1.50 per day. We prefer white help because they are more intelligent as a rule; our experience with negroes is that they stay away from and neglect their work for very trivial reasons. They are not ambitious and do not try to better their condition. We have succeeded in keeping some good negro help by weeding out the trash. During the packing season in the Fall we employ about fifty men, ten of whom are negroes. They do the rough work, such as scalding tomatoes, etc., and are as good at it as white men, but not so reliable. They are apt to remain away without notice. We employ a few negro women to peel tomatoes; their work is very satisfactory as they are very painstaking, but they are slow; earning about $1.00 per day to the $1.50 and $2.00 earned by white women, who, however, do poorer work in consequence of their greater speed. Our experience hardly affords material for a fair comparison, as we draw our colored help from a class that used to be connected with the business of horse racing up to the time Monmouth Park was closed. These people had to find other employment after racing was discontinued."

A leather manufacturer writes: "We employ no negroes simply because we have never received an application for employment from one of that race."

. . . A pottery company: "We have never employed negroes in our line. For some unknown reason they do not appear to have ever sought employment in pottery manufacture, at least not to our knowledge."

A manufacturer of sash, doors, and blinds: "I do not employ any negroes at present. I have tried them as drivers and found them very good around horses, but in general very lazy. This laziness seems to increase with age."

A company engaged in the manufacture of paints and varnish writes: "We do not at present, nor have we at any time, employed negroes. We have no particular objection to negroes, and have no reason for their non-employment other than that they have never made application for work."

. . . A manufacturer of tools and hardware: "We have no negroes in our employ, not from any prejudice on our part, but we do not think our men would make it agreeable for them. This we believe to be the reason why negroes do not enter the field of skilled mechanics."

A manufacturer of boilers says: "We never have, nor should we ever employ negroes such as are to be found in this quarter."

A brick manufacturer: "Have no negroes employed at our works and have made no attempt to use negro labor. We prefer white foreign help such as Hungarians, Polanders, etc."

Manufacturers of terra cotta: "Our work is done by skilled white mechanics; we have not and do not intend to introduce negro labor, believing that they never could be trained up to taking the places of white men in skilled labor."

. . . Manufacturer of food products: "There is no department of our works where negroes could be employed advantageously."

Manufacturer of hats: "We do not employ negroes in the hat manufacturing business; do not believe they could be trained to do the work . . . ."

. . . Shoe manufacturers: "We have no negroes in our employ because there is a strong prejudice against them. Think, however, it would be better to employ them than to encourage them to steal by keeping them in idleness."

Watch case manufacturers: "We do not employ negroes in any capacity, except as porters and laborers."

. . . It will be noticed that only a comparatively few of the employers quoted above declare themselves opposed to negroes as workmen on grounds arising from experience with them in that capacity. Those who write against them in positive terms, do so for the most part on the assumption that, as a matter of course, white employees would revolt against working side by side with negroes.

"Laziness" and "unsteadiness at work" are the most serious short-comings specifically urged against the race, in the opinions given by employers, who now have negro workmen or have had them in the past. Only a few intimate rather than plainly express a disbelief in the negroe's ability to acquire such skill in mechanical occupations as to ever make him a desirable workman. But how far one or even a greater number of employers in a given industry may fall short of accurately expressing the sentiments of all is shown by the fact that while four manufacturers of brick and terra cotta declare that negro labor would not do in their business, and that none had been or ever would be employed in their several establishments the table of occupations in which negroes are employed shows that in fifteen establishments engaged in the same industry men of that race are now employed in large numbers, and, presumably, giving satisfaction . . . .

To test the sentiment of the local organizations toward the negro as a workman and co-laborer, and also with a view to showing whether or not his absence from the skilled industries is due to their opposition, a circular was sent to the secretaries of all local unions in New Jersey under the jurisdiction of the American Federation of Labor . . . .

The following are some of the replies received:

Bookbinders—"Negroes are eligible."

Carriage and Wagon Makers—"Have never had an application or membership from a negro, but think if one were made it would not be looked on favorably by members."

Saw Smiths—"Negroes are not eligible; do not regard them as a desirable class of people."

Folders of Textiles—"Negroes not eligible. Folders are finishers of all goods classed as textiles; these goods are 'yarded ' on a machine by girls and passed on to the folder. He takes the goods and puts them up in style ordered for shipment to market. The machine girls would never consent to work for a negro."

Machinists—"Negroes not admitted; they and all races but whites are excluded by the constitution of the union."

Wet Leather Tackers' Union—"Negroes not admitted. If one were to apply he would be blackballed. The chief objection to them is that in tacking leather on frames the workmen fill their mouths with tacks as shoemakers do, and take them from there to be driven through the leather into the frame. As the tacks are used over and over again the thought that a negro had had them in his mouth previously proved so disgusting that white men refused to work with them."

Potters—"Negroes not admitted, although nothing in the constitution or by-laws forbids their admission. If one were to apply he would be blackballed."

Terra Cotta Workers—"Negroes not admitted. Their admission is forbidden by the by-laws and by general custom."

Typographical Union—"There is nothing in the constitution or by-laws to prevent the admission of a negro if otherwise qualified. Two unions of the craft, however, state that negroes would surely be blackballed if any of them applied for membership."

Five other unions of the same trade say that applications for admission on the part of negroes if good workmen and of clean character would receive fair treatment.

Barbers—Negroes are eligible to membership as a general thing, but restrictions of a certain kind are imposed by some of the locals; thus, in one of them it is the rule that a negro barber who conducts a shop for persons of his own race exclusively, is expected to join a union made up entirely of men of his own color, or he may become directly connected with the International Union. But, if he conducts a shop in which white men only are worked upon, he may join the local with barbers of the white race.

Most of the communications received from barbers show a spirit of friendliness toward the negro as a fellow-craftsman.

Painters, Decorators and Paperhangers—There is nothing in the constitution of the national organization that prevents the admission of negroes as members if they should be otherwise qualified. Regulations relating to membership are, however, left to the locals, each of them being at liberty to make these as they see fit. Out of nineteen locals reporting thirteen unqualifiedly declare their readiness to admit negroes who know the trade and are up to the standard in other respects; the other six state that negroes would not be admitted as members under any circumstances.

Bakers and Confectioners.—Out of four reports received from as many local unions, three admit negroes and one does not. The constitution of the national union does not discriminate against the negro, and he is not excluded from the single objecting local by any by-law; there is simply a general understanding among the members that one applying for admission shall be black-balled.

Textile Workers.—Negroes are not admitted to membership in the union, although it is admitted that one man of the race is working as a designer in the rug factory at which a large majority of the members are employed. This negro is not in the union and would not be admitted to it as a member.

Cotton Spinners.—Negroes are not admitted to membership; their exclusion is brought by a general understanding that an applicant of that race shall be black-balled, the sentiment of the whites being against them as fellow workmen.

Longshoremen and Marine Transport Workers.—The two unions of this organization that have reported, state that negroes would be gladly admitted to membership if they desired to connect themselves with the locals. Apparently, however, they do not wish to join, although many of them are working as longshoremen along the water front of New York and Philadelphia where they successfully compete with white men on the basis of lower wages. Longshore work is done in all southern sea coast cities almost entirely by negroes.

The officers of the unions are very anxious to bring the negroes into their organizations and will cheerfully admit them on terms of perfect equality with white men.

The secretary of one of these locals writes that in the cities of Philadelphia and Camden there are now about three thousand negroes working on the docks as longshoremen who might be persuaded to join a union but for the opposition of their employers and the consequent fear that by doing so they would loose their jobs. The negroes also appear to believe that if they demanded the same wage as white men, employers would prefer the latter, and that they should thereby loose the employment entirely.

Wood, Wire and Metal Lathers.—One union out of five reporting does not admit negroes. Their admission is not prevented by the constitution or by-laws, but, it is stated, if one should apply for membership he would be black-balled.

In striking contrast to this policy are the liberal views on the subject of the admission of negroes expressed by another union of the same trade, the secretary of which states that "negro applicants would not be excluded if any should offer themselves, and it is only exceedingly narrow minded persons who would object to them." The same official summarizes the race question in this direct and forceful way: "The only difference I see between a negro and a white man is that one can be a *black* gentleman and the other can be a *white* gentleman; if neither one can be a gentleman, then both are alike loafers."

3   MIGRATION FROM THE RURAL SOUTH, 1917

For over a century, Newark has settled more blacks than any other municipality in the state. Beginning in the 1830s, it rapidly developed a remarkably diversified industrial economy attracting thousands of European immigrants, and also Afro-Americans from the southern seaboard states. Yet the black experience in New Jersey's largest city has been an anomaly and in many respects a tragic story. Helen Pendleton's account focuses on the difficulties of the migrant population during World War I. Black migrants, in spite of sanguine promises given to migrants by industrial agents in the South, were largely viewed as undesirables by Newark residents. As Pendleton observes, the migrants could obtain housing only in the central city's unwholesome tenement district. Rarely could they acquire employment in the skilled trades; and, as a mark of their lowly status, they suffered diseases and illnesses at a much greater rate than whites. Pendleton was a white social worker in Newark and a member of the city's Urban League. In that capacity she approached the problems of the migrants with considerable compassion and insight. The following is an early account of the social crisis that by the 1960s earned for Newark a reputation as the nation's most troubled city.

Helen B. Pendleton,
"Cotton Pickers in Northern Counties,"
Survey 34 (17 February 1917): 569-71.

Early last spring, when a marked shortage of labor was felt, northern industries turned to the South and began to import Negroes by the thousand. Railroads and industrial plants furnished transportation and offered undreamed-of wages to the simple farm hands from the cotton fields of Georgia and Alabama.

Estimates of the number of Negroes that have come north vary anywhere from two hundred and fifty thousand to half a million. So far there seem to be no trustworthy figures. Newark, it is said, has absorbed about ten thousand. How many are living in the adjoining boroughs no one knows.

At first the railroad and other companies furnished the transportation, sending agents all through the South, who painted in glowing terms— who knows how highly colored?—the high wages and advantages of the North. But apparently that was not long necessary. The news spread like wildfire; it was like the gold fever in '49. The Negroes sold their simple belongings, and, in some instances, valuable land and property, and flocked to the northern cities, even though they had no objective work in sight. And they are still coming. Enough money has been saved from their unprecedented wages to send for wives and children. Almost every day one may see in the Pennsylvania station groups of Negro women sitting patiently, surrounded by bundles and babies and shivering in cotton garments, waiting for night to come, which will bring the men to meet them.

While getting ready to crowd up here, the Negroes composed a chant down in Dixie which ran like this:

"New Jersey, New Jersey, the land where the fritters Fall into the syrup right off of the trees!"

"But I ain't seen the fritters nor the syrup!" exclaimed one of these dusky Southerners the other day.

The high cost of living has soared far beyond the reported rise of 18 per cent in wages. The corner grocery, with its bewildering bright-colored canned goods, and other dazzling shops offer unusual opportunities for getting rid of money. The instalment houses, too, are reaping a harvest. The stores of "hog and hominy," corn meal, syrup and sweet potatoes which the migrants in many instances clubbed together and brought on with them in freight cars are gone by this time. The process of learning to use hard coal, which they must buy in small quantities, is wasteful. And the saloons welcome them heartily. No one draws the color line there! Negro ministers and social workers who are among them report with sorrow and amazement the amount of whiskey (no beer) that these people have already formed the habit of buying. Evil tentacles, too, have grasped young southern Negro girls, who have disappeared into houses of ill fame.

A number of undesirable, helpless folk, including widows and deserted wives, have "come along in the excitement," as one old cripple remarked. These the Associated Charities workers are trying to send back to the sunny South. One old man, totally blind, is easily recognized as belonging to the type of itinerant beggars familiar on the streets in southern towns, where they sit, making a cheerful noise on some screeching instrument. He says Newark is a wicked city, because the accustomed nickels and pennies do not fall readily into his hand, and is therefore quite willing to return to his native land.

Many of the older men did not intend to engage in hard labor, because they had a number of strong young sons in the family group. But illness has overtaken some of these young people, and the older ones have been obliged to take heavy work, with the result that they too have fallen ill. The native Negro residents of the city and suburban towns have been kind and generous in helping the southern strangers. They have collected money to send numbers back home, and, when the bitter cold weather began, they collected and distributed thousands of garments. Resident colored people have also taken hundreds of newcomers into their own homes until rooms could be found for them.

But while different churches and kind-hearted people have been most active in helping individually, there was no concerted movement to bring all these forces together until recently, when the Negro Welfare League of New Jersey was organized.

On the other hand, there are unscrupulous Negroes who have not hesitated to take advantage of the trust the strangers have reposed in them.

On January 6, a voluble, well-dressed Negro, representing himself as a house-agent, got $80 in first payments for rooms and then disappeared. White sharpers, too, have been active. A favorite method of getting money is to pretend to be a secret-society agent and secure membership fees from the unwary.

Almost all newcomers are from southwest Georgia and the adjoining counties. It seems impossible that a Negro is left in Dothan, Alabama. In fact, a white farmer writes from near there: "There has been lots of darkies left here and nearly all the good ones is gone."

They are country folk by every implication of their being, with the slow southern speech that to the northern ear is at first unintelligible. Already they are the despair of housewives, who eagerly welcomed much-needed houseworkers, innocently supposing that these people, whose chief labor had heretofore been picking cotton, would readily adapt themselves to city homes. In the factories and freight-yards the men and boys, when overheated, throw off their outer clothing, just as they would in the mild South, only to be laid up as a consequence with grip and pneumonia. With swollen feet from the unaccustomed roads and pavements and long hours of toil, they are obliged to lose many days' work. The Municipal Employment Bureau reports that they are now only applying for indoor work, as they have begun to realize the hardships of outdoor labor in a northern winter. To the outdoor worker the snow, too, is a disagreeable hindrance. "All this stuff flyin' 'round in the air confuses me!" they say. When we read in trade journals of the difficulty of inducing these laborers to stick to their jobs, we are not entirely convinced that it is altogether "because they cannot stand prosperity," as one journal puts it.

Moreover, the fumes in the munition factories have made many of them temporarily ill, and they have therefore sought other places and accepted lower wages. The recent destruction of several ammunition plants has thrown a number out of work and frightened away more, so that the difficulties and real hardships attached to their new jobs, added to the strangeness of their surroundings, have been the chief cause of the irregularity of their labor. We know of many families that have been obliged to move again and again in order to find a home, while the breadwinner has had to accept lower wages for that reason.

The industries of New Jersey went after these laborers because they needed them in their business. But, although the Negro is warmly welcomed as a laborer, it is increasingly apparent that as a Negro he is unwelcome. In a suburb of Newark there are forty Negro families who are better housed than the average and who thus have a chance to develop proper home life. When the white ministers of the place were asked to invite the colored children to their Sunday schools, they demurred, saying it "would not work." So a separate building was hired by the Negroes themselves and they are carrying on their own Sunday school.

Soon after the migration began to be noticeable, suddenly, mysteriously, almost in a night, the signs To Let and For Rent in the part of the city where small houses and flats were available were changed to "For Sale," and a recent advertisement for rooms, inserted by Negroes, brought only two replies, neither of them from Newark. These humble newcomers, therefore, have been forced into finding lodgings in basements and in the worst parts of our city.

Several generations ago, when the Negro was a human chattel, the master was considered a bad business man who did not properly house his slaves. He lost money by it and the community did not prosper. But industries of New Jersey have utterly failed to provide the housing which would enable their Negro help to live decently and in enough comfort so that, while growing accustomed to their unusual work, they might be stimulated to become useful and efficient.

In the last two weeks the Negro Welfare Committee,[1] with the help of trained investigators from the Associated Charities, has visited 120 self-supporting families, all of whom were found in the worst sections of the city. A close study of fifty-three of these families reveals that 166 adults—only twenty of whom are over forty years of age—and 134 children, a total of 300 souls, are all crowded into unsanitary, dark quarters, averaging four and two-sevenths persons to a room. These fifty-three families pay a total rent per month of $415.50, an average of $7.86. The average wage of these people is $2.60 a day. In not one of the 120 families was there a wage-earner making the maximum wage of $3 and $4 a day. Here are some of the notes brought back by visitors who recently made these studies:

"Wife and three children living over a stable. Husband earning $11 a week." "Three families in four rooms." "A little house, not fit for a chicken-coop." "A sorry-looking house for so much money—$15 a month; doors off the hinges; water in the cellar; two families in five rooms." "Indescribable; so dark they must keep the light burning all day." "This family lives in three rooms on the second floor of a rickety frame house, built on the side of a hill, so that the back rooms are just above the ground. The entrance is in a muddy, disorderly yard and is through a tunnel in the house. The rooms are hard to heat because of cracks. A boy of eighteen was in bed breathing heavily; very ill with pneumonia; delirious at times."

And so the list goes on, describing the difficulties and tragedies that would be sure to overtake numbers of unsophisticated country people recently arrived from a part of Georgia and Alabama not far from the Gulf of Mexico. Unused to city life, crowded into dark rooms, their clothing and household utensils unsuitable, the stoves they have bought being all too small to heat even the tiny rooms they have procured (the instalment houses are charging from $20 to $30 for these stoves), shivering with the cold from which they do not know how to protect themselves, it is small wonder that illness has overtaken large numbers.

The health department's report for December states that excessive labor and bronchial pneumonia were responsible for more than one-third of the 975 cases of diseases reported last month. There were 287 more cases of sickness reported than in the preceding month. The deaths from the malady numbered ninety-four.

Health Officer Craster said the cause of pneumonia increase must be laid to the severe weather in December and to the increasing number of colored laborers from the South who are employed in large industrial plants of the city. He continued: "It is unfortunate that these people have been allowed to come here without any advice as to how to live and keep themselves in health in this climate. The colored man has a natural predisposition to chest diseases, such as tuberculosis and pneumonia, and to the latter he falls an easy victim."

Dr. Craster said also that old, dilapidated buildings, long closed as undesirable for habitation, have been opened and rented to them. "These houses," he said, "are rented out as housekeeping apartments irrespective of the fact that there are no facilities for such purposes. Kitchen ranges, lavatories, baths and toilets are either altogether absent or inadequate. There is no heat in a majority of these places, with the consequence that whole families are found crowded around a small kerosene or coal stove in stuffy rooms, with no ventilation, where all the housekeeping is done and where frequently the whole family sleep together to keep warm."

The health inspectors report that wherever these conditions were discovered they directed the inhabitants to get better quarters and notified the owners of the premises, by written notice, that the rooms were not again to be rented. They further recommended that a campaign of education be instituted by the health department for better homes. "They (the Negroes) seem to be a simple, easy-going, honest sort of people who know no better."

It is all very well to tell them that they must not live in such abominable buildings, but, ignorant as these people are and much as they need instruction as to how to live in this climate and in a strange city, they are with few exceptions anxious and willing to move into decent homes and neighborhoods. *There are no decent houses for them to rent.*

Many have burned their ships behind them, others had no ships to burn, and many came north because of a desire to get away from parts of the South where race troubles are acute. All are dazzled by the lure of city life. They are here to stay. It is reported that thousands more are preparing to come in the spring.

There are nearly one million Negro farm operators in the South and it is estimated that the total wealth of the Negroes of the United States is about one billion dollars. They own twenty-one million acres of land, or more than thirty-two thousand square miles—an area greater than that of the state of South Carolina. The pall of illiteracy is slowly being removed from the South and higher and secondary education are becoming increasingly obtainable for the Negro. A Negro farmer at Albany, Georgia, is the owner of 10,000 acres of land. Ninety families reside on his plantations. A fourteen-year-old Negro boy won the first prize for cotton at the Oklahoma State Fair. The champion corn grower of Missouri is the principal of the Bartlett Farm and School for Negroes of Dalton, Mo.

But while Negro farmers are 29 per cent of the total farmers in the

South, Negro farm owners are still only 7 per cent of the total owners.

The South is more prosperous today than she has ever been before, with diversified agriculture making rapid progress, railroad expansion inevitable and factories fully employed. But there is also a shortage of labor there, and the South can ill afford to lose a half million farm laborers who are adapted to the southern climate. The Negro has made his best progress down South. The southern people should strive to keep him there, not by laws and lock-ups, but by better wages and by more and better opportunities of profit sharing, and above all by the cultivation of the spirit that will make it more and more possible for the Negro to accumulate property and to live in peace with his neighbors, especially his white neighbors. To that end it is hoped that the citizens of southern states will search for and put into office such public officials as the present governor of Kentucky.

On the other hand, there is no doubt that the Negro laborer from the South between the ages of twenty and forty will be able to compete successfully with the northern laborer if he becomes properly acclimated. But one cannot fail to see that the overcrowded, unhealthful and often evil surroundings in which the little children of these people are already placed are sure to result disastrously for them, and that no large increase of wages or other advantages of city life can compensate. It is not entirely a Negro problem. It is the city laborer's problem. The Slav and Italian and Russian Jew face the same difficulty. The influx of a number of people who happen to be Negroes merely augments it.

This migration from the South will be a blessing in disguise if it will show the people of this community the absolute necessity of getting together not only to improve living conditions among these strangers, but to begin to solve the whole problem of providing proper housing for the great mass of the people whose labor is the chief asset of the city. Meanwhile there is trouble brewing for the municipalities that have invited southern Negroes to become residents of the most crowded parts of the United States, without any other preparation than a pay envelope.

---

1. The Negro Welfare Committee, actually called the Negro Welfare League, was formed on January 8, 1917. In January 1919 it became the New Jersey Urban League with William M. Ashby as executive secretary.

4   PROBLEMS IN PUBLIC HEALTH, 1932

One of the worst manifestations of the poor living conditions of blacks in New Jersey between the two wars was the incidence of tuberculosis. This was largely the result of the relatively high population density of blacks in substandard housing and their inability to secure adequate medical assistance—tragic consequences of poverty and racial discrimination. Many hospitals in the state restricted the number of black patients and doctors, or managed to exclude them entirely. These problems are explored in the following article by Beatrice A. Myers and Ira De A. Reid. It is the most disturbing exposé of the connection between racial discrimination and inferior health conditions for blacks in New Jersey during the inter-war period. Tuberculosis was the major disease of blacks between 1917 and 1940 despite substantial improvements made in its detection and cure. The disease was especially acute among blacks in Newark, the state's largest city. Between 1917, when Helen Pendleton criticized the health standards of migrants, and 1932, when the Myers-Reid study was presented, conditions actually worsened. In the larger cities, blacks sought to ameliorate health problems by establishing small hospitals and by protesting the exclusionary practices of the public and private medical institutions. Some improvements were made in their health care during the 1940s. But the first massive assault against tuberculosis and a host of other diseases having their origins in poor living conditions came as recently as the 1960s.

Beatrice A. Myers and Ira De A. Reid, "The Toll of Tuberculosis among Negroes in New Jersey," *Opportunity* 10 (1932): 279-82.

It is becoming more and more apparent as research advances that tuberculosis is a disease of poverty and ignorance. No one is surprised when the death rate from this disease is higher in a slum neighborhood than in a wealthy neighborhood. Yet when the question of tuberculosis among Negroes is discussed, it is too often taken for granted that the high death rate in this group is due not to environmental factors but to some "racial susceptibility." This paper, however, is presented not from the angle of *Dies Irae,* but with consideration of the social aspects and environmental factors related to the problem.

That a high tuberculosis death rate among the Negroes is a societal indictment, and a heavy one, is apparent from one glance at the crude death rate. In New Jersey during 1930, 264 Negroes died from tuberculosis for each 100,000 in the population, while 58 white people per 100,000 died from this disease. In other words, the colored population of New Jersey is dying 4.6 times as fast from tuberculosis as the white population.

In 1927, the latest date for which figures are available, only three of the southern states had colored tuberculosis death rates higher than that in New Jersey. The other eight states for which the Census Bureau gives the figures all had rates under 200 per 100,000 though for that year the rate in New Jersey was 237.

If the tuberculosis death rates for the white and colored populations since 1910 are put on a logarithmic chart to show the trend, three periods come to light. From 1910 to 1918 the two lines follow similar paths, with the Negro rate having perhaps a slight advantage in rate of decline. The phenomenal drop from 1918 to 1921, which occurred universally, is not so pronounced in the Negro line and did not reach its lowest point until 1922. Since 1922 there has been no appreciable decline in the Negro trend. On the contrary, there is a very definite tendency for the rate to rise, as is shown by the high point of 1925 and the fact that the last two years have shown decided increases.

In 1930 the white tuberculosis death rate was 45.2 per cent lower than that in 1920. The rate for Negroes in 1930, however, was only 7.9 per cent lower than the 1920 figure. If we take 1921 as the end of the phenomenon following 1918 for the white rate and 1922 as the end of the Negro period of greatest decline, we find that in 1930 the white rate is 41 percent *lower* and the Negro rate 14 percent *higher* than their respective bases.

The significance of these figures is further enhanced by an examination of the specific death rates by age. Although the colored population of New Jersey according to the last census was only 5 per cent of the total, colored deaths from tuberculosis made up 20 per cent of all tuberculosis deaths. Colored infants under 5 years of age accounted for over one-third of the total tuberculosis deaths in that age group; namely, 25 per cent. Nearly one-half of the deaths in the age group 5 to 14 years were of colored children—47 per cent. Young people from 15 to 24 years of age who died from tuberculosis were colored in 31 per cent of the deaths, while adults 25 years and over were colored in 15 per cent of the deaths.

The specific death rates show the terrific toll of this disease among Negro children and young adults. It is especially noticeable that the death rate for colored children under 5 is six and one-half times that for whites, 137 compared to 21. The highest point in the colored death rate is reached at the age group 15 to 19 where it is eight times the white rate. The first high point for the white population is reached in the 20 to 24 year age group, where the colored rate is still four times as high. The colored rate gradually falls after that, while the white rate continues to rise until age group 55 to 64, when the colored rate is over twice as high.

An examination of the chart showing the sex and age of the deaths from tuberculosis by color reveals some striking differences. The number of deaths for young Negro women is exceptionally high, remaining so for three age groups, from 15 to 29. In fact, the deaths in these age groups are over 50 per cent of the total tuberculosis deaths among Negro women, although the corresponding age groups account for only 41 per cent among white women. The curve for white women drops rapidly after age group 20 to 24, but for colored women the curve rises to age group 25 to 29, after which it drops even more rapidly than that for white women. In proportion to the population, however, the number of colored women dying is considerably greater in each group than that of white women.

Young colored men also have a very high rate of death, especially noticeable in the three age groups between 20 and 34. White males, on the other hand, have the greatest number of deaths, in age group 40-44.

In 1928 a study of the living cases of tuberculosis in the State was made by the New Jersey Tuberculosis League. This revealed a high fatality rate among the Negro population, there being only four living cases per death compared to eight living cases per death of the whites. A great number of Negro cases alive in the population was shown. In age group 15-19, in spite of the high death rate, there were four times as many living cases. In age group 25-29 there were nearly five times as many living cases as deaths.

The sex and age distribution of the living cases was shown to be somewhat different from that of the deaths, with the number of colored male cases almost equaling the number of female cases in the early age groups. This was especially noticeable in age group 25-29 where the highest point of both cases and deaths among colored females occurs. The number of living cases of males in this age group was only very slightly below that for females, although in the case of the deaths there were only 28 males compared to 41 females of this age group, a considerable difference.

Although the condition of the Negroes in New Jersey may be very bad, it might be possible that these are so concentrated that the problem presents itself to only a small section of the state. As a matter of fact, however, the Negro problem presents itself to the entire area. New Jersey has the largest percentage of its population Negro of any northern state except Missouri.

Essex County has the largest number of Negroes, but Atlantic County has the highest percentage of its population Negro. Camden, Hudson, Mercer, Monmouth, and Union Counties all have more than 10,000 Negroes. In eleven counties Negroes are more than 5 per cent of the population. Two countries, Sussex and Warren, have less than 1 per cent Negro population, and with Hunterdon there are less than 500 Negroes in each.

It is not surprising that Essex County and Hudson County, both counties of great density of population and heavy industry, should have the highest Negro tuberculosis death rates. Atlantic County is third in rank in the three-year period 1928 to 1930. Its concentrated Negro population has been attracted by the hotels and other features of a resort section. Left with nothing to do in the winter months, hit hard by the depression, it is not surprising that there should be a high tuberculosis death rate there. The lower rates in Middlesex and Camden Counties, in spite of the industrial nature of these areas, may be due in part to the presence of rural sections which make unnecessary the intense crowding present in other counties. This favorable condition is not present in the cities of these counties, as New Brunswick and Perth Amboy both have rates for Negroes of over 200, while the rate for the city of Camden is 178.

All of the twenty-one counties in the state have colored tuberculosis death rates considerably higher than those for their white population. Even in Salem County, where the colored death rate is 126 per 100,000, this is two and one-half times the white rate of 51. Cape May County, with the exceptionally low white rate of 39, has a colored rate of 206— over five times as high.

The colored tuberculosis mortality rate in Essex County is nearly five times as high as the white, while for the city of Newark it is over five times as high in the three-year period under consideration. East Orange, a suburban city, has a white tuberculosis mortality of only 32 per 100,000, with the colored mortality rate at 158. This, again, while low, is nearly five times the white rate. Orange, with a white rate of 77, reports a colored rate of 212, nearly three times as high. The differences in rates between the cities of this county are very significant. Congestion and heavy industry produce high rates for both races; the better living conditions and higher standard of living of a suburban community produce comparatively low rates for both races.

The city of Newark has one of the highest rates for tuberculosis among Negroes in the entire country. The average rate for the three-year period 1928–1930 was 407, 25 per cent higher than the rate for Essex County; and 70 per cent higher than the rate for the state. The rate in the last two years has increased sharply, moreover, registering 491 for 1930. The highest rate recorded by the Census Bureau in 1926 for those cities in which the data are given was 331 for New Orleans. In that year the rate for Newark was 329.

The city of Newark contains 19 per cent of the colored population of the state, but from 1928 to 1930, 32 per cent of the colored deaths from tuberculosis occurred there. At present, the rate is higher than it has been since 1917. The 1930 rate is 1.3 per cent higher than that for 1920, and 53.1 per cent higher than in 1924 when it reached its lowest point.

The colored population of Newark makes up less than one-tenth of the total. Yet 37 per cent of the deaths from tuberculosis in 1929 to 1930 were of Negroes. *Two-thirds of the deaths* under 5 years of age were of Negro infants and over that proportion—namely 69.4 per cent of those between 5 and 14 were of colored children. Deaths among Negro young people accounted for nearly half of all deaths between 15 and 25 years of age.

The scourge which this disease is among the Negroes of Newark, if shown graphically in a chart comparing the rates (for 1929 and 1930), age group for age group with those for white people would reveal that in each five-year age group through 19, the rate for Negroes is over 10 times that for white people. If all tuberculosis deaths under 15 are considered together, the Negro rate is twenty-two times the white rate.

That this situation is unnecessary is shown by a comparison of the rates for the city of Newark with those for the state as a whole. Urban communities ordinarily have higher mortality rates than rural, and likewise the rates for the cities of a state are usually higher than those for the state as a whole. The rates for tuberculosis mortality among the white people of Newark, however, are only very slightly above those for the state as a whole, while the Negro rate for the city of Newark is more than one and three-fourths times as high as that for the state as a whole, great as that is.

The situation being what it is in Newark, it is important to know in what sections of the city the problem is worst. An analysis by wards has therefore been made, but for this purpose we have to use the mortality data from the Newark Department of Health, which is not the same as that from the State Department of Health. These figures give a total average death rate for the years 1927 to 1929 of 308.5 per 100,000.

Five of the wards of the city have rates over 400 per 100,000. These are the Second, Fifth, Tenth, Twelfth and Fifteenth. The Twelfth Ward, with a Negro population of only 418 returns a rate of 549.0. While this should not be considered final, as it is based on a total of only 7 deaths for the three years, it cannot be greatly questioned after one sees the conditions along the dumps where these people try to keep alive. The Second and the Fifteenth Wards are on the edges of the Black Belt of Newark, where evidently conditions were worse than at its heart.

Six Wards return rates between 250 and 400, including the Third, Ninth, Fourth, Eighth, Eleventh and Sixteenth. The Third Ward, where nearly one-third of all the Negroes in the city live, shows a tuberculosis mortality rate for them of 282.7, which is three and one-third times the white rate for the Ward, 84.2. The Eighth and Ninth Wards, each have over 2,000 Negroes, making up respectively 5 per cent and 3 per cent of their population. The other three Wards under consideration have only a few over 1,000 Negroes, who in the Fourth Ward are 15 per cent of the total. The actual number of Negroes in each Ward is evidently not a valuable criteria of their living conditions. We really should know on how many blocks in each Ward they are concentrated and what is the extent of congestion in these blocks.

There are five Wards remaining with Negro tuberculosis mortality rates of less than 250. Four of these are adjoining—the Thirteenth, Fourteenth, Sixth and Seventh. It cannot be considered accidental that the Thirteenth Ward, on the outskirts of Newark and primarily suburban in character, should have reported no colored deaths during the three years considered. The white death rate in this ward is only 55.

In every city ward the Negro mortality rate is considerably higher than that for whites. The Ninth Ward, with the low rate of 35 for white people shows a rate of 346 for the colored, nearly ten times as high. In the Fourth Ward, where the colored rate is 305, the white rate is very high, 229. The Sixth Ward has comparatively low rates for both colored and white, 130 and 64 respectively. In the Twelfth Ward, where the unusual rate of 549 prevails for the colored people, the white rate is also high, though less than one-fourth of the former, at 128.

No doubt, if Newark were divided into health areas and analyzed on that basis, a correlation between living conditions and mortality rates would be found. In spite of all studies which purport to prove that there is no correlation between housing and tuberculosis mortality, it is only common sense to see that where there is congestion, unsanitary conditions, and lack of sunshine; combined with undernourishment, poor food and ignorance of health laws, there the tubercle bacillus will thrive.

Despite the fact that the situation is as it has been pictured here, very little actual work is being done outside of two counties—Essex and Hudson—though the colored people need much more attention than do white people, and work among them would give larger returns.

A study made by the Department of Institutions and Agencies in 1928 shows that 11 per cent of the first admissions to the institutions of the state were Negroes, though we have shown that tuberculosis deaths are 20 per cent of the total. A study of the New Jersey Tuberculosis League shows that in 1930, while there were 478 admissions of Negro residents of the state to all institutions, including those outside the state, compared to 3,349 of white residents, or 13 per cent of the total, only 8 per cent of the patient days in the sanatoria were spent by Negroes. It is at once evident that admissions of Negroes to sanatoria is not sufficient information to judge the extent of sanatorium care given them. There were only 126 patient days per colored case admitted as contrasted to 207 patient days per white case admitted. In Essex County 21 per cent of the admissions and 12 per cent of the patient days were for Negroes, compared to 33 per cent of the deaths.

The study also shows that of the pulmonary cases which were diagnosed on admission, 16 per cent of the white and only 8 per cent of the colored cases were in the minimal stage. On the other hand, 46 per cent of the white and 67 per cent or over two-thirds of the colored cases were far advanced when admitted to the institutions. Is it any wonder that the prognosis for the colored case is so much worse than for the white?

There are no figures available as to the number of Negroes examined in the clinics of the state. Newark has long had special Negro clinics. For the six months—April to September, 1931—an average of 253 cases were seen each month in the Negro clinic. Thirty-one per cent of all visits and 22 per cent of all new cases in the clinics in this period were of Negroes.

Hudson County rather than open a clinic labeled "Negro Clinic," has established clinics in areas largely populated by colored people but admitting both colored and white cases. There are two Negro nurses on the staff, and Negro doctors are present at these clinics. A large number of white people appear at these clinics, which are very well attended. This plan has proved very satisfactory.

Little special health education propaganda had been carried on by the tuberculosis leagues of the state. The Essex County League is the only organization with a special colored worker, although she has been able to stimulate interest in the problem in neighboring counties. Hudson County clinics, with the cooperation of the County Tuberculosis and Health League, conducted a series of health meetings in Negro neighborhoods. Bergen County has also put on a few such special meetings. Outside of Essex County, however, the work is sporadic and not consistently followed up.

The problem of tuberculosis among the Negro population is one of tremendous proportions. At present no consistent, thought-out plan has been introduced to meet it. Yet this is a situation where a minimum of effort would reap a maximum reward. Only a beginning in health education for Negroes, only a little attention to getting them into sanatoria in the minimal stage of disease and making their life there sufficiently pleasant so that they would remain, only a modicum of effort in forcing landlords of colored tenements and city health departments to uphold the sanitary laws in colored areas, is necessary to bring down the tuberculosis death rate for this underprivileged minority.

5   ORGANIZING THE URBAN COMMUNITY, 1932

On the eve of the New Deal, the Interracial Committee of the New Jersey Conference of Social Work, a private social service agency, released the study, *The Negro in New Jersey*. It was the most comprehensive examination ever attempted of black life in the state and stood as a scholarly affirmation of racial equality with an enduring impact on race relations. In keeping with the liberalism of the New Deal generation, *The Negro in New Jersey* championed interracial cooperation and urged that an effort be made to ameliorate imperfections in the social order arising from racial injustices. In the following chapter taken from the study, the institutional structure of black communities in New Jersey is examined, probably for the first time in New Jersey history, as complex entities of social, economic, and cultural life. Not surprisingly, the church was found to be the paramount institution of the race; however, the study also shed light on many secular organizations. It explored the legal history of racial equality in New Jersey and provided evidence of persistent racial indignities. The book benefited from the exhaustive analysis of Ira De A. Reid, the research director of the National Urban League. Reid, who directed the study, headed a staff of fifteen—nine blacks and six whites—that conducted over 2,000 interviews of black families in sixty communities.

New Jersey Conference of Social Work, "Aspects of the Negro Community," *The Negro in New Jersey* (Newark, N.J., 1932), pp. 62-64.

THE MOST important and the financially strongest institution among Negroes in New Jersey is the church. The Federal Census of Religious Bodies, 1926, revealed that 412 (11.2 per cent) of the 3,670 churches in New Jersey were Negro. These 412 churches, 370 of which had church edifices, had a membership of 71,221 persons. They represented 19 different denominations, chief among which were the Baptist bodies, with 159 churches and 41,129 members.

Recently the Negro church in New Jersey has become a social center, ministers have become more interested in social and political affairs, and the members have endeavored to have less of the "other worldliness" and more of a practical religion. There has also arisen a number of esoteric cults and highly emotional religious groups during the last decade. The rapid influx of a new Negro population was also responsible for an increase in the number of meeting places. In urban centers, particularly, it has been responsible for the "store-front" church, so called because the group's meetings are held in buildings normally used for stores.

The relative importance of the church in Negro life in New Jersey is noted in the following distribution: There is one church for every 1,374 persons in the total population, but one for every 567 persons of the Negro population. The average membership of all churches in New Jersey is 541, while the average membership of all Negro churches is 173.

A concise picture of the relation of the Negro church to the population is shown in an analysis made of sixty-one churches of ten denominations, having an aggregate membership of 25,336 persons. During the twelve year period 1920–1931 the average membership increased from 284 to 432 or 52 per cent.

Returns from fifty-three of the churches in 1930 showed that they controlled real property, chiefly church buildings and parsonages, having an estimated value of $3,766,000, an average per church of $71,056. But on these properties there were indebtedness amounting to $1,865,273, an average per church of $35,194. The total receipts of these institutions during 1930 was $276,817 or an average per church of $5,223. More so than any other institution, the Negro church in New Jersey with its rapid growth in congregations, its rise in membership and its increase in church properties; its heavy indebtedness and its per capita membership income from 1930 ($10.92) represents the economic and social struggle of the Negro masses. Yet, of the sixty-one churches reporting in 1931, only four have a general social program with paid workers, while only sixteen carry on any kind of extension programs with volunteer workers.

SOCIAL, CULTURAL AND FRATERNAL

Less compact in their organization than the church, but exercising a much wider influence, are the Negro clubs and lodges. Within recent years the mania for joining lodges and clubs has been less pronounced, but the importance of these organizations within the life of the group has waned but little. They provide, in many instances, the only opportunity for group expression outside of the church. These social groups vary from branches of national organizations, to the independent local and civic groups found in every community.

Among the national organizations is the National Association for the Advancement of Colored People with nineteen branches in New Jersey. This organization through its locals in such centers as Asbury Park, Atlantic City, Camden, Elizabeth, Jersey City, Long Branch, Morristown, Newark, Paterson, Plainfield, Orange, Roselle, South Bergen County, Summit, South Orange, Trenton and Westfield, is particularly active in matters of political action and racial segregation. Local branches have successfully protested racial segregation as in Plainfield where a sign was displayed in a cemetery designating a special section for Negroes, and in Paterson where an amusement park endeavored to restrict Negro attendance to one day a week.

Outstanding among the state-wide organizations is the New Jersey State Federation of Colored Women's Clubs, which in 1930 had seventy-two affiliated bodies. While interests of the local groups are varied including social, political, reading, civic, religious, domestic art, and welfare units, all are combined on a state-wide program for the welfare of Negro girls. Many local branches also provide educational scholarships for their high school graduates.

The Federation of Colored Organizations of New Jersey was organized in 1915 to encourage racial unity and to stimulate civic pride and consciousness. It is particularly interested in the political rights of the Negro and the progress of Negro business enterprises.

Of relatively recent interest are the various interracial committees of the state. Aside from the committee sponsoring this survey, there are (1) the New Jersey Interracial Committee of Church Women, under the auspices of the Federal Council of Churches, and (2) local interracial groups, frequently sponsored by a few liberals, or by the activity of a character-building agency as the Y.M.C.A. or the Y.W.C.A. The Negro work of the Y.M.C.A. is under the auspices of the Interracial Committee of the State Committee. All these groups have created and stimulated discussion and action on various phases of Negro-white relations throughout the state. The interracial conferences of the New Jersey Church Women, and the state-wide conference of the Y.M.C.A. are outstanding examples of this effort.

Foremost in members among the fraternal organizations in New Jersey are the Independent Benevolent Protective Order of Elks and the Ancient Free and Accepted Masons with their auxiliaries for women and children. Other fraternal orders include, the Odd Fellows, Knights of Pythias, Independent Order of Saint Luke's, Court of Calanthe, Order of Menelik, Order of Moses, the Good Samaritans, American Woodmen, Sons and Daughters of Africa and the Household of Ruth. A conservative estimate of the membership of these orders is forty-five thousand.

Special groups include the American Legion and the Veterans of Foreign Wars for ex-service men, the former being particularly active in South Jersey where there are separate posts. Professional persons are also organized racially, aside from holding membership in state-wide organizations. Examples of this type of organization are the North Jersey Medical Association and the New Jersey Organization of Teachers of Colored Children.

Since the World War there has been a tremendous growth in Negro Greek letter societies, composed of college students and alumni. While the interest of these groups is basically social, they have often formed the nucleus for constructive civic action.

POLITICAL

There are approximately 135,000 Negroes of voting age in New Jersey who in the past have aligned themselves largely with the Republican party. A group of Negro women are organized into the Negro Women's Republican Clubs of New Jersey. Negro Assemblymen have been elected to the State Legislature from Essex County on the Republican ticket. During the gubernatorial campaign of 1931, Democratic groups were organized among Negroes in Atlantic, Essex and Hudson counties. The Independent Political Progressive Organization of New Jersey claimed 20,000 members. Negroes have a state-wide Republican organization, and are members of several county committees. Neither Socialism nor Communism has developed any appreciable voting strength among Negroes in New Jersey.

The political and racial consciousness of New Jersey's Negroes was evidenced in 1931 when under the guidance of the National Association for the Advancement of Colored People, a Republican candidate, David Baird, Jr., was opposed because of his vote while a member of the U.S. Senate to sanction the nomination of Judge John J. Parker of North

Carolina to the U.S. Supreme Court. Meanwhile, Democratic representatives accused Republicans of "quieting the colored people" through the creation of a Migrant Welfare Commission with a grant of $15,000 to study employment conditions among Negroes.

From many sections of the state, however, there are frequent evidences of the exploitation of the Negro vote by both white and Negro politicians. In the opinion of many public officials and lay leaders, political matters are "a field that should become reason for grave concern among the Negroes themselves. They much too easily become the easy prey of the influence of the self-seekers in political affairs." "They lack effective political organizations and the discipline of definite political and racial objectives." Others maintain, as in Monmouth County, that "at different times Negroes have proven to be the balance of power under intelligent and wise leadership, and have taken an active and intelligent part in political affairs."

Evidence of the political power of the Negro group is shown in Atlantic County where it had 546 members on the state, county and city payrolls, with annual salaries in October 1931 of approximately $875,000 and in Camden where there were 683 Negro public employees earning a total of $775,000. In Newark, Negroes have little political advantage. According to one observer, "Aside from two men in the Department of Public Welfare; two in the Water Department; three on the police force; seven nurses and three physicians in the Department of Health; one clerk, one nurse, two janitors and six teachers in the Department of Education, there are no Negroes employed in any positions of importance in the city."

The reason for this failure to make gains politically is attributed to "(1) the lack of a Negro leader, (2) the domination of Negro politicians who practice their professions in Newark, but who reside elsewhere in Essex County." As an example of this situation it may be noted that Negroes in the Third Ward of Newark, where they form more than eighty per cent of the population, register no influence beyond having a few district leaders.

6   CIVIL RIGHTS ACTIVISM, 1934–45

Harold A. Lett (1896–1974) was the executive secretary of the New Jersey Urban League from 1934 to 1945 and a leading advocate of interracial cooperation in the civil rights struggle. A native of Adrian, Michigan, he was the industrial secretary of the Pittsburgh Urban League before he came to Newark to assume one of the most important positions in the black community.

Prior to the 1930s the New Jersey Urban League refrained from direct protest activities and concentrated its efforts on social work and job placement. These concerns were enhanced by the rise of civil rights advocacy during the 1930s and 1940s. Under Lett's leadership the League expanded its social work activities and supported the protest movement spurred by the National Association for the Advancement of Colored People, the National Negro Congress, and the March on Washington Movement. In the following interview Lett discusses his role in the civil rights movement in Newark.

Interview with Harold A. Lett,
4 January, 20 February 1974
(Newark Public Library, New Jersey Reference Division).

INTERVIEWER:
    . . . Let's go to the integration of hospitals, the staff, which was something you'd worked for for many years with the Newark Interracial Council.
LETT:
    Yes, that's right. Because when I came to Newark in 1934 there wasn't a single black physician on the staff of any hospital in the Newark area. There wasn't a school for nurses available to a black girl anywhere in New Jersey. These were the conditions. This was before the war, of course, and we hadn't gotten into such a thing as blood donations and blood supplies. But even as late as World War II the Red Cross, in collaboration with the hospitals, segregated and labeled blood as from Negroes and from whites.
    So here was a total fight across the front, first of all for Negro physicians, on staff; the hospitals that claimed to have Negro staff, extended only what they called courtesy privileges. Meaning to say, technically and practically that a Negro doctor sending his patient to any one of our Essex County hospitals, lost that patient because he couldn't treat that patient in the hospital. A white physician took over or the hospital staff took over and from that point that patient was theirs. The Negro physician could only go in, look at the chart, and talk with his patient and go home, period. Now, this was the situation in every hospital. There was not a single black nurse in any of the hospitals nor were there any teaching facilities.
    My two daughters became nurses a few short years thereafter. Both of them had to go to New York for their training, and there were only two hospitals in New York that trained black nurses. Lincoln and Harlem. So, my two daughters are graduates of Lincoln.

Well, that meant then, all kinds of pressures through the committees, on doctors, on boards of directors, a continuing pressure until, one by one, they began to move. I think Beth Israel—which had two or three Negro doctors on courtesy staff—I think Beth Israel was the first one to break and admit a black doctor on staff. And, of course, as you know, access to the facilities of a hospital was absolutely imperative to the successful work of any physician anywhere. So, you can't find a responsible physician in the neighborhood any more, who isn't a member of some staff, somewhere, because his destiny depends upon that.

INTERVIEWER:

This was quite a concerted effort by the Interracial Council and several other groups.

LETT:

That's right. Well, ultimately we had formed—I say we had, I was the moving spirit in each instance—three different interracial committees and this was the theme of, first of all, the speech that I made to the Massachusetts Conference of Social Workers that later appeared in the Harvard Educational Review in pointing out the consistency of having as many interracial committees as you have problems that call for specialized attention. And this was what we had developed here in Newark.

We had, this first Interracial Council which is sort of a broad-based thing and then we had a council, an interracial council on education and then another one against the hostile activity between groups because that one was formed at the time of a riot here in the north side between Italians and Negroes, teenagers.

INTERVIEWER:

About what year was that?

LETT:

That was in the early '40's. I couldn't name the exact year. There's a sheet that I usually have that isn't with me here now and I think I could tell you the exact year from that, but it was in the early '40's.

INTERVIEWER:

Was there any particular thing that set off the rioting?

LETT:

Except the bad blood that existed, as it exists now. And it got out of hand and these were kids, high school kids, upper teenagers, high school age, and it was in the North 5th and 6th Street, Barringer High School area, and there were a number of little skirmishes, and then the big one. And I remember distinctly of one youth, black youth, being killed, I think there were two killed in that situation.

INTERVIEWER:

It was teenagers only, it didn't spread to the adults?

LETT:

No, it didn't spread to the adults. No, it was kept within that particular general area and in that one particular incident, except for all of the little spot incidences that had preceded and came to fruition in that one big one.

INTERVIEWER:

At this time, when you had organized the campaign with the Inter-racial Council to integrate the hospital staff, what was your position? Were you on the Urban League still at that time?

LETT:

Oh, yes. I was still Urban League and the Jewish agencies, the Jewish Congress, B'nai Brith, each of them had a professional worker occupy-ing the same sort of category as mine in the Urban League and we worked together, along with some of the non-Jewish whites who had a personal interest in the things we were doing. They were attracted to us individually because we had no central white Christian agency to work with as we did in the Jewish agencies, you see. Defense organizations in other words.

But we did have recruits from the YWCA. I don't recall ever having any help during that period from the YMCA. Actually, the YW and YM were not seeing eye to eye because of the liberal views of the YWCA. We weren't getting any of that kind of help from the Community Chest or its agencies because they were looking down their noses at us. This was a time when there were no camp facilities for black children but every year black people were called to make contributions for the camping pro-gram, and so on.

INTERVIEWER:

Maybe this would be the time to speak of some of the other agencies as you have been doing. First of all, I'd like to start with some of the black organizations. What sort of cooperation or non-cooperation did you get with the black ministers council and the NAACP?

LETT:

Yes. There was a black Baptist ministers organization that met every week. The Methodists and one Episcopalian, either were active members, fringe members of white associations or they had no association. The sprinkling of Methodists may come together just occasionally but not as did the Baptist because the Baptist was the large contingent of Chris-tians, Black Christians, in the community. They were passively friendly. I would get an invitation to one of their sessions during the year, maybe once a year, and always I had something to say about our social prob-lems, that was my only reason for being there in the idea of activating them something outside of their tightly religious preoccupations. So I would talk about the combining of forces for housing—this was before housing developments—I would talk with them about, say for instance, the physician deal in the hospitals.

Now, I never knew, really, how much effect these talks had because I was never called in in a consultative capacity for any action program that they may have devised. If they had an actions program I never knew unless just by sheerest of accident and it usually was an individual affair.

There were two, three, four of these ministers, these Baptist ministers, who saw themselves as budding politicians or persons with political influence. So that they would be working in and out of city hall on who happened to be the commissioner that they wanted to seek favors of. So it was a disorganized thing as far as the church was concerned. I never knew of any activity on the part of non-Baptist Negro ministers in terms of social activities out in the community.

Then, of course, there was the NAACP, and one of my first tasks, first moves, when I came to Newark was to discover that there was not good blood between the NAACP and the Urban League. So, I set about correcting that and one of the things I did was to open the Urban League building to the NAACP, free of charge, for all of its meetings. This had never occurred before.

They would get a room now and then from the YWCA or something of this sort. The Negro YWCA was a little cramped thing with virtually no room for meeting facilities. The black YMCA had taken over Court Street Armory so this was a big, almost barn-like structure with just a couple of offices. Now, these two black agencies were the step-children of our entire social machinery structure of Newark.

INTERVIEWER:

So, you let the NAACP come in and use your facilities of the Urban League.

LETT:

And we then reached a point of cooperative venture. I would appeal to them when I had something that needed their activist approach because in the Urban League my activism was on a different level completely. I mean, mine was totally persuasion without mass pressures, per se, except as they were accomplished through civic organizations. That was the reason for the interracial committees, the three different ones. Because they could get out into the community and do the things that as one Urban League secretary, without a constituency as such, could not possibly have accomplished.

So my relationship then with the NAACP was, as it was with the interracial committees, with the Jewish agencies, and now with the NAACP. My efforts to get the ministry to move were futile in a general sense. So this was the way then that was a coordination of civic pressures, and awareness, and sensitivity that flowed out of the things we were trying to accomplish in the Urban League.

INTERVIEWER:

Another social agency, and I'm not certain they were still active by the time you got to Newark—I know they were earlier—was the Friendly Fuld House.

LETT:

Oh yes. That was the neighborhood house. They were not activists in the sense of social pressures or anything of this sort. They attended to their duties of taking care of the kids and the parents in the various club activities in the neighborhood house. It was functioning then and we've just lost, within the past month, a very wonderful women who was a fledging in the Friendly Neighborhood House when I came in 1934. Mrs.Churchman, Gladys Churchman.

Garnet Henderson, who is long retired and is living out in Montclair, was the director of Friendly Neighborhood House when I came here. And we always had the very best of relationships.

INTERVIEWER:

I understand they helped to get the camps opened for black kids.

LETT:

Yes. Well, they were a part of the many forces that got into that because at the time, in '34, up until, I guess, 1940, '41 or '42, the only recreational leadership that black children had in the Essex County community were in such places as the Friendly Neighborhood House. The suburbs had something corresponding but on a smaller scale, even out as far as Morristown, Summit. But, as I say, they were small, independent operations, not quite compared to Friendly Neighborhood House in size.

Then, of course, a few years later, I don't remember just when, but Fuld House came into being. I think that was after the project was built though. I don't think Fuld House was in operation before the first housing projects were built in '39, '40, thereafter.

INTERVIEWER:

I'm amazed that several indignities you've mentioned. I just can't understand how human beings can treat other human beings that way. How can you maintain your dignity through all of this?

LETT:

Well, this is the great dilemma within the Negro world, has been for centuries because I can say centuries because of the revolts during the slave regime and long before there was any thought of emancipation. But it's the dilemma that has occurred, and the strength of the individual is the only thing that determines whether he turns out a good citizen or a bad citizen.

This is the hardest lesson for the white world to accept, to comprehend, to believe in, that the human spirit, subjected to a constant barrage of indignity, humiliation, dehumanization, is bound to crack under certain circumstances and among certain individuals. The mystery of American life today is the great number, the vast number, the great majority of black citizens who are good citizens yet despite this constant barrage. Now, to try to get this over to white society it's almost futile because they're not willing to accept—there's a guilt complex there— they're not willing to accept that they've been responsible for these things.

So, that when they talk today about drug addicts, muggers, purse snatchers, they don't realize that this is the product they have created. And that nothing we have or possess, or can do in the black world, can change that tide where this individual doesn't have the stamina and the strength to resist and to fight back on a different level. Now, no matter how so-called intelligent blacks may be measured by the white world, deep down inside them rankles this resentment and it depends upon our up-bringing, our teachings, our philosophy, how we bring it out. Now, this is the difference.

So, when you ask a question, how do we do it, God only knows except that which we learned during the slave regime that for survival, you learn to accept certain things no matter how deeply it rankles. So we have survived. One of the bitterest pages of history we have survived because of this. And the choices that individuals have made as against the kind of provocation that was theirs throughout their lifetime . . . .

7   OPPOSITION TO STATE REGULATION OF BUSINESS, 1938

The Depression seriously threatened black businesses in New Jersey. Many of them, especially vulnerable to the economic crisis, closed during the 1930s and never reopened. Those that survived often faced another danger from the plethora of new federal and state regulations on minimum wages, maximum working hours, and safety standards. In the following editorial from the *New Jersey Herald News,* a threat to the black beauty business by "greedy whites" is alleged. At this time a number of New Jersey cities considered the adoption of ordinances believed to be unfavorable to black beauticians. The *Herald News* was ever the guardian of black business interests in the state, a position of possible self-interest since beginning in 1939 its owners, Fred and Richard Martin, were manufacturers of a hair compound. The editorial calls on Governor A. Harry Moore to appoint a black member to the State Board of Beauty Culture Control.

"Protect Beauty Business," *New Jersey Herald News,* 23 July 1938.

The Colored Beauty Business in America is the biggest commercial enterprise that is owned and operated by the American Negro. Every year we spend over $100,000,000 for Beauty products alone. This money is not spent to "turn white," or to get "long, stringy, straight hair," but to present to the community a neat, clean and attractive appearance.

It is a business that is rapidly approaching the glorifying angles of a "New Profession." Cities, states and counties throughout the country are now considering and passing laws and ordinances of cosmotology. They have set up taxes, special fees, special requirements and special qualifications in all branches of the industry. Last but not least they have set up "special deceptions" for the poor colored beauty shop operators.

Thus, the growth and development of a great Negro business, which should be viewed with tolerant friendliness is now faced with deceit and disaster. We regret to say that the motive is not without its precedents. In this case the "greedy whites" of America have again joined hands to "fleece the Race" of its largest and juiciest plum.

In most cities and states the new laws to regulate the Beauty Shops have particularly distinguished themselves for lack of any consideration for the colored operators. The shorter hours and compensation laws deliberately set out to hamstring and thus subsidize this lucrative field into the hands of white ownership.

At the present time Beauticians in our own state are awaiting the appointment by Governor Moore of the new colored member to the State Board of Beauty Culture Control. Let us hope that such appointee qualifies in training and experience as a protector of Black Business in this world of "white greed."

8 EXERTING ECONOMIC PRESSURE, 1938

In many northern cities during the Depression, blacks organized Don't-Buy-Where-You-Cannot-Work campaigns. These actions were designed to force white-owned businesses in black communities suffering high employment to desegregate their work forces. In the following editorial from the *New Jersey Herald News,* this early effort of economic coercion is supported. In cities such as Newark, Jersey City, and Trenton, the direct action imposed by a boycott was successful. While blacks were using the ballot to their own advantage, they were also beginning to apply economic pressure.

"Negroes Must Work,"
New Jersey Herald News, 20 August 1938.

Newark colored citizens should jubilantly hail the decision of the local unit of the National Negro Congress to continue its job-finding program, and the HERALD NEWS commend the group for their successful efforts of the past few months. Recognizing the imperative need of more employment opportunities for Negroes, the Newark Negro Congress, in its program, has done much to direct the interest of the Negro masses toward SPENDING THEIR MONEY WHERE THEY CAN WORK.

It was less than five years ago that the present publishers of the HERALD NEWS, then sponsoring another local paper, first began to urge members of the race to unite in a campaign to create employment and opportunities. Partial success was obtained, which saw several large chain stores giving employment to Negroes as clerks for the first time. But it was over a year ago that the Newark Council of the Negro Congress, stirred into action by the decreasing of race employables, accepted the challenge which had been ignored by other better known organizations. The Congress planned a program, and they inflamed the Negroes of New Jersey as well as Newark to unite in a campaign that MUST succeed, if the race is to retain security and respectability.

NEGROES MUST WORK, and with private industry gradually closing its doors to race workers, new avenues of employment must be created. Other races gain employment from business firms where they spend their money, and the Negro is only asking for his rightful recognition. This is the program of the HERALD NEWS; this is the program of the Newark Council of the National Negro Congress; and this must be the program of all race organizations, including our religious bodies.

If more employment opportunities for Negroes are to be created we must SPEND OUR MONEY WHERE WE CAN WORK, thereby showing our appreciation to those merchants who recognize their obligation to their colored patrons. WE MUST do this!

Beginning with next week's issue the HERALD NEWS will publish a series of stories relating to those stores which employ Negro workers. This is YOUR fight. We can only show the way.

9 CROSSING THE COLOR LINE, 1938

By the 1930s, discriminatory actions against blacks met with aroused indignation and protest, as the following editorial from the *Newark Herald News* demonstrates. In August 1938 blacks attempting to use a public pool in Elizabeth were assailed and molested by whites, a vestige of earlier racial customs in that town. But the black bathers would not be intimidated, and the color line was soon crossed. The *Herald News* often reported such victories in the stuggle for civil rights and reminded its readers of the importance of a vigilant black press.

"Doing Our Bit,"
Newark Herald News, 27 August 1938.

Immediately upon discovery last week that Negroes were being assailed by whites when they attempted to swim in the city-owned Dowd Natatorium in Elizabeth . . . and that tomatoes had been hurled at women of our race . . . the NEWARK HERALD dispatched a representative[1] to that locality to see why the police of that locality were not rendering protection to members of our group.

Chief Frank Brennen of the Elizabeth Police Department told our representative that there was no excuse for the reign of disorder at the Dowd Pool and that from then on law and order would prevail there regardless of race, creed or color.

It is particularly gratifying to note that Negroes utilized the pool on Saturday and Sunday . . . AND WERE NOT MOLESTED. We feel that our efforts along with that put forth by residents in that immediate vicinity have succeeded in breaking down the open discrimination that previously held sway at that particular spot.

Another interesting feature concerning the pool discrimination fights being waged in both Elizabeth and Trenton, is the large amount of pride and enthusiasm for victory that have been expressed in letters sent to the NEWARK HERALD.

One letter from Asbury Park read, in part: "It is very pleasing to see members of our race stand up for their rights, and it is extraordinary to see a race newspaper assist us in our battles. There should be no discrimination—and with the NEWARK HERALD playing an important part in each of our fights, it won't be long before we will hold the position in the state that rightfully belongs to us.

There are other predicaments that confront us in this sector of the state, and it is the hope of this publication that they can be remedied . . . at any rate we will do our bit in an effort to vanquish them. Judging from the way in which members of our race have been co-operating during the course of the past few months, it will not be long before all New Jersey will discover that the Negroes are not marking time any longer.

If we continue to portray co-operation, all of us will discover that less discriminatory practices will be attemped. We are definitely a powerful race . . . if only we "stick together" . . . and no stone will be left unturned in the battle to mold us into one strong force.

---

1. George Thompson of Newark, currently a staff writer for the Mayor's Office of Employment and Training in Newark.

10   THE POLITICAL MACHINE, 1938

The election of black mayors, city councilmen, county freeholders, and state legislators came to New Jersey after years in which the political strength of black voters was wasted and manipulated by entrenched political interests. Nowhere was this more evident than in Jersey City, which was under the boss rule of Mayor Frank Hague from 1917 to 1947. As noted by Lester Granger in the following article, Hague's Hudson County machine practiced one of the oldest political arts; that is, the delivery of patronage, services, and other benefits in return for support at the polls on election day. In the case of blacks in Jersey City, though, the relationship with the machine was of diminishing value to the voters. Black support for Hague, however, was rewarded by a relatively open city, free from the Jim Crow practices plaguing other urban areas.

Yet Granger argues that the mayor opposed the more progressive segment of the labor movement, which sought an improvement in the working conditions of the race, and he was contemptuous of black politicians who dared challenge his political authority. Granger also notes that, although housing was allegedly open in Jersey City, most blacks were mired in the city's dilapidated areas. Probably the most important aspect of this document is Granger's discussion of Hague's use of anti-communist rhetoric to discredit the Congress of Industrial Organizations (CIO) in Jersey City. Granger, like A. Philip Randolph, realized that the fortunes of the civil rights movement were hinged on the right of trade unions to organize workers.

Lester Granger was one of New Jersey's and the nation's best-known social reformers between the two world wars. He was a frequent contributor to *Opportunity* magazine, a former administrator at the Bordentown School, and industrial secretary of the National Urban League.

Lester B. Granger,
"Mayor Hague and the Negro,"
***Opportunity* 16 (1938): 244-46, 255.**

Slowly, and somewhat unwillingly, the Negro voters of New Jersey are beginning to consider, from the standpoint of their own racial interests, the amazing controversy which has developed between Mayor Frank

Hague of Jersey City and the liberal forces of New Jersey and the nation. It may be thought that this interest is a belated one, for "the Hague affair" has been developing for over six months—since the 1937 Fall election—and several times its issues have cut directly across the interests of the 225,000 Negroes who live in New Jersey.

It is natural, however, that these colored voters should have postponed judgment on the issues of the affair until the last possible moment. This would be the attitude of any weak minority group placed in the position where Negroes find themselves in New Jersey and in most northern states. The shadow of Mayor Hague lies darkly across all political situations in New Jersey, regardless of whether they be Democratic or Republican-controlled. Through manipulation of his tremendous "vote-factory" in Hudson County, Frank Hague has been able to produce locally, on important occasions, as large a Democratic majority as is needed to offset the Republican majority which the down-state counties frequently muster. Thus his Hudson County dictatorship has enabled the Jersey City Mayor to become veritable ruler of the State, no matter what party may be temporarily in the titular seat of power. He can block or advance the program of a Republican governor; he can produce favors for complaisant State Senators and Assemblymen, or he can embarrass those who are obstinate. Hague seldom has trouble in getting what he wants out of Trenton, the state capital, and Trenton has learned not to court trouble with the Lord of Hudson County.

So, likewise, with the powerful financial and industrial interests of the State. Mayor Hague has built a formidable political machine which can, if he chooses, make considerable trouble for the financial giants who hold New Jersey's economic reins. Instead, he has offered them a political alliance which they, like shrewd business men, have accepted. A truce exists—has existed for a long time—between Big Business and Big Politics in New Jersey, and both parties to the truce have reaped handsome benefits therefrom.

Under such conditions Negro voters should not be expected to stick their necks out to the extent of taking active sides in the original controversy surrounding the Hague administration. The dispute began with the claims of the Reverend Lester Clee, defeated Republican candidate for Governor in the fall elections of 1937, that the Hague machine had accomplished his defeat by unusually crooked polling methods— unusual, that is, even for Hudson County. Negro voters gave the minister scant sympathy, for as a reform candidate Mr. Clee had shown little concern for the desperate conditions faced by New Jersey's Negro population. Though he was more liberal than the unbelievable Governor Hoffman, his campaign was far removed from the bread-and-butter problems of a minority group fifty percent unemployed, and with a median family income of less than $600.

In the beginning, therefore, Negro voters had their choice of taking sides with the corrupt Hague machine and the Democratic politics of the

State; or giving their allegiance to an equally corrupt Republican machine which, if it won, would immediately make a deal with Hague; or standing with a "reform" Republican organization which represented the businessman's idea of governmental economy and a checkmating of the New Deal program. It was small wonder that these colored citizens either ignored the scrap completely or gave their casual sympathy to the New Deal's official representative in New Jersey—the head of the Democratic Party.

Suddenly and surprisingly, however, the picture changed. New Jersey's C.I.O. was engaged in organizing the industries of Jersey City and these labor leaders found themselves in sudden conflict with the police and courts of that city. Political sharps will tell you that the C.I.O. fell into a trap set for them by the wily Hague. He opposed the unions, hoping for their public protest so that he could put on a show that would divert attention from the investigation of his flagrant violation of the election laws. Planned or not, this was the actual outcome. The Jersey City police force, which Mr. Clee claimed had done such efficient strong-arm work at the polls, transferred its strong-arm tactics to the labor organizers. Labor lawyers descended upon Jersey City with legalistic briefs; labor sympathizers and other liberals made the trek from New York City and neighboring communities to play their part in defending the constitutional rights of American citizens. All of this made meat in the Hague pie. A few weeks previously thousands of well-meaning New Jersey citizens had seen Hague as a semi-literate, crooked political boss defending a corrupt machine. Today those same citizens have forgotten the civic angle; Hague has become an earnest American official who is defending his city against an attempted invasion of Communists and other dangerous radicals.

For many Negroes, this new interpretation of the Hague affair has increased the indifference with which they view the proceedings. Say some, "Hague might be a corrupt politician, but he has been a friend to the Negro." To support this view they point to the fact, admittedly true, that less Jim-Crowism is to be found in Jersey City than in any other large New Jersey city. There are perhaps two dozen colored teachers in its mixed schools; one is an assistant principal. Theatres and restaurants are more prone to obey the State's Civil Rights Law. There is less restriction of Negro residence.

Others say, "This business is a fight between a practical politician and a bunch of Reds. There's no reason for us to stick our noses into something that can't benefit us one way or the other." The Bill of Rights? Negroes will smile and remind you that there has never been an effective Bill of Rights for the darker brother in the Garden State. When Labor becomes effectively concerned about equal rights for Negroes, then will be time for Negroes to begin fighting Labor's battles.

Of course, both of these views stray considerably from the actual facts in the case. Democratic politicians who have worked with Hague for years will tell you confidentially that he is far from being a "friend of the Negro." The leader of Negro Democrats in one important city told this writer, for instance, that Mayor Hague has an indifference toward Negroes that amounts almost to contempt. He is reported to have publicly remarked that any Negro leader can be bought—and it is to be admitted that many of his experiences have somewhat justified this view. What favors colored voters in his own bailiwick receive come to them as the usual grist which is ground out of the political machine.

It must be remembered, also, that for twenty years Hague has been in control of New Jersey's legislation and its elected officials that during all this time New Jersey has been ranked as one of the chief Jim Crow states of the North, so far as politics is concerned. Even in states like Missouri and Ohio Negroes have received more political recognition and occupied positions of more strategic importance than in the state dominated by the Mayor of Jersey City.

Equally trivial is the excuse that only "a bunch of Reds" are opposed to Mayor Hague. Any intelligent person who cares to put in a few hours of research will find that the C.I.O. is almost as free of true Communist leadership as the A.F. of L. It would be a daring advocate, moreover, who would seriously charge that Congressman Jerry O'Connell, who was "deported" from Jersey City, or President Roosevelt, who inferentially condemned Mayor Hague's tactics in a recent speech, are in the ranks or under control of the Communist Party.

But even if both statements were true, it would be a shortsighted position for Negro voters to remain on the Hague bandwagon for such reasons. It has been long since proved, by experience in a hundred American cities, that a corrupt political machine cannot in the last analysis be friendly to the interests of such a group as the Negro community. Crooked politics means a crooked police force, with favors for the rich and powerful and brutality for the weak—i.e., the Negro. The political machine means a controlled judiciary; rascals escape their just deserts and honest defendants find themselves railroaded into fines and prison sentences. Corrupt politics mean graft in administration of official duties, in construction of public works; they produce high taxes, which in the end are paid by the poor consumer in higher prices or by the poor worker in lower wages. Machine politics, whether in New York, Kansas City, Philadelphia or Jersey City, produce blighted slums, where Negro families search for bread, fall into disease and crime, and pay the price which the poor always pay for mismanaged city government.

Naturally Negro voters take pride in seeing one or two of their number elevated to positions of minicipal prominence—as several have been during the past few years in Jersey City—even though it be as cogs in a political machine. The recognition of these leaders by the Democratic organization of New Jersey has had its effect upon the rank and file of the voters. It is a high price, however, that the man in the street pays for the honors and rewards given to a few of his race.

Throughout the entire State there is terrific suffering among the unemployed as a result of New Jersey's out-moded relief practices. Negroes compose one-fourth of the unemployed group. When the Hague-dominated Legislature cut off relief two years ago and turned its management back to bankrupt communities that were unable to take care of it, Negro families were faced with literal starvation. Enlightened persons are still shocked to remember that Ewing Township gave begging licenses to families that had been on relief and that were suddenly dropped through the Legislature's action. In Monmouth, Atlantic, Gloucester and Cumberland Counties farmers who sought cheap labor gleefully offered fifteen and twenty cents an hour as wages to family heads who could no longer claim assistance from the public treasury. Negroes who blandly state today that "Mayor Hague is all right" with them, cannot afford to forget these conditions, or the fact that Mayor Hague controls the State which produced them.

Nor can Negroes afford to look with complacency upon the denial of constitutional rights to labor leaders because they happen to be called "Reds." The spectacular riots which have been so efficiently organized in Jersey City by so-called respectable elements in the community hold a serious threat against the personal and civil security of every colored citizen in the state.

Negroes have already learned to their sorrow—and they constantly warn their white neighbors—that the lynch spirit breeds easily and spreads rapidly. The mob which attacked Congressman O'Connell and the hoodlums who rioted through Journal Square on several occasions waiting for C.I.O. organizers to show up were perfectly ready to carry out a lynching with the same gusto as would be shown by their fellows in Mississippi and Alabama. The methods which were used by newspapers and orators to whip up the mob spirit were exactly the methods used in small Southern towns and described by Walter White in his vivid articles on lynching.

The lynch mobs which were organized by the Hague machine in Journal Square a few months ago have already over-flowed into Newark's Military Park. This has been done through applying the Communist tag to labor organizers and liberal speakers. If such a tag may be successfully applied to those who seek the constitutional rights of workers, that same tag may be applied with equal success to the NAACP president and the Urban League secretary who seeks the constitutional rights of Negro citizens.

It is difficult, therefore, to see how the colored voters of Hudson County can continue to give allegiance—and votes—to Mayor Hague, or how those in other counties can support his henchmen, and still claim to be interested in improving the economic and civil status of the Negro race. It is hard to forget how Colonel Kelly, a Hague satellite who is active in veterans' organizations, promised frequently and publicly to raise a mob of Legionnaires that would lynch any C.I.O. "Reds" daring to invade the precincts of Jersey City. Negroes seeking the passage of a Federal Anti-Lynching Bill will show a disheartening inconsistency if they fail to fight against the lynch spirit as it appears in the councils of New Jersey's Democratic leadership.

Now it is to be admitted that consideration of these problems poses difficult questions for those thoughtful voters who honestly desire a solution. The writer is a former Jerseyite of thirty-one years residence, and he knows from intimate acquaintance the local dilemmas that perplex voters in southern as well as northern counties. The iniquitous relationship existing between the state Republican and Democratic machines usually offers a Hobsons choice to the voter. He may give his vote to a Hague candidate, or he may give it to an "opposing" candidate who will usually sell out to the Hague influence. He may vote for the New Deal program as "protected" by one of the country's worst political corruptionists, or he may vote for a reactionary program of opposition which will be controlled by short-sighted and selfish business interests.

In either case the Negro voter loses—and it is no wonder that he frequently gets rid of his puzzlement by simply voting the straight ticket of that party which happens to control his local district. In this way he achieves party regularity and is eligible for such crumbs of political reward as he may some day need.

Fortunately, however, such a defeatist attitude toward politics in New Jersey and countless other states of the Union is no longer justified or necessary. Without question the issues which have been raised in the Hague trial and in the disgraceful Jersey City proceedings will have their reflection in the elections this Fall.

There may arise a strong third-party movement; opposition candidates may run against Hague men in both the Democratic and Republican primaries. In either case those voters who are dissatisfied with the kind of Americanism which is promulgated in New Jersey politics today will have their chance to express themselves at the polls. It will be a serious reflection upon the foresight of Negro citizens in New Jersey, and a disheartening example for others elsewhere, if they continue to look upon Mayor Hague as an unimportant issue in deciding how to cast their votes. The New Deal and its continuance should not be allowed to obfuscate the political scene.

It has been aptly said that the New Deal is a program of social reform which need not necessarily be the property of any one party. The past Congressional session has shown us that the New Deal has some of its worst enemies among the ranks of the Democratic Party. Certainly, until the politics of New Jersey have been purified and the influence of Frank Hague's machine has been considerably lessened, there is scant prospect for civic decency in State or municipal government. Until such decency shall have been produced there can be no New Deal for the thousands of desperate or defeated Negroes who watch for the dawn of a new day.

11 DISCRIMINATION IN THE MILITARY, 1939

In keeping with its militant advocacy of racial equality, the *Herald News* expressed doubt over the propriety of America's defending democracy aboard at a time when black Americans were the victims of racial discrimination. In the following editorial, the paper attacked the exclusionary practices of the West Point and Annapolis military academies. On the eve of World War II, there were fewer than ten black officers in federal service and less than 5,000 blacks out of a total enlistment of 230,000 men. The newspaper warned that the mistreatment of blacks in peacetime would imperil the military readiness of the United States in war.

"Shall We Fight?"
Newark Herald News, 25 February 1939.

President Roosevelt has sent an urgent request to Congress for $552,000,000 to finance a minimum program for the necessity of Defense in DEMOCRATIC AMERICA.

Since world democracy is on the defensive America's frontiers are not on the Rhine, the Panama Canal, or any other particular spot, but are to be found, as Benjamin Franklin rightly says: wherever the principles of democratic government are at stake.

Speaking of DEMOCRATIC FRONTIERS, we as a Race feel that QUITE A FEW INSIDE THE U.S.A. NEED DEFENDING. PERHAPS WE SHOULD SAY—THAT NEED ATTENTION.

First—we would like to know when WILL AMERICAN DEMOCRATS see the ABSURDITY OF THEIR pretensions to DEMOCRATIC PRINCIPLES IN THE FACE OF THE SCANDAL OF NEGRO YOUTH at WEST POINT and ANNAPOLIS?

Our personal feelings towards war, war-makers, and the conditions that lead to war, are not of great concern here.

What we are concerned mightily with here is: the right of Negro Youth who desire to serve their country in the military—to be given equal, democratic treatment.

The other FRONTIER is the right of Negro Youth to share in the training to be offered the 20,000 young flyers the President is asking for. Let any so-called Democrat come forth with any argument against the right of Negroes to this training.

Segregate Negroes NOW and Negroes may draw the COLOR LINE IN 1940, or whenever THAT WAR does come.

Make the U.S. Safe for Democracy; and the U.S.A.—black and white—may be solid-minded for making the WORLD safe for democracy.

An undemocratic America is scarcely in a position to aid the embattled DEMOCRACY OF THE WORLD.

VII
The Modern Civil Rights Movement

AFTER the Allied victory over Germany in May 1945, the state's leading black newspaper, the *New Jersey Afro-American,* proclaimed: "War Ends in Europe. On Land. On Sea. In The Air. We Did Our Part."[1] That was the Afro-American role in protecting democratic values. The end of World War II and the triumph over fascism brought racial injustice in the United States into greater disfavor. Against the background of global devastation and human misery, the Allies professed faith in a new world order devoted to human freedom. It was a great task, one which promised an end to racial inequality and the prejudices upon which injustice toward blacks and other oppressed groups was based.

In April 1945, a month before Germany surrendered, the civil rights movement in New Jersey achieved a major victory with the passage of the Act Against Discrimination. **[doc. 1]** It was the most important guarantee of civil rights in New Jersey in over half a century. The measure, patterned after a law enacted earlier in New York, prohibited racial discrimination in employment and established a Division Against Discrimination in the Department of Education, the first agency in the state's history created to eradicate racial and ethnic discrimination.

During the next several years the legislature extended the provisions of the act to include guarantees against discrimination in housing, education, and public accommodations. In May 1949, Governor Alfred E. Driscoll, whose support of civil rights made him one of New Jersey's most popular political leaders among blacks, aided the passage of the Freeman Act, which allowed a person to file a complaint with the Division Against Discrimination in the event of unfair treatment on account of race or national origin.[2] Meanwhile, a movement for constitutional reform gained momentum in the state. For many years there had been criticism of poor state government. In 1946, Governor Driscoll urged that a constitutional convention be held to reform the Constitution of 1844 or submit a new document to the citizens. As a result of his efforts and those of civil libertarians and political reformers, a convention met in New Brunswick in 1947.

Black leaders in New Jersey, much like their forebears a century earlier, vigorously advocated constitutional reforms, particularly civil rights guarantees, and they sought to inform the general public of the indignities from which black residents suffered. A few months before the constitutional convention was convened, the New Jersey State Conference of the NAACP Branches released a study pointing out the existence of illegal forms of school segregation in nearly all of the eighteen counties investigated. Separate school systems for blacks and whites, the study found, were widespread in Atlantic, Camden, Cumberland, and Cape May counties. Although black and white children were enrolled in the same schools in Burlington and Bergen counties, they were taught in separate classrooms. The study also revealed that black teachers often were required to teach three times the load of white teachers. Though classrooms in the Newark school system, the state's largest and ostensibly most progressive, were racially integrated, black teachers were treated as permanent substitutes.[3] An equally damaging blow to the pretense of racial equality in New Jersey's public schools had been made in 1941, when Marion Thompson Wright of Howard University published *The Education of Negroes in New Jersey*. This seminal study of race relations in a northern state traced the impact of race on education in New Jersey and the efforts on behalf of racial justice by black and white residents.[4]

As the constitutional convention assembled in the summer of 1947, black organizations supported the adoption of a civil rights provision identical to the one included in the New York Bill of Rights. [doc. 2] On July 8, 1947, Fred W. Martin of Jersey City [see chap. 6, doc. 5-7] represented the State Council of the NAACP before the convention's Committee on Rights and Privileges. He reminded the delegates: "Since we are now holding up to the countries of the world that the democratic way is the right way and the correct form of government, we ask you to let us have that form of government in America. First and above all, we ask that New Jersey lead the way in that democratic process."[5]

The next day the committee heard from former Assemblyman J. Mercer Burrell, a lawyer, on behalf of the Essex County Colored Republican Council. He too called for the adoption of a civil rights provision and, in much the same fashion as Martin, associated his appeal with the ideals of American foreign policy. [doc. 3]

As a result of appeals by black organizations, Governor Driscoll's enthusiastic support of civil rights, the affirmation of racial equality by the Division Against Discrimination, and, most important, the urgency given to the movement for democratic rights by World War II, the convention drafted the following provision in the new constitution (article I, paragraph 5), which was ratified by the voters on November 4, 1947:

> No person shall be denied the enjoyment of any civil or military right, nor be discriminated against in the exercise of any civil or military right, nor be segregated in the militia or in the public schools, because of religious principles, race, color, ancestry or national origin.

The provision made New Jersey the first state in the Union to forbid segregation in its public schools and the State Militia. In the years following the ratification of the constitution, the state's troubled legacy of racial segregation ended on several fronts. The most dramatic improvement occurred in public school education. For the first time in southern counties, black students and teachers were assigned to schools and classes without regard to race. Governor Driscoll ordered the desegregation of the State Militia on February 1, 1948.

The judicial foundation of the civil rights movement in New Jersey was established much earlier than the legislation enacted in the 1940s and early 1950s and the adoption of the state constitution of 1947. In *Raison v. Board of Education, Berkeley Township* (1927), the New Jersey Supreme Court ended its customary reluctance to interpret the School Law of 1881 in favor of blacks seeking redress from racial discrimination, when it ruled that a child could not be excluded from a school on the basis of color. In 1933 another case based on that law was brought in *Patterson v. Board of Education, Trenton*. It involved a black student who was denied the use of the high school swimming pool. The Supreme Court ruled that this practice was illegal: "To say to a lad you may study with your classmates," Justice Ralph W.E. Donges wrote, "you may attend the gymnasium with them, but you may not have swimming with them because of your color is unlawful discrimination.''[6]

In 1939 the issue of equal rights in public accommodations was raised in *Bullock v. Wooding,* in which the Supreme Court held that the black plaintiff was entitled to a writ of mandamus to force the defendants to allow her use of a segregated part of the beach at Long Branch. In 1944 and 1948 the Supreme Court upheld the state's attempt to outlaw racial discrimination in public education and accommodations. In *Seawell v. MacWithey* (1949), the Superior Court of New Jersey ruled that it was illegal for the City of East Orange to exclude black veterans from a public housing project set aside for white veterans.[7] [doc. 4]

Encouraged by the support given to their rights as citizens, blacks in New Jersey viewed their advancement as a part of a general elevation of the race throughout the country. When the U.S. Supreme Court in 1954 outlawed public school segregation in the landmark case of *Brown v. Board of Education of Topeka, Kansas,* the decision was seen not only as a victory for racial justice in the South, but also as a vindication of the crusade for freedom in New Jersey. [doc. 5] Between December 1953 and September 1954, for example, the Division Against Discrimination received six complaints from black parents in Englewood. They charged the Englewood Board of Education of that nominally quiet, middle-class suburban community with deliberately fostering racial segregation in the elementary schools through a change in school zoning. The action by the school board and the protests it sparked in the city marked the beginning of a protracted struggle for equal educational rights which lasted well into the 1960s and drew national attention.[8]

The dramatic improvement in the legal status of blacks in New Jersey inspired a view of the state which was in sharp contrast with the pessimistic outlook of the past. New Jersey, one observer claimed, had become in a few short years a new laboratory in race relations. A similar view was held by Myra A. Blakeslee, the educational director of the Division Against Discrimination, who, along with other civil rights advocates in New Jersey, believed the cause of equality to be more successful there than in most northern states. Indeed, the post-war years were generally marked by the confidence of black leaders and their white supporters, who worked together to improve race relations in their communities. Particularly in the cities, the civil rights movement spawned programs, meetings, and organizational functions directed toward these ends.[9]

In February 1948, for example, Montclair observed "Freedom Week" to celebrate its racial diversity. In Trenton an interracial group, the Committee for Unity, was established in 1946. In 1947 and 1948 the Newark Board of Education sponsored a series of radio broadcasts confidently entitled "One World in Newark." Three years later, Perth Amboy formed its own Civil Rights Commission. In the field of social work, the relationship between racial prejudice and juvenile delinquency was examined in 1958 in public hearings held by the New Jersey Youth Study Commission.

Business interests too sought to become identified with improved race relations. In 1963 the Business and Industrial Coordinating Council, an agency of business and community organizations, was formed to promote the employment of minorities in the commercial and building trades of Newark. Four years later, one of the largest employers in the state, the New Jersey Bell Telephone Company, submitted a "Plan for Progress" which foresaw a similar employment effort. In the field of public employment, Governor Richard J. Hughes issued Executive Order No. 21 on June 25, 1965, which adopted the Governor's Code of Fair Practices in the administration of the state government.

Yet, despite the overall improvement in civil rights and race relations in the post-war years, vestiges of profound racial inequality persisted and increasingly troubled the life of New Jersey. Between 1948 and 1953 the state became the center of controversy over the fortunes of blacks in the North, as the result of the trial of six young black men accused of the murder of a white man in Trenton on January 27, 1948. Popularly known as the trial of the Trenton Six, the case raised doubts about the fair treatment of black suspects in police custody and their ability to obtain a fair trial in the state capital. It brought to wide public attention the fragile legal rights of poor, uneducated blacks in the cities of New Jersey. "All six of these men are manual workers, at the bottom of the social scrap heap," observed a reporter for *The New Republic.* Moreover, as a result of the emotions stirred by the trial, civil rights groups and communist organizations clashed over the case. It was a conflict symptomatic of the domestic tensions in the United States during the Cold War.[10] **[doc. 6]**

The number of poor blacks in New Jersey grew dramatically as a result of the great migration from the South during and after the war years. Between 1940 and 1950 the state's black population rose from 226,973 to 318,565, an increase of 40.3 percent. By 1960 it reached 514,875, an increase of 61.6 percent. The census for 1970 placed the number of blacks in New Jersey at 770,292, a 49.6 percent increase. During the thirty-year period between 1940 and 1970 the total black population in the state had grown by 239.9 percent, with the greatest number of newcomers settling in the industrial cities of northern New Jersey. Like the first great tide of migrants between the two world wars, the second generation of newcomers found that New Jersey was not a land of opportunity, and they were the most adversely affected by the diminishing employment prospects. "The Negro migrant," the National Advisory Commission on Civil Disorders observed in 1967, "unlike the immigrant, found little opportunity in the city; he arrived too late, and the unskilled labor he had to offer was no longer needed."[11]

Civil rights advocates in the state also found that despite a decrease in the practice of total exclusion of black workers, resistance to anti-discrimination laws existed in areas where black and white workers competed for employment. In 1961, Harold A. Lett [see chap. 6, doc. 4] of the Division Against Discrimination noted: "Token placement of a hand picked few; quota placement of limited percentages; promotional limitations within the work force; operation of job ceilings; and exclusion from the more desirable and lucrative occupations, are discriminatory practices to which minority group workers . . . are exposed."[12]

For many black families settling in New Jersey's cities during this period, decent housing was unavailable. There were successful attempts at neighborhood integration in several New Jersey communities, most notably in Morristown, Teaneck, and Willingboro's Levittown development. In most cities, however, where blacks were living in significant numbers, tacitly segregated neighborhoods were the norm. Living conditions were no better in predominantly black communities than they ever had been.

Growing black ghettos were made worse by the housing policies of the federal government. The Housing Act of 1949 favored middle class and predominantly white suburbs at the expense of the central city where most of the black newcomers lived. Suburban New Jersey prospered largely as a result of the settlement of white-collar and blue-collar workers, whose flight from the city was made possible by federal mortgage assistance. The sum effect of the unequal consideration given to cities and suburbs was that the suburbs became comfortable communities for white families, while the cities, struggling to offset the loss of revenues once provided by labor-intensive industries and homeowners, faced an impending social disaster.[13]

By the 1960s the problems of the black poor came dramatically to the surface along with other concerns of the national conscience. Events during these years assumed an urgency seldom witnessed in the past. The southern civil rights movement entered its most critical and dangerous stage, pitting black freedom marchers and their white supporters against local police authorities and whites bent on preserving the color line. The deeper meaning of these struggles for full citizenship rights was brought into focus by the Reverend Martin Luther King, Jr., and, in a decisively ominous fashion, by Malcolm X. King's espousal of Christian love and non-violence may have popularized the civil rights movement in the nation, but these ideals were betrayed by developments far beyond his control.

In the northern industrial states, blacks became disgruntled by the dubious opportunities for them in employment, housing, and education, and they expressed a lack of faith in long-term gains made possible through legal and cooperative civil rights efforts. Such frustrations had been building over many years in some New Jersey communities. In May 1963, Englewood, a town with racial problems of long standing, became the object of civil rights activities then spreading across the northern states. About thirty black students there, with the support of their parents and much of the black community, began a sit-in at the predominantly white Cleveland Elementary School. Protesting Englewood's de facto segregation in education and other concerns, blacks also conducted a boycott of downtown stores, a sit-in at the school superintendent's office, demonstrations at the governor's office in Trenton, and other activities designed to dramatize their concern over racism in the town. Vincente Tibbs, the only black on the Englewood City Council, claimed the town was ". . . the battleground of the Northern suburbs. We have here the subtle (segregation) line. It's in housing, employment, government. There are people here who don't even admit there's a problem."[14]

Ironically, the belief that racial equality for black Americans was an unfulfilled promise had its staunchest supporters in the northern states, where civil rights advocacy had been first established. The problems of blacks, argued Amiri Baraka, the prominent writer and social activist from Newark, had less to do with questions of civil rights than with the unequal distribution of political and economic power and the racial self-interest of whites. [doc. 7] Baraka and an increasing number of young black spokesmen and women in New Jersey cities espoused a militant form of black nationalism manifesting black self-esteem, sought an increase in black political and economic power, and adapted aspects of traditional African culture to the black American experience. These beliefs, which fell under the rubric of Black Power, were not new or unique to New Jersey. Black Power was a revival of earlier themes in Afro-American thought and action.[15] What distinguished the revival of race-consciousness among blacks in the 1960s from most, if not all, earlier expressions of racial identity was the fervor of its exponents and the often embittered reaction it provoked from many whites.

Against the background of an intense civil rights campaign in the South and the growing militancy and frustration of blacks in the North, serious disorders erupted in several American cities during the early 1960s, including Jersey City, Elizabeth, and Paterson. Each disturbance was precipitated by local racial difficulties, which were generally local manifestations of national problems. In the spring and summer of 1967 violent confrontations between blacks and white police occurred in Nashville, Tennessee; Jackson, Mississippi; Houston, Texas; Tampa, Florida; Cincinnati, Ohio; and Atlanta, Georgia.[16] Coming at a time of heightened American military involvement in southeast Asia and anti-war activities at home, these disturbances appeared all the more frightening to many white Americans. The nation, it seemed, was threatened from within by black insurrectionists.

One of the most serious civil disorders of 1967 occurred in Newark where, ironically, much of the state's civil rights activity had been centered. Newark's mayor, Hugh J. Addonizio, had a liberal voting record on civil rights measures as a congressman. The black voters who helped elect him mayor in 1962 anticipated a greater role in the administration of city government. By the late 1960s, however, the mayor was under attack for failing to make the concerns of Newark's large and predominantly poor black population an administration priority.

A fundamental dilemma facing blacks and whites in Newark, yet one which they seldom viewed in the same way, was the decline in the city's economic vitality and its adverse impact on the social and political character of the city. Changing economic conditions in the nation ended Newark's industrial grandeur and that of other cities in New Jersey. With prospects for employment dimmed by the exodus of factories and businesses, black residents were trapped in the worst areas of a city whose golden era had passed long ago. The city's economic problems carried bleak social implications. Newark's public school system, once considered the most progressive in New Jersey and among the leading educational systems in the nation, had fallen upon bad times, with a dropout rate of nearly thirty-three percent. Health conditions, which were never enviable in predominantly black communities, worsened in the years after World War II. The same was true of housing for the poor, city services, and public safety in the central city.

There were, in effect, two Newarks: one consisting of white ethnic groups long resident in the city, who exercised some control over political affairs; the other, predominantly black and poor, with considerably less political influence, and looked upon as a burden to the city. As in other American cities experiencing changes in racial composition, the mistrust which existed between the older, established white communities and the emerging black ghetto in Newark could, with a sufficient catalyst, explode into violence.[17]

The incident which ignited the disorders in Newark occurred on July 12, 1967, when a black cab driver, under arrest for a traffic violation, was allegedly beaten by Fourth Precinct police in the predominantly black Central Ward. At first the altercation triggered the anger of blacks against the police, who for years had been accused by community spokesmen of using unnecessary force against blacks in their custody. In a matter of hours, that anger was directed against other symbols of white authority in the ghetto. During the next five days, Newark and its environs were gripped by fear. Scores of small business establishments located in the Central Ward were looted. Fires, presumably started by arsonists, lit the night sky, giving Newark's inner city the appearance of a battle zone.

There was considerable confusion over the means to end the turbulence. The local police, according to the Report of the National Advisory Commission on Civil Disorders, were insufficiently staffed for the situation and responded badly at critical points during the disorders. In the view of black residents, the police used excessive force against looters and hurled racial insults at blacks during the melee. The National Guard, which was ordered into Newark by Governor Richard J. Hughes on Friday,

July 14, 1967, and the State Police were both criticized for their role during the disorders. Both units were unprepared for civil disorders and responded in a provocative manner to unruly crowds and sporadic gunfire. Adding to their difficulties in the ghetto, the National Guard and State Police were overwhelmingly white; less than two percent of 17,529 state National Guard members were black.[18]

When the disorders ended in Newark on Monday, July 17, twenty-three persons had lost their lives. Property damage exceeded $10,000,000, and the city's Central Ward lay virtually in ruins. More than twenty years of civil rights work in Newark also seemed to be in shambles. The Newark *Star Ledger,* like most newspapers in the state, expressed shock at the wanton destruction the riot caused. "The regrettable incident," it editorialized, "comes at a time when a genuine effort at constructive leadership and achievement has been launched in Newark."[19] The newspaper, in contrast to the view held by many black leaders, condemned the disorders as anarchy and chided local and state officials who urged law enforcement agencies to use restraint in restoring order. The city's leading newspaper, the *Newark Evening News,* saw racial issues behind the disturbances, and it urged the residents of Newark to begin the difficult task of repairing the extremely strained race relations. [doc. 8]

The disturbances in Newark and their legacy of racial bitterness aggravated an already tense situation in other New Jersey cities. In Jersey City, Elizabeth, Englewood, and New Brunswick there were outbreaks of pilfering and angry confrontations between black residents and police officers, but those incidents were not as serious as the trouble in Newark. On the other hand, just as the riot in Newark was brought under control, Plainfield experienced seven days of widespread looting and sporadic violence which attracted national attention. In its report on these disturbances, the National Advisory Commission on Civil Disorders found that, like Newark, the troubles in Plainfield were precipitated by an incident involving the police and that racial and economic problems in the city were the root causes. [doc. 9]

In the months following the summer of 1967, a cross section of New Jersey residents realized that the efforts on behalf of interracial cooperation, civil rights, and social work among blacks had been weakened, and they began the difficult task of revitalizing concern for the problems of the race and preventing future racial outbreaks. Efforts toward these ends were made in police and community relations and in housing, recreation, and employment training programs. But they were not always successful or looked upon favorably by local residents. Black power advocates, whose numbers increased after the disturbances in 1967, attacked some programs because they failed to address the fundamental problems of poverty and racism. Some white spokesmen believed that more social programs in the ghetto were unwarranted and called for more effective law enforcement. Nonetheless, real progress was made out of the impasse which existed in New Jersey communities following the summer of discontent.

As the 1960s drew to a close considerable unity among blacks was achieved over the issue of political power. Much of the emphasis in this direction was made, not surprisingly, in Newark, the site of a National Conference on Black Power in 1967, and a city where blacks were now in the majority. In 1968 black voters were instrumental in the election of Kenneth A. Gibson as mayor of New Jersey's largest city, a victory which heralded a greater role for blacks in the American political process.

But despite Gibson's election and the infusion of funds from federal and state programs designed to improve the living conditions of poor families, many of the old problems remained. Generations of neglect, racial discrimination, and poverty had compounded the social and economic crisis of many black communities. Ameliorative efforts by public and private agencies were usually not designed to attack the root causes of racial inequality. In 1968 at a public policy forum on civil disorders held at Rutgers University in New Brunswick, one of the forum participants, Robert Curvin, director of the Community Action Intern Program at the University, spoke for many blacks when he observed: "It is time that we saw how deeply related the plight of the ghetto is to white racism in the suburbs and the government and the legislature. If we could do something about white racism, we could do something about the ghetto . . . . Those of you who are in a position to make policy," he advised, "must begin to recognize that this may be our last chance to move cooperatively and constructively toward a society of peace and harmony."[20] Black participants at the forum submitted a resolution which claimed that white racism was "the single most pervasive attitude in New Jersey society . . . ." It was a resolution not unlike the appeals made by black leaders in the state since the nineteenth century. [doc. 10]

The vital parts of the black struggle have been an affirmation of group pride and a faith in democracy, ideals which are deeply rooted in the American experience. Among blacks, the ideals of democracy, the plea for justice, and the desperate frustration which results when, in the words of John Rock, they "are looked upon as things," has been voiced not only by the leadership and the articulate. In 1972 several young black men incarcerated at the Bordentown Correctional Facility were enrolled in a writing class to encourage and develop their literary skills.[21] In the main, their works reflected the other side of the American dream, and, as products of the black experience in New Jersey and America, they expressed indisputable truths and hopes. [doc. 11]

1   LAW AGAINST DISCRIMINATION, 1945

With the precedent for direct government intervention in civil rights matters set by President Franklin D. Roosevelt's Executive Order 8802 in 1941, blacks in the United States sought more permanent guarantees against racial discrimination after the war. In March 1945, New York became the first state to enact a fair employment law, which attested both to the increased political influence of black voters and to the growing belief that racial discrimination was legally indefensible and abhorrent to the public good. New Jersey passed a similar law on April 16, 1945. The act, printed in part below, marked a watershed in the history of civil rights legislation. Racial discrimination in employment was prohibited, and a Division Against Discrimination was created to enforce the law's provisions. In subsequent years the legislature amended the act to prohibit discrimination in places of public accommodation (1949), the armed forces (1953), and public housing (1954).

An Act to prevent and eliminate practices of discrimination in employment and otherwise against persons because of race, creed, color, national origin or ancestry; to create a division in the Department of Education to effect such prevention and elimination; and making an appropriation therefor, *New Jersey Laws*, **16 April 1945.**

BE IT ENACTED *by the Senate and General Assembly of the State of New Jersey:*

1. This act shall be known as "Law Against Discrimination."

2. The enactment hereof shall be deemed an exercise of the police power of the State for the protection of the public safety, health and morals and to promote the general welfare and in fulfillment of the provisions of the Constitution of this State guaranteeing civil rights.

3. The Legislature finds and declares that practices of discrimination against any of its inhabitants, because of race, creed, color, national origin or ancestry, are a matter of concern to the government of the State, and that such discrimination threatens not only the rights and proper privileges of the inhabitants of the State but menaces the institutions and foundation of a free democratic State.

4. The opportunity to obtain employment without discrimination because of race, creed, color, national origin or ancestry is recognized as and declared to be a civil right.

5. As used in this act, unless a different meaning clearly appears from the context:

a. "Person" includes one or more individuals, partnerships, associations, corporations, legal representatives, trustees, trustees in bankruptcy or receivers.

b. "Employment agency" includes any person undertaking to procure employees or opportunities to work.

c. "Labor organization" includes any organization which exists and is constituted for the purpose, in whole or in part, of collective bargaining or of dealing with employers concerning grievances, terms or conditions of employment, or of other mutual aid or protection in connection with employment.

d. "Unlawful employment practice" includes only those unlawful practices specified in section eleven of this act.

e. "Employer" does not include a club exclusively social or a fraternal, charitable, educational or religious association or corporation, if such club, association or corporation is not organized for private profit nor does it include any employer with fewer than six persons in his employ.

f. "Employee" does not include any individual employed by his parents, spouse or child, or in the domestic service of any person.

g. "Division" means the State "Division against Discrimination" created by this act.

h. "Commissioner" means the State Commissioner of Education.

6. There is created in the State Department of Education a division to be known as "The Division against Discrimination" with power to prevent and eliminate discrimination in employment against persons because of race, creed, color, national origin or ancestry by employers, labor organizations, employment agencies or other persons and to take other actions against discrimination because of race, creed, color, national origin or ancestry, as herein provided; and the division created hereunder is given general jurisdiction and authority for such purposes.

7. The said division shall consist of the Commissioner of Education and a council. The council shall consist of seven members; each member shall be appointed by the Governor, with the advice and consent of the Senate, for a term of five years and until his successor is appointed and qualified, except that of those first appointed, one shall be appointed for a term of one year, one for a term of two years, one for a term of three years and two for a term of four years. Vacancies caused other than by expiration of term shall be filled in the same manner but for the unexpired term only. Members of the council shall serve without compensation but shall be reimbursed for necessary expenses incurred in the performance of their duties. The first chairman of the council shall be designated by the Governor and thereafter, the chairman shall be elected by the members, annually . . . .

---

2   CLUB WOMEN APPEAL FOR CIVIL RIGHTS, 1947

The New Jersey State Federation of Colored Women's Clubs was organized in 1915. By World War II it was one of the most influential black organizations in the state. Its growth was attributable to two interrelated developments—the nascent movement by women for sexual equality in American democracy and the increasing concern over racial injustice. In the following resolution to the New Jersey Constitutional Convention, the Federation appealed for the adoption of a civil rights provision patterned after the one provided in the Bill of Rights of New York.

"Resolution of the New Jersey State Federation of Colored Women's Clubs," *State of New Jersey Constitutional Convention of 1947,* **vol. 3, Committee on Rights, Privileges, Amendments and Miscellaneous Provisions (Trenton, N.J., 1947), pp. 421-22.**

WHEREAS, it is the object of the New Jersey State Federation of Colored Women's Clubs to "Work and Serve the Hour" in helping solve the many problems confronting the race, and to study the conditions in cities and counties, with a view to raising the educational, industrial and economic standards of all people and improve the public health and general welfare of the people of the State; and

WHEREAS, for the past 32 years this organization has conducted a program working toward equal opportunity for all people and the full enjoyment of the rights, privileges and benefits of the State of New Jersey; and

WHEREAS, it has long been recognized that the restrictive covenant is a device used by real estate interests in conformity with narrow community attitudes, to confine certain housing areas to favored racial groups and for the exclusion of other groups, most frequently the Jewish and Negro segments of our population; and

WHEREAS, a large percentage of the population of the State of New Jersey, in a general way, was denied opportunity for business and industrial employment (public utilities included) under the existing State Constitution until Executive Order 8802, superseding our state laws, was issued by the late President Roosevelt during the emergency, making such practices unlawful; and

WHEREAS, the recent survey of the school systems of the State of New Jersey, made by the N.A.A.C.P., showed the great extent of the segregation and discrimination in education as practiced in the State of New Jersey; and

WHEREAS, not much success has come out of remedies sought by education and legislation, because the average man holds hard to his prejudices, it is agreed that a strong and forthright declaration set forth in the Bill of Rights of the proposed new Constitution is needed, and will provide for all the people the instrument through which all rights and privileges accorded a citizen might be realized;

BE IT THEREFORE RESOLVED, that we do respectfully submit to and urge the adoption by the 1947 Constitutional Convention, the following:

1. That this paragraph, as written in the new New York Bill of Rights, be added to section 5 under "Rights and Privileges":

"No person shall be denied the equal protection of this State or any subdivision thereof. No person shall, because of race, creed, color or religion, be subject to any discrimination in his civil rights by any other person or by any firm, corporation or institution, or by this State or any agency or subdivision of this State."

2. That the following sentence be added to section 17 under "Rights and Privileges";

"Property taken for public use shall be enjoyed without discrimination because of race, color, religion or national origin."

BE IT FURTHER RESOLVED, that a copy of this resolution be forwarded to the Constitution Convention, the subcommittee on Rights and Privileges, the press, and a copy recorded in the minutes of our 32nd Annual Convention.

The above resolution was ordered and adopted at the St. James A.M.E. Church, Court and High Streets, Newark, N.J., July 18, 1947.

Respectfully submitted,

N.J. STATE FEDERATION OF COLORED WOMEN'S CLUBS
(MRS.) RUSSELL C. CAUTION, *President,*
400 N. Indiana Ave., Atlantic City, N.J.

MRS. ELIZ. B. THOMAS,
Chairman, Legislative Committee

---

3   TESTIFYING FOR THE BILL OF RIGHTS, 1947

The following presentation by former Assemblyman J. Mercer Burrell of Essex County was made before the Committee on Rights and Privileges of the New Jersey Constitutional Convention on July 9, 1947. Burrell, who spoke on behalf of the Essex County Colored Republican Council, urged the adoption of a constitutional provision on civil rights identical to one in the Bill of Rights of New York. Like many black leaders during the early years of the modern civil rights movement, Burrell was an astute observer of world events. The basic rights of racial minorities and women, he asserted, could not be denied in a nation claiming leadership of the free world. This argument, which black leaders had espoused since World War I, was considerably more effective in the years following the Allied defeat of fascism. Assemblyman Burrell advocated the nineteenth-century black ideal of improvement in the civil rights of all New Jersey's citizens, resting his appeal upon noble principles to which most Americans subscribed. Under questioning from members of the committee, Burrell discussed the technical aspects of the constitutional guarantee which most black organizations supported. The convention recommended the adoption of a civil rights provision encompassing the intent of the one proposed by black groups and extending protection against racial segregation.

State of New Jersey Constitutional Convention
of 1947. **vol. 3, Committee on Rights,**
Privileges, Amendments and Miscellaneous Provisions
(Trenton, N.J., 1947), pp. 89-96.

MR. BURRELL:

May I restate our proposal? (*Reading*):

"No person shall be denied the equal protection of the laws of this State or any subdivision thereof. No person shall, because of race, color, creed or religion, be subjected to any discrimination in his civil rights by any other person or by any firm, corporation, or institution, or by this State or any agency or subdivision of the State."

There appears to be a very definite necessity for a restatement of the principle against discrimination here in New Jersey. When the Constitution of 1844 was enacted there had not been the Civil War amendments to the Federal Constitution, namely, the 13th, 14th and 15th Amendments, and therefore, in our opinion, a great segment of our body politic was not considered in the enactment of the 1844 Constitution. We may say several segments, because it was before the enactment and the amendment concerning suffrage for the women of our State. We therefore feel that very definitely there should be a restatement—a restatement in line with not only national but international principles.

We are greatly concerned in selling democracy to the United Nations, to the inhabitants of Timbuktu, Afghanistan, Albania, Bulgaria and other places, and they are to see that democracy actually lives and that the inhabitants of these far away lands are protected in their civil rights. Should we not be equally and far more concerned in seeing that these basic fundamental laws of our State declare in unequivocal terms that all citizens of the State are of the same status, regardless of accidental questions of race, creed, color, or national origin? It is for that purpose and in line with the sentiment which was evidenced by the use of these words by the President of these United States speaking in Washington before the great national convention of the National Association for the Advancement of Colored People, where the President said very definitely that we could not delay action against discrimination to wait for the most laggard and backward community or section to catch up, but that a definite, vigorous and progressive action was necessary at this time.

The Constitution of New Jersey should forbid discrimination of all kinds, including discrimination in housing, discrimination in educational institutions, discrimination in admission to hospitals, and discrimination in opportunities for employment. All of those broad discriminations are interdicted by this proposed amendment, and this is not, in our opinion, a radical proposal. It does not come to you from a group of wild-haired radicals, but comes to you from substantial citizens of your State. The president of our organization who just preceded me is a present member of the Legislature of this State.[1] And I have served two terms in the Legislature of this State. We are not wild-eyed radicals, but we are persons who have been citizens of the State who have met with the problem and studied it, and feel we offer to you the best solution of something that cannot be avoided, and that we hope that this Constitutional Convention will attack it with courage.

To quote from a statement made in New York at the time of their constitutional convention which adopted a similar amendment, in the language of this amendment let us announce to the millions of our citizens that there shall be no discrimination in our democracy in this great State. We are citizens of a common country and a common State. We are entitled to equal opportunity regardless of the race from which we spring, the color of our skin, and the faith in God that we profess. It is our sincere hope that you will carefully consider this provision which is supported not only by our group but by many organizations which have carefully considered the problem over a period of time, and we ask that the New Jersey Constitution be modernized in the thought of 1947—after the Civil War, after the adoption of the 13th, 14th and 15th Amendments, after the emancipation of a segment of our population from chattel slavery, and after the emancipation of our women from the slavery of denial of the ballot.

Thank you for this opportunity. We'll be glad to discuss it further, if desired.

CHAIRMAN:

Are there any questions at this time that any of the members of the Committee have to ask?

MR. LAWRENCE N. PARK:

I believe you state that you are a member of the bar.

MR. BURRELL:

I am—for 25 years.

MR. PARK:

Yesterday a man advocated the same thing but confessed that he was not a lawyer and was not in a position to offer us any technical information.[2] As I read your proposal—and I've read it—it appears to be identical with the proposal submitted yesterday by the Department of Education representative of the Divison against Discrimination. Now, you have advanced to us the theory that the rights and privileges to which you are referring ought to be in general language. Are you familiar with the proposal which was advanced by the Urban Colored Population Commission?

MR. BURRELL:

I am, sir.

MR. PARK:

Is it your opinion that the proposal violates your own idea—that it is too detailed in terms?

MR. BURRELL:

I would not say so. In fact, there is one provision of that proposal I very heartily desire to endorse, although not ensconced in our own proposal. And that follows: "and any writing, agreement or practice in violation hereof shall be void and unenforceable." That strikes against the very way of discrimination, whose practice is increasing, according to the restrictive covenants in real estate law. I do feel that, as a matter of pure language, there could be some possible condensation in the amendment submitted by the Urban Colored Population Commission. But in effect and in principle, we are behind that as much as behind our own.

MR. PARK:

But your specific proposal is that which is contained in the mimeographed copy here.

MR. BURRELL:

Right, sir.

MR. PARK:

Now, since you are a lawyer you are going to be cross-examined.

MR. BURRELL:

Proceed, sir.

MR. PARK:

We have the difficulty—assuming we are in favor of the principle which you are advocating—we have the difficulties of technical draftsmanship. You will note your first paragraph starts out by saying that no person shall be denied the equal protection of the laws of the State or any subdivision thereof. Now, is it not true that that is the law of New Jersey because it is incorporated into the 14th Amendment?

MR. BURRELL:

I differ with you slightly. There is a question as to whether the 14th Amendment extends to discriminations practiced by individuals against individuals within a state. The denial of protection of the laws by the state itself is, in my opinion, prohibited by the 14th Amendment, but not the practice of discrimination by individuals, corporations or subdivisions of the state.

MR. PARK:

Well, I agree with you on that, but I'm talking now about your first sentence. What I wanted to know is your advice on the question, since you agree that brevity is a very desirable thing, and if there is already as part of the organic law of the State the content of the first sentence of your recommendation, where is the need to repeat it? I agree that the 14th Amendment is a limitation on governmental actions, not individuals; but since you have already incorporated in the second sentence the limitations imposed upon the State, as an agency, are you not thereby repeating?

The criticism I make is, first, this: that your first sentence is surplusage, that you are only repeating in that paragraph what already is the law of the land, the law of the State. Secondly, that if you are stating it at first as a general principle and then you are repeating it again in those details, what about the possible argument that the specific controls the general and that the general might lose some if its force and effect?

MR. BURRELL:

May I direct your attention to the words "or any subdivision thereof." That is not at present contained in any constitutional provision under the 1844 Constitution.

MR. PARK:

I don't want to argue, but I want to get it cleared up in my mind. The point that I make is that you are putting in your next sentence the same thought you put in your first sentence. Now, why won't you get everything that you want by eliminating the first sentence? Starting off with the second sentence, does that not give you everything that you are after and can't take anything away from you?

MR. BURRELL:

There is the possibility that we hope to gain strength by a restatement of the principle in specific terms, whereas the first sentence is general. I agree on that.

MR. PARK:

Can you give us any good legal reason why the first sentence should be in?

MR. BURRELL:

There is a difference of verbiage. One says, "No person shall be denied the equal protection." The other says, shall not "be subjected to any discrimination." Those things may not be definitely synonymous. Denial of the protection of a law, and subjection to discrimination may be different. For that reason I feel that the two statements might well be contained. One is denial of equal protection of the law and the other one subjection to discrimination.

MR. PARK:

We already have the first one by the 14th Amendment. And the second one—

MR. BURRELL:

I previously made the statement that the 14th Amendment only limits the action of the State and does not extend to the actions of the individual, the corporation, or a subdivision of the State against another individual.

MR. PARK:

But it does extend to every activity of the State, all the way down the chain, as long as they are acting under a color of office. Isn't that right?

MR. BURRELL:

There may be some discussion there where the State has delegated certain powers—whether the superintendent of a hospital for the insane, for instance, could refuse to admit a person because his name ended in "izky." The question would be whether the superintendent of the institution would violate the 14th Amendment, or whether we would go to the Constitution of New Jersey in that particular instance. Then there are quasi-public institutions, which are frequent malefactors in the matter of discrimination; and it is a question whether they come under the prohibition of the 14th Amendment which extends only to the State. I think that your argument as to surplusage is good on the surface, but if it is desired to give us a strong amendment, no harm will be done by keeping in both sentences.

MR. PARK:

Thank you very much.

CHAIRMAN:

Any other questions?

MR. JOHN H. PURSEL:

You spoke of restrictions in deeds as to colored people buying in certain sections. Am I not correct in the thought that there are United States Supreme Court decisions that make such restrictions illegal?

MR. BURRELL:

I only wish that you were correct, sir. I am a member of the committee of the National Bar Association which is presently preparing a brief in an appeal from Circuit Court of Appeals in Michigan, which may be taken to the Supreme Court on that subject. The Supreme Court has not declared a restrictive covenant legally unenforceable.

MR. PURSEL:

How about the New Jersey courts?

MR. BURRELL:

The New Jersey courts have not definitely acted on the question of restrictive covenants. There is a decision in the State of California which is now being appealed, which outlaws restrictive covenants. The decision recently in the Supreme Court in Michigan is to the contrary, and one in the state court of Illinois is to the contrary. I've cooperated in the brief *amicus curiae* in both Michigan and Illinois, representing the National Bar Association.

MR. PARK:

While you are preparing the brief you might look up that case in New Jersey. There is a ruling in New Jersey and you can find it if you locate that case in the District of Columbia. I think it's *May* v somebody.

MR. BURRELL:

Thank you; I appreciate that greatly.

MRS. MARIE H. KATZENBACH:

May I ask you a question? Would not the statement that "no person shall because of race . . ." be sufficient?

MR. BURRELL:

I do not think so. Persons may be designated by racial designations, which are not always synonymous with designations as to color. A person may be sometimes of one race but his color is decidedly different. I think it is necessary to use both words, as they are definitely not synonymous.

MR. PURSEL:

How would it be if you used race and color and then left those other terms out?

MR. BURRELL:

Oh, very definitely we want the prohibition against creed and religion. That is equally important. It is one of our great discriminations. We could not at all leave out creed or religion. Creed and religion must be in.

MR. PARK:

I don't want to be too oppressive on this thing, but you are one of the few lawyers who has been here. You can appreciate the difficulties the lawyers have on this thing, and I would like you to give, if you wish, your concept of what is included within the idea of a civil right, because obviously this is going to be discussed a great deal. What do you mean by civil right? What does it include and not include?

MR. BURRELL:

That is a question that is rather difficult to answer. To go back to the original constitutional concept of right of enjoyment of life, liberty, and the pursuit of happiness, of those things which go to the exercise of the right of liberty, pursuit of happiness, would be the beginning of civil rights. Take first the right of the individual to enjoy public accommodations—contra-distinction to private accommodations. Under civil rights we do not assert the right of any individual to invade the home of any other person, or to invade his club, or his fraternity, or lodge; but in places of public accommodation, which are licensed by the State or by a subdivision thereof, every citizen should have equal accommodations— not one to pay ten cents for a beverage and the other to pay a dollar, one to enter and the other not to enter.

The question of civil rights is rather broad. We might extend them in some cases, as some states have, even to the quesion of discrimination in the ownership of property. Our own State has a civil rights law which governs largely the question of the use of public accommodations. Whether public accommodations should extend to hospitals, schools, and other things is a matter of discussion. Recent amendments have been introduced, but unfortunately were not adopted. Doctor Hill, who just preceded me, introduced an amendment to include hospitals, schools and others, but the amendment was not successful. If you have a specific question, I'd be very happy to answer it. I don't want to take too much time of the Committee. We might talk on this subject for minutes and it might go into hours.

COMMITTEE MEMBER:

Would it be asking too much for you to give us some kind of brief, setting out the rights of colored people under the New Jersey legislation? Could it be done?

MR. BURRELL:

I wouldn't like to limit it to colored people. I'm not appearing strictly for colored people. I'm appearing for citizens of New Jersey. Accidentally, I'm colored; but I'm equally interested in discriminations against women, against persons of one religion, against a person's national origin. I believe that which is good for all of the citizens will eventually be good for any specific minority.

I do not wish to limit my argument to color, but I will tell you that there are numerous statutory enactments which protect persons of minority groups. I happen to be the author of several—the fair labor bill with regard particularly to discrimination in employment. This was a law introduced by me and enacted in 1933. Mr. Randolph is the author of a law with respect to riots in assemblage. The Stackhouse law was against discrimination in employment, particularly during the war years. The Urban Colored Population Commission, which is the investigating body, has some measure of power in the way of protection; and we have of course the latest, the Division against Discrimination under the Department of Education. We discussed that, I believe, yesterday and representatives of that group are here today. May I also say that there are laws prohibiting various discriminations. There are laws prohibiting discrimination in admitting children to schools, and there are decisions under these various laws.

COMMITTEE MEMBER:

I think all of that would be very helpful to know about, as far as I'm concerned. I don't know much about it.

MR. BURRELL:

I shall be very happy to see if we cannot find a compilation of that and get it to you today or tomorrow, and to any other members of the Committee who may be interested. But we still feel that in adopting statutes from time to time you are attacking symptoms; that when you are making a constitutional enactment you are attacking basic causes. I believe it would be better to have a constitutional enactment reaching the cause, rather than continually treating symptoms, in effect, as we do for the moment by our legislative enactments.

CHAIRMAN:

Are there any other questions? . . . Thank you Mr. Burrell.

---

1. Assemblyman James O. Hill of Newark.
2. The man referred to here was Fred W. Martin of Jersey City, who spoke to the Committee on behalf of the State Council of the NAACP.

---

4   COURT OUTLAWS DISCRIMINATION IN PUBLIC HOUSING, 1949

The following decision by New Jersey Superior Court Justice Alfred A. Stein marked a significant victory for civil rights advocates in New Jersey. Charles Seawell and eight other black veterans, who were refused apartments in segregated public housing projects in East Orange, asked the court to rule whether it was legal to restrict blacks to a "separate but equal" housing facility, claimed to be the equal of projects set aside for the families of white veterans. In keeping with earlier civil rights decisions by the state's Supreme Court, Justice Stein ruled that racial segregation in public housing projects in New Jersey was a violation of federal and state law. "By the Fourteenth Amendment of the Constitution of the United States," he declared, "the colored race was raised to the dignity of citizenship and equality, and the states were prohibited from abridging the privileges and immunities of persons of that race." Justice Stein also noted that the laws establishing public housing projects in New Jersey specifically prohibited racial discrimination in their operation. This decision established the legal basis for non-discriminatory public housing in the state.

Seawell v. MacWithey,
New Jersey Superior Court, 2: 258-65.

STEIN, J.S.C. Before the court is the complaint brought on behalf of nine Negro veterans of World War II for injunctive and other relief. Plaintiffs are honorably discharged veterans and are and have been residents of East Orange, both at the time of their entry into and their discharge from service. Each of them is a citizen of the United States, married, and each has at least one child. Plaintiffs are regularly employed and each receives monthly wages at least four times the monthly rental fixed for the project. They are in need of housing and have made timely application to the City of East Orange for accommodations in the emergency housing project. None has been accepted as tenants in the South Arlington Avenue project solely because that project admittedly has been reserved by the City of East Orange for occupancy by white veterans.

Four housing projects have been commenced under *R.S.* 55:14G-1. *et seq., P.L.* 1946, *c.* 323, in the City of East Orange located as follows: 146-158 South Arlington Avenue containing 44 dwelling units; 68-78 Elmwood Avenue containing 40 dwelling units; Rhode Island Avenue and Chelsea Place containing 20 dwelling units; and 291-295 North Clinton Street containing 14 dwelling units. Of these only one, the project on South Arlington Avenue has reached the state of completion where families have been accepted as tenants and are in possession of their apartments. All such families admitted as tenants to this apartment are white. In leasing apartments in this project the plan followed by the City of East Orange was to exclude Negroes. William M. McConnell, a member of the City Council of East Orange, and chairman of the Veterans Housing Committee, in his reply affidavit says: "It was the intent and policy of the City to assign the first Negro tenants recommended by the Screening Committee and whose applications have been and are being investigated, to site No. 2 (North Clinton Street) which affords at least equal dwelling facilities to the other three sites. This policy was established by the City after careful study and consideration of the experience and general tenant relationships obtained by the governing body in temporary veterans' housing projects heretofore furnished by the City under both Federal and State temporary housing programs.''

Under *R.S.* 55-14*G*-2, *P.L.* 1946, *c.* 323, the "authority" mentioned in the act is defined to mean the Public Housing and Development Authority in the State Department of Economic Development. "Administrator" means the administrator of the Public Housing and Development Authority who is the Commissioner of the Department of Economic Development. The present administrator is the defendant, Charles H. Erdman, Jr. His deputy is the defendant, William T. Vanderlipp.

The administrator has promulgated regulations under which priorities for tenants are to be established as follows: (a) distressed veterans or families of veterans; (b) distressed servicemen or families of servicemen; (c) distressed families of non-veterans or servicemen; (d) non-distressed veterans or families of veterans; (e) non-distressed servicemen or families of servicemen; (f) non-distressed families other than veterans or servicemen.

The City of East Orange, by the members of its City Council and the mayor, are the agencies charged with the renting of the several projects. The individuals composing the City Council, the mayor, the Commissioner of the Department of Economic Development of the State of New Jersey, and his deputy administrator, and the City of East Orange are named herein as defendants.

Plaintiffs seek injunction enjoining the defendants from denying to plaintiffs and other qualified Negro applicants equal opportunity to be considered for admission to the various emergency housing projects under their control and supervision where such denial is solely because of the race or color of such applicants, and from asking information on or anywise considering race, creed, color, national origin or ancestry in any application for occupancy in such projects under their control and supervision and from considering race, creed, color, national origin or ancestry in processing, investigating or acting upon any such application.

The South Arlington Avenue project was commenced October 27, 1947 and according to William M. McConnell, chairman of the veterans' permanent housing committee of the City of East Orange, the structure, although not yet fully completed or accepted by the state agency, was, by agreement with the state agency because of the dire need for housing by qualified veterans, recommended by the screening committee for immediate occupancy, and thereupon 26 families were placed in the finished units of that project. It is not denied that the families thus placed in that housing project are exclusively white. None of the other projects have as yet reached the stage of completion. Each of the plaintiffs has filed his application for admission to the housing projects constructed and under construction, and from all that appears before me they are qualified for consideration. No reason for their disqualification is presented and I must assume that none exists, unless the color of the plaintiffs can be regarded as a valid reason justifying their exclusion from three of the four housing projects and their segregation into one of those projects. That the latter represents the view of the municipal authorities admits of no doubt.

The complaint is that in the selection of tenants for occupancy in the South Arlington Avenue project, which has been completed, and for other projects at Elmwood Avenue and Chelsea and Rhode Island Avenue, the defendants have adopted a policy of refusing to admit qualified Negro applicants solely because of their color and have for the same reason refused to consider their applications for admission to such projects. The policy thus complained of is admitted in the replying affidavit of the chairman of the municipal committee. It is admitted that Negro applicants were to be assigned to the North Clinton Street project and thus segregated from the white applicants.

Under *section* 3 of the act the Public Housing and Development Authority in the Department of Economic Development is given complete power and authority to coordinate "all the programs, planning and construction contemplated by the provisions of this act, and to do and to authorize all things incidental, desirable or necessary to effect the purposes thereof in accordance with such rules and regulation as may be established by the Administrator and approved by the Economic Council of the Department of Economic Development."

By *section* 12 of the act, when an emergency housing project is available for occupancy the administrator may commit to any public corporation, municipality or other public agency such property for operation and management as emergency housing at such rentals "and with such preferences as to occupancy and upon such terms and conditions as shall be for the best interests of the public."

Section 21 of the act provides: "For all of the purposes of this act, no person shall because of race, creed, color, national origin or ancestry be subject to any discrimination."

[1] The defendant, City of East Orange, and the defendant members of the City Council are respectively a municipal corporation and public officials performing a necessary public function under the act. Their acts are the acts of the State within the purview of section 1 of the Fourteenth Amendment of the Constitution of the United States which provides in part:

"**No state shall make or enforce any law which shall abridge the privileges or immunities of citizens of the Untited States; nor shall any state deprive any person of life, liberty or property without due process of law; nor deny to any person within its jurisdiction the equal protection of the laws."

Thus, in *Virginia v. Rives*, 100 *U.S.* 313, 318, 25 *L. Ed.* 667, 669, the court stated "It is doubtless true that a State may act through different agencies—either by its legislative, its executive, or its judicial authorities; and the prohibitions of the amendment extend to all action of the State denying equal protection of the laws, whether it be action by one of these agencies or by another." In *Shelley v. Kraemer* (1948), 334 *U.S.* 1, 92 *L. Ed.* 1161, it was said: "In the Civil Rights Cases, 109 *U.S.* 3, 11, 17, 27 *L. Ed.* 835, 841, this Court pointed out that the Amendment makes void 'state action of every kind' which is inconsistent with the guaranties therein contained, and extends to manifestation of 'state authority in the shape of laws, customs, or judicial or executive proceedings.' Language to like effect is employed no less than eighteen times during the course of that opinion."

In *Home Telephone & Telegraph Co. v. City of Los Angeles*, 227 *U.S.* 278, the United States Supreme Court held that acts done under the authority of a municipal ordinance passed in virtue of power conferred by a state are embraced by the Fourteenth Amendment to the Federal Constitution.

The four projects above referred to are not a private enterprise, financed with private funds, as was the situation in the case of *Dorsey v. Stuyvesant Town Corporation*, 190 *Misc. (N.Y.)* 187, affirmed by the New York Supreme Court, Appellate Division, on December 20, 1948. Here all four projects are financed by public funds furnished in part by the State and in part by the municipality. The question therefore posed in the case at bar is whether a municipality, charged with the management of several public housing projects being erected with public funds, may, in the face of the Federal Constitution and of our own statute *(R.S. 55:14G-21, P.L. 1946, c. 323, sec. 21)*, exclude persons of the colored race from three of those projects and segregate them within the fourth of those projects. Is such segregation unlawful discrimination?

In the briefs of counsel appear many citations from the federal jurisdiction. I do not consider it necessary to discuss them in detail. They may all be summarized by the single statement that by the Fourteenth Amendment the colored race was raised to the dignity of citizenship and equality and the states were prohibited from abridging the privileges and immunities of persons of that race. This amendment has uniformly been held to protect all persons, white or black, against discriminatory legislation or action by the states. We need not step out of our own decisions to determine whether in this State segregation constitutes unlawful discrimination. Two decisions are deemed controlling. In *Bullock v. Wooding*, 123 *N.J. Law* 176, *(Sup. Ct.* 1939), the court dealt with the complaint of a colored person who sought to be admitted to the facilities of public beach No. 1 at Long Branch, New Jersey. The municipal authorities had divided the bathing beach into four sections, all of equal facility and desirability, but under an ordinance had pursued the policy of segregating colored persons within beach No. 3. The plaintiff was denied access to the beach of her choosing. She brought certiorari to review the ordinance. Although the court held that mandamus was the proper remedy to compel the City of Long Branch to grant to the plaintiff a permit or license to the beach of her choosing, the court nonetheless passed upon the meritorious question involved. It said: "It is, of course, settled that the dignities, equalities and rights of citizenship cannot legally be denied to members of the negro race. *Cf. Buchanan v. Warley,* 245 *U.S.* 60; 62 *L. Ed.* 149; *Patterson v. Board of Education, Trenton,* 11 *N.J. Misc. R.* 179, 164 *Atl. Rep.* 892; affirmed, 112 *N.J.L.* 99, 169 *Atl. Rep.* 690."

In the cited case of *Patterson v. The Board of Education of the City of Trenton* our courts dealt with a policy of the Trenton Board of Education which permitted the students of a high school to enjoy indiscriminately the advantages of the classroom and the facilities of the gymnasium but would not permit the colored students to take swimming lessons during such periods as the white students received such instruction. The colored students were permitted to take swimming lessons only with those of their own race. This was held to be unlawful discrimination. Mandamus was allowed and that action was affirmed.

Here the State itself has not offended. Quite the contrary. Under the very law permitting these public projects there is an explicit prohibition against discrimination because of race, creed, color, national origin or ancestry. By this legislation the people of this State declared its policy that such public housing projects, financed in whole or in part with public funds, shall be equally and commonly available to all citizens, free of that discrimination condemned by the statute. Is this not as it should be? The public funds emanate from common sources, without distinction of color, race or creed. The duties and responsibilities or citizenship are discharged alike by the white and colored citizens, witness the effort made, the blood shed, and the lives sacrificed on common battle fields by citizens of all kinds of color, creed and race. Man's sense of justice, coupled with an enlightened understanding of our common humanity, would dictate that if there be no segregation in the field of civic duty and sacrifice, there be none in the realm of human dignity and equality.

[2] The defendants herein, other than the State of New Jersey and its said officials who are made parties hereto, insist that segregation in the East Orange housing project is not discriminatory because the facilities made available to colored applicants are of equal, if not better, character than those furnished to white applicants. This argument lacks validity. In the two cases last cited the facilities offered by the municipalities were of like character and equal quality. In fact, in the Trenton school case the facility offered to the colored students (the swimming pool) was the same facility made available to the white students. There only the time for utilization was different. Yet that single circumstance was held to be an act of unlawful discrimination. The holdings in these two cases settle the law on the point in controversy in the present case and I hold that the segregation, frankly admitted by the city authorities, is unlawful discrimination and violates not only our general policy of the law but

also the provisions of the very statute under which these projects have been erected. The City of East Orange and its municipal agents and agencies will be restrained from taking any action in furtherance of the city's admitted policy and purpose of segregation. The motion to strike the complaint as insufficient in law is denied.

[3] In the brief for the State and its two officials it is conceded that the segregation here complained of is unlawful discrimination. It is claimed, however, that the State has not approved the municipality's policy and acts of segregation, that the state officials learned of it only by the fact of the bringing of the within suit, and that the State has the matter under factual investigation. It therefore would appear that the State has neither done nor threatened to do any act violative of plaintiffs' rights. The motion to strike the complaint as against the State and Charles R. Erdman, Jr., Commissioner of the Department of Economic Development, and William T. Vanderlipp, Deputy Administrator of the Public Housing and Development Authority in the Department of Economic Development of the State of New Jersey, is granted.

An order of preliminary injunction and the other orders contemplated by the foregoing views should be presented on notice to adverse parties.

5 SCHOOL DESEGREGATION LAUDED, 1954

Although the public schools in New Jersey had been legally desegregated before the U.S. Supreme Court handed down its unanimous decision in *Brown v. Board of Education of Topeka, Kansas,* on May 17, 1954, the state's black communities praised that decision more than any other event in over a generation. Many saw the Supreme Court's invalidation of racial segregation in public schools as a long-sought victory for all black Americans and, as the following editorial from the *New Jersey Afro-American* makes clear, the harbinger of the collapse of Jim Crow in American life. After the decision was announced, extensive coverage of the opinion, and the briefs submitted by the lawyers of the Legal Defense Fund of the NAACP, appeared in the *Afro-American,* the longest running and most widely read black newspaper in New Jersey. By calling on New Jersey blacks to demonstrate their support of the civil rights cause by acquiring a life membership in the NAACP, the *Afro-American* recognized the increased capacity of the black middle class to bear the financial burden of major civil rights activities. The cause of freedom, the newspaper reminded its readers, was a costly matter. Indeed, it was and became more so, as the pace of the civil rights movement increased in the coming years.

"$500 For Freedom," Newark, *New Jersey Afro-American,* 29 May 1954.

Let's prove to the NAACP and the nation that the joy in our hearts over the abolition of segregated schools by the Supreme Court is genuine in the most effective practical manner.

Let's feel ashamed about our token membership in the NAACP and make it more substantial in the light of the magnitude of the Supreme Court's decision.

Let us in New Jersey show our gratitude to Thurgood Marshall and his brilliant legal staff by taking out $500 life memberships in the NAACP right now.

This is a good time to do so. The annual meeting of the New Jersey State Conference of NAACP Branches will be held in Atlantic City from June 4 to 6.

Walter White, the national executive secretary, will climax the meeting Sunday afternoon, June 6, with interpretation of our responsibilities to be on guard against all efforts by the Southern states to sabotage or circumvent the Supreme Court's decision.

The Association, therefore, will need many more thousands of dollars to successfully meet the challenges from Dixie.

And, if our slogan, "Freedom by 1963" is to become a reality, there can be no moratorium on large memberships in and gifts to the NAACP, whose Freedom Fund goal is one million dollars.

Freedom is a very costly heritage as the history books record. But, in our case, a $500 life membership in the NAACP is not costly by any yardstick—indeed it is a paltry sum beside the goal we seek to achieve.

Most of us throw away $500 a year without any serious consequences.

None of us are so poor that we cannot take out a life membership in the NAACP. We can pay for it in full or by installments.

It would only cost you $2.00 per week yearly for five years, or $1.00 per week for ten years.

The New Jersey AFRO-AMERICAN strongly recommends that as many organizations, churches, clubs, business and professional leaders and individuals as possible stop now and revise their budgets to include a $500 life membership in the NAACP.

We recommend further that you time your subscription for the annual meeting of the State Conference of Branches in Atlantic City, so that New Jersey, which has the nation's best civil rights legislation, can give a challenging impetus to the nationwide drive for NAACP life membership.

A fine start has already been made in this direction.

Bravell M. Nesbitt, president of the NAACP Branch in Elizabeth, was presented with a paid-up life membership certificate Sunday, May 16, at a Freedom Rally by Judge Hubert Delany of NYC, national membership chairman.

Another NAACP life membership was paid in full by members of the New Jersey State Medical Association at their Spring session held May 12 at Bordentown Manual Training School.

If you can't get to the annual meeting of the State Conference of Branches in Atlantic City, send your life membership check, or your down payment by proxy, or through the editor of this newspaper, who is a member of the Board of Directors of the NAACP Branch in Newark.

On to Atlantic City with at least 100 NAACP life memberships!

6 STRUGGLE FOR LEGAL JUSTICE, 1951

The right of blacks in New Jersey to equal justice under the law came under public scrutiny in the case popularly known as the trial of the Trenton Six. No other racial case in the history of the state troubled public opinion so deeply and provoked such widespread reaction outside the state. Some civil rights advocates, seeking to draw attention to the case, compared it with the infamous trials of the Scottsboro Boys in which nine black youths were unjustly accused of sexually assaulting two white women near Scottsboro, Alabama, on March 25, 1931. Actually, the differences far outweighed the similarities in the two cases, but in both, the issue of fair trial for blacks was at stake.

In the first trial of the Trenton Six, all of the defendants were found guilty of murdering seventy-two-year-old William Horner (called Fred Horner in **doc. 6**) on January 27, 1948. On appeal to the New Jersey Supreme Court, the verdict was reversed because the trial judge had improperly sentenced the six to death and doubt had been cast on the confessions of five of the defendants. The second trial began on February 1, 1951, but ended in a mistrial after the Mercer County prosecutor became seriously ill. By the end of the fifteen-week third trial on June 14, 1951, the case of the Trenton Six was a cause célèbre among civil rights organizations, labor unions, and radical groups. The verdict in the trial found four of the six not guilty; the two other men, Ralph Cooper and Collis English, were found guilty and sentenced to life imprisonment. The following appeal, which appeared in the *New York Times*, questioned whether Cooper and English had received a fair trial because the prosecution had produced no substantive evidence against the defendants.

The case precipitated a clash between the Civil Rights Congress (an allegedly subversive organization of the Communist Party which had defended the Trenton Six during the first trial), the NAACP, and the American Civil Liberties Union. The Civil Rights Congress was accused of using the case to discredit the American legal system and of giving secondary importance to gaining an acquittal for the defendants. Moderate civil rights advocates also feared that the association of communists with the defense of the Trenton Six made it more difficult for them to obtain a fair trial. "There is some evidence," observed the reporter for the *New Republic,* "that many people in New Jersey have a feeling that anybody defended by the Communists is guilty *ipso facto,* or at the very least, that nobody else should soil his hands by interfering in a case the Communists have taken up and on the same side." Under pressure from the civil rights groups, the Civil Rights Congress removed its lawyers from the second case. But its interest and propaganda on behalf of the defendants continued.

The guilty verdict against Cooper and English in the third trial was also reversed by the New Jersey Supreme Court, which found errors in the case. In an unexpected and tragic turn of events, Collis English, the first youth arrested for Horner's murder, died while in prison awaiting his fourth trial. On February 24, 1953, Ralph Cooper, the last defendant in the case, unexpectedly pleaded no defense and claimed that the other five men had also been involved in Horner's murder. Cooper was then sentenced to six to ten years' imprisonment beginning with his arrest in August 1948. Cooper's admission of guilt brought the Trenton Six case to an incredible, and for many, unsatisfactory conclusion. The defense attorneys in the first three trials claimed that Cooper's plea and his implication of the other defendants was a confession of dubious merit, and they called on the state attorney general to investigate the matter. Nearly seven years after the first trial, Ralph Cooper was paroled in November 1955.

"The Case of the Trenton Six," *New York Times,* 28 November 1951.

Two Americans face life in prison for a crime of which millions of men and women throughout the world believe them innocent. They are Negroes. Their names are Ralph Cooper and Collis English. They have been imprisoned for almost four years. They are the two remaining imprisoned members of the now world-famous Trenton Six, the jury at a second trial having acquitted four of the original Trenton Six.

The purpose of this advertisement is to secure justice, through a new trial for Ralph Cooper and Collis English, whom the three undersigned organizations believe to be innocent and the victims of a great miscarriage of justice.

ROUGH JUSTICE

It is argued "what matter that two young Negroes are condemned to spend the rest of their lives in prison for a crime which they did not commit? Far better to drop the case and pretend that justice has been done. Four of the original Trenton Six have been exonerated. Is not this a sort of rough justice?" This was the evident reasoning of the jury at the second trial which acquitted four men and condemned two, neither of whom had been accused of striking the murder blows.

But it matters. Believing these men to be innocent, no decent American can rest until justice is secured through the medium of a fair trial, in which a jury upon consideration of the evidence arrives at a verdict, without trading the lives of some for the liberty of others.

A GREAT AMERICAN TRADITION

There is a great American tradition that all of our citizens whether rich or poor, Negro or white, shall have equal justice under law. It is the task of each generation to preserve and pass on to posterity that tradition so long as America shall endure. That is our principal objective in this effort to secure a new trial for Ralph Cooper and Collis English, the tragic Trenton Two.

Above all, the four year long agony of Ralph Cooper and Collis English speaks to every decent American who learns of this miscarriage of justice and invests all of us with a share of the responsibility for the life and death of these stricken men.

THE FACTS IN THE CASE

The case of the Trenton Two began on the morning of January 27, 1948, when a 72-year-old junk dealer named Fred Horner was clubbed to death in the back room of his store in Trenton, N.J. Since then, two trials have been held, in the first of which six Negroes arrested and charged with the crime were convicted and condemned to death. Following an appeal and reversal of this verdict, a second trial was held in the spring of 1951, at which four of the original "Trenton Six" were acquitted, while Ralph Cooper and Collis English were convicted and sentenced to life imprisonment.

It is impossible to understand the case of the Trenton Two without taking into account the background of city politics from which it emerged. In 1948 Trenton was enduring a crime wave, Mayor Donal

Connally was under indictment for bribery and his police department under attack for a long series of unsolved crimes. The press was clamoring for reform. An editorial in the Trenton TIMES headed "The Idle Electric Chair" pointed out that no man had been convicted and sentenced to death in New Jersey for a crime since December 11, 1945. The Police Department, stung into action by this record of unsolved crime, and by attacks on corruption in the city administration, began frenzied efforts to round up suspects. Within 15 days six men were arrested, all Negroes, all of whom had alibis. They were the Trenton Six.

There were no eye witnesses to the crime. The dead man's common-law wife, Elizabeth Maguire, who had seen "three light complected Negroes" enter the store, failed to identify either Cooper or English when confronted with the suspects ten days after the crime. Cooper and English are dark-skinned—the darkest of the six men arrested. She said she had never seen either Cooper or English before.

HELD INCOMMUNICADO

The Police Department held the Trenton Six incommunicado for days. Testimony at subsequent trials by Dr. J. Minor Sullivan, who had been called to witness the signing of confessions and to examine the men for marks of physical violence, indicated that the men were under the influence of drugs. Held under arrest, refused access to legal counsel, presumably drugged, interrogated for long periods of time (English for 19 hours at a stretch) without sleep, five of the six Negroes signed utterly confusing confessions, all at variance. It is believable that almost any six Negroes of a comparable cultural level in the hands of the police, fearful, without friends and denied access to counsel would have confessed to this or any other crime.

It was upon this flimsy evidence that the Trenton Six were first rushed to trial before an all-white jury in June 1948. They were defended by court-appointed attorneys. The verdict was Guilty—the sentence Death.

It was at this juncture that the Communist Party, through the Civil Rights Congress, their legal defense arm, entered the case. Out of this case they attempted to build support for the Communist Party. They engaged lawyers, founded a propaganda mill, organized a nationwide collection of funds with which to finance the defense, and took it to the New Jersey Supreme Court. At this point the American Civil Liberties Union and the National Association for the Advancement of Colored People entered the case through the filing of separate briefs amicus. In June 1949, the Supreme Court of New Jersey reversed the verdict of guilty, stating that the trial record was a "judgment tainted with error." The Communists' legal defense was withdrawn subsequently.

THE SECOND TRIAL

Before the opening of the second trial on May 5, 1951, a group of Princeton University and Princeton Theological Seminary educators, under the chairmanship of Dr. Edward S. Corwin, as the Princeton Committee for the Defense of the Trenton Six, undertook the defense. Their purpose was and is to secure to these humble men equal justice under law and not to leave the defense in the hands of Communists who attempted to exploit the case for their own ends. The Princeton Committee defended three of the men. At the same time the National Association for the Advancement of Colored People undertook the defense of two of the accused. The sixth accused was defended by a court-appointed attorney.

This second trial occasioned the longest criminal procedure in the history of New Jersey, covering 15 weeks and 3 days. Nearly 10,000 pages of testimony were recorded. Its result was the acquittal of four of the Trenton Six who had been previously convicted, and the conviction and sentence to life imprisonment of Ralph Cooper and Collis English. It is from this verdict that the organizations interested in the present defense are appealing. This appeal holds that the verdict is against the weight of evidence, that it was entered into as a result of horsetrading on the part of the jury with the lives of the two men.

Neither Ralph Cooper nor Collis English have been accused of striking the fatal blow. The man who was accused was acquitted. Both Ralph Cooper and Collis English were confronted by Miss Maguire, 10 days after the tragedy. She stated that she had never seen them before. Weeks later, at the urging of police, she changed her story and stated English and Cooper had been present, as well as two others of the four men now acquitted. This is the basis of the prosecution's case, which is founded on an actual political necessity to find victims.

THE PRESENT APPEAL

The present appeal is taken to the New Jersey Supreme Court against the conviction of Ralph Cooper and Collis English, and their sentence to life imprisonment. A distinguished array of attorneys, including Arthur Garfield Hays, General Counsel of the American Civil Liberties Union; Mercer Burrell, representing the National Association for the Advancement of Colored People; and Judge George Pellettieri, counsel to the Princeton Committee for Defense of the Trenton Six, will serve without fee to carry the case to the U.S. Supreme Court, if necessary.

JUSTICE COSTS MONEY

Had Cooper and English been condemned to *death* the Court would have provided for appeal expenses. But the Court cannot so provide in the case of life sentences. To print the full record of the 15-week trial, required by New Jersey law for appeal to the Supreme Court, will cost more than $20,000. It will cover 24 bound volumes of 400 pages each, each volume costing about $750. Additional expenses will be minimal. There is no money available for this purpose from any source.

THIS IS A CALL TO EVERY AMERICAN TO JOIN IN HELPING SECURE FOR RALPH COOPER AND COLLIS ENGLISH EVERY LEGAL RIGHT WHICH IS THEIR DUE AS AMERICAN CITIZENS. Four men of the original Trenton Six, once adjudged Guilty and condemned to death, have since been exonerated by due process of American law. The three organizations which have assumed responsibility for the appeal, all of which have made intensive investigations into the facts, believe Ralph Cooper and Collis English to be innocent. Whatever the opinion of any American as to the innocence or guilt of these men, all can join in helping to secure for them the ultimate redress at law. This is the best possible answer to the Communist outcry that American justice turns its face from the Negro.

JUSTICE CAN BE SECURED

The Communists have sought to make capital of this case by whipping up a worldwide hysteria against American treatment of Negro citizens. But the history of this case refutes the Communist thesis. It proves that justice can be secured through the normal processes of law. It also proves that sincere and informed public opinion must be aroused on occasion to secure to humble and helpless defendants their full rights under law, especially when police officers abuse their powers.

Believing in the innocence of Ralph Cooper and Collis English, we call on every American for help in making possible this appeal for a new trial through your contribution to the Joint Defense Fund.

PLEASE HELP BY SENDING YOUR CONTRIBUTION TODAY

Joint Committee to Free the Trenton Two[1]

American Civil Liberties Union

Princeton Committee for Defense of the Trenton Six

N.A.A.C.P. Legal Defense & Educational Fund, Inc.

---

1. Signatories of the appeal included a number of distinguished Americans: for the American Civil Liberties Union, Ernest Angell, Whitney North Seymour, Walter Gellhorn, and Arthur Garfield Hays; for the National Committee to Free the Trenton Two, Roger N. Baldwin, Pearl S. Buck, Lloyd K. Garrison, and The Right Reverend Edward L. Parsons; for the Princeton Committee for the Defense of the Trenton Six, Edward S. Corwin; and for the NAACP Legal Defense and Educational Fund, Inc., Arthur B. Spingarn, Hubert H. Delany, Mrs. Franklin D. Roosevelt, Walter White, Roy Wilkins, and Thurgood Marshall.

7   VOICE OF BLACK NATIONALISM, 1969, 1972

Amiri Baraka has been the most controversial poet, playwright, and social activist in New Jersey in the last two decades. His early writings presaged the militancy and emerging racial consciousness of Afro-Americans in the 1960s and placed him in the forefront of the black cultural and nationalist movement of the late 1960s and early 1970s. Born Everette LeRoi Jones in Newark in 1934, Imamu Amiri Baraka (the name he took around 1968) briefly attended Rutgers University, was graduated from Howard University, and served in the U.S. Air Force from 1954 to 1957. In 1958 he moved to Greenwich Village in New York City, where he pursued his intellectual and artistic talents through poetry and writings on social issues and Afro-American music. In 1965 he moved to Harlem, where for a short time he headed the Black Arts Repertory Theater/School. That year his play, *Dutchman,* was awarded the Obie Award as the best off-Broadway play of 1964.

In the late 1960s, Baraka espoused black separatism and assailed the racial and economic injustices that prevented the uplift of blacks in the United States. Returning to Newark during these years, the writer-turned-social-activist helped to form the Spirit House, a self-help organization devoted to Kawaida and Nguzo Saba, the black cultural and nationalist principles espoused by Ron Karenga. The political arm of the organization's efforts in Newark was the Committee for a Unified Newark. Baraka's advocacy of black community consciousness often brought him into sharp disagreement with city officials and moderate black leaders who deplored what they regarded as his revolutionary ideas. Nonetheless, the efforts of Baraka and scores of young Newarkers who joined his organization greatly assisted the emergence of political maturity among blacks in the city.

The following writings reflect Baraka's nationalist ideas during the late 1960s and early 1970s. By the mid-1970s he espoused a revolutionary Marxist-Leninist position which he has since articulated in his literary and theatrical works and polemical writings. The first poem, "Young Soul," beseeches black youth to discover their identity. "Beautiful Black Women" is a tribute and plea to black women; it was recorded in the late 1960s by the writer and a voice ensemble, the Jihad. In his essay, "The Practice of the New Nationalism," Baraka discussed the role of black nationalists in Newark in the years after the summer of 1967, proposing that a program devoted to the principles of black nationalism would help unify the race and set the stage for its eventual liberation.

a.   LeRoi Jones, *Black Magic, Collected Poetry, 1961–1967* (New York, 1969), pp. 49, 148.

YOUNG SOUL

First, feel, then feel, then
read, or read, then feel, then
fall, or stand, where you
already are. Think
of your self, and the other
selves . . . think
of your parents, your mothers
and sisters, your bentslick
father, then feel, or
fall, on your knees
if nothing else will move you,

> then read
> and look deeply
> into all matters
> come close to you
> city boys—
> country men
>
> Make some muscle
> in your head, but
> use the muscle
> in yr heart

BEAUTIFUL BLACK WOMEN . . .

Beautiful black women, fail, they act. Stop them, raining.
They are so beautiful, we want them with us. Stop them, raining.
Beautiful, stop raining, they fail. We fail them and their lips
stick out perpetually, at our weakness. Raining. Stop them. Black
queens, Ruby Dee weeps at the window, raining, being lost in her
life, being what we all will be, sentimental bitter frustrated
deprived of her fullest light. Beautiful black women, it is
still raining in this terrible land. We need you. We flex our
muscles, turn to stare at our tormentor, we need you. Raining.
We need you, reigning, black queen. This/terrible black ladies
wander, Ruby Dee weeps, the window, raining, she calls, and her voice
is left to hurt us slowly. It hangs against the same wet glass, her

sadness and age, and the trip, and the lost heat, and the grey cold
buildings of our entrapment. Ladies. Women. We need you. We are still
trapped and weak, but we build and grow heavy with our knowledge.
Women.
Come to us. Help us get back what was always ours. Help us   women.
Where
are you, women, where, and who, and where, and who, and will you help
us, will you open your bodysouls, will you lift me up mother, will you
let me help you, daughter, wife/lover, will you

b. Imamu Amiri Baraka (LeRoi Jones),
"The Practice of the New Nationalism,"
Kawaida Studies, The New Nationalism
(Chicago, 1972), pp. 33-38.

The struggle for Black political power in Newark is not limited to the
ideas white people have about public political participation. We are not
white people. This is not a simple dissociation; people are dying today
because they do not understand this. The Black cultural revolution was
created to teach this lesson more forcefully to negroes and colored
people—that we are not white people. So Adolph Saxe's invention of a
dour lamentation sounding "a-phone," and that projection of it did not
in the end say anything about what John Coltrane could produce.

Newark is a key because it is a test of the new nationalism. A test of
how "fluidized" pure nationalism can be and still prove effective at raising the race. We have no doubts that it will be effective.

All over the country nationalism in many forms is activating Black
people (& white people too, in various reactions) & propelling them con-
sciously and not into higher levels of life participation.

The most profound value system of the new nationalism is called
Kawaida, the doctrine of Maulana Karenga. It is this value system which
is the atom hot nucleus of positive political movement in Newark.

Negroes & elections are not new, they are depressingly familiar in any
random recollection. But Black people galvanized & given positive motion by a Black value system, a Black ideology of change, is a new &
vitally rejuvenating phenomenon.

We will not be manipulated by anything but the purest Black need.
Though the new nationalist must believe in and practice, to a sometimes
maddening degree of aggravation, operational unity, we cannot lose our
values and become negroized. Our task is to nationalize our brothers,
and operational unity is one way of getting close enough to them to do it.

But the new nationalist must be the hard nondiminishable core that
proves the limit to any collapse of Black national spirit and projection.
And this is the place for battle, the actualities of negro political potential
as envisioned by negroes. The nationalist must begin with the people (to

paraphrase Maulana Karenga's quote of Mao), and transform their desires into a fulfillment of their needs. Black politics Black nationalist politics must provide the moral guideline for negro politics, otherwise all that will result is negro egos aggrandized at the expense of the ultimate development of the Black nation.

We are not interested merely in who is the mayor of Newark, but the consciousness that can be given the people as a result of a heightened political involvement.

We can mobilize the people around elections—they are, in the 20th century world, almost "natural" occurrences. But the emphasis must be changed, the approach differently proposed, to excite our real consciousness.

What can be achieved in Black reality? Political power. Cultural revolution. The transfer of Economic Institutional and Coercive Power. (These last three, as Maulana points out, are sure clear goals of the would be revolutionary party).

The new nationalism must be the strong brew that flavors and defines the mixture of Black movement. There are many levels of involvement in and comprehension of what National Liberation entails. The people themselves are the material force that will bring it about. Ideas are relevant only in proportion to how much of this material force they can mobilize along a broad but nevertheless specific path toward national liberation. So that even if the *theories* of nationalism might say, as theories, alienate negroes, as working stratagems they much have exactly the opposite effect. There are people who could not possibly *say they are nationalists* who we get *to function as nationalists* every day. This is what operational unity *really* means.

In the mad swirl of craziness that passes as the day to day lifeclimate of America, the nationalist has as his focus of sanity a Black value system. It is this value system that he must throw into every game, with which he must color every discussion, out of which he must be coming all the time. If somebody say "election," we got a nationalist interpretation and *use* for that. If somebody say Alpha Kappa Alpha, we got a program, a *use,* for them too. Understanding the need for National Liberation should not make it necessary in and of itself to alienate Black people. The ultimate goal of the nationalist is the empowerment of Black *people.* Think about that. Unless they move, it is impossible. The nationalist must take what movement actually exists and give it identity, purpose and direction.

There is a use to the nation in the Urban League, NAACP, negro frats, welfare mothers, as well as the slick dudes athletic and social club. Think. They are organized bodies. The negro *is* organized. The ubiquitous churches, social clubs, associations, mark us as one of the most organized, in the sense of gathered together, people on the continent. True these organizations do not lead the vanguard for National Liberation, but that is the nationalist's responsibility. But it is also the nationalist's responsibility to see that the entire nation races along toward National Liberation, or, and this is crucial, *none of us will.*

Fragmented and alienated, we are losers, whether we are shot down in super radical headquarters or are mentally assassinated and content, in whatever superficial characterization (whether a 3 button suit or cowboy fringe jacket) to float around america eating . . . & loving it, for a dying.

Say that to say better a nationalist is trying to join with the NAACP or join *behind* the NAACP to bring real change, where possible, than discussing theoretical nationalism in coffee shops, or smoking bush with "revolutionary" devils.

Where necessary the nationalist must work *behind the scenes*, moving what has to be moved through the weight of the entire community. If you are in the AØA or the Lil Darlin ASC don't split, mobilize and nationalize. Make these groups more relevant to Black national priorities.

In the cities, political power is a national priority. The nationalist aims for an organized community. This is our only survival. *You cannot organize Black people* by shouting "Kill The Pig." I know. You can only get the pig to look at you very closely, and try to kill you. But more important you will alienate great amounts of the unconscious.

What is the community itself doing? We must be doing that, but also we must be practicing a value system which by its presence will transform negro activities into Black moves toward National Liberation.

Involve all levels of the community in nationalist programs. Involve nationalism in possibly accomodationist seeming programs. The *strongest content* will dominate. The "integration" of a school *administration* can be a nationalist program. Integrationists must dig it (except the ones who are just emotionally committed to white control, these are pathological "integrationists" who are not really even integrationists but simply in favor of white domination even of themselves). Most Black people are not social integrationists they just want the same goods and services the white nation has. We must not alienate this mass of Blacks who constitute the majority of us. So that a program for "integrating" administrations of this or that are good programs for nationalists to get behind, because in so doing they can hook up with great segments of the community, usually segments that include professionals as well as the unemployed.

The nationalist vision is as Maulana Karenga says "progressive perfection." The election in Newark of a Black and Puerto Rican slate ie a mayor and 7 of 9 possible councilmen is not to us an end in itself. It is the beginning of national construction. We must develop the theory and vision of nation building even with a city of 500,000 people.

Newark, New Ark, the nationalist sees as the creation of a base, as example, upon which one aspect of the entire Black nation can be built. We will build schools or transform present curriculum to teach National Liberation. We will create agencies to teach community organizing, national & local politics, and send brothers all over the country to recreate the model. We will nationalize the city's institutions as if it were liberated territory in Zimbabwe or Angola. There are nations of less than 300,000 people.

We will build a "city-state," or make alliances throughout the area to develop regional power in the scatter of Black cities of northern New Jersey.

Control of institutions (schools, hospitals, &c) and coercive (police) mental-spiritual development & defense, is control over two major aspects of life. Economic control will be gained by reversing tax priorities so that the capitalists will pay for the cities needs, and the suburban dwellers pay tax on their city salaries. All the transportation and communications industries must be highly taxed and/or "nationalized." The Port of Authority and Newark Air Port are vast money makers for suburbia, they will become even vaster money makers for the city. Change municipal priorities so that they will reflect the need to raise a people & rebuild a city in an image more modern than most of dying America. More than this is unwise to go into in public.

December 1969   January 1970
Year of Reconstruction   Year of Separation

8   A CALL FOR RECONCILIATION, 1967

In the immediate aftermath of disorder in Newark, the complex forces that produced an uprising of so many black residents were difficult to ascertain. In the following editorial, the *Newark Evening News* recognized two contributory issues: the controversy surrounding the Newark Board of Education's failure to appoint a highly qualified black man, Wilbur Parker, as its secretary; and the relocation of hundreds of black families in the central ward in order to make room for the College of Medicine and Dentistry of New Jersey. The official studies of the disorders by the federal government and the state also viewed these developments as having an adverse impact on the black community. But, unlike the local press and most political leaders, the careful analysis following the disorders led to the conclusion that deeply rooted racial inequality in Newark had fostered the troubles. Finding causes for the troubles, though, was a less difficult task than solving them. The *Newark Evening News,* in a tone of reconciliation, asked the city's black and white residents to work toward rebuilding their shattered relationships.

"Repairing the Damage,"
Newark Evening News, 18 July 1967.

On the assumption that the worst is over, Gov. Hughes has withdrawn most of the National Guard troops from Newark streets.

Only one serious incident, the shooting of a looter, has disturbed the peace. Tensions have diminished and the city has enjoyed its longest period of calm since the rioting broke out six days ago.

Sooner or later the violence had to end, as it has ended in other American cities that have endured similar racial convulsions. Next will come the task in Newark as it has elsewhere of rebuilding, a task that goes far beyond the physical restoration of burned and looted shops.

At the heart of the city's immediate problem is the reconstruction of shattered relationships between the Negro and white communities. This will call for modernization of riot hardened attitudes, which, in turn, will require time, patience and good will. It is a mission that will not be expedited by the lectures, aired and printed, of outside experts none of whom may claim home to be a model city.

Throughout its ordeal Newark has been continually reminded in a superior sort of way of its manifold faults and omissions, and there is no disposition to protest that mistakes have not been made. And while Newark knows substandard housing, obsolete schools and unemployment are not exclusive with Newark, it also is not blind to the fact that its Negro relationships have been too often mired in politics. In this particular the denied appointment of Wilbur Parker as secretary to the board of education is too recent an example of political injustice to be ignored.

The new state medical college is also an advertised cause of Negro resentment. Perhaps the city has not made adequate provision as claimed for the relocation of displaced families, although the fault may reside more with the Housing Authority's failure to make its plans and intentions incontrovertibly clear. But if it is a crime to raze slums, Newark in this instance must plead guilty. How a city is to abolish slums except by abolishing them is otherwise not apparent.

Yet these and other issues are certainly more susceptible of resolution around a conference table than in bullet-pocked streets. And Newark's future will be more suitably and gainfully served by reasonable negotiation than by recrimination about the vandalism and looting which are all too visible to any who travel the city's stricken areas.

Finally, while charges of "police brutality" fill the air, Newark might remember that it was these same police, along with the national guardsmen, who risked their lives for the public's protection.

9   PLAINFIELD—JULY 1967

The racial disorders that gripped Plainfield in July 1967 were nearly as shocking to New Jersey residents as was the violence in Newark. Although few persons in responsible positions realized it, Plainfield, like other New Jersey cities in the post-war years, had undergone profound social changes, resulting in virtually distinct black and white communities. As more blacks settled in the city, the indifference of city officials toward their problems added to frustration over such local issues as the lack of decent housing and recreation for blacks on Plainfield's West Side. Poor blacks became increasingly distrustful of city government and police. In addition, the West Side was apparently without a respected leadership capable of articulating its concerns to city officials. Months before the outbreak of rage in the black community, as the following report of the National Advisory Commission on Civil Disorders shows, Plainfield reached an uncomfortable impasse. When violence erupted, efforts by the police to quell the disorders were counterproductive. The National Guard's search for arms in the black community proved unsuccessful and, in light of its dubious legality, outraged blacks across the state. These problems, to be sure, were not unique to Plainfield, for they existed in varying degrees elsewhere in urban New Jersey. What really distinguished the troubles in Plainfield was the city's essentially middle-class character, which obscured its social ills and racial inequities.

U.S. National Advisory Commission on Civil Disorders, "Plainfield," *Report* **(Washington, D.C., 1968), pp. 41-45.**

New Jersey's worst violence outside of Newark was experienced by Plainfield, a pleasant, tree-shaded city of 45,000. A "bedroom community," more than a third of whose residents work outside the city, Plainfield had had relatively few Negroes until 1950. By 1967, the Negro population had risen to an estimated 30 percent of the total. As in Englewood, there was a division between the Negro middle class, which lived in the East side "gilded ghetto," and the unskilled, unemployed and underemployed poor on the West side.

Geared to the needs of a suburban middle class, the part-time and fragmented city government had failed to realize the change in character which the city had undergone, and was unprepared to cope with the problems of a growing disadvantaged population. There was no full-time administrator or city manager. Boards, with independent jurisdiction over such areas as education, welfare and health, were appointed by the part-time mayor, whose own position was largely honorary.

Accustomed to viewing politics as a gentleman's pastime, city officials were startled and upset by the intensity with which demands issued from the ghetto. Usually such demands were met obliquely, rather than head-on.

In the summer of 1966, trouble was narrowly averted over the issue of a swimming pool for Negro youngsters. In the summer of 1967, instead of having built the pool, the city began busing the children to the county pool a half-hour's ride distant. The fare was 25 cents per person, and the children had to provide their own lunch, a considerable strain on a frequent basis for a poor family with several children.

The bus operated only on 3 days in midweek. On weekends the county pool was too crowded to accommodate children from the Plainfield ghetto.

Pressure increased upon the school system to adapt itself to the changing social and ethnic backgrounds of its pupils. There were strikes and boycotts. The track system created *de facto* segregation within a supposedly integrated school system. Most of the youngsters from the white middle-class districts were in the higher track, most from the Negro poverty areas in the lower. Relations were strained between some white teachers and Negro pupils. Two-thirds of school dropouts were estimated to be Negro.

In February 1967 the NAACP, out of a growing sense of frustration with the municipal government, tacked a list of 19 demands and complaints to the door of the city hall. Most dealt with discrimination in housing, employment and in the public schools. By summer, the city's common council had not responded. Although two of the 11 council members were Negro, both represented the East side ghetto. The poverty area was represented by two white women, one of whom had been appointed by the council after the elected representative, a Negro, had moved away.

Relations between the police and the Negro community, tenuous at best, had been further troubled the week prior to the Newark outbreak. After being handcuffed during a routine arrest in a housing project, a women had fallen down a flight of stairs. The officer said she had slipped. Negro residents claimed he had pushed her.

When a delegation went to city hall to file a complaint, they were told by the city clerk that he was not empowered to accept it. Believing that they were being given the run-around, the delegation, angry and frustrated, departed.

On Friday evening, July 14, the same police officer was moonlighting as a private guard at a diner frequented by Negro youths. He was, reportedly, number two on the Negro community's "10 most-wanted" list of unpopular police officers.

(The list was colorblind. Although out of 82 officers on the force only five were Negro, two of the 10 on the "most-wanted" list were Negro. The two officers most respected in the Negro community were white.)

Although most of the youths at the diner were of high school age, one, in his mid-twenties, had a reputation as a bully. Sometime before 10 p.m., as a result of an argument, he hit a 16-year-old boy and split open his face. As the boy lay bleeding on the asphalt, his friends rushed to the police officer and demanded that he call an ambulance and arrest the offender. Instead, the officer walked over to the boy, looked at him, and reportedly said: "Why don't you just go home and wash up?" He refused to make an arrest.

The youngsters were incensed. They believed that, had the two participants in the incident been white, the older youth would have been arrested, the younger taken to the hospital immediately.

On the way to the housing project where most of them lived, the youths traversed four blocks of the city's business district. As they walked, they smashed three or four windows. An observer interpreted their behavior as a reaction to the incident at the diner, in effect challenging the police officer: "If you won't do anything about that, then let's see you do something about this!"

On one of the quiet city streets, two young Negroes, D.H. and L.C., had been neighbors. D.H. had graduated from high school, attended Fairleigh Dickinson University and, after receiving a degree in psychology, had obtained a job as a reporter on the Plainfield *Courier-News.*

L.C. had dropped out of high school, become a worker in a chemical plant, and, although still in his twenties had married and fathered seven children. A man with a strong sense of family, he liked sports and played in the local baseball league. Active in civil rights, he had, like the civil rights organizations, over the years, become more militant. For a period of time he had been a Muslim.

The outbreak of vandalism aroused concern among the police. Shortly after midnight, in an attempt to decrease tensions, D.H. and the two Negro councilmen met with the youths in the housing project. The focal point of the youths' bitterness was the attitude of the police—until 1966 police had used the word "nigger" over the police radio and one officer had worn a Confederate belt buckle and had flown a Confederate pennant on his car. Their complaints, however, ranged over local and national issues. There was an overriding cynicism and disbelief that government would, of its own accord, make meaningful changes to improve the lot of the lower-class Negro. There was an overriding belief that there were two sets of policies by the people in power, whether law enforcement officers, newspaper editors, or government officials: one for white, and one for black.

There was little confidence that the two councilmen could exercise any influence. One youth said: "You came down here last year. We were throwing stones at some passing cars, and your said to us that this was not the way to do it. You got us to talk with the man. We talked to him. We talked with him, and we talked all year long. We ain't got nothing yet!''

However, on the promise that meetings would be arranged with the editor of the newspaper and with the mayor later that same day, the youths agreed to disperse.

At the first of these meetings, the youths were, apparently, satisfied by the explanation that the newspaper's coverage was not deliberately discriminatory. The meeting with the mayor, however, proceeded badly. Negroes present felt that the mayor was complacent and apathetic, and that they were simply being given the usual lip service, from which nothing would develop.

The mayor, on the other hand, told Commission investigators that he recognized that "citizens are frustrated by the political organization of the city,'' because he, himself, has no real power and "each of the councilmen says that he is just one of the 11 and therefore can't do anything.''

After approximately 2 hours, a dozen of the youths walked out, indicating an impasse and signaling the breakup of the meeting. Shortly thereafter, window smashing began. A Molotov cocktail was set afire in a tree. One fire engine, in which a white and Negro fireman were sitting side by side, had a Molotov cocktail thrown at it. The white fireman was burned.

As window smashing continued, liquor stores and taverns were especially hard hit. Some of the youths believed that there was an excess concentration of bars in the Negro section, and that these were an unhealthy influence in the community.

Because the police department had mobilized its full force, the situation, although serious, never appeared to get out of hand. Officers made many arrests. The chief of the fire department told Commission investigators that it was his conclusion that "individuals making fire bombs did not know what they were doing, or they could have burned the city.''

At 3 o'clock Sunday morning, a heavy rain began, scattering whatever groups remained on the streets.

In the morning, police made no effort to cordon off the area. As white sightseers and churchgoers drove by the housing project there was sporadic rock throwing. During the early afternoon, such incidents increased.

At the housing project, a meeting was convened by L.C. to draw up a formal petition of grievances. As the youths gathered it became apparent that some of them had been drinking. A few kept drifting away from the parking lot where the meeting was being held to throw rocks at passing cars. It was decided to move the meeting to a county park several blocks away.

Between 150 and 200 persons, including almost all of the rock throwers, piled into a caravan of cars and headed for the park. At approximately 3:30 p.m., the chief of the Union County park police arrived to find the group being addressed by David Sullivan, executive director of the human relations commission. He "informed Mr. Sullivan he was in violation of our park ordinance and to disperse the group."

Sullivan and L.C. attempted to explain that they were in the process of drawing up a list of grievances, but the chief remained adamant. They could not meet in the park without a permit, and they did not have a permit.

After permitting the group 10 to 15 minutes grace, the chief decided to disperse them. "Their mood was very excitable," he reported, and "in my estimation no one could appease them so we moved them out without to much trouble. They left in a caravan of about 40 cars, horns blowing and yelling and headed south on West End Avenue to Plainfield."

Within the hour, looting became widespread. Cars were overturned, a white man was snatched off a motorcycle, and the fire department stopped responding to alarms because the police were unable to provide protection. After having been on alert until midday, the Plainfield Police Department was caught unprepared. At 6 p.m., only 18 men were on the streets. Checkpoints were established at crucial intersections in an effort to isolate the area.

Officer John Gleason, together with two reserve officers, had been posted at one of the intersections, three blocks from the housing project. Gleason was a veteran officer, the son of a former lieutenant on the police department. Shortly after 8 p.m., two white youths, chased by a 22-year-old Negro, Bobby Williams, came running from the direction of the ghetto toward Gleason's post.

As he came in sight of the police officers, Williams stopped. Accounts vary of what happened next, or why Officer Gleason took the action he did. What is known is that when D.H., the newspaper reporter, caught sight of him a minute or two later, Officer Gleason was two blocks from his post. Striding after Williams directly into the ghetto area, Gleason already had passed one housing project. Small groups were milling about. In D.H.'s words: "There was a kind of shock and amazement," to see the officer walking by himself so deep in the ghetto.

Suddenly, there was a confrontation between Williams and Gleason. Some witnesses report Williams had a hammer in his hand. Others say he did not. When D.H., whose attention momentarily had been distracted, next saw Gleason he had drawn his gun and was firing at Williams. As Williams, critically injured, fell to the ground, Gleason turned and ran back toward his post.

Negro youths chased him. Gleason stumbled, regained his balance, then had his feet knocked out from under him. A score of youths began to beat him and kick him. Some residents of the apartment house attempted to intervene, but they were brushed aside. D.H. believes that, under the circumstances and in the atmosphere that prevailed at that moment, any police officer, black or white, would have been killed.

After they had beaten Gleason to death, the youths took D.H.'s camera from him and smashed it.

Fear swept over the ghetto. Many residents—both lawless and law-abiding—were convinced, on the basis of what had occurred in Newark, that law enforcement officers, bent on vengeance, would come into the ghetto shooting.

People began actively to prepare to defend themselves. There was no lack of weapons. Forty-six carbines were stolen from a nearby arms manufacturing plant and passed out in the street by a young Negro, a former newspaper boy. Most of the weapons fell into the hands of youths, who began firing them wildly. A fire station was peppered with shots.

Law enforcement officers continued their cordon about the area, but made no attempt to enter it except, occasionally, to rescue someone. National Guardsmen arrived shortly after midnight. Their armored personnel carriers were used to carry troops to the fire station, which had been besieged for 5 hours. During this period only one fire had been reported in the city.

Reports of sniper firing, wild shooting, and general chaos continued until the early morning hours.

By daylight Monday, New Jersey state officials had begun to arrive. At a meeting in the early afternoon, it was agreed that to inject police into the ghetto would be to risk bloodshed; that, instead, law enforcement personnel should continue to retain their cordon.

All during the day various meetings took place between government officials and Negro representatives. Police were anxious to recover the carbines that had been stolen from the arms plant. Negroes wanted assurances against retaliation. In the afternoon, L.C., an official of the human relations commission, and others drove through the area urging people to be calm and to refrain from violence.

At 8 p.m., the New Jersey attorney general, commissioner of community affairs, and commander of the state police, accompanied by the mayor, went to the housing project and spoke to several hundred Negroes. Some members of the crowd were hostile. Others were anxious to establish a dialog. There were demands that officials give concrete evidence that they were prepared to deal with Negro grievances. Again, the meeting was inconclusive. The officials returned to City Hall.

At 9:15 p.m., L.C. rushed in claiming that—as a result of the failure to resolve any of the outstanding problems, and reports that people who had been arrested by police were being beaten—violence was about to explode anew. The key demand of the militant faction was that those who had been arrested during the riot should be released. State officials decided to arrange for the release on bail of 12 arrestees charged with minor violations. L.C., in turn, agreed to try to induce return of the stolen carbines by Wednesday noon.

As state officials were scanning the list of arrestees to determine which of them should be released, a message was brought to Colonel Kelly of the state police that general firing had broken out around the perimeter.

The report testified to the tension: an investigation disclosed that one shot of unexplained origin had been heard. In response, security forces had shot out street lights, thus initiating the "general firing."

At 4 o'clock Tuesday morning, a dozen prisoners were released from jail. Plainfield police officers considered this a "sellout."

When, by noon on Wednesday, the stolen carbines had not been returned, the governor decided to authorize a mass search. At 2 p.m., a convoy of state police and National Guard troops prepared to enter the area. In order to direct the search as to likely locations, a handful of Plainfield police officers were spotted throughout the 28 vehicles of the convoy.

As the convoy prepared to depart, the state community affairs commissioner, believing himself to be carrying out the decision of the governor not to permit Plainfield officers to participate in the search, ordered their removal from the vehicles. The basis for his order was that their participation might ignite a clash between them and the Negro citizens.

As the search for carbines in the community progressed, tension increased rapidly. According to witnesses and newpaper reports, some men in the search force left apartments in shambles.

The search was called off an hour and a half after it was begun. No stolen weapons were discovered. For the Plainfield police, the removal of the officers from the convoy had been a humiliating experience. A half hour after the conclusion of the search, in a meeting charged with emotion, the entire department threatened to resign unless the state community affairs commissioner left the city. He acceded to the demand.

On Friday, 7 days after the first outbreak, the city began returning to normal.

10   A BLACK POWER RESOLUTION, 1968

Nearly a year after the disorders of the summer of 1967, a conference on the causes and remedies of racial violence in New Jersey and other states was held at Rutgers University in New Brunswick. A number of distinguished scholars and black community activists discussed the origins of black discontent, the problem of racism and poverty in New Jersey society, and the impact of public policy on the state's troubled democracy. A group of approximately twenty-five black participants formed an ad hoc caucus to present the following resolutions to the conference. In a sense this document represented a continuation of earlier expressions of black protest in New Jersey. Like black spokesmen and women during the World War II years, the black caucus protested racial injustice in the state and called for an immediate improvement in the status of blacks there. But considerably more urgent concerns were also expressed. The resolutions reflected the contemporary emphasis on black power in the economy, politics, and education. Significantly, they were adopted by a majority of the conference participants, most of whom were white. In the context of the period, the resolutions and their acceptance at that public forum reveal the militancy spawned by the riots and the influence which black agitation had upon the white population.

Rutgers, The State University, Bureau of Government Research and the University Extension Division, *Proceedings of the Public Policy Forum on Civil Disorders: Causes and Remedies* **(New Brunswick, N.J., 1968), pp. 80-81.**

WHEREAS in the State of New Jersey, racism has produced a system which makes people of color the major "clients or problems" of our state and

WHEREAS white racism is the single most pervasive attitude in New Jersey society and

WHEREAS it is incumbent upon the Governor and other elected and appointed officials to exercise leadership to improve race relations for the good and health of the entire state,

THEREFORE, BE IT RESOLVED:

1. That the governor should forthwith appoint black persons to his cabinet and fully integrate the state official policy-making apparatus.

2. That the Division of Civil Rights be elevated to a department of the State of New Jersey and a black person be appointed as Commissioner and it be given all powers and authority to aggressively seek and eliminate all racial bias in the State of New Jersey.

3. That the State of New Jersey immediately assume administrative control of the Newark school system and fully involve the community of Newark in policy formulation.

4. That the State of New Jersey immediately investigate the fatal shooting of the young black student, Harlen Joseph, of Trenton, New Jersey during the recent disturbances.

5. That the governor and the state legislature increase the number of trustees on the Board of the New Jersey College of Medicine and Dentistry to provide the immediate appointment of two black persons from the City of Newark.

6. That the Department of Higher Education and the State of New Jersey and all other relevant departments in the State of New Jersey influence and compel New Jersey State colleges to appoint black admis-

sions officers to insure the maximum possible enrollment of black students in New Jersey colleges. Where necessary, scholastic aptitude tests and other presently used criteria should be adjusted or ignored. Immediate steps should be taken to increase the enrollment of black students at Newark-Rutgers, where they are only 60 out of 2,900.

7. That the State of New Jersey Department of Civil Services revise its qualifications for administrative posts in the State, county and municipal governments to allow the appointment of black persons to administrative posts.

8. That the State of New Jersey immediately institute a massive program of economic development in ghetto areas providing money and technical assistance to black corporations.

9. That the State Department of Education appoint black people to administrative positions.

10. That the welfare system be reorganized and a majority of the welfare directors be black people.

11. That these resolutions adopted be forwarded immediately to Governor Hughes, to cabinet members, to leaders of the New Jersey legislature and the President of Rutgers University.

11 PRISON POETRY, 1973

In spring 1972 the New Jersey State Council on the Arts sponsored a creative writing program at the Bordentown Correctional Facility. The program and the poetry which it produced was rather extraordinary; no state agency had ever attempted such a rewarding project on behalf of the creative expressions of blacks in prison. The Bordentown Correctional Facility is a moderate security penal institution whose inmate population is overwhelmingly black, young, and male. The fact that the following poems were created by black prisoners and that they reveal exceptional literary talent is of singular importance. Life in the black ghetto and imprisonment generally discourages literary expression.

The first poem by James Black, "The Sisters is Mean, Man," is a tribute to black women. In the context of black colloquial expression, the word "mean" may be used to express a diversity of attitudes. In this poem, however, it refers to the strength, support, insight, and patience of black women ("the sisters") toward black men. James E. Beatty's poems, of which two are included here, employ surrealism to depict the black urban experience. His first poem, which is untitled, portrays the ghetto in a disturbing light and as a place that offers little peace to the poet. Beatty's second poem, "Color Me Jail Bait," in keeping with the contemporary emphasis on black power, expresses defiance and black identity.

New Jersey State Council on the Arts,
Creative Writing Program,
Prison Poetry **(Trenton, N.J., 1973), pp. 36-38, 71-72.**

THE SISTERS IS MEAN, MAN
—James Black

The sisters is mean, man.
I mean like
they're into something
and we ain't ready.
I mean like
they eyes.
You ever look into a sister's eyes, man?
They know what's happening, man.
Ya know?
It's like they're laying for something.
Waiting.
All kinds of things going on in their minds.
Like when we're wrong
and shamming
and jivving
and into things we know we ain't supposed to be into.
But they don't say nothing, man.
They're putting the weight on us.
Laying for us—to get right.
Like it's us who ain't together
and they're waiting on us
—to—dig—it.
Like my woman, man.
She is in my corner
and I know I been wrong
a whole lot of times.
But she just run it down
and then lay.
And like
it ain't nothing I can say,
I just look at her, man.
Her eyes . . .
Wow, man!

Ya know?
She loves me, man.
I mean like . . .
Ya know?
The sisters is mean, man.

UNTITLED
—James E. Beatty

Faceless
nomads have gathered
to water
              withering lives
while houris seem mirages disappearing
              behind the resting
                        camels of the city,
as blue eunuchs
              spur their steel steeds
                    one fiery red eye forward
alms! alms!
       the dark putrid smell
              of the doorway is speaking
"tizen-izand-thrizee."
Pardon?
              where might a poet rest
                    only
                              his thoughts
       in this midtowncaravanserai?
O' lovely one . . .

COLOR ME JAIL BAIT
—James E. Beatty

color me jail bait
    cause i got swallowed.
then color me prisoner
    using black hued days.
but remember to keep coloring me man
    & don't spare the black.

Epilogue

THE high expectations of the post-war generation gave way among New Jersey blacks in the 1970s to a widespread pessimism. Federal and state support of civil rights declined as the nation grew more conservative. Political leaders sought to diminish government intervention on many fronts, including civil rights. The civil rights movement's coalition of blacks, white ethnic groups, labor, and religious organizations also weakened during the 1970s in the face of the complex tensions in the areas of employment, housing, foreign policy, and political ideology. Many whites believed that the blacks had made extraordinary progress over recent years, and this made them increasingly impatient with continued black discontent. This attitude of many whites complicated the work of Afro-American organizations which, especially after the assassinations of Malcolm X and Martin Luther King, Jr., were unable to keep the problems of blacks squarely in public view.

Although the civil rights movement no longer captured the nation's conscience, blacks continued their call for racial justice and equality. Much of the urgency of the 1970s resulted from the activities of younger blacks—high school and college students to whom long-standing racial problems appeared as evils ready to be destroyed. On campuses throughout the state, young blacks, sometimes joined by white students, called for reforms designed to make educational institutions more responsive to minority group needs and aspirations. Changes were called for in admissions policies, curricula, administration, and other areas of academic life. Drawing their inspiration from the black power and youth movements of the 1960s and early 1970s, these young advocates broadened the struggle for equality to educational institutions from which blacks had historically been excluded.

The 1970s was a time of sharpened protests from the more established black organizations in New Jersey. A profusion of professional organizations augmented the civil rights advocacy of established groups such as the NAACP, the National Urban League, the State Federation of Colored Women's Clubs, and religious groups. Although the emphasis on black power has customarily been associated with the young and intemperate, black professional groups, such as the New Jersey Association of Black Educators and the New Jersey Association of Black Social Workers, were in the 1970s and are today deeply influenced by the racial consciousness of the 1960s. To these groups, token desegregation of white institutions and egalitarian rhetoric are unsatisfactory solutions to deeply rooted racial inequalities in New Jersey.

Civil rights organizations during the 1970s also mounted legal challenges to various forms of discrimination in housing. Most attention was focused on the Mount Laurel decision, in which the New Jersey Supreme Court ruled that municipal zoning ordinances could not be used by localities to obviate housing for low-income and middle-income families. The 1975 decision, which was subsequently allowed to stand by the U.S. Supreme Court, forced several New Jersey towns to revise their zoning ordinances. Sanguine forecasts, however, that the decision would provide desperately needed housing opportunities to the urban poor have not been borne out. As the 1970s closed few of New Jersey's 567 municipalities had new, low-income housing. For many black families today, as in the past, housing opportunities are very dim and, because of an increasingly troubled housing market, growing worse.

The ability of blacks to use the political system to further their interests was enhanced during the 1970s by their greater political visibility in state government. Made possible by the emergence of large black voting blocks in Essex, Hudson, and Mercer counties, the growth of black political leadership in the state legislature has been perhaps one of the most significant developments for New Jersey's Afro-Americans since World War II. Despite their small numbers, black political leaders have brought to public attention both the aspirations and frustrations of their constituents.

In 1970, Kenneth A. Gibson became the first black mayor of Newark, the state's largest city. Three years later, S. Howard Woodson of Trenton became the first black speaker of the New

Jersey Assembly. By 1980 the black caucus in Trenton comprised four assemblymen—Willie B. Brown, Mildred B. Garvin, Charles Mays, and Eugene Thompson—from Essex and Hudson counties and one state senator, Wynona M. Lipman, from Essex County. These legislators recently presented an overview of problems faced by blacks in the state. Examining an array of public concerns, they found that blacks were still victimized by past inequality. In an unpublished report they observed:

> As has historically been the case, Blacks in New Jersey during the 1970's, have patiently awaited progressive governmental action, that would assist us in entering the state's mainstream. We have made great strides in the development of a positive self perception as a result of the activism our young people inspired in us in the 1960's. The issues we faced in the decade of the sixties, however, were dramatically different from those of the past ten years. In fact, some gains achieved by our community during the turbulent period of civil rights achievement were cruelly taken away.[1]

A nineteenth-century observer of the contemporary scene would undoubtedly be amazed at the improved status of Afro-Americans in New Jersey society. Past abuses waned in the face of civil rights legislation enacted during the 1960s and 1970s. Yet, racial inequality is still very much a part of New Jersey today. Blacks remain economically disadvantaged, with chronic unemployment, especially among the young. Poverty, which had been a constant barrier to black aspirations, is evident on a relatively large scale in black communities. In 1970 the U.S. Census found that 22.6 percent of New Jersey blacks were below the national poverty level, compared with 6.4 percent of whites. This grim statistic is mirrored in the state's larger municipalities—Newark, Trenton, Camden, Atlantic City, Passaic, Paterson, Elizabeth, and Jersey City—to which blacks have migrated in search of employment and other opportunities. As in the last century, many black families are struggling to escape the cycle of economic deprivation, public neglect, and the despair of an underclass existence.

Admittedly, conditions have improved for blacks. From the vantage point of a nineteenth-century observer, there are now many social service agencies, health facilities, and charitable groups providing critically needed services where once blacks were either viewed with indifference or hostility. Yet, that observer would also be struck by the seemingly vast social problems within the black community and the gross inequalities far from solution.

The historic Afro-American protest against injustice as well as a frustrated idealism spawning discontent remain features of our times. They have, on some fronts, taken on a more impatient and disquieting character. It may be true that, after generations of faith that fundamental progress was within the reach of black New Jersey, that freedom was not far distant, recent years have fostered severe disillusionment and anger. It is certainly true that blacks view solutions to their inequality as very complex, requiring fundamental reforms of the nation's political economy. Between the early nineteenth and early twentieth centuries, black leaders stressed commonly held democratic ideals. New Jersey was in their view a highly principled society, except for its miserable treatment of blacks. But as discrimination mounted against large numbers of blacks, a broader attack against the treatment of Afro-Americans was articulated. The democratic idealism, which is at the heart of the American story, is still challenged by the racial antipathies, the injustices, and the failures of our times.

Notes

CHAPTER I: BIRTH OF A SLAVE SOCIETY

1. See Dorothy Cross, "The Indians of New Jersey," *Proceedings of the New Jersey Historical Society* 70 (1952): 1-16; and Frank J. Esposito, "Indian-White Relations in New Jersey, 1609–1802" (Ph.D. dissertation, Rutgers University, 1976).

2. J.P. Snell, *History of Sussex and Warren Counties, N.J.* (Philadelphia, 1881), p. 76. For early studies of slavery in New Jersey see Henry S. Coolcy, *A Study of Slavery in New Jersey*, Johns Hopkins University Studies, ser. 14, 9-10 (Baltimore, 1896); Alfred M. Heston, *Story of the Slave, Paper Read before the Monmouth County Historical Association on October 30, 1902 . . .* (Camden, N.J., 1903); and William Alexander Linn, "Slavery in Bergen County," *Papers and Proceedings of the Bergen County Historical Society*, 4 (1907–1908): 23-40.

3. George H. Budke, "The History of the Tappan Patent," *The Rockland Record* 2 (1931–32): 40. A more recent and complete study is David S. Cohen, *The Ramapo Mountain People* (New Brunswick, N.J., 1974).

4. A useful study of the religious and socio-economic differences between East and West Jersey is Wesley Frank Craven, *New Jersey and the English Colonization of North America*, New Jersey Historical Series 3 (Princeton, N.J., 1964). Another introduction to the history of colonial New Jersey is Richard P. McCormick, *New Jersey from Colony to State, 1609–1789*, New Jersey Historical Series 1 (Princeton, N.J., 1964). A scholarly examination of New Jersey as a royal colony is Donald L. Kemmerer, *Path to Freedom: The Struggle for Self-Government in Colonial New Jersey, 1703–1776* (Princeton, N.J., 1940).

5. Frances D. Pingeon, *Blacks in the Revolutionary Era*, New Jersey's Revolutionary Experience 14 (Trenton, N.J., 1975): 5-6. Another excellent study of the growth of slavery in New Jersey is Simeon F. Moss, "The Persistence of Slavery and Involuntary Servitude in a Free State, 1695–1866," *Journal of Negro History* 35 (1950): 289-314.

6. Pingeon, pp. 6-7.

7. An informative article on Quaker views of slavery and treatment of blacks is Henry J. Cadbury, "Negro Membership in the Society of Friends," *Journal of Negro History* 21 (1936): 151-213; see also Marion Thompson Wright, "The

Quakers as Social Workers among Negroes in New Jersey from 1763 to 1804,"
Bulletin of Friends Historical Association 30 (1941): 79-88. An invaluable contribution to the study of early resistance to slavery by Quakers in the North is Arthur Zilversmit, *The First Emancipation: The Abolition of Slavery in the North* (Chicago, 1967), pp. 24-32; and a more recent treatment of northern slavery, Edgar J. McManus, *Black Bondage in the North* (Syracuse, N.Y., 1973).

8. Hunterdon County was an exception in West Jersey. As the result of the settlement of slaveholders from East Jersey and Pennsylvania, approximately seven percent of its population was black by 1790. Peter O. Wacker, *The Cultural Geography of Eighteenth Century New Jersey*, New Jersey's Revolutionary Experience 4 (Trenton, N.J., 1975): 15, 19.

9. Zilversmit, pp. 12-24, gives an informative discussion of New Jersey's black codes.

10. The sentence was handed down by John Johnstone, presiding justice of the Monmouth Court of Sessions. Andrew D. Mellick, *The Story of an Old Farm; Or Life in New Jersey in the Eighteenth Century* (Somerville, N.J., 1889), p. 225.

11. Winthrop D. Jordan, *White Over Black: American Attitudes toward the Negro, 1550–1812* (Chapel Hill, N.C., 1968), pp. 272-76. The most useful collection of Woolman's works may be found in Phillips P. Moulton, ed., *The Journal and Major Essays of John Woolman* (New York, 1971).

CHAPTER II: AFRICANS IN A STRANGE LAND

1. Samuel B. How, *Slaveholding Not Sinful. Slavery, the Punishment of Man's Sin, Its Remedy, the Gospel of Christ, An Argument Before the General Synod of the Reformed Protestant Dutch Church, October, 1855* (New Brunswick, N.J., 1856), p. 80.

2. Kenneth M. Stampp, *The Peculiar Institution: Slavery in the Ante-Bellum South* (New York, 1956), p. 13.

3. John W. Blassingame, *The Slave Community: Plantation Life in the Ante-Bellum South* (New York, 1972), p. 13. For a more complete and critical discussion of African religion, see John S. Mbiti, *African Religion and Philosophy* (Garden City, N.Y., 1970). For an informative overview see John S. Mbiti, *Introduction to African Religion* (New York, 1975), pp. 2-18.

4. Blassingame, p. 17.

5. Arthur Zilversmit has observed that New York and New Jersey were exceptional in their treatment of blacks. "The harsh slave codes of the middle colonies, devised at the beginning of the eighteenth century, were designed to control an alien population, regarded as heathen in origin and barbarous by nature." Zilversmit, p. 23.

6. Pingeon, pp. 6, 11.

7. "Traditions of Our Ancestors," *Hunterdon Republican,* 27 January 1870; Leonard P. Stavisky, "Negro Craftsmanship in Early America," *American Historical Review* 54 (1949): 322; and by the same author, "The Origins of Negro Craftsmanship in Colonial America," *Journal of Negro History* 32 (1947): 417-29.

8. Eileen Southern, *The Music of Black Americans: A History* (New York, 1971), p. 53.

9. LeRoi Jones (Amiri Baraka), *Blues People: The Negro Experience in White America and the Music that Developed from It* (New York, 1963), pp. 27-28.

10. Moss, p. 311.

11. John Bodine Thompson, "Readington Negroes," *Historical Discourse and Addresses Delivered at the 175th Anniversary of the Reformed Church,* 17 October 1894 (Somerville, N.J., 1894), p. 55.

12. Hubert G. Schmidt, "Slavery and Attitudes on Slavery, Hunterdon County, New Jersey," *Proceedings of the New Jersey Historical Society* 58 (1940): 159-60.

13. Zilversmit, p. 11; *New Jersey Archives,* ser. 3, 2:28. During the Civil War, in 1864, the legislature enacted a measure "to prevent the admixture of races in the state of New Jersey."

14. Anna Bustill Smith, "The Bustill Family," *Journal of Negro History* 10 (1925): 638-40; Cadbury, pp. 162-63; Schmidt, pp. 161-63; Zilversmit, p. 28.

15. Zilversmit, pp. 9-11.

16. *Boston Weekly Post-Boy,* 11 May 1741, cited in *New Jersey Archives,* ser. 1, 12: 92.

CHAPTER III: BONDAGE AND THE REVOLUTION

1. Cooley, p. 23.

2. Frances D. Pingeon argues in *Blacks in the Revolutionary Era* that resistance to manumission was caused in part by the state's pivotal role in the war. "In the impending conflict with England," she notes, "New Jersey would be placed in an exposed and defenseless position, with a population sorely divided." Pingeon, p. 17. For a discussion of the legal status of blacks in New Jersey during the Revolution see Marion Thompson Wright, "New Jersey Laws and the Negro," *Journal of Negro History* 28 (1943): 169-72; Moss, pp. 298-302.

3. Zilversmit, p. 141.

4. *Ibid.*

5. For a discussion of the military role of blacks in colonial New Jersey see Robert J. Gough, "Black Men and the Early New Jersey Militia," *New Jersey History* 88 (1970): 227-38.

6. John Hope Franklin, *From Slavery to Freedom, A History of Negro Americans*, 4th ed. (New York, 1974), p. 93; "An Important Revolutionary Record of a Negro Soldier," *Journal of Negro History* 17 (1932): 379-81. The seminal treatment of the role of blacks during the Revolution is Benjamin Quarles, *The Negro in the American Revolution* (Chapel Hill, N.C., 1961); see also Lorenzo J. Greene, "The Negro in the Armed Forces of the United States to 1865," *Negro History Bulletin* 14 (1951): 125. For a discussion of the New Jersey context see Atalanta Brown Liscomb, "Status of the Negro in New Jersey during the Period 1763-1804" (M.A. thesis, Columbia University, 1942).

7. Edwin Salter, *A History of Monmouth and Ocean Counties . . .* (Bayonne, N.J., 1890), pp. 429-30. Contemporary sources show that blacks assisted

Loyalist forces in raids on the East Jersey coast, Elizabeth, Newark, and New Brunswick.

8. It was not "to be wished, much less expected," announced the Society's president in 1804, "that sudden and general emancipation would take place." Cooley, p. 24.

9. D. H. Gardner, "The Emancipation of Slaves in New Jersey," *Proceedings of the New Jersey Historical Society* 9 (1924): 15-16; Zilversmit, pp. 193-94.

CHAPTER IV: TWILIGHT OF SLAVERY

1. Larry A. Greene, "The Emancipation Proclamation in New Jersey and the Paranoid Style," *New Jersey History* 91 (1973): 119; Peter O. Wacker, "The Changing Geography of the Black Population of New Jersey, 1810–1860: A Preliminary View," *Proceedings of the Association of American Geographers* 3 (1971): 174; Moss, "Slavery and Involuntary Servitude," p. 303.

2. Sabbath School for Coloured People in the Newark Academy. Female Department, Reports (MG 1003), Manuscript Collections, The New Jersey Historical Society.

3. For an extensive examination of the colonization movement see P. J. Staudenraus, *The African Colonization Movement, 1816–1865* (New York, 1961). An early, sympathetic view of Robert Finley may be found in Isaac Van Arsdale Brown, *Biography of the Reverend Robert Finley, D.D., of Basking Ridge, N.J.* (Philadelphia, 1857); also for the role of blacks in the movement see Sheldon H. Harris, *Paul Cuffe: Black America and the African Return* (New York, 1972). An examination of the colonization movement in New Jersey is made by Wright, "New Jersey Laws and the Negro," pp. 179-184.

4. *Historical Notes on Slavery and Colonization: With Particular Reference to the Efforts Which Have Been Made in Favor of African Colonization in New Jersey* (Elizabeth, N.J., 1842), p. 28.

5. A compelling discussion of the anti-colonization views of American blacks is made by Benjamin Quarles, *Black Abolitionists* (New York, 1969), chap. 1; a more recent study is Leonard I. Sweet, *Black Images of America, 1784-1870* (New York, 1976), chaps. 3-4.

6. The New Jersey Constitution of 1776 provided "That all Inhabitants of this Colony of full Age, who are worth Fifty Pounds, proclamation Money, clear Estate in the same, and have resided within the County, in which they claim to Vote for twelve Months immediately preceding the Election, shall be entitled to vote for Representatives in Council and Assembly; and also for all other publick Officers that shall be elected by the People of the County at Large." Julian P. Boyd, *Fundamental Laws and Constitutions of New Jersey* (Princeton, N.J., 1964), p. 158. This article did not exclude blacks and women from voting and was liberally applied in the state to permit not only free black men to vote, but women as well. A black woman reportedly voted in Newark as late as February 1807. Joseph Atkinson, *The History of Newark, New Jersey* (Newark, N.J., 1878), p. 143.

7. Marion Thompson Wright, "Negro Suffrage in New Jersey, 1776–1875," *Journal of Negro History* 33 (1948): 177-83.

8. The New Jersey Constitution of 1844 declared that: "All men are by nature free and independent, and have certain natural and unalienable rights, among which are those of enjoying and defending life and liberty, acquiring, possessing and protecting property, and of pursuing and obtaining safety and happiness." But in 1845 the State Supreme Court ruled in *State v. Post* that slavery was not outlawed by the above section, that the "framers of the constitution never designed to apply this language to man in his private, individual or domestic capacity; or to define his individual rights or interfere with his domestic relations, or his individual condition." *New Jersey Law Reports,* 20: 357. A discussion of the case and the legal status of blacks in ante-bellum New Jersey is made by Lee Calligaro, "The Negro's Legal Status in Pre-Civil War New Jersey," *New Jersey History* 85 (1967): 167-80; see also Helen Tunnicliff Catterall, ed., *Judicial Cases Concerning American Slavery and the Negro,* 4 (Washington, D.C., 1936), pp. 319-50.

9. U.S. Works Projects Administration, New Jersey, *The Negro Church in New Jersey* (Hackensack, N.J., 1938); Norman H. Maring, *Baptists in New Jersey* (Valley Forge, Pa., 1964); Andrew E. Murray, *Presbyterians and the Negro* (Philadelphia, 1966); Mt. Zion African Methodist Episcopal Church, *One Hundred Thirty-Second Anniversary of Mt. Zion African Episcopal Church, 1827–1959* (New Brunswick, N.J., 1959); Wright, "Negro Suffrage in New Jersey," pp. 184-85, 187. For a more extensive study of the black church in nineteenth-century America see Carter G. Woodson, *The History of the Negro Church,* 2d ed. (Washington, D.C., 1945); E. Franklin Frazier, *The Negro Church in America* (New York, 1964); Leonard Haynes, *The Negro Community within American Protestantism, 1619–1844* (Boston, 1953).

10. Marion Thompson Wright, "Mr. Baxter's School," *Proceedings of the New Jersey Historical Society* 59 (1941): 116.

11. John S. Rock was a delegate to the Negro Convention in Trenton in 1849. For a biographical sketch of him see William Wells Brown, *The Black Man, His Antecedents, His Genius and Achievements* (Boston, 1863), pp. 266-70. Writings by Rock are included in James M. McPherson, *The Negro's Civil War: How American Negroes Felt and Acted during the War for the Union* (New York, 1967).

12. Federal Writers Project, New Jersey, "The Underground Railroad in New Jersey," *Stories of New Jersey,* 1939–40 ser., bulletin no. 9; see also John T. Cunningham, *The New Jersey Sampler: Historic Tales of Old New Jersey* (Upper Montclair, N.J., 1964), pp. 128-32; William Still, *The Underground Rail Road. A Record of Facts, Authentic Narratives, Letters. etc. . . . .* (Philadelphia, 1872) includes material relating to the escape of slaves through New Jersey. For a revisionist view which argues that the Railroad was not as widespread in the North as slaveholders and abolitionists claimed see Larry Gara, *The Liberty Line: The Legend of the Underground Railroad* (Lexington, Ky., 1961). Wilbur H. Siebert, *The Underground Railroad from Slavery to Freedom* (New York, 1898; reprint ed., New York, 1968), pp. 123-25.

13. Walter Measdale, "Cape May and the Underground Railroad," *The Cape May County Magazine of History and Genealogy* 7 (1975): 140-42; see also Earl Conrad, *Harriet Tubman* (Washington, D.C., 1943).

14. Boonton, *New Jersey Freeman,* 11 February 1846.

15. An excellent discussion of the problem of race in New Jersey during the Civil War era is Greene, "The Emancipation Proclamation in New Jersey and

the Paranoid Style"; see also Richard P. McCormick, "The Emancipation Proclamation: New Jersey's Reaction," in "Views on the Emancipation Proclamation, Selected Papers Presented at the Second Annual American History Workshop of the New Jersey Civil War Centennial Commission," 8 December 1962 (mimeographed); and Wright, "Negro Suffrage in New Jersey," pp. 198-201.

16. Trenton, *Daily True American,* 13 January 1863; for an informative discussion of David Naar see Carl E. Hatch, "Editor David Naar of Trenton: Profile of the Anti-Negro Mind," *New Jersey History* 86 (1968): 71-87.

17. Benjamin Quarles, "The Emancipation Proclamation: A Centenary Appraisal," in "Views on the Emancipation Proclamation, Selected Papers Presented at the Second Annual American History Workshop of the New Jersey Civil War Centennial Commission," 8 December 1962 (mimeographed). William S. Stryker, *Record of Officers and Men of New Jersey in the Civil War, 1861-1865,* 2 (Trenton, N.J., 1876): 1496, 1574; Franklin, *From Slavery to Freedom,* p. 231. William C. Wright, "New Jersey's Military Role in the Civil War Reconsidered," *New Jersey History* 92 (1974): 204-5. For a compelling view of the meaning of the Civil War to black Americans see McPherson, *The Negro's Civil War.*

CHAPTER V: QUEST FOR RACIAL IDENTITY

1. Wright, "Negro Suffrage in New Jersey," pp. 217-18; Abner J. Gaines, "New Jersey and the Fourteenth Amendment," *Proceedings of the New Jersey Historical Society* 52 (1952): 36-55. For a compelling revisionist interpretation of Reconstruction, which emphasizes the political motives of the Republican Party's support of the Fifteenth Amendment in the northern states, see William Gillette, *The Right to Vote: Politics and the Passage of the Fifteenth Amendment* (Baltimore, 1965).

2. Trenton *State Gazette,* 3 May 1870, in Wright, "Negro Suffrage in New Jersey," pp. 219-20.

3. See Rayford W. Logan, *The Betrayal of the Negro* (New York, 1965). Also see C. Vann Woodward, *The Strange Career of Jim Crow,* 3rd rev. ed. (New York, 1974), chaps. 2-3.

4. The definitive interpretation of the changing character of black thought in the late nineteenth century is August Meier, *Negro Thought in America, 1880-1915: Racial Ideologies in the Age of Booker T. Washington* (Ann Arbor, Mich., 1963). A very useful anthology of writings by black leaders in the nineteenth and early twentieth centuries is Howard Brotz, ed., *Negro Social and Political Thought, 1850-1920* (New York, 1966).

5. John H. Bracey, Jr., August Meier, and Elliott Rudwick, *Black Nationalism in America* (New York, 1970), p. xxvi. For a perceptive discussion of early black nationalist expression see Sterling Stuckey, comp., *The Ideological Origins of Black Nationalism* (Boston, 1972), pp. 1-29.

6. Edwin S. Redkey, *Black Exodus; Black Nationalist and Back-to-Africa Movements, 1890-1910* (New Haven, Conn., 1969), pp. 31-41, 171.

7. W.E.B. DuBois, "Strivings of the Negro People," *Atlantic Monthly* 53 (August 1897): 194.

8. Meier, *Negro Thought in America,* pp. 100-18. An excellent biography of Booker T. Washington is Louis R. Harlan, *Booker T. Washington: The Making of a Black Leader, 1856-1901* (New York, 1972).

9. Richard R. Wright, Jr., "The Economic Conditions of Negroes in the North: III, Negro Communities in New Jersey," *Southern Workman* 37 (1908): 385-89; also see "The Lees from Gouldtown," *Negro History Bulletin* 10 (1946-47): 99-100, 108, 119; and William Steward, *Gouldtown, A Very Remarkable Settlement of Ancient Date* (Philadelphia, 1913).

10. Wright, "The Economic Conditions of Negroes in the North," pp. 390-91.

11. *Ibid.,* pp. 391-93; the most helpful study of a black settlement in New Jersey is Charles C. Smiley, *The True Story of Lawnside, N.J.* (Camden, N.J., 1921). Smiley claims that Lawnside was the "oldest colored town in New Jersey, probably dating back to early liberated slaves of Friends of this section." *Ibid.,* p. 32.

12. Lester B. Granger, "Race Relations and the School System (A Study of Negro High School Attendance in New Jersey)," *Opportunity* 3 (1925): 327-29; also see New Jersey State Conference of the National Association for the Advancement of Colored People Branches, "A Survey of the Public School Systems in the State of New Jersey" (np., 28 February 1947).

13. See Frazier, *The Negro Church in America,* chaps. 3-4; Clement A. Price, "The Afro-American Community of Newark, 1917-1947: A Social History," (Ph.D. dissertation, Rutgers University, 1975), pp. 74-80. Brief contemporary perspectives on black life in New Jersey towns include: Anna Bustill Smith, *Reminiscences of Colored People of Princeton, N.J., 1800-1900* (Philadelphia, 1913), and Amorel E. O'Kelly Cooke, *Faded Foliage and Fragrant Flowers from the Heart of Bethany* (Newark, N.J., 1922).

14. Paul Robeson, Jr., "Paul Robeson: Black Warrior," in *Paul Robeson: The Great Forerunner,* ed. Editors of Freedomways (New York, 1978), pp. 3-16; for an informative study of Robeson's experiences while he was a student at Rutgers University see George Fishman, "Paul Robeson's Student Days and the Fight Against Racism at Rutgers," *Freedomways* 9 (1969): 221-29.

15. See William C. Wright and Paul A. Stellhorn, comps., *Directory of New Jersey Newspapers, 1765-1970* (Trenton, N.J., 1977).

16. The most useful studies of Woodrow Wilson's policies toward blacks while he served as president are Henry Blumenthal, "Woodrow Wilson and the Race Question," *Journal of Negro History* 48 (1963): 1-21; and Nancy J. Weiss, "The Negro and the New Freedom: Fighting Wilsonian Segregation," *Political Science Quarterly* 84 (1969): 61-79; also for an indispensable study of Wilson's political career see Arthur S. Link, *Wilson: The New Freedom* (Princeton, N.J., 1956).

CHAPTER VI: NEWCOMERS BETWEEN THE WARS

1. "The N.A.A.C.P.," *Crisis* 2 (June 1911): 60; William M. Ashby, "What Happened at Carteret," *Opportunity* 4 (1926): 191-92.

2. Emmett J. Scott, *Negro Migration during the War* (New York, 1920; reprint ed., New York, 1969); also see Florette Henri, *Black Migration: Move-*

ment North, 1900–1920 (Garden City, N.Y., 1976); and Carter G. Woodson, *A Century of Negro Migration* (Washington, D.C., 1918; reprint ed., New York, 1969). For an extensive discussion of black migration to New Jersey, particularly its impact on Newark, see George W. Groh, *The Black Migration: The Journey to Urban America* (New York, 1972); on Newark see Clement A. Price, "The Beleaguered City as Promised Land: Blacks in Newark, 1917–1947," in *Urban New Jersey since 1870,* ed. William C. Wright (Trenton, N.J., 1975), pp. 13-24. The best personal account on race relations in a New Jersey community (Hackensack) during the migration is E. Frederick Morrow, *Way down South up North* (Philadelphia, 1973); for a contemporary view of the same in Burlington see Linton Satterthwait, "The Color-Line in New Jersey," *Arena* 35 (1906): 394-400.

3. Kenneth T. and Barbara B. Jackson, "The Black Experience in Newark: The Growth of the Ghetto, 1870–1970," in *New Jersey since 1860, New Findings and Interpretations,* ed. William C. Wright (Trenton, N.J., 1972), pp. 41-46; The Interracial Committee of the New Jersey Conference of Social Work, *The Negro in New Jersey* (Newark, N.J., 1932; reprint ed., New York, 1969), p. 28. For a general discussion of the problem of racial exclusion in the American Federation of Labor see Sterling D. Spero and Abram L. Harris, *The Black Worker* (New York, 1959), pp. 53-86; and Julius Jacobson, ed., *The Negro and the American Labor Movement* (New York, 1968), chaps. 1-4.

4. New Jersey Conference of Social Work, *Negro in New Jersey,* p. 26.

5. William M. Ashby, private interview with Clement A. Price, 19 June 1972. At the (Newark) Brotherhood Day program in 1939, William Pickins, the former field secretary of the NAACP observed that "Jersey is nobody's heaven, but it is better than Mississippi." Newark, *New Jersey Herald News,* 18 February 1939, p. 1

6. New Jersey Conference of Social Work, *Negro in New Jersey,* pp.78, 80.

7. The most extensive treatment of blacks in Newark during the World War I period is Price, "The Afro-American Community of Newark, 1917–1947," chaps. 2-4. For an excellent study of the role of blacks in the public school system of Newark see John R. Anderson, "Negro Education in the Public Schools of Newark, N.J. during the 19th Century" (Ed.D. dissertation, Rutgers University, 1972); also Wright, "Mr. Baxter's School," pp. 116-33.

8. William M. Ashby, "The Housing of the Negro—Is It Wise to Group by Nationalities," *Proceedings of the New Jersey Conference for Social Welfare* (1919), p. 113.

9. E.U. Essien-Udom, *Black Nationalism: A Search for an Identity in America* (Chicago, 1962), p. 33.

10. See Wright and Stellhorn, pp. 7-13, 149-71.

11. Newark, *New Jersey Herald News,* 21 May 1938: pp. 2, 9; 30 July 1938; 27 August 1938.

12. New Jersey Urban Colored Population Commission, *Annual Report* 1943 (Newark, N.J., 1943), n.p.

13. A very useful analysis of the impact of the New Deal on black Americans is Leslie H. Fishel, "The Negro in the New Deal Era," *Wisconsin Magazine of History* 48 (Winter 1964): 111-26; also for an indispensable study of the treatment of blacks under the Agricultural Adjustment Act and the National Industrial Recovery Act see Raymond Wolters, *Negroes and the Great Depression: The Problem of Economic Recovery* (Westport, Conn., 1970). A contemporary

insight into the ideals of the New Deal regarding American blacks is found in Harold L. Ickes, "The Negro as Citizen," *Crisis* 93 (1936): 230-31, 242. Eleanor R. Roosevelt, "The Negro and Social Change," *Opportunity* 14 (1936): 22-23.

14. Gordon F. Allison, "New Jersey's Negro Battalion," *Newark Sunday Call,* 5 March 1944.

15. Edmund L. Drago, "American Blacks and Italy's Invasion of Ethiopia," *Negro History Bulletin* 41 (1978): 883-84.

16. For an analysis of the war's impact on American blacks see Richard M. Dalfiume, "The 'Forgotten Years' of the Negro Revolution," *Journal of American History* 55 (June 1968): 90-106. A few national black organizations, most notably the National Negro Congress, were opposed to the Negro's participation in World War II. Francis L. Broderick and August Meier, eds., *Negro Protest Thought in the Twentieth Century* (New York, 1965), pp. 196-201. In Newark, members of the House of Israel, a black religious sect, were arrested in January 1943 when they refused to be drafted into the armed services. A month later the Federal Bureau of Investigation arrested three black conscientious objectors of the Allah Temple of Islam in Newark. Newark, *New Jersey Herald News*, 14 January 1943, p. 1; 27 February 1943, p. 1; 30 January 1943, p. 1.

CHAPTER VII: THE MODERN CIVIL RIGHTS MOVEMENT

1. *New Jersey Afro-American,* 12 May 1945, p. 1.

2. For an overview of the early history of the Division Against Discrimination see Marion Thompson Wright, "Extending Civil Rights in New Jersey through the Division Against Discrimination," *Journal of Negro History* 38 (January 1953): 96-107; also a brief but informative discussion of the work of the Division is found in Myra A. Blakeslee, "The New Jersey Division Against Discrimination," *American Unity* 4 (December 1945): 10-11, and Joseph L. Bustard, "The Operation of the New Jersey Law Against Discrimination, 1947-1948," *Journal of Negro Education* 18 (1949): 123-33. For a review of Governor Alfred E. Driscoll's efforts on behalf of civil rights in New Jersey see Clifford R. Moore, "Full Citizenship in New Jersey," *Crisis* 56 (1949): 272-73, 284; and Alfred E. Driscoll, "More than a Law on the Books," *American Unity* 7 (April–May 1949): 3-4.

3. New Jersey State Conference of NAACP Branches, "A Survey of the Public School Systems in the State of New Jersey" (28 February 1947).

4. Marion Thompson Wright, *The Education of Negroes in New Jersey* (New York, 1941).

5. *State of New Jersey Constitutional Convention of 1947,* 3, Committee on Rights, Privileges, Amendments and Miscellaneous Provisions (Trenton, N.J., 1947), p. 71.

6. Patterson v. Board of Education, Trenton, *New Jersey Miscellaneous Reports,* 11: 179.

7. John P. Milligan, "Perspective On: Civil Rights in New Jersey," *New Jersey Educational Association Review* 29 (1955–56): 294-96.

8. "Englewood School Bias Charges," *Crisis* 61 (1954): 608-10.

9. George C. Morse, "New Jersey, New Laboratory in Race Relations," *Negro History Bulletin* 13 (1949–50): 156-63. Myra A. Blakeslee, "One State's Fight for Unity," *American Unity* 9 (Nov.-Dec. 1950): 3-6.

10. Bruce Bliven, "The Trenton Murder Case," *New Republic* 120 (May 1949): 12; also see by the same author "27 Who Believed in Justice," *New Republic* 125 (October 1951): 13-15. An attack against communists for allegedly attempting to exploit the Trenton Six case for propaganda purposes is found in "Communists Trying for a Northern 'Scottsboro,' " *Christian Century* 66 (1949): 548. The U.S. Communist Party view of the case is found in Elwood M. Dean, *The Story of the Trenton Six* (New York, 1949). An extensive undergraduate study is Chester Apy, Jr., "The Trenton Six" (senior thesis, Princeton University, 1954). The NAACP's role in the case is discussed in National Association for the Advancement of Colored People, Legal Defense and Educational Fund, Inc., *The Fantastic Case of the Trenton Six* (New York, 1951).

11. National Advisory Commission on Civil Disorders, *Report* (Washington, D.C., 1968), p. 143.

12. Harold A. Lett, "Civil Rights in New Jersey," paper submitted at the National Conference of Christians and Jews, Washington, D.C., 1 August 1961.

13. Kenneth T. and Barbara B. Jackson, "The Black Experience in Newark," pp. 51-52; Frances Fox Piven, "The Shaping of Our Newarks," in *Newark: An Assessment, 1967–1977,* ed. Stanley B. Winters (Newark, N.J., 1978), pp. 29-33.

14. Paul Hope, "Englewood, New Jersey—A Case Study in De Facto Segregation," in *Freedom Now! The Civil-Rights Struggle in America,* ed. Alan F. Westin (New York, 1964), pp. 140, 142.

15. Harold Cruse, *Rebellion or Revolution* (New York, 1968), chap. 13; Bracey, Meier, and Rudwick, eds., *Black Nationalism in America,* pt. 5.

16. National Advisory Commission on Civil Disorders, *Report,* chap. 1; "Black Rage in New Jersey," *Time* 84 (21 August 1964): 19; "White Boycott," *Newsweek* 64 (24 August 1964): 27, 30.

17. Among the more useful studies on Newark during this period are the New Jersey Governor's Select Commission on Civil Disorder, *Report for Action* (Trenton, N.J., 1968), pt. 1; Robert Curvin, "Black Ghetto Politics in Newark after World War II," *Cities of the Garden State: Essays in the Urban and Suburban History of New Jersey,* eds. Joel Schwartz and Daniel Prosser (Dubuque, Iowa, 1977), pp. 146-50; and National Advisory Commission on Civil Disorders, *Report,* pp. 30-32.

18. There has been a great deal of interest in the 1967 disorders in Newark. Among the more successful analyses are the Governor's Select Commission on Civil Disorders, *Report for Action,* pp. 104-44; National Advisory Commission on Civil Disorders, *Report,* p. 32-38; Tom Hayden, *Rebellion in Newark, Official Violence and Ghetto Response* (New York, 1967). A controversial treatment of the disorders is Sol Chaneles, "The Meaning of Two Predictions: An Historical Perspective," in *Newark,* ed. Winters, pp. 383-90; and the more useful Ron Porambo, *No Cause for Indictment; An Autopsy of Newark* (New York, 1971). An insightful doctoral thesis on the disorders is Daniel E. Georges, "Arson: The Ecology of Urban Unrest in an American City" (Ph.D. dissertation, Syracuse University, 1974).

19. Newark *Star Ledger,* 14 July 1967, p. 9.

20. Robert Curvin, "A View from the Ghetto," in *Proceedings of The Public*

Policy Forum on Civil Disorders: Causes and Remedies (New Brunswick, N.J., 1968), p. 14.

21. In 1973 the United States Department of Justice in a census of prisoners in state correctional facilities found that in New Jersey approximately 36 percent were white and 63 percent non-white (mostly black). U.S. Department of Justice, *Census of Prisoners in State Correctional Facilities, 1973* (Washington, D.C., 1973), p. 135.

EPILOGUE

1. "Blacks in New Jersey: 1980" ([Trenton, N.J., 1980]), p. ii.

Suggested Readings

T HE growing interest in the history of Afro-Americans in New Jersey
   has been spurred by two related developments: the emergence of
black Americans into the mainstream of contemporary American society; and the civil rights movement in the years following World War II.
Readers are urged to consult *New Jersey and the Negro: A Bibliography,
1715–1966* (Trenton, N.J., 1967), an excellent and indispensable guide to
published sources on the subject. Other useful bibliographies are the
basic compilation of Monroe N. Work, *A Bibliography of the Negro in
Africa and America* (New York, 1928; reprint ed., New York, 1966); and
Jefferson B. Kellogg, "Selected Secondary Sources," *American Studies
International* (Summer 1979): 25-28.

The most extensive coverage of the history of Afro-Americans in New
Jersey has been in the area of slavery, where several useful studies are
available. A very readable and informed account of the attempts to end
slavery in New Jersey and in other northern states, as well as the problem
of slave crimes and the economic vitality of the institution in the North,
is by Arthur Zilversmit, *The First Emancipation: The Abolition of
Slavery in the North* (Chicago, 1967). Zilversmit's brief discussion of the
problem of slavery in New Jersey during the American Revolution is also
useful: "Liberty and Property: New Jersey and the 'Self-Evident
Truths,' " in *New Jersey in the American Revolution: Political and
Social Conflict,* ed. William C. Wright (Trenton, N.J., 1970; rev. ed.,
1974). A more recent and extensive study of slavery in the northern states
is Edgar J. McManus, *Black Bondage in the North* (Syracuse, N.Y.,
1973). Among the concise treatments of New Jersey slavery are Frances
D. Pingeon, *Blacks in the Revolutionary Era,* New Jersey's Revolutionary Experience, ed. Larry R. Gerlach, 14 (Trenton, N.J., 1975); and,
by the same author, "Slavery in New Jersey on the Eve of Revolution,"
in *New Jersey in the American Revolution: Political and Social Conflict,*
ed. William C. Wright (Trenton, N.J., 1970; rev. ed., 1974); also see Lee
Hagan, Larry A. Greene, Leonard Harris, and Clement A. Price, "New
Jersey Afro-Americans: From Colonial Times to the Present," in *The*

New Jersey Ethnic Experience, ed. Barbara Cunningham (Union City, N.J., 1977).

There is only one monograph specifically on slavery in New Jersey. Although dated, it is still quite useful: Henry Scofield Cooley, *A Study of Slavery in New Jersey,* Johns Hopkins University Studies, ser. 14 (Baltimore, 1896). A personal account which provides some interesting insights into black life under slavery in eighteenth-century New Jersey is Andrew D. Mellick, *The Story of an Old Farm; Or Life in New Jersey in the Eighteenth Century* (Somerville, N.J., 1889); see also Francis Bazley Lee, *New Jersey As a Colony and As a State, One of the Original Thirteen,* vol. 4 (New York, 1903). There are several early articles on slavery in New Jersey. Among the most useful are D. H. Gardner, "The Emancipation of Slaves in New Jersey," *Proceedings of the New Jersey Historical Society* 9 (1924): 1-21; Hubert G. Schmidt, "Slavery and Attitudes on Slavery, Hunterdon County, New Jersey," *Proceedings of the New Jersey Historical Society* 58 (1940): 151-69, 240-53. Simeon F. Moss, "The Persistence of Slavery and Involuntary Servitude in a Free State (1685-1866)," *Journal of Negro History* 35 (1950): 289-314.

New Jersey slavery is covered in the following dissertations: Emma Lou Thornbrough, "Negro Slavery in the North; Its Legal and Constitutional Aspects" (Ph.D. dissertation, University of Michigan, 1946); Hubert G. Schmidt, "An Economic History of Hunterdon County, New Jersey" (Ph.D. dissertation, Rutgers University, 1946); and Oscar Renal Williams, "Blacks and Colonial Legislation in the Middle Colonies" (Ph.D. dissertation, Ohio State University, 1969).

Considerably less work has been done on the life of free blacks in New Jersey, the institutions they formed, and the problems they encountered. The most useful studies are those by Marion Thompson Wright, who published a pioneer study on the history of blacks in the state in 1941. See Wright, *The Education of Negroes in New Jersey* (New York, 1941); also in the field of education, by the same author, "Mr. Baxter's School," *Proceedings of the New Jersey Historical Society* 59 (1941): 116-33; and John R. Anderson, "Negro Education in the Public School System of Newark, N.J. during the 19th Century" (Ed.D. dissertation, Rutgers University, 1972). Two informative and extensive discussions of the problem of race and civil rights in New Jersey by Wright are "Negro Suffrage in New Jersey, 1776-1875," *Journal of Negro History* 33 (1948): 168-224; and "New Jersey Laws and the Negro," *Journal of Negro History* 28 (1943): 156-99. A more recent treatment of black settlement patterns in the nineteenth century is Peter O. Wacker, "The Changing Geography of the Black Population of New Jersey, 1810-1860: A Preliminary View," *Proceedings of the Association of American Geographers* 3 (1971): 174-78. A further exploration of this subject by the same author is "Patterns and Problems in the Historical Geography of the Afro-American Population of New Jersey, 1726-1860," in *Pattern and Process: Research in Historical Geography,* ed. Ralph Ehrenberg (Washington, D.C., 1975). An overview of the origins of free black communities is found in the previously cited Lee Hagan, et al., "New Jersey Afro-Americans"; also for a recent study of blacks in Burlington County see Ernest Lyght, *Path of Freedom: The Black Presence in New Jersey's Burlington County, 1659–1900* (Cherry Hill, N.J., 1978). A rather dated but still essential account of the history of New Jersey's best-known community of free blacks is William Steward, *Gouldtown, A Very Remarkable Settlement of Ancient Date . . .* (Philadelphia, 1913); the only study of Lawnside is Charles C. Smiley, *A True Story of Lawnside, N.J.* (Camden, N.J., 1921). A personal account of the black community of Princeton is Anna Bustill Smith, *Reminiscences of Colored People of Princeton, N.J., 1800–1900* (Philadelphia, 1913).

New Jersey's racial attitudes toward blacks during the nineteenth century are explored in the following articles: Larry A. Greene, "The Emancipation Proclamation in New Jersey and the Paranoid Style," *New Jersey History* 91 (1973): 108-24; Carl E. Hatch, "Editor David Naar of Trenton: Profile of the Anti-Negro Mind," *New Jersey History* 86 (1968): 70-87; Lee Calligaro, "The Negro's Legal Status in Pre-Civil War New Jersey," *New Jersey History* 85 (1967): 167-80; Frances D. Pingeon, "Dissenting Attitudes toward the Negro in New Jersey—1837," *New Jersey History* 89 (1971): 197-220; and Richard P. McCormick, "The Emancipation Proclamation: New Jersey's Reaction," in "Views on the Emancipation Proclamation, Selected Papers Presented at the Second Annual American History Workshop of the New Jersey Civil War Centennial Commission," 8 December 1962 (mimeographed).

The migration of blacks to New Jersey is discussed in the standard work on the World War I migration, Emmett J. Scott, *Negro Migration during the War* (New York, 1920; reprint ed., New York, 1969). Recent treatments on the subject having information on New Jersey are George W. Groh, *The Black Migration: The Journey to Urban America* (New York, 1972); and Florette Henri, *Black Migration: Movement North, 1900–1920* (Garden City, N.Y., 1975). For census data on the migration see U.S. Bureau of the Census, *Negro Population, 1790–1915* (Washington, D.C., 1918).

Twentieth-century black urban life is covered by Kenneth T. and Barbara B. Jackson's overview study of the black community in Newark, "The Black Experience in Newark: The Growth of the Ghetto, 1870–1970," in *New Jersey since 1860, New Findings and Interpretations,* ed. William C. Wright (Trenton, N.J., 1972); on Newark, see also Clement A. Price, "The Beleaguered City As Promised Land: Blacks in Newark, 1917–1947," in *Urban New Jersey since 1870,* ed. William C. Wright (Trenton, N.J., 1975).

Two useful dissertations on the Newark black community during the twentieth century are Clement A. Price, "The Afro-American Community of Newark, 1917–1947: A Social History" (Ph.D. dissertation,

Rutgers University, 1975); and Robert Curvin, "The Persistent Minority: The Black Political Experience in Newark" (Ph.D. dissertation, Princeton University, 1975).

For an insightful discussion of early black protest see August Meier and Elliott M. Rudwick, "Early Boycotts of Segregated Schools: The East Orange, New Jersey, Experience, 1899–1906," *History of Education Quarterly* 7 (1967): 22-35; a brief but interesting article on a civil rights case in Paterson is by Michael H. Ebner, "Mrs. Miller and 'The Paterson Show': A 1911 Defeat for Racial Discrimination," *New Jersey History* 86 (1968): 88-91.

The problems encountered by New Jersey blacks in employment during the Depression is the object of an extensive contemporary study by Egerton E. Hall, "The Negro Wage Earner of New Jersey . . ." (Ed.D. dissertation, Rutgers University, 1933); also William R. Valentine, Jr., "A Place for Negro Youth in Industry," *Opportunity* 18 (1940): 177-79; State of New Jersey, *Report of the New Jersey State Temporary Commission on the Condition of the Urban Colored Population . . .* (Trenton, N.J., 1939); and Interracial Committee of the New Jersey Conference of Social Work, *The Negro in New Jersey* (Newark, N.J., 1932).

There is no comprehensive study of the civil rights movement in New Jersey. Part of the story—efforts in Newark—are discussed in the previously cited work by Clement A. Price, "The Afro-American Community of Newark"; also Robert Curvin, "Black Ghetto Politics in Newark after World War II," in *Cities in the Garden State: Essays in Urban and Suburban History of New Jersey,* eds. Joel Schwartz and Daniel Prosser (Dubuque, Iowa, 1977). Civil rights gains in the state after World War II are discussed by Marion Thompson Wright, "Extending Civil Rights in New Jersey through the Division Against Discrimination," *Journal of Negro History* 38 (1953): 96-107.

For insights into the work of the New Jersey Division Against Discrimination see the various reports of that agency which are widely available in New Jersey's major repositories. The causes for the civil disorders of the early 1960s and 1967 have been explored by many scholars, community activists, and governmental agencies. Among the more useful treatments are the National Advisory Commission on Civil Disorders, *Report* (Washington, D.C., 1970); Governor's Select Commission on Civil Disorder, *Report for Action* (Trenton, N.J., 1968); Ron Porambo, *No Cause for Indictment, An Autopsy of Newark* (New York, 1971); and Tom Hayden, *Rebellion in Newark, Official Violence and Ghetto Response* (New York, 1967). One New Jersey city's attempt to study its past problems and assess its future is Stanley B. Winters, ed., *Newark: An Assessment, 1967–1977* (Newark, N.J., 1978); republished as *From Riot to Recovery: Newark after Ten Years* (Washington, D.C., 1979).

There are, unfortunately, few manuscript collections pertaining to the life of blacks in New Jersey. Most of the materials available cover slavery and the anti-slavery and African colonization movements. The New Jersey Historical Society has a substantial number of miscellaneous documents on blacks in eighteenth- and nineteenth-century New Jersey. Included in the manuscript collections are slave bills of sale and other business transactions involving slaves; deeds to land purchased by or willed to blacks; certificates of manumission; sundry correspondence concerning the colonization of blacks in Africa; minutes of the Essex County Anti-Slavery Society, 1839–42, and of the New Jersey State Anti-Slavery Society, 1839–45; and photographs of middle-class black families in West Orange and Newark from about 1880 to 1930.

Manuscript materials dealing with blacks in New Jersey are in the Special Collections of Alexander Library, Rutgers University, New Brunswick. Included are miscellaneous papers of the African Association of New Brunswick, 1817–24. The Association, formed in 1816 by the Presbyterian Synod of New York and New Jersey, was devoted to the support of the African School in Parsippany. Also in the Special Collections are records of the New Brunswick Colonization Society; archives of the New Jersey Welfare Council, Newark; and in the Rutgers Archives are materials relating to the student days of Paul Robeson at Rutgers College.

The New Jersey Reference Division of the Newark Public Library contains manuscript materials on the history of blacks in twentieth-century Newark, including the records of the New Jersey Urban League, circa 1917–1955; photocopies of the *New Jersey Herald News,* circa 1939–1944; miscellaneous papers of William M. Ashby and Harold A. Lett; and photographs of blacks in Newark in the early 1940s.

The New Jersey State Library, Trenton, contains original materials such as petitions on the slavery issue; bills of sale for slaves; indentures; legislative records; and sundry public documents. A valuable source of material in the State Library, but not yet indexed, is the data accumulated by a WPA study on blacks in Newark and Atlantic City in about 1940.

Most black newspapers in New Jersey have not been preserved. Three of the most important, though, are available. The *New Jersey Herald News* has been mentioned above. The *Sentinel,* a newspaper published in Trenton from 1880 to 1882, is available in photocopy at the Alexander Library, Rutgers University, and the Schomburg Collection of the New York Public Library. The *New Jersey Afro-American* is widely available.

Oral history is a relatively recent resource on black history in New Jersey. For a recent guide to such collections see *Oral History in New Jersey: A Directory, 1979,* comp. Ronald J. Grele (Trenton, N.J., 1979). Though meager, the material on New Jersey Afro-Americans in these collections is growing. The Newark Public Library holds transcribed interviews on the Newark NAACP and civil rights in New Jersey; the New Jersey Historical Society holds tapes of the meetings of its Afro-American Committee and interviews with its members. Tapes pertaining

to the New Brunswick black community during World War II are held by
the Middlesex County Cultural and Heritage Commission in New
Brunswick; and tapes relating to Gouldtown are held by Cumberland
County College in Vineland.

Index